TH

EXPLORERS

SACRAMENTO PUBLIC LIBRARY

D0447265

828 "I" STREET
SACRAMENTO, CA 95814

JAN   2001   JAN   2001

OTHER BOOKS BY THE AUTHOR

Mammals of New Guinea

Tree Kangaroos: A Curious Natural History
with R. Martin, P. Schouten and A. Szalay

The Future Eaters

Possums of the World: A Monograph
of the Phalangeroidea with P. Schouten

Mammals of the South West Pacific and Moluccan Islands

Watkin Tench, *1788* (ed.)

The Life and Adventures of John Nicol, Mariner (ed.)

Throwim Way Leg

The Birth of Sydney

THE
EXPLORERS

STORIES OF DISCOVERY AND ADVENTURE
FROM THE AUSTRALIAN FRONTIER

EDITED AND WITH AN INTRODUCTION BY

TIM FLANNERY

GROVE PRESS
New York

Copyright © 1998 by Tim Flannery

All rights reserved. No part of this book may be reproduced in any form or by any electronic or mechanical means, including information storage and retrieval systems, without permission in writing from the publisher, except by a reviewer, who may quote brief passages in a review. Any members of educational institutions wishing to photocopy part or all of the work for classroom use, or publishers who would like to obtain permission to include the work in an anthology, should send their inquiries to Grove/Atlantic, Inc., 841 Broadway, New York, NY 10003.

Originally published in 1998 by The Text Publishing Company, Melbourne, Victoria, Australia

Published simultaneously in Canada
Printed in the United States of America

FIRST AMERICAN EDITION

Library of Congress Cataloging-in-Publication Data

The explorers : stories of discovery and adventure from the Australian frontier / edited and introduced by Tim Flannery.
    p.   cm.
    Originally published: Melbourne, Vic. : Text Pub. Co., 1998.
    Includes bibliographical references.
    ISBN 0-8021-3719-9
    1. Australia—Discovery and exploration. 2. Explorers—Australia. I. Flannery, Tim F. (Tim Fridtjof), 1956–

DU97 .E96 2000
994.01—dc21

00-041742

Designed by Anthony Vandenberg

Grove Press
841 Broadway
New York, NY 10003

00 01 02 03 10 9 8 7 6 5 4 3 2 1

ACKNOWLEDGMENTS

Sincere thanks are due to my editor Michael Heyward who conceived the idea of this book, edited the pieces I selected, sculpted and polished my contributions, checked original sources, located new material, and asked the really important questions. George Thomas and Alexandra Szalay proofread the manuscript, greatly improving it with their suggestions. Emma Gordon Williams has been tireless in her efforts to locate the most obscure works.

Some of the most significant material herein was drawn from extremely rare books or unpublished archival records. Such material is priceless and access to it quite rightly restricted. Carol Cantrell (rare books), May Robertson (archives) and the other staff of Information Services at the Australian Museum deserve special thanks for giving me their time, and access to the material in their care. Jennifer Broomhead of the Mitchell Library, and Tim Robinson of the Sydney University Archives also deserve special thanks for their help in locating and contextualising important archival records. I am also very grateful to Des Cowley and Gerard Hayes of the State Library of Victoria who found many important books for me.

To Anna—may all your explorations be happy ones

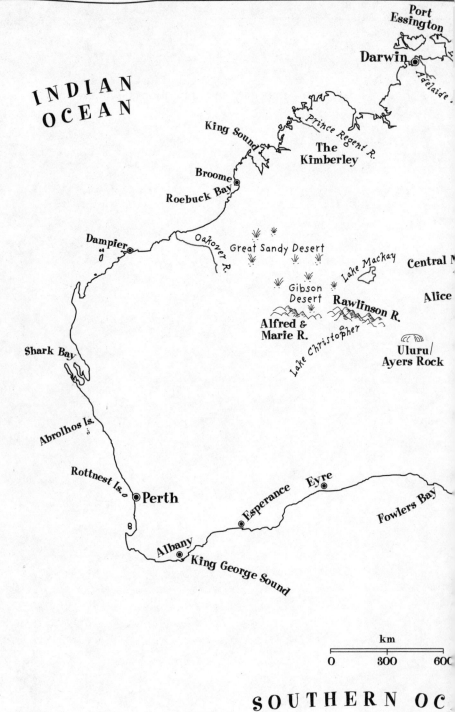

INDIAN
OCEAN

Port
Essington

Darwin

Adelaide R.

King Sound

Prince Regent R.

The
Kimberley

Broome

Roebuck Bay

Dampier

Oakover R.

Great Sandy Desert

Lake Mackay

Central M

Gibson
Desert

Rawlinson R.

Alice

Alfred &
Marie R.

Lake Christopher

Uluru/
Ayers Rock

Shark Bay

Abrolhos Is.

Rottnest Is.

Perth

Esperance

Eyre

Fowlers Bay

Albany

King George Sound

km

0   300   600

SOUTHERN OC

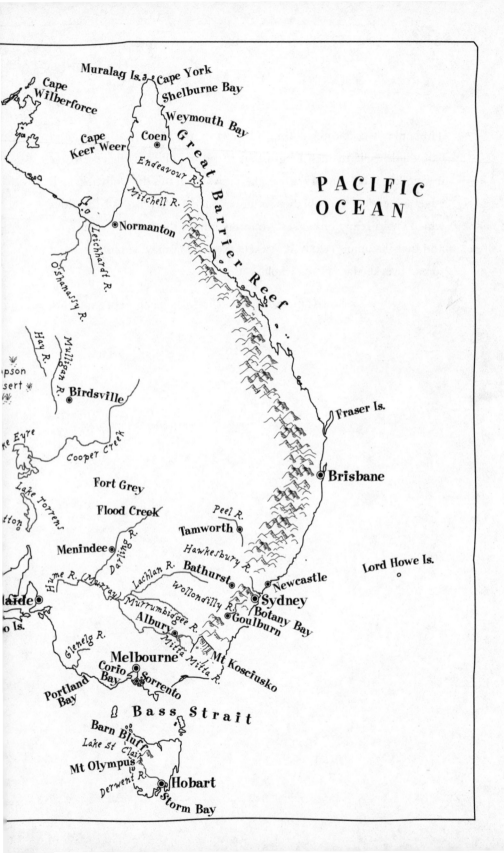

Muralag Is. Cape York
Cape Wilberforce
Shelburne Bay
Weymouth Bay
Cape Keer Weer
Coen
Endeavour R.
Great Barrier Reef
Mitchell R.
Normanton
Leichhardt R.
O'Shanassy R.
Hay R.
Mulligan R.
...pson ...sert
Birdsville
...ke Eyre
Cooper Creek
Lake Torrens
...tton
Fort Grey
Flood Creek
Peel R.
Tamworth
Menindee
Darling R.
Hawkesbury R.
Hume R. (Murray)
Lachlan R.
Bathurst
Newcastle
...laide
Murrumbidgee R.
Wollondilly R.
Sydney
Botany Bay
Albury
Goulburn
...o Is.
Glenelg R.
Mitta Mitta R.
Mt Kosciusko
Melbourne
Corio Bay
Sorrento
Portland Bay
Bass Strait
Barn Bluff
Lake St Clair
Mt Olympus
Derwent R.
Hobart
Storm Bay

PACIFIC OCEAN

Fraser Is.

Brisbane

Lord Howe Is.

This unknown country is the fifth part of the terrestrial globe, and extendeth itself to such length that in probability it is twice greater in kingdoms and seignories than all that which at this day doth acknowledge subjection and obedience unto your Majesty...to all the titles which you already do possess you may adjoin this which I represent, and that the name TERRA AUSTRALIS INCOGNITA may be blazoned and spread over the face of the whole world.

PEDRO DE QUIROS, REPORT TO KING PHILLIP III OF SPAIN, 1610

CONTENTS

THIS EXTRAORDINARY CONTINENT
by Tim Flannery

Drunken camels were the bane of the Burke and Wills expedition. They consumed prodigious quantities of rum, better used perhaps to soothe the pillows of the doomed explorers. The only female member of Ernest Favenc's expedition to Queensland's Gulf country in 1882–83 never got to publish her remarkable story of endurance in the face of sickness, death and privation. Her journal lies all but forgotten in the archive of Sydney's Mitchell Library, the list of baby clothes at the back suggesting she was pregnant for at least part of the journey. In February 1869 G. W. Goyder, surveyor-general of South Australia and martinet, was dispatched to survey and found the settlement of Darwin. He was watched by the Larrakia people who, when they decided it was safe to contact the strangers, held a corroboree, giving pitch and word perfect renditions of 'John Brown's Body', 'The Glory, Hallelujah', and 'The Old Virginia Shore'. This 'white-fella corroboree' had been traded from the Woolna people, who memorised the tunes while lying prone in the wet grass at night, spying on surveyors who were working near the Adelaide River. Who, in this instance, were the explorers?

It's an illustration of just how rich the stories of Australian exploration are that neither the Larrakia's corroboree nor Burke's camels made it into this book. In assembling these accounts I had wanted to offer the reader the experience of being a fly on the wall at exemplary moments in Australia's history. To be there, looking over Governor Phillip's shoulder as he chooses the location for the infant settlement of Sydney; to accompany John McDouall Stuart in his moment of triumph at reaching the centre of the continent; and to join the young William Wills as he lies alone, dying of starvation on a full stomach, at Cooper Creek. But then I discovered that the records of Australia's explorers offer so much more. In them, the unexpected is commonplace. So much that is new and extraordinary, both trivial and profound, crowds in on the reader. Events, glimpsed across the barriers of time, language and environmental alienation, continue to puzzle weeks later. One finds humanity at its extreme; acts of unimaginable cruelty are juxtaposed with those of compassion and self-sacrifice. George Evans played games with frightened Aboriginal children to cheer them up. Other explorers were murderers.

Why were the explorers there? What made them do it? The answers are as varied as the explorers themselves. Some were simply obeying orders. Others had set out in search of new grazing land, illusory cities or imaginary seas. Some were careful calculators of risk, while others played a terrifying sport of brinkmanship with their own lives. Some were looking for lost comrades, while a few were made explorers by fate, having set out to do something completely different.

For all its wonder, Australia's exploration history has been bowdlerised, debased and made insipid for generations of Australians by those with particular political and social agendas. In my last year of primary school I fidgeted whenever stern Miss Conway raised the topic of the explorers. A map of Australia would be produced, across which ran a confusion of dotted, dashed and coloured lines. I was bored because I did not know the country the map represented. The men were just names, their journeys snail-trails across paper. No attempt was made to bring exploring to life, perhaps because the inconvenient details about Aborigines and barren wastes would have simply got in the way of the main message: that the Europeans had triumphed. Somehow, those lines granted possession of a continent. And in that message, all of the subtlety, the excitement and wonder of exploration was lost.

Perhaps it is the very realisation that exploration was a sort of conquest which has caused it to fall so far out of favour with many contemporary Australians. It is now commonly thought of as a kind of abomination—the penetration of a fragile continent by ruthless, rough-handed, pale-skinned men who probed, desecrated and killed in their quest for personal vainglory. Yet as I read the words of the men and women, black and white, who carried the endeavour, I find that this is as far from the true heart of Australian exploration as were the deadly boring history lessons of my childhood.

For me, Australian exploration is a very different thing. It is heroic, for nowhere else did explorers face such obdurate country; and it depended on black people far more than on white. In the end it was a failure, for few discovered the fertile soil and abundant water they so yearned for. Yet it has enriched us immeasurably, for it turned the lens on that most fascinating other—a whole continent as it was on the day of European arrival. A continent that, through vast transformations, was to become my home.

With one notable exception, all of the accounts included here are by eyewitnesses. Some were written on the moment, by the light of a candle after a punishing day's work, in unbearable heat or flooding rain, or with the author unable to sit because of massing ants. Only those who know the total exhaustion that such work brings can understand the sheer effort of will needed to write in such circumstances. Other narratives are reminiscences, made fragrant by the smoky atmosphere of Victorian reading rooms or beery hotels. There are precious few accounts by female explorers, and even fewer were ever published, but they are often luminous and fresh and different. For once we see the Aboriginal child, wandering lost and frightened as his parents are held at gunpoint. For once we get the whole-body fear, the loss of nerve that all explorers must have experienced at times of crisis. And we get to hear about the barely edible hairy beef, the loathing at not having washed in a week. Creaghe, Pink and Davidson are names to watch out for.

Australian exploration does not lack light relief. Figures like John Lhotsky and William Wall can be thought of as the comic explorers whose exploits are more suited to a Gilbert and Sullivan opera than the hard grind of exploration. Mark Twain said that Australian history was like so many beautiful lies, but it all actually happened. There is no fiction in this book except for one outrageous hoax, published as a factual adventure in 1899 by the pseudonymous Louis de Rougemont, who claimed, amongst other things, to have found the lost explorer Gibson. He describes new kinds of animals, discovers gold and marries an Aboriginal wife during his bizarre mind-travels. His is the pastiche jewel deliberately threaded on the necklace, so that the genuine diamonds can shine all the more brightly.

Australian exploration literature is so vast and varied that ten volumes the size of this could be filled with riveting accounts. The selection of materials presented here does not pretend to be comprehensive. Rather, it consists of fragments that pleased me, either for their lucidity, their drama or their ability to surprise. Some were chosen because they speak about the greater, evolving Australia, and some are here simply because they are old friends.

Many of the explorers knew they were writing in a mainstream tradition: they knew their journals were as important as their walking boots. There are some wonderful writers in this book who were aware that a thing is not truly discovered until it is written about, for only then does it take shape in the minds of those who have no direct experience of it. Giles, Eyre, Mitchell, Leichhardt and Sturt are marvellous describers. Giles' account of the death of Gibson is one of the most powerful things in our literature. Sturt, a plain and sturdy writer, memorably tells us how in the grotesque desert heat his horses lacked 'the muscular strength to raise their heads'. Eyre, despite exhaustion and illness, seems always to have been able to see another's point of view, and to write beautifully about it.

But what to make of Mr Gosse, who wrote, 'I was compelled to turn south, crossing Mr Giles's track several times...and on to a high hill east of Mt Olga, which I named Ayers Rock'?

Mr Gosse was the first European to lay eyes on the largest rock on the planet: Uluru, an epicentre of Aboriginal dreaming, a place almost hallucinogenic in its grandeur. Any account which could call such a place 'a high hill' finds no home in this book.

European explorers got to carry the ink, pens and journals, and you could easily get the impression that they were the most indispensable members of any expedition. Yet a careful reading of these accounts reveals that Aborigines were the real, albeit unacknowledged, explorers of much of Australia. They generally carried the guns that fed and defended the expedition, they found the water, and they made the peace. In tribute to them, I have coloured the mix of this anthology as far as the written accounts will permit. Sadly, it is rare to hear an account of exploration from an Aborigine's own mouth. The exceptions are usually cases where the Europeans perished, and only the Aboriginal explorer remained to tell of the fate of the party. Their accounts are startling, unforgettable. They come from the ancient tradition of oral storytelling, and they have a liveliness, rhythm and drama all of their own. Lest anyone imagine that Aboriginal explorers' first hand accounts were relegated to the rubbish bin of history because they were somehow inferior to those of literate Europeans, just listen to Jackey Jackey on the death of John Kennedy in 1848:

> I asked him, 'Mr Kennedy, are you going to leave me?' and he said, 'Yes, my boy, I am going to leave you.' He said, 'I am very bad, Jackey; you take the books, Jackey, to the captain, but not the big ones—the governor will give anything for them.' I then tied up the papers. He then said, 'Jackey, give me paper and I will write.'
>
> I gave him paper and pencil, and he tried to write, and then he fell back and died, and I caught him as he fell back and held him, and I then turned round myself and cried.

There is a certain moment in Australian exploration which has always transfixed me. It is the instant when white looks on black, and black on white, for the first time. Neither knows it, but such meetings bridge an extraordinary temporal gulf, for they unite people who became separated at least 50,000 years ago. That's 40,000 years longer than people have been in the Americas or Ireland, 20,000 years before the Neanderthals finally surrendered Europe to my ancestors, and 25,000 years before the worst of the last ice age turned most of Australia into a howling desert, a vast dunefield. No other cultures, meeting on the frontier, have been separated by such an unimaginable chasm of time.

The thing that fascinates me about such meetings is just how clearly both sides managed to make themselves understood. A smile, anger or fear are immediately comprehended—as if the separation of the millennia never existed. That understanding is a tribute to the great commonality of experience that shaped humanity on the African savannah for a million years before the diaspora of the late Pleistocene brought people to Australia. It speaks to me of a common humanity that makes differences in colour, race and culture almost invisible in their triviality.

That magic second of reunion between black and white in Australian exploration has resolved itself in as many different ways as there are explorers. James Cook watched the Aborigines behave as if it never happened. They simply kept fishing or walking, not looking up, as the *Endeavour* passed by a few hundred yards offshore. Sometimes, a spear or a gun saw this remarkable reunion terminated in bloodshed and shame; yet, at its best, the moment was followed by a celebration, a gift or a song.

And then there were the eccentric, almost comic, responses. John McDouall Stuart records that one fine morning in 1858 near Lake Torrens he surprised an Aboriginal man who was hunting: 'What he imagined I was I do not know...in an instant, he threw down his waddies, and jumped up into a mulga bush...He kept waving us off with his hand...I expected every moment to see the bush break with his weight.' What, indeed, did he imagine this white spectre on a horse was? Did the hunter divine (correctly as it turns out) that horses could not climb?

Robert Logan Jack, geologist explorer in north Queensland, records an even more astonishing encounter. What in heaven's name were the Aboriginal women he met near Coen trying to convey to him? They stood in a line and began a chant, then 'all at once each caught hold of her breasts and squirted milk towards us in copious streams'.

The reactions of the Europeans were frequently just as peculiar. Sir Joseph Banks is reputed to have taken a handkerchief (moistened with saliva at one end, one imagines) and applied it to the skin of an Aboriginal man, to discover if the blackness rubbed off. Tasman's party heard gongs and trumpets, and found evidence of giants on the strange mountainous island they called Van Diemen's Land, while several explorers mistook campfires or cremations for evidence of cannibalism.

But the most delightful if confused European response is surely that of Surgeon W. H. Leigh 'maggot-hunter extraordinaire'. Leigh travelled to Kangaroo Island in 1836, where he:

> observed...that the natives frequently stopped and examined a tree...I watched one of them, and found that he forced a little stick into a hole in the tree, whence he drew it two or three times, and sucked the end of it. I had little doubt that he had discovered wild honey, but resolving to ascertain the fact I got a little twig resembling his, and used it as he did. When I withdrew it, I saw nothing on the end of it; yet not trusting to sight alone I put it to my tongue, but it had no taste. Supposing therefore that I had not guided the stick aright, I made two or three more attempts with as little success.
>
> My black squire was all the time watching my movements, and when he saw me suck the bare end of the stick and look so wise about it, he laughed to that degree that he was unable to support himself. I now began to suspect that it was all a joke; but on seeing me turn to go away, he pulled me back, and was about to introduce his stick when I discovered that it had a little fish-bone hooked at its end; and the reason he put it into his mouth appeared to be to keep a bit of grass firm with which it was bound on. He now forced it far into the tree as it would reach and, on withdrawing it, there was on the end an enormous maggot.

That maggot, of course, was a witchetty grub. But such easy relations between the races were impossible two centuries earlier when Australia was first discovered by Europeans. The earliest explorers were Dutch mariners, and they had a terror of the Aborigines. Their main objective seems to have been to kidnap them for interrogation and removal to Java. At this time, Australia was a land of boundless possibilities. In 1688 Dampier did not even know whether it was 'an island or a main continent', but had at least realised that it was not joined to Asia, Africa or America. The seventeenth-century Dutch navigators fully expected to encounter such marvels as mermaids, giants and other human monstrosities in the South Land, for these creatures regularly appeared on maps, and even in scientific texts of the time. As late as 1697 Willem de Vlamingh found 'a miraculous fish, about two feet long with a round head and arms and legs of a kind, nay even something like hands'.

There is a lacuna in Australian exploration between 1699 and 1770. There were no European visits. The Dutch had lost interest and economic muscle, and the English and French were yet to regularly travel so far. So Australia remained as it always had been, an isolated land, unvisited by the outside world except perhaps for adventurous Macassans in search of trepang.

With the establishment of a European beachhead in 1788, the pattern of Australian exploration changed, for a frontier had been created. By 1791 sufficient relations had been established between Europeans and Aborigines for a partnership in exploration to commence. In the early days, the Aborigines had the upper hand. Watkin Tench records a joint expedition in search of the Hawkesbury River in 1791. Colbee and Boladeree, both Eora men from Sydney Harbour, accompanied nineteen Europeans, including Governor Phillip, on a trip inland. From the beginning, the Europeans were the packhorses for, as Tench explains, the Aborigines refused to carry their own supplies, yet laughed to excess when any of the heavily laden Europeans stumbled. 'Our perplexities afforded them an inexhaustible fund of merriment and derision. Did the sufferer, stung at once by nettles and ridicule, and shaken nigh to death by his fall, use any angry expressions with them, they retorted in a moment by calling him by every opprobrious name which their language affords.' Tench explains that their general term of reproach was *gonin-patta*—shit-eater.

To Tench's chagrin, he also found that the Eora knew nothing of the country inland from the harbour. Instead of helping, they plagued him with laments. ' "At Rose Hill," said they, "are potatoes, cabbages, pumpkins, turnips, fish and wine; here are nothing but rocks and water." These comparisons constantly ended with the question of "Where's Rose Hill? Where?" '

Despite this unpromising start, European explorers continued to take Aborigines with them who often earned the undying gratitude and admiration of their fellow expeditioners. Yet it never earned them the respect of society at large. Typical of their fate in this respect, perhaps, is Tommy Windich, guide and closest companion of John Forrest during his three arduous expeditions through the worst of Australia between 1869 and 1874. Upon their arrival in Adelaide, after crossing the southern margin of the continent from Perth in 1870, a banquet was given in honour of the party. During the official speeches a Mr Barlee arose to salute the explorers and, after some opening remarks, mocked Tommy Windich, accusing him of excessive pride in his achievement. Windich, he said, claimed to be 'the man who had brought Mr Forrest to Adelaide, and not Mr Forrest him', and intimated that it was an act of condescension for Windich even to look upon a man such as Barlee. The speech elicited roars of laughter.

It was doubtless considered inappropriate for a savage to eat at the same banquet table as Europeans, so Windich was probably spared the embarrassment of Mr Barlee's arrogant speech. But, after reading Forrest's account, I'm sure that Windich was justified in his statements. He repeatedly found water for the party when they were in dire distress, provided most of the fresh meat they consumed, and risked his life in confronting other

Aborigines who wished to deny the expeditioners passage. Windich probably could have made the journey alone. I doubt that any of the Europeans in Forrest's party could have done the same.

The relationships between the European explorers and their Aboriginal companions varied enormously. Sometimes an Aboriginal guide was simply dragooned into accompanying an expedition. Inevitably, such people had to travel beyond their own country into the territory of enemy tribes where they were in far greater danger than the Europeans. Other explorers picked up local guides who volunteered their services, leaving them and acquiring a replacement at a tribal boundary. Wherever they went, explorers in this country were almost always setting out to enter someone else's territory—another person's home. Like any visitors, their manners and the introduction they brought with them often determined the reception they got.

There is no clearer illustration of this than the experiences of Charles Sturt on his exploration of the Murray in 1830. The exploring expedition had been passed from group to group by Aboriginal emissaries who smoothed the way for them, but at one point Sturt's boat moved faster than the emissaries could make their way along the banks. Arriving unannounced, they were on the point of being massacred until, at the very last possible second, their belated emissary arrived.

Of course, the European forays across the frontier into Aboriginal lands are only half of the story, for Aborigines were constantly crossing the frontier in the opposite direction. The greatest of all eighteenth-century Aboriginal expeditions were Bennelong's visit to Norfolk Island and his journey with Yemmerrawanie to England. Yemmerrawanie was to die during his peregrinations in the English wilderness, and was buried near Eltham in Kent. Bennelong, however, survived two years in England, and returned to his native home.

Almost nothing is known of his visit, except that he met King George III at St James, and that he was ill and was nursed by a Mrs Phillips, Lord Sydney's steward, who resided at Frognal near Eltham.

One slender thread of first-hand evidence of Bennelong's travels survives. It is a letter headed 'Sidney Cove, N.S. Wales, Aug'st 29, 1796'. Bennelong doubtless used an amanuensis. Apparently directed to Mr Phillips the letter reads in part:

> Sir,
> I am very well. I hope you are very well. I live at the governor's. I have every day dinner there. I have not my wife; another black man took her away. We have had murry doings; he speared me in the back, but I better now; his name is Carroway.[†] All my friends alive and well. Not me go to England no more. I am at home now.
>
> I hope Mrs Phillips is very well. You nurse me madam when I sick. You very good madam; thank you madam, and hope you remember me madam, not forget. I know you very well madam. Madam I want stockings, thank you madam. Sir, you give my duty to Ld Sydney. Thank you very good my Lord; hope you well all family very well. Sir. Bannelong.

If only we could include here some of Bennelong's tales about England, told round a campfire on Sydney Cove to entranced listeners. Alas, none survive.

Other unexpected explorers have emerged during the compilation of this anthology. One recounted that for him and his companion 'life was so uncomfortable, that they wished to die'. No, this is not a quote from a dying Burke or a lost Leichhardt, but the words of quite another kind of explorer who was quietly doing a perish in the vicinity of George Street, Sydney, in 1805. Paloo Mata Moigna and his wife Fatafehi had left the comfort of a royal existence in Tonga, and had set off to explore the new society which they heard had been established on the shores of Port Jackson. They were possibly Australia's first royal visitors, but barriers of language and prejudice meant that they were accepted by Governor King only as lowly black freeloaders. Starving, exhausted and disoriented in an apparently barren and hostile land, their wanderings round

---

† Murry: great.

11

Circular Quay in 1805–6 almost cost them their lives. But unlike Burke and Wills, who actually did perish amidst plenty, the Tongans adapted, and lived to return home and tell their tale to King Finau.

I make no apology for including Paloo's rather unconventional tale of exploration in this anthology, for in its own way it is a story as noble, courageous, even heroic, as those of Mitchell or Sturt. But the story of the Tongans is important for another reason. It makes plain that explorers cannot exist without a frontier, and the frontier of Australian exploration has almost always been between two cultures. True it is that Australian exploration in the Antarctic, or even on Lord Howe Island, has involved the penetration of a truly virgin, uninhabited land, and that the exploration of Kangaroo, Flinders, and a few other Australian islands has involved the investigation of a place which has lain uninhabited for a few thousand years. But pure geographic exploration in this sense is a relative rarity in Australasia.

Behind the European-Aboriginal-Pacific frontier developed a series of other, lesser frontiers; for throughout the nineteenth century Australia was developing its own distinctive culture. For this reason, I consider the visit of François Péron to Sydney in 1802 as a form of exploration. Exploration, indeed, continues even today, but now it is largely the natural frontier—between humanity and nature—which provides the challenge. The principal frontier—between Aboriginal and European Australia—closed in 1977 when William Peasley went in search of the last of the nomads, removing them from their desert home and bringing them to Wiluna. His account is the last entry in this anthology.

Earlier generations of Australians viewed the continent's exploration very differently. They knew what an explorer was—and he certainly wasn't an Aborigine or a Tongan. To them, the famous figures of the classic phase of exploration—from about 1817 to 1874, that is from Oxley to Giles—were celebrated as the makers of modern Australia. They were seen as being in the very vanguard of the inexorable European advance and, by traversing the land, they were transferring tenure to the Europeans.

Even these classic explorers, however, tend to fall in and out of fashion. Sir Thomas Mitchell seems to be the latest to suffer a fall from grace. During my primary school days, he was held up as a paragon, an explorer of the first water. Yet in the last few years he has been severely criticised. Some suggest that his meticulous measuring of distances and directions indicate that he did not instinctively 'know' where he was, and he has been castigated as a Luddite for travelling with bullock drays rather than horses. Most recently he has been pilloried as a monster for shooting at an Aboriginal war party. So what was this man— a fool, a savage?

Mitchell was, like many explorers, a complex personality. He was surveyor-general of New South Wales, fluent in Portuguese, a lover of poetry and inventor of curious devices. He was also virtually alone in his time in recognising and wishing to perpetuate a sense of prior Aboriginal ownership of Australia. It was he, after all, who admonished his survey staff that they should be 'particular in noting the native names of as many places as you can in your map...The natives can furnish you with names for every flat and almost every hill...the names of new parishes will also be taken in most cases from the local names of the natives'. Mitchell was a key player in retaining Aboriginal names for 70 per cent of Australia's four million place names. Were it not for his efforts, unfashionable at the time, our cultural geography would be much the poorer.

If in Mitchell, and before him Banks and Tench, we meet men of the enlightenment, by the middle of the nineteenth century we are encountering men of the frontier. All too often they were rough men, ill-educated and prejudiced. Some were bragging, self-confessed murderers. Abominations, such as the Jardine brothers' account of the 'Battle of the Mitchell' form some of the blackest pages in our history, but they must be included here. The goldfields of north Queensland seem to be a particularly rich ground for such dismal pickings, while David Carnegie's habit of capturing

Aborigines (even aged women) and depriving them of water until they led the party to a soak, passed, with variations, as normal practice for many Western Australian explorers.

The third of November, 1874, arguably marks the apogee of this classic phase of exploration. Beginning about midday, a remarkable parade made its way through the streets of Adelaide. The good citizens of the city had decked the route with flags, flowers and streamers to honour the arrival of John Forrest's expedition. The four Europeans and two Aborigines had left the Murchison district of Western Australia eight months earlier, and had pushed west towards the Adelaide–Darwin telegraph line, in the process traversing some of the most inhospitable country on the face of the earth. They were accompanied at the head of the procession by the glitterati of the town, while behind came a remarkable miscellany of exploration participants. Members of Stuart's exploring expeditions bore standards marked with the dates January 1862 and 25 July 1862. Next rode R. E. Warburton (the son of the famous colonel who was absent overseas) and Charley, the Aborigine who performed such remarkable service on Peter Warburton's expedition. Next came William Gosse, European discoverer and namer of Ayers Rock, and the irascible yet poetic Ernest Giles. Even the equine explorers were well represented, for Mr Waterhouse rode astride the horse which had carried 'poor Burke on his ill-fated expedition', and Mr Thring on 'a horse which had crossed the continent with Stuart'.

When the Hon. Arthur Blyth rose to speak at the celebratory dinner that night, he compared the occasion to an 'old Roman Triumph...how the conquerors, when they went forth, and were successful, were granted a triumph, and in this triumph were accompanied by the most beautiful of their captives'. It seems that explorers like John Forrest were Australia's conquistadors. Most often they returned without riches, but they brought a sense of real ownership of the entire continent to those Europeans that clustered around the edge, and for that they were feted.

Whatever the intent of the explorers of the classic period, the consequences of their work were clear. They were the vanguard of an army of invaders who, with disease, the rifle and poisoned flour, would utterly sweep away the unique world of which the explorers give us the briefest glimpse. We can see in their writing how little of this complex world the explorers knew, and how few were their opportunities to learn about it before the full-scale European invasion began.

It is one of the great ironies of the classic age of exploration that, by its end, the sum of human knowledge about Australia had been diminished. In 1817 it was still possible to find somebody, somewhere, who could tell you in detail about their society, the animals, plants and history of their particular part of Australia. The driest desert was as comprehensible to its inhabitants as your street is to you. Then, almost all of the country was lived in and used. But by 1874 vast new wildernesses had been created: areas which had become depopulated, or where people only very occasionally ventured. Moreover, these new 'nomadic', mostly European inhabitants knew little about the land they occasionally crossed. Today, there is no-one who can interpret that land for us. It's true that what knowledge has survived, in writings such as those presented here, is more widely known; but that is the advantage which every literate society has over pre-literate ones.

As you peruse these accounts, I hope that you discover or rediscover something of Australia yourself. Its history is varied beyond belief. Eora warriors, Polish patriots, French aristocrats, currency lads and lasses, fools and wise men, black and white, have all played their part in shaping what the dying William Wills called 'this extraordinary continent'. It's a continent we are just beginning to explore.

Although the explorers often refer to Aborigines in terms which today we find unacceptable—'gins', 'blacks', 'savages', 'niggers', not to mention the strange but surprisingly popular 'children of nature'—the use of such expressions is not always intended to diminish. I have left the judgment of these instances to the reader. Where necessary, I have modernised punctuation and spelling, silently corrected a handful of obvious errors, inserted the occasional explanatory date, and sometimes added a word or two of clarification in a footnote, marked by a dagger (†). The explorers' own footnotes are indicted by an asterisk (*). Otherwise, their writings are presented as they were first printed, with any omissions of text indicated by an ellipsis (...).

WILLEM JANSZ
Uncultivated, Savage, Cruel, 1606

 Sometime during the first half of 1606, the Dutch ship *Duyffken*, under the command of Willem Jansz, made landfall on the western side of Cape York, then known as Nova Guinea. Jansz had entered a great and hitherto unknown gulf—the Gulf of Carpentaria. No eyewitness account of the voyage survives, which is a great pity, for Jansz seems to have been an interesting man. Born a foundling, he became an admiral who, from a pecularity of his speech, was known to his friends as 'I say, I say'.

This, the first authenticated visit to Australia by a European, foreshadowed later visits in being marred by bloodshed. The brief account given here is drawn from expedition instructions given to Abel Tasman by the Dutch East India Company in January 1644.

Both by word of mouth and through the perusal of journals, charts and other writings, it is in the main well known to you how the successive governors of India...have, in order to the aggrandisement, enlargement and improvement of the Dutch East India Company's standing and trade in the east, divers times diligently endeavoured to make timely discovery of the vast country of Nova Guinea and of other unknown eastern and southern regions; to wit, that four several voyages have up to now with scant success been made for this desired discovery...

The first was undertaken in the year 1606 with the yacht *Duyffken*...on which voyage...the unknown south and west coasts of Nova Guinea were discovered over a length of 220 miles from 5 to $13^{3}/_{4}$ degrees southern latitude, it being only ascertained that vast regions were for the greater part uncultivated, and certain parts inhabited by savage, cruel, black barbarians who slew some of our sailors, so that no information was obtained touching the exact situation of the country and regarding the commodities obtainable and in demand there; our men having, by want of provisions and other necessaries, been compelled to return and give up the discovery they had begun, only registering in their chart the name of Cape Keer-weer, the extreme point of the discovered land...

JAN CARSTENSZ
Coal-Black and Stark Naked, 1623

 In 1623 another Dutch mariner Jan Carstensz, sailing in the yacht *Pera*, entered the Gulf of Carpentaria, pushing further south than Jansz. After passing the verdant Spice Islands and glimpsing the eternal snows of New Guinea's highest mountains, he was gravely disappointed by the arid country of western Cape York. Worse, the 'coal-black and stark naked' inhabitants were implacable, repulsing Carstensz's attempts to go 'landinward' in order to complete his explorations. The crew of the *Pera* kidnapped an Aboriginal man, whose fate, like that of so many others, is not recorded. The theme of kidnapping was to become a recurring tragedy of Australian exploration.

We join Carstensz on a deserted and forbidding part of the coast.

May—On the 3rd...I went ashore myself with ten musketeers, and we advanced a long way into the wood without seeing any human beings. The land here is low-lying and without hills as before, in latitude 15° 20'. It is very dry and barren for, during all the time we have searched and examined this part of the coast to our best ability, we have not seen one fruit-bearing tree, nor anything that man could make use of: there are no mountains or even hills, so that it may be safely concluded that the land contains no metals, nor yields any precious woods, such as sandalwood, aloes or columba.

In our judgment this is the most arid and barren region that could be found anywhere on the earth. The inhabitants, too, are the most wretched and poorest creatures that I have ever seen in my age or time; as there are no large trees anywhere on this coast, they have no boats or canoes whether large or small. This is near the place which we touched at on the voyage out on Easter Day, April the 16th; in the new chart we have given to this spot the name Waterplaets.[†] At this place the beach is very fine, with excellent gravelly sand and plenty of delicious fish...

In the morning of the 5th the wind was E, course held N; at noon we were in 14° 5' latitude; shortly after the wind went over to W, upon which we made for the land and cast anchor in two fathom; I went ashore myself in the pinnace which was duly armed. The blacks here attacked us with their weapons, but afterwards took to flight, upon which we went landinward for some distance, and found divers of their weapons, such as assegais and callaways, leaning against the trees. We took care not to damage these weapons, but tied pieces of iron and strings of beads to some of them, in order to attract the blacks who, however, seemed quite indifferent to these things, and repeatedly held up their shields with great boldness and threw them at the muskets. These men are, like all the others we have lately seen, of tall stature and very lean to look at, but malignant and evil-natured...

In the morning of the 7th the wind was SE with fine weather. The skipper went ashore with the pinnace, with strict orders to treat the blacks kindly, and try to attract them with pieces of iron and strings of beads; if practicable, also to capture one or more. When at noon the men returned they reported that on their landing more than 100 blacks had collected on the beach with their weapons, and had with the strong arm tried to prevent them from coming ashore. In order to frighten them, a musket

† Possibly the Mitchell River.

was accordingly fired, upon which the blacks fled and retreated into the wood, from where they tried every means in their power to surprise and attack our men. These natives resemble the others in shape and figure: they are quite black and stark naked, some of them having their faces painted red and others white, with feathers stuck through the lower part of the nose...

In the morning of the 8th, the wind being ESE with good weather, I went ashore myself with ten musketeers. We saw numerous footprints of men and dogs (running from south to north). We accordingly spent some time there, following the footprints aforesaid to a river where we gathered excellent vegetables or pot-herbs. When we had got into the pinnace again, the blacks emerged with their arms from the wood at two different points; by showing them bits of iron and strings of beads we kept them on the beach, until we had come near them, upon which one of them, who had lost his weapon, was by the skipper seized round the waist, while at the same time the quartermaster put a noose round his neck, by which he was dragged to the pinnace.

The other blacks, seeing this, tried to rescue their captured brother by furiously assailing us with their assagais. In defending ourselves we shot one of them, after which the others took to flight, upon which we returned on board without further delay. These natives resemble all the others in outward appearance: they are coal-black and stark naked with twisted nets round their heads...

We cannot, however, give any account of their customs and ceremonies, nor did we learn anything about the thickness of the population, since we had few or no opportunities for inquiring into these matters. Meanwhile I hope that with God's help Your Worships will in time get information touching these points from the black we have captured, to whose utterances I would beg leave to refer you.

FRANÇOIS PELSAERT
Woeful Diurnal Annotations, 1629

 François Pelsaert described his account of the loss of the *Batavia* on the Abrolhos Islands off the coast of Western Australia as his 'woeful diurnal annotations'.

After the shipwreck he took the pinnace, leaving most of the survivors on the islands, and made his way to Batavia (now Jakarta). In his absence these first Europeans to live in Australia turned on each other—conspirators massacred 125 of their fellows, thereby proving that the Dutch could be every bit as barbarous and cruel as the Aborigines of their imaginings.

Pelsaert returned some months later to rescue the survivors and punish the miscreants. He was no deliberate explorer but this time he had more leisure to examine the nature of the strange islands where his ship had met disaster. The 'cats' he encountered were tammar wallabies, the first members of the kangaroo family to be observed closely by Europeans.

On the 4th of June, it being Whitmonday, with a light, clear full moon, about two hours before daybreak...I felt the ship's rudder strike the rocks with a violent horrible shock...I rushed up on deck, and found all the sails atop, the wind south-west. Our course during the night had been north-east by north, and we were now lying amidst thick foam. Still, at the moment, the breakers round the ship were not violent, but shortly after the sea was heard to run upon us with great vehemence on all sides.

When day broke, we found ourselves surrounded by cliffs and shoals...I saw no land that I thought would remain above water at high tide, except an island, which by estimation was fully three miles from the ship. I therefore sent the skipper to two small islets or cliffs in order to ascertain whether our men and part of our cargo could be landed there. About nine o'clock the skipper returned, informing me that it was well-nigh impossible to get through the rocks and cliffs, the pinnace running aground

21

in one place, and the water being several fathom deep in another. As far as he could judge, the islands would remain above water at high tide. Therefore, moved by the loud lamentations raised on board by women, children, sick people and faint-hearted men, we thought it best first to land the greater part of our people...

It was determined, as shown by the resolution, that we should try to find fresh water in the neighbouring islands or on the mainland coast in order to save their lives and our own; and that, if no water should be found, we should in that case at the mercy of God with the pinnace continue our voyage to Batavia, there to make known our calamitous and unheard-of disasters...

November 1629—On the 15th the wind was SSW, with seemingly fine weather. Therefore, in the name of God, we weighed anchor and set sail from these luckless Abrolhos for the mainland on an ENE course...The sea abounds in fish in these parts: they are mainly of three kinds, but very different in shape and taste from those caught on other coasts. All the islands about here are low-lying atolls or coral-islets and rocks, except two or three...

We found in these islands large numbers of a species of cats, which are very strange creatures; they are about the size of a hare, their head resembling the head of a civet-cat; the forepaws are very short, about the length of a finger, on which the animal has five small nails or fingers, resembling those of a monkey's forepaw. Its two hindlegs, on the contrary, are upwards of half an ell in length, and it walks on these only, on the flat of the heavy part of the leg, so that it does not run fast. Its tail is very long, like that of a long-tailed monkey; if it eats, it sits on its hindlegs, and clutches its food with its forepaws, just like a squirrel or monkey.

Their manner of generation or procreation is exceedingly strange and highly worth observing. Below the belly the female carries a pouch, into which you may put your hand; inside the pouch are her nipples, and we have found that the young ones grow up in this pouch with the nipples in their mouths. We have seen some young ones lying there which were only the size of a bean, though at the same time perfectly proportioned, so that it seems certain that they grow there out of the nipples of the mammae, from which they draw their food, until they are grown up and are able to walk. Still, they keep creeping into the pouch even when they have become very large, and the dam runs off with them when they are hunted.

In these two islands we also found a number of grey turtle-doves, but no other animals. Nor is there any vegetation beyond brushwood, and little or no grass. This and what has hereinbefore been related is all that we have experienced and met with about these Abrolhos.

ABEL TASMAN
Men of Extraordinary Stature, 1642

 In 1642 Abel Tasman, wanderer on the sea from Batavia, sailed into a great blank on the world map. At latitude 42° s he sighted a mountainous island. Among the tall timbers, his men found a tree with notches cut at five-foot intervals. They heard the sounds of trumpets and small gongs, and saw the pawprints of an animal like a tiger. Tasman's island is rather like the magical place Shakespeare dreamed up in *The Tempest*, 'full of noises, sounds and sweet airs', a land of preternatural imaginings and monstrous possibilities.

Tasman left the island destined to bear his name convinced it was inhabited by giants and, to judge by the gongs and tigers, somewhat similar to Java. He was not to know that he had crossed the most profound zoological barrier on the planet—Wallace's Line—the imaginary divide that separates the Australian region (with its eucalypts and kangaroos) from Asia (with its elephants and tigers). In Tasmania, men climbed trees by leaps and bounds, ascending from notch to notch with their toes and a stone hatchet. There, the currawong and bellbird called their melodious songs, and of course there were tigers—Tasmanian Tigers. We join Tasman near Storm Bay in the south-east of the island.

24 November—Good weather and a clear sky...In the afternoon, about four o'clock, we saw land bearing east by north of us at about ten miles distance from us by estimation. The land we sighted was very high...

25 November—This land being the first land we have met with in the South Sea, and not known to any European nation, we have conferred on it the name of Anthoony van Diemenslandt in honour of the Hon. Governor-General, our illustrious master, who sent us to make this discovery...

2 December—Early in the morning we sent our pilot-major Francoys Jacobsz in command of our pinnace, manned with four musketeers and six rowers, all of them furnished with spikes and side-arms, together with the cockboat of the *Zeehaen* with one of her second mates and six musketeers in it, to a bay, situated north-west of us at upwards of a mile's distance, in order to ascertain what facilities (as regards fresh water, refreshments, timber and the like) may be available there.

About three hours before nightfall the boats came back, bringing various samples of vegetables which they had seen growing there in great abundance, some of them in appearance not unlike a certain plant growing at the Cabo de Bona Esperance and fit to be used as pot-herbs, and another species with long leaves and a brackish taste, strongly resembling *persil de mer* or samphire. The pilot-major and the second mate of the *Zeehaen* made the following report, to wit:

That they had rowed the space of upwards of a mile round the said point, where they had found high but level land, covered with vegetation (not cultivated but growing naturally by the will of God), abundance of excellent timber, and a gently sloping watercourse in a barren valley; the said water, though of good quality, being difficult to procure because the watercourse was so shallow that the water could be dipped with bowls only.

That they had heard certain human sounds and also sounds nearly resembling the music of a trump or a small gong not far from them, though they had seen no one.

That they had seen two trees about two or two and a half fathom in thickness, measuring from sixty to sixty-five feet from the ground to the lowermost branches, which trees bore notches made with flint implements, the bark having been removed for the purpose. These notches, forming a kind of steps to enable persons to get up the trees and rob the birds' nests in their tops, were fully five feet apart, so that our men concluded that the natives here must be of very tall stature, or must be in possession of some sort of artifice for getting up the said trees; in one of the trees these notched steps were so fresh and new that they seemed to have been cut less than four days ago.

That on the ground they had observed certain footprints of animals, not unlike those of tiger's claws; they also brought on board certain specimens of animal excrements voided by quadrupeds so far as they could surmise and observe, together with a small quantity of gum of a seemingly very fine quality, which had exuded from trees and bore some resemblance to gum-lac...

That in the interior they had in several places observed numerous trees which had deep holes burnt into them at the upper end of the foot, while the earth had here and there been dug out with the fist so as to form a fireplace, the surrounding soil having become as hard as flint through the action of the fire.

A short time before we got sight of our boats returning to the ships, we now and then saw clouds of dense smoke rising up from the land, which was nearly west by north of us, and surmised this might be a signal given by our men because they were so long coming back; for we had ordered them to return speedily, partly in order to be made acquainted with what they had seen and partly that we might be able to send them to other points, if they should find no profit there, to the end that no precious time might be wasted.

When our men had come on board again, we inquired of them whether they had been there and made a fire, to which they returned a negative answer, adding, however, that at various times and points in the wood they also had seen clouds of smoke ascending. So there can be no doubt there must be men here of extraordinary stature.

WILLIAM DAMPIER
The Miserablest People in the World, 1688

 William Dampier, privateer, provided the first extended account in English of the Great South Land and its inhabitants when he landed on the northern Western Australian coast in January 1688. Both the land and the people clearly appalled him. His realistic description stands in contrast to the fantastical Dutch interpretations. Perhaps Dampier's bleak account helped create the great lacuna in the exploration of Australia, from the late seventeenth century until Cook arrived on the eastern seaboard in 1770.

New Holland is a very large tract of land. It is not yet determined whether it is an island or a main continent; but I am certain that it joins neither to Asia, Africa nor America. This part of it that we saw is all low even land, with sandy banks against the sea. Only the points are rocky and so are some of the islands in this bay.[†]

The land is of a dry sandy soil, destitute of water except you make wells, yet producing diverse sorts of trees; but the woods are not thick nor the trees very big...We saw no sort of animal, nor any track of beast, but once; and that seemed to be the

---

† King Sound.

tread of a beast as big as a great mastiff dog. Here are a few small land birds, but none bigger than a blackbird; and but few sea fowls. Neither is the sea very plentifully stored with fish unless you reckon the manatee and turtle as such.[†] Of these creatures there is plenty, but they are extraordinarily shy; though the inhabitants cannot trouble them much, having neither boats nor iron.

The inhabitants of this country are the miserablest people in the world. The Hodmadods of Monomatapa, though a nasty people, yet for wealth are gentlemen to these, who have no houses, and skin garments, sheep, poultry, and fruits of the earth, ostrich eggs, etc., as the Hodmadods have.[††] And, setting aside their human shape, they differ but little from brutes. They are tall, straight-bodied and thin, with small long limbs. They have great heads, round foreheads and great brows. Their eyelids are always half closed to keep the flies out of their eyes; they being so trouble-some here that no fanning will keep them from coming to one's face and, without the assistance of both hands to keep them off, they will creep into one's nostrils and mouth too, if the lips are not shut very close. So that from their infancy being thus annoyed with these insects, they do never open their eyes as other people, and therefore they cannot see far unless they hold up their heads as if they were looking at something over them.

They have great bottle noses, pretty full lips and wide mouths. The two fore-teeth of their upper jaw are wanting in all of them, men and women, old and young; whether they draw them out, I know not. Neither have they any beards. They are long-visaged, and of a very unpleasing aspect, having no one graceful feature in their faces. Their hair is black, short and curled like that of the negroes, and not long and lank like the common Indians. The colour of their skins, both of their faces and the rest of their body, is coal-black, like that of the negroes of Guinea...

[†] Manatee: Dampier is referring to the dugong.
[††] Hodmadods: the Hottentots of South Africa.

These people speak somewhat through the throat; but we could not understand one word that they said. We anchored, as I said before, on January the 5th, and seeing men walking on the shore, we presently sent a canoe to get some acquaintance with them, for we were in hopes to get some provision among them. But the inhabitants, seeing our boat coming, run away and hid themselves...

At last we went over to the islands, and there we found a great many of the natives. I do believe there were forty on one island, men, women and children. The men at our first coming ashore threatened us with their lances and swords, but they were frighted by firing one gun which we fired purposely to scare them. The island was so small that they could not hide themselves, but they were much disordered at our landing, especially the women and children, for we went directly to their camp. The lustiest of the women, snatching up their infants, ran away howling, and the little children run after squeaking and bawling; but the men stood still.

WILLEM DE VLAMINGH
A Land of Miracles, 1696–97

 At the time of de Vlamingh's visit, unicorns, mermaids and giants were still found in the pages of respectable books of natural history. Despite Dampier's pragmatic assessments, the possibilities raised by the Great South Land remained monstrous: fish with arms and legs—even hands—like men, footprints half a metre long, and water as red as blood.

Willem de Vlamingh, master of the *Geelvinck*, captained the last large-scale voyage of exploration made by the Dutch East India Company. He had been despatched to investigate the fate of an East Indiaman lost off the coast of Western Australia. The expedition gives us a glimpse of the land beyond the shore, for de Vlamingh's men were the first Europeans to penetrate any distance inland. They found the uncanny 'Land of Eendracht', with its elusive inhabitants and eerie environment, little to their liking. Here we join him as he sights Rottnest Island—his first taste of Australia.

December 1696—The 29th in the morning on the fifth glass...we raised the South Land ENE of us, about four to five miles, being low land and the shore here reaching s and n. Here our people saw a miraculous fish about two feet long with a round head and arms and legs of a kind, nay even something like hands; likewise several branches of vegetation. And we came to anchor at fourteen to fifteen fathoms, about half a mile off the island, on the south coast, good bottom, the wind sw by s...

The 31st I rowed ashore again with our skipper, and having gone some distance into the interior of the island I found there a great variety of herbs of which a great many were not unknown to me and some of which were similar in smell to those at home; likewise also several trees and among these a kind whose wood had an aromatic fragrance, almost like *Lignum rhodii*.[†] The ground is covered with little or no soil, mostly white sand and rocky, in my opinion unsuitable for cultivation. There are few if any birds to be seen and no animals except a kind of rat as large as a common cat, whose dung is to be found in abundance all over the island;[††] also very few seals and fish other than a kind of sardine and grey rock bream...While returning to the beach, the people found a piece of Dutch timber with nails still sticking in it, which it seems must be from a wrecked ship. On the mainland coast smoke was seen to rise up in several places, about three to four miles from us. The country appears much higher than it really is and looks like that of Holland.

---

† A hardwood, thought previously to have great medicinal qualities.
†† These were quokkas.

The 1st January our people fetched firewood and again saw smoke rising in several places on the mainland; also observed that there is a high and low tide here...

The 3rd after sunset we saw many fires burning along the entire mainland coast...

The 5th in the morning at sunrise the resolution made was put into execution and with the boats of the three South Land ships we, I again in company of the skipper, made for the mainland coast, where having stepped ashore, we found ourselves to amount to eighty-six men (both soldiers and seamen and two of the abovementioned blacks whom we had brought from the Cape) all well provided with weapons. We marched eastward and encountered after about an hour's advance a small hut quite as bad as those of the Hottentots; somewhat further on a large basin with brackish water, which later was found to be a river on whose banks we saw several footprints, no larger than ours, as well as some holes in which there was fresh and somewhat brackish water. But however thoroughly we explored everything, we found no people. Further on we found still more poor huts and footprints. Towards the evening it was resolved to remain ashore that night and so we camped in a wood in a place where we found a fire started by the inhabitants, whom, however, we did not see. It was kept going by throwing on wood while in the meantime four guards were posted every quarter of an hour...

The 7th all the people were ferried back to the ships in the boats, bringing along two young black swans...

The 12th two hours before sunrise I went ashore again with our upper-steersman, several seamen and the said two blacks, upon seeing several fires. We met...no people, wherefore recognising that nothing was to be achieved by us here, we returned to our ship, which we came to at noon. Concerning the country, it is sandy and, in the area where we have been, wooded with many trees, among which some as much as three to four fathoms thick, but without fruit: in short, full of thistles and thorns. Several of these trees yielded a kind of resin, almost like lacquer, brownish-red in colour. Everything was timid in our presence, both men and birds, swans, brent-geese, pelicans, cockatoos, parakeets, etc. The best part of it is that no vermin is found here, but by day the flies are a terrible torment...

The 15th...saw much smoke and vapour rising up in several places. About midday we went ashore...We were inland about a mile and a half, but found no people, nor fresh water, but several human footprints and such as of a dog and cassowary; further no trees and nothing but thistles and thorns. One of our people said that he had seen a red snake, some others that just when we arrived at the beach they had seen a yellow dog jump out of the scrub and throw itself into the sea as if to enjoy a swim. I do not know what truth there is in this: for I saw neither...

The 21st our boat once again went ashore, but without discovering anything new...

The 25th early in the morning I went ashore...Having come to the beach, we found many oysters and started at once out on our march but sometimes had to rest through fatigue caused by the heat of the sun and the heavy going through thick scrub, until we came to the mountain range, where we camped. But if the march had been hard, the greatest grief struck us now, for finding no water, we thought we would perish from thirst. We could see our ships clearly from here and wished a thousand times to be back on board. Meanwhile, the commander of the soldiers had descended with another two men and brought back a report, with a cheerful face when he returned, that he had found fresh water as well as a hut and footprints eighteen inches long, about an hour's march from our camp. Whereupon it was resolved to march there even though it began to grow dark, which was not done without great trouble because of the scrub and nightfall. Having arrived at the watering place, we found it to be a large hole but the water slightly brackish. We camped by it and, having properly posted guards all the time, passed the night as well as we could.

The 26th in the morning before sunrise we started marching again and arrived at the said hut after a while, around which we found a great many eggshells, but those eighteen-inch footprints changed into ordinary ones. We also passed this night on shore,

31

camped again by the waterhole mentioned, without, although having split up, finding either humans or animals, there being nothing but scrub.

WILLIAM DAMPIER
Crying *Pooh, Pooh, Pooh*, 1699

 Dampier seems to have matured as an explorer by the time of his second voyage to Australia in 1699, this time representing the British Admiralty. His careful descriptions of wildlife indicate that he had overcome his initial horror at the sterility of the country, and he was filled with regret at the first spilling of blood between Aborigines and the English, at Roebuck Bay near Broome, an event he recounts here. When homeward bound, his ship sprang a leak and had to be run ashore on Ascension Island. Dampier finally reached England in 1701. Fittingly, he later rescued Alexander Selkirk, better known as that most famous of castaways, Robinson Crusoe.

August—The 28th day we had between twenty and forty fathom. We saw no land this day, but saw a great many snakes and some whales. We saw also some boobies and noddy-birds; and in the night caught one of these last. It was of another shape and colour than any I had seen before. It had a small long bill, as all of them have; flat feet like ducks' feet; its tail forked like a swallow but longer and broader, and the fork deeper than that of the swallow, with very long wings.

The top or crown of the head of this noddy was coal-black, having also small black streaks round about and close to the eyes; and round these streaks, on each side, a pretty broad white circle. The breast, belly and underpart of the wings of this noddy were white; and the back and upper part of its wings of a faint black or smoke colour...

32

The 30th day, being in latitude 18° 21', we made the land
again, and saw many great smokes near the shore; and having
fair weather and moderate breezes I steered in towards it. At
four in the afternoon I anchored in eight fathom water, clear
sand, about three leagues and a half from the shore. I presently
sent my boat to sound nearer in, and they found ten fathom
about a mile farther in; and from thence still farther in the water
decreased gradually to nine, eight, seven, and at two-mile distance
to six fathom. This evening we saw an eclipse of the moon...

The 31st of August betimes in the morning I went ashore
with ten or eleven men to search for water. We went armed
with muskets and cutlasses for our defence, expecting to see
people there; and carried also shovels and pickaxes to dig wells.
When we came near the shore we saw three tall black naked
men on the sandy bay ahead of us, but as we rowed in they
went away. When we were landed, I sent the boat with two men
in her to lie a little from the shore at an anchor, to prevent
being seized; while the rest of us went after the three black men,
who were now got on the top of a small hill about a quarter of
a mile from us, with eight or nine men more in their company.
They, seeing us coming, ran away. When we came on the top
of the hill where they first stood, we saw a plain savannah, about
half a mile from us, farther in from the sea. There were several
things like haycocks standing in the savannah, which at a distance
we thought were houses, looking just like the Hottentot's houses
at the Cape of Good Hope—but we found them to be so many
rocks. We searched about these for water, but could find none,
nor any houses, nor people, for they were all gone. Then we
turned again to the place where we landed, and there we dug
for water.

While we were at work there came nine or ten of the natives
to a small hill a little way from us, and stood there menacing
and threatening of us, and making a great noise. At last one of
them came towards us, and the rest followed at a distance. I
went out to meet him, and came within fifty yards of him,
making to him all the signs of peace and friendship I could; but

then he ran away, neither would they any of them stay for us to come nigh them, for we tried two or three times.

At last I took two men with me, and went in the afternoon along by the seaside, purposely to catch one of them, if I could, of whom I might learn where they got their fresh water. There were ten or twelve of the natives a little way off, who, seeing us three going away from the rest of our men, followed us at a distance. I thought they would follow us: but there being for a while a sandbank between us and them, that they could not then see us, we made a halt, and hid ourselves in a bending of the sandbank. They knew we must be thereabouts and, being three or four times our number, thought to seize us. So they dispersed themselves, some going to the seashore, and others beating about the sandhills.

We knew by what rencounter we had had with them in the morning that we could easily outrun them; so a nimble young man that was with me, seeing some of them near, ran towards them; and they for some time ran away before him. But, he soon overtaking them, they faced about and fought him. He had a cutlass, and they had wooden lances; with which, being many of them, they were too hard for him. When he first ran towards them I chased two more that were by the shore; but fearing how it might be with my young man I turned back quickly, and went up to the top of a sandhill, whence I saw him near me, closely engaged with them.

Upon their seeing me, one of them threw a lance at me that narrowly missed me. I discharged my gun to scare them, but avoided shooting any of them; till, finding the young man in great danger from them, and myself in some; and that, though the gun had a little frighted them at first, yet they had soon learnt to despise it, tossing up their hands, and crying *pooh, pooh, pooh*, and coming on afresh with a great noise.

I thought it high time to charge again, and shoot one of them, which I did. The rest, seeing him fall, made a stand again; and my young man took the opportunity to disengage himself, and come off to me; my other man also was with me, who had done nothing all this while, having come out unarmed; and I returned back with my men, designing to attempt the natives no farther, being very sorry for what had happened already.

They took up their wounded companion; and my young man, who had been struck through the cheek by one of their lances, was afraid it had been poisoned; but I did not think that likely. His wound was very painful to him, being made with a blunt weapon, but he soon recovered of it.

JAMES COOK
Botany Bay, 1770

 James Cook is justly regarded as the greatest maritime explorer of his age, perhaps of all time. In 1770 he charted the east coast of Australia, touching land five times—first of all at what is now Botany Bay. Cook initially named it Stingray Bay, for the enormous stingrays caught there, and he correctly surmised that these creatures were never hunted by the Aborigines. After giving the botanists Banks and Solander time to collect a cornucopia of plant specimens, he changed the name in honour of their work, set sail, and coasted serenely past a safe anchorage he named Port Jackson—thus failing to discover Sydney's astonishing harbour.

6 May—In the evening the yawl returned from fishing having caught two stingrays weighing near 600 pounds. The great quantity of new plants etc. Mr Banks and Dr Solander collected in this place occasioned my giving it the name of Botany Bay. It is situated in the latitude of 34° 0' south, longitude 208° 37' west. It is capacious, safe and commodious.

It may be known by the land on the sea coast which is of a pretty even and moderate height, rather higher than it is farther inland with steep rocky cliffs next to the sea and looks like a long island lying close under the shore. The entrance of the harbour lies about the middle of this land; in coming from the southward it is discovered before you are abreast of it which you cannot do in coming from the northward; the entrance is little more than a mile broad and lies in WNW...

We anchored near the south shore about a mile within the entrance for the conveniency of sailing with a southerly wind and the getting of fresh water, but I afterwards found a very fine stream of fresh water on the north shore in the first sandy cove within the island, before which a ship might lay almost landlocked, and wood for fuel may be got everywhere. Although wood is here in great plenty yet there is very little variety; the largest trees are as large or larger than our oaks in England and grows a good deal like them and yields a reddish gum; the wood itself is heavy, hard and black like lignum vitae; another sort that grows tall and straight something like pines, the wood of this is hard and ponderous and something of the nature of American live oaks; these two are all the timber trees I met with.

There are a few sorts of shrubs and palm trees and mangroves about the head of the harbour. The country is woody, low and flat as far inland as we could see and I believe the soil is generally sandy; in the wood are a variety of very beautiful birds such as cockatoos, lorikeets, parrots etc., and crows exactly like those we have in England. Waterfowl are no less plenty about the head of the harbour where there are large flats of sand and mud on which they seek their food: the most of these unknown to us, one sort especially which was black and white and as large as a goose but most like a pelican.

On the sand and mud banks are oysters, mussels, cockles etc., which I believe are the chief support of the inhabitants, who go into the shoaled water with their little canoes and pick them out of the sand and mud with their hands and sometimes roast and eat them in the canoe, having often a fire for that purpose as I suppose, for I know of no other use it can be for. The natives do not appear to be numberous, neither do they seem to live in large bodies but dispersed in small parties along by the water side; those I saw were about as tall as Europeans, of a very dark brown colour but not black, nor had they woolly frizzled hair, but black and lank like ours. No sort of clothing or ornaments were ever seen by any of us upon any one of them, or in or about their huts, from which I conclude they never wear any. Some we saw that had their faces and bodies painted with a sort of white paint or pigment.

Although I said that shellfish is their chief support yet they catch other sorts of fish, some of which we found roasting on the fire the first time we landed; some of these they strike with gigs and others they catch with hook and line; we have seen them strike fish with gigs, and hooks and lines were found in their huts. Stingrays I believe they do not eat because I never saw the least remains of one near any of their huts or fireplaces. However, we could but know very little of their customs as we were never able to form any connections with them; they had not so much as touched the things we had left in their huts on purpose for them to take away.

During our stay in this harbour I caused the English colours to be displayed ashore every day and an inscription to be cut in one of the trees near the watering place setting forth the ship's name, date, etc. Having seen everything this place afforded we at daylight in the morning weighed with a light breeze at NW and put to sea, the wind soon after coming to the southward. We steered alongshore NNE and at noon we were by observation in the latitude of 33° 50' S about two or three miles from the land and abreast of a bay or harbour wherein there appeared to be safe anchorage which I called Port Jackson.

JOSEPH BANKS
The *Endeavour* Holed, 1770

 Perhaps it's his well-known portrait as the corpulent, bewigged and gouty president of the Royal Society that makes us think of Sir Joseph Banks as stuffy. His *Endeavour* writings, however, reveal a lively, enquiring young man with a delightful sense of humour, fully worthy of the maidens bestowed upon him by Queen Purea of Tahiti.

The holing of the *Endeavour* on the Great Barrier Reef in June 1770 is one of the most dramatic events in Australian exploration history. Banks's account of the catastrophe is full of life, wonderment and terror. In it we meet a landlubber faced with the prospect of a watery death, and the marvelling of an outsider at the coolness of the ship's crew in a moment of crisis.

Banks was perhaps secretly jubilant at the enforced stay at the Endeavour River in north Queensland, where Cooktown now is. It must have been frustrating for the great botanist to watch the coastline slip by for weeks at a time, with a captain unwilling to land. It was at Endeavour River that a European first saw a kangaroo, and where a sailor from the *Endeavour* encountered what appeared to be the devil himself!

8 June 1770—Still sailing between the main and islands; the former, rocky and high, looked rather less barren than usual and by the number of fires seemed to be better peopled. In the morn we passed within a quarter of a mile of a small islet or rock on which we saw with our glasses about thirty men, women and children standing all together and looking attentively at us. The first people we have seen show any signs of curiosity at the sight of the ship.

9 June—...After dinner came to an anchor and went ashore, but saw no people. The country was hilly and very stony affording nothing but fresh water, at least that we found, except a few plants that we had not before met with. At night our people caught a few small fish with their hooks and lines.

10 June—Just without us as we lay at an anchor was a small sandy island laying upon a large coral shoal, much resembling the low islands to the eastward of us but the first of the kind we had met with in this part of the south sea. Early in the morn we weighed and sailed as usual with a fine breeze along shore,

the country hilly and stony. At nightfall rocks and shoals were seen ahead, on which the ship was put upon a wind offshore. While we were at supper she went over a bank of seven or eight fathom water which she came upon very suddenly; this we concluded to be the tail of the shoals we had seen at sunset and therefore went to bed in perfect security, but scarce were we warm in our beds when we were called up with the alarming news of the ship being fast ashore upon a rock, which she in a few moments convinced us of by beating very violently against the rocks.

Our situation became now greatly alarming: we had stood offshore three hours and a half with a pleasant breeze so knew we could not be very near it: we were little less than certain that we were upon sunken coral rocks, the most dreadful of all others on account of their sharp points and grinding quality which cut through a ship's bottom almost immediately. The officers, however, behaved with inimitable coolness void of all hurry and confusion; a boat was got out in which the master went and after sounding round the ship found that she had ran over a rock and consequently had shoal water all round her. All this time she continued to beat very much so that we could hardly keep our legs upon the quarterdeck; by the light of the moon we could see her sheathing-boards etc. floating thick round her; about twelve her false keel came away.

11 June—In the meantime all kind of preparations were making for carrying out anchors, but by reason of the time it took to hoist out boats etc. the tide ebbed so much that we found it impossible to attempt to get her off till next high water, if she would hold together so long; and we now found to add to our misfortune that we had got ashore nearly at the top of high water and as night tides generally rise higher than day ones we had little hopes of getting off even then.

For our comfort, however, the ship as the tide ebbed settled to the rocks and did not beat near so much as she had done; a rock, however, under her starboard bow kept grating her bottom making a noise very plainly to be heard in the fore storerooms.

This, we doubted not, would make a hole in her bottom; we only hoped that it might not let in more water than we could clear with our pumps.

In this situation day broke upon us and showed us the land about eight leagues off as we judged; nearer than that was no island or place on which we could set foot. It, however, brought with it a decrease of wind and soon after that a flat calm, the most fortunate circumstance that could possibly attend people in our circumstances. The tide we found had fallen two feet and still continued to fall. Anchors were, however, got out and laid ready for heaving as soon as the tide should rise but to our great surprise we could not observe it to rise in the least.

Orders were now given for lightening the ship which was begun by starting our water and pumping it up; the ballast was then got up and thrown overboard as well as six of our guns (all that we had upon deck). All this time the seamen worked with surprising cheerfulness and alacrity; no grumbling or growling was to be heard throughout the ship, no not even an oath (though the ship in general was as well furnished with them as most in His Majesty's service). About one, the water was fallen so low that the pinnace touched ground as she lay under the ship's bows ready to take in an anchor, after this the tide began to rise and as it rose the ship worked violently upon the rocks so that by two she began to make water and increased very fast. At night the tide almost floated her but she made water so fast that three pumps, hard worked, could but just keep her clear and the fourth absolutely refused to deliver a drop of water. Now in my own opinion I entirely gave up the ship and packing up what I thought I might save prepared myself for the worst.

The most critical part of our distress now approached. The ship was almost afloat and everything ready to get her into deep water but she leaked so fast that with all our pumps we could just keep her free. If (as was probable) she should make more water when hauled off she must sink and we well knew that our boats were not capable of carrying us all ashore, so that some, probably the most of us, must be drowned: a better fate maybe than those would have who should get ashore without arms to defend themselves from the Indians or provide themselves with food, on a country where we had not the least reason to hope for subsistence had they even every convenience to take it as nets etc., so barren had we always found it; and had they even met with good usage from the natives and food to support them, debarred from a hope of ever again seeing their native country or conversing with any but the most uncivilised savages perhaps in the world.

The dreadful time now approached and the anxiety in everybody's countenance was visible enough. The capstan and windlass were manned and they began to heave: fear of death now stared us in the face. Hopes we had none but of being able to keep the ship afloat till we could run her ashore on some part of the main where out of her materials we might build a vessel large enough to carry us to the East Indies.

At ten o'clock she floated and was in a few minutes hauled into deep water where to our great satisfaction she made no more water than she had done, which was indeed full as much as we could manage, though no one there was in the ship but who willingly exerted his utmost strength.

12 June—The people who had been twenty-four hours at exceeding hard work now began to flag; myself, unused to labour, was much fatigued and had laid down to take a little rest; was awaked about twelve with the alarming news of the ship's having gained so much upon the pumps that she had four feet water in her hold. Add to this that the wind blew off the land a regular land breeze so that all hopes of running her ashore were totally cut off. This, however, acted upon everybody like a charm: rest was no more thought of but the pumps went with unwearied vigour till the water was all out, which was done in a much shorter time than was expected, and upon examination it was found that she never had half so much water in her as was thought, the carpenter having made a mistake in sounding the pumps.

We now began again to have some hopes and to talk of

getting the ship into some harbour as we could spare hands from the pumps to get up our anchors; one bower, however, we cut away but got the other and three small anchors far more valuable to us than the bowers, as we were obliged immediately to warp her to windward that we might take advantage of the sea breeze to run in shore.

One of our midshipmen now proposed an expedient which no one else in the ship had seen practised, though all had heard of it by the name of fothering a ship, by the means of which he said he had come home from America in a ship which made more water than we did; nay so sure was the master of that ship of his expedient that he took her out of harbour knowing how much water she made and trusting entirely to it.

He was immediately set to work with four or five assistants to prepare his fother which he did thus. He took a lower studding sail and, having mixed together a large quantity of oakum chopped fine and wool, he sticked it down upon the sail as loosely as possible in small bundles each about as big as his fist: these were ranged in rows three or four inches from each other. This was to be sunk under the ship and the theory of it was this: wherever the leak was must be a great suction which would probably catch hold of one or other of these lumps of oakum and wool and, drawing it in either partly or entirely, stop up the hole. While this work was going on the water rather gained on those who were pumping which made all hands impatient for the trial.

In the afternoon the ship was got under way with a gentle breeze of wind and stood in for the land; soon after the fother was finished and applied by fastening ropes to each corner, then sinking the sail under the ship and with these ropes drawing it as far backwards as we could; in about half an hour to our great surprise the ship was pumped dry and upon letting the pumps stand she was found to make very little water, so much beyond our most sanguine expectations had this singular expedient succeeded.

At night came to an anchor, the fother still keeping her almost clear so that we were in an instant raised from almost despondency to the greatest hopes. We were now almost too sanguine, talking of nothing but getting her into some harbour where we might lay her ashore and repair her, or if we could not find such a place we little doubted to the East Indies.

During the whole time of this distress I must say for the credit of our people that I believe every man exerted his utmost for the preservation of the ship, contrary to what I have universally heard to be the behaviour of seamen who have commonly as soon as a ship is in a desperate situation began to plunder and refuse all command. This was no doubt owing entirely to the cool and steady conduct of the officers, who during the whole time never gave an order which did not show them to be perfectly composed and unmoved by the circumstances howsoever dreadful they might appear.

13 June—One pump, and that not half worked, kept the ship clear all night. In the morn we weighed with a fine breeze of wind and steered along ashore among innumerable shoals, the boats keeping ahead and examining every appearance of a harbour which presented itself; nothing, however, was met with which could possibly suit our situation, bad as it was, so at night we came to an anchor. The pinnace, however, which had gone far ahead was not returned, nor did she till nine o'clock, when she reported that she had found just the place we wanted, in which the tide rose sufficiently and there was every natural convenience that could be wished for either laying the ship ashore or heaving her down. This was too much to be believed by our most sanguine wishes: we, however, hoped that the place might do for us if not so much as we had been told yet something to better our situation, as yet but precarious, having nothing but a lock of wool between us and destruction.

14 June—Very fresh sea breeze. A boat was sent ahead to show us the way into the harbour, but by some mistake of signals we were obliged to come to an anchor again of the mouth of it without going in, where it soon blew too fresh for us to weigh. We now began to consider our good fortune; had it blown as

fresh the day before yesterday or before that we could never have got off but must inevitably have been dashed to pieces on the rocks.

The captain and myself went ashore to view the harbour and found it indeed beyond our most sanguine wishes: it was the mouth of a river the entrance of which was, to be sure, narrow enough and shallow but, when once in, the ship might be moored afloat so near the shore that, by a stage from her to it, all her cargo might be got out and in again in a very short time; in this same place she might be hove down with all ease, but the beach gave signs of the tides rising in the springs six or seven feet which was more than enough to do our business without that trouble. The meeting with so many natural advantages in a harbour so near us at the very time of our misfortune appeared almost providential; we had not in the voyage before seen a place so well suited for our purpose as this was, and certainly had no right to expect the tides to rise so high here that did not rise half so much at the place where we struck, only eight leagues from this place; we therefore returned on board in high spirits...

17 June—Weather a little less rough than it was. Weighed and brought the ship in but in doing it ran her twice ashore by the narrowness of the channel; the second time she remained till the tide lifted her off. In the meantime Dr Solander and myself began our plant gathering. In the evening the ship was moored within twenty feet of the shore afloat and before night much lumber was got out of her...

20 June—Weather cleared up so we began to gather and dry plants of which we had hopes of as many as we could muster during our stay...

21 June—Fine clear weather: began today to lay plants in sand. By night the ship was quite clear and in the night's tide (which we had constantly observed to be much higher than the day's) we hauled her ashore.

22 June—In the morn I saw her leak which was very large: in the middle was a hole large enough to have sunk a ship with twice our pumps, but here providence had most visibly worked

in our favour, for it was in great measure plugged up by a stone which was as big as a man's fist. Round the edges of this stone had all the water come in which had so near overcome us, and here we found the wool and oakum or fothering which had relieved us in so unexpected a manner. The effects of the coral rock upon her bottom is difficult to describe but more to believe; it had cut through her plank and deep into one of her timbers, smoothing the gashes still before it so that the whole might easily be imagined to be cut with an axe. Myself employed all day in laying in plants. The people who were sent to the other side of the water in order to shoot pigeons saw an animal as large as a greyhound, of a mouse colour and very swift.[†] They also saw many Indian houses and a brook of fresh water.

23 June—The people who went over the river saw the animal again and described him much in the same manner as yesterday.

24 June—Gathering plants and hearing descriptions of the animal which is now seen by everybody. A seaman who had been out in the woods brought home the description of an animal he had seen, composed in so seamanlike a style that I cannot help mentioning it: it was (says he) about as large and much like a one gallon cagg, as black as the devil and had two horns on its head; it went but slowly but I dared not touch it.[††]

25 June—In gathering plants today I myself had the good fortune to see the beast so much talked of, though but imperfectly; he was not only like a greyhound in size and running but had a long tail, as long as any greyhound's; what to liken him to I could not tell, nothing certainly that I have seen at all resembles him...

29 June—One of our midshipmen, an American who was out a shooting today, saw a wolf, perfectly he said like those he had seen in America; he shot at it but did not kill it.[†††] The seine was hauled today for the first time and 150 pounds of fish caught in it...

[†] The first European sighting of a kangaroo. Previous explorers had seen only various kinds of wallabies.
[††] This was probably the black flying fox.
[†††] The midshipman was James Maria Magra (Matra). He probably saw a dingo.

1 July—Being Sunday all hands were ashore on liberty; many animals were seen by them. The Indians had a fire about a league off up the river...

The ship was now finished and tomorrow being the highest spring tide it was intended to haul her off, so we began to think how we should get out of this place, where so lately to get only in was our utmost ambition. We had observed in coming in innumerable shoals and sand all round us, so we went upon a high hill to see what passage to the sea might be open. When we came there the prospect was indeed melancholy: the sea everywhere full of innumerable shoals, some above and some under water, and no prospect of any straight passage out. To return as we came was impossible, the trade wind blew directly in our teeth. Most dangerous then our navigation must be among unknown dangers. How soon might we again be reduced to the misfortune we had so lately escaped! Escaped indeed we had not till we were again in an open sea...

6 July—Set out today with the second lieutenant resolved to go a good way up the river and see if the country inland differed from that near the shore. We went for about three leagues among mangroves, then we got into the country which differed very little from what we had seen. From hence we proceeded up the river which contracted itself much and lost most of its mangroves; the banks were steep and covered with trees of a beautiful verdure particularly what is called in the West Indies mohoe or bark tree (*Hibiscus tiliaceus*). The land within was generally low, covered thick with long grass, and seemed to promise great fertility were these people to plant and improve it. In the course of the day Tupia saw a wolf, so at least I guess by his description, and we saw three of the animals of the country but could not get one; also a kind of bats as large as a partridge but these also we were not lucky enough to get.[†] At night we took up our

---

[†] Tupia was a Tahitian who had joined the expedition. The animals they saw were probably a dingo and flying foxes.

lodgings close to the banks of the river and made a fire, but the mosquitoes, whose peaceful dominions it seems we had invaded, spared no pains to molest as much as was in their power: they followed us into the very smoke, nay almost into the fire, which hot as the climate was we could better bear the heat of than their intolerable stings.

Between the hardness of our beds, the heat of the fire and the stings of these indefatigable insects the night was not spent so agreeably but that day was earnestly wished for by all of us; at last it

7 July—came and with its first dawn we set out in search of game. We walked many miles over the flats and saw four of the animals, two of which my greyhound fairly chased, but they beat him owing to the length and thickness of the grass which prevented him from running while they at every bound leaped over the tops of it. We observed much to our surprise that instead of going upon all fours this animal went only upon two legs, making vast bounds just as the jerboa (*Mus jaculus*) does.

We returned about noon and pursued our course up the river, which soon contracted itself into a freshwater brook where, however, the tide rose pretty considerably; towards evening it was so shallow, being almost low water, that we were obliged to get out of the boat and drag her, so finding a convenient place for sleeping in we resolved to go no farther. Before our things were got up out of the boat we observed a smoke about a furlong from us; we did not doubt at all that the natives, who we had so long had a curiosity to see well, were there. So three of us went immediately towards it, hoping that the smallness of our numbers would induce them not to be afraid of us. When we came to the place, however, they were gone, probably upon having discovered us before we saw them. The fire was in an old tree of touchwood; their houses were there, and branches of trees broken down, with which the children had been playing, not yet withered; their footsteps also upon the sand below the high-tide mark proved that they had very lately been there; near their oven, in which victuals had been dressed since morn, were shells of a kind of clam and roots of a wild yam which had been cooked in it.

Thus were we disappointed of the only good chance we have had of seeing the people since we came here by their unaccountable timidity, and night soon coming on we repaired to our quarters, which was upon a broad sandbank under the shade of a bush where we hoped the mosquitoes would not trouble us. Our beds of plantain leaves spread on the sand as soft as a mattress, our cloaks for bedclothes and grass pillows, but above all the entire absence of mosquitoes made me and, I believe, all of us sleep almost without intermission; had the Indians came they would certainly have caught us all napping but that was the least in our thoughts...

10 July—Four Indians appeared on the opposite shore; they had with them a canoe made of wood with an outrigger in which two of them embarked and came towards the ship but stopped at the distance of a long musket shot, talking much and very loud to us. We hollored to them and waving made them all the signs we could to come nearer; by degrees they ventured almost insensibly nearer and nearer till they were quite alongside, often holding up their lances as if to show us that if we used them ill they had weapons and would return our attack. Cloth, nails, paper etc. etc. was given to them all which they took and put into the canoe without showing the least signs of satisfaction.

At last a small fish was by accident thrown to them on which they expressed the greatest joy imaginable, and instantly putting off from the ship made signs that they would bring over their comrades, which they very soon did and all four landed near us, each carrying in his hand two lances and his stick to throw them with. Tupia went towards; they stood all in a row in the attitude of throwing their lances; he made signs that they should lay them down and come forward without them; this they immediately did and sat down with him upon the ground. We then came up to them and made them presents of beads, cloth, etc. which they took and soon became very easy, only jealous if anyone attempted to go between them and their arms. At dinner time we made signs to them to come with us and eat but they refused; we left them and they going into their canoe paddled back to where they came from.

11 July—Indians came over again today, two that were with us yesterday and two new ones who our old acquaintance introduced to us by their names, one of which was Yaparico. Though we did not yesterday observe it they all had the septum or inner part of the nose bored through with a very large hole, in which one of them had stuck the bone of a bird as thick as a man's finger and five or six inches long, an ornament no doubt, though to us it appeared rather an uncouth one. They brought with them a fish which they gave to us in return I suppose for the fish we had given them yesterday. Their stay was but short for some of our gentlemen being rather too curious in examining their canoe they went directly to it and pushing it off went away without saying a word. At night the boat which had been sent to the reef for turtle came home and brought three.

12 July—Indians came again today and ventured down to Tupia's tent, where they were so well pleased with their reception that three stayed while the fourth went with the canoe to fetch two new ones; they introduced their strangers (which they always made a point of doing) by name and had some fish given them. They received it with indifference, signed to our people to cook it for them, which was done, and they eat part and gave the rest to my bitch. They stayed the most part of the morning but never ventured to go above twenty yards from their canoe. The ribbands, by which we had tied medals round their necks the first day we saw them, were covered with smoke; I suppose they lay much in the smoke to keep off the mosquitoes.

They are a very small people or at least this tribe consisted of very small people, in general about five feet six in height and very slender; one we measured five feet two and another five feet nine, but he was far taller than any of his fellows. I do not know by what deception we were to a man of opinion, when we saw them run on the sand about a quarter of a mile from us, that they were taller and larger than we were. Their colour was nearest to that of chocolate, not that their skins were so dark but the smoke and dirt with which they were cased over, which I suppose served them instead of clothes, made them of that colour.

Their hair was straight in some and curled in others; they always wore it cropped close round their heads; it was of the same consistence with our hair, by no means woolly or curled like that of Negroes. Their eyes were in many lively and their teeth even and good; of them they had complete sets, by no means wanting two of their foreteeth as Dampier's New Hollanders did.

They were all of them clean limned, active and nimble. Clothes they had none, not the least rag, those parts which nature willingly conceals being exposed to view completely uncovered; yet when they stood still they would often or almost always with their hand or something they held in it hide them in some measure at least, seemingly doing that as if by instinct. They painted themselves with white and red, the first in lines and bars on different parts of their bodies, the other in large patches. Their ornaments were few: necklaces prettily enough made of shells, bracelets wore around the upper part of their arms, consisting of strings lapped round with other strings as what we call gimp in England, a string no thicker than a pack thread tied round their bodies which was sometimes made of human hair, a piece of bark tied over their forehead, and the preposterous bone in their noses which I have before mentioned were all that we observed. One had indeed one of his ears bored, the hole being big enough to put a thumb through, but this was peculiar to that one man and him I never saw wear in it any ornament.

Their language was totally different from that of the islanders; it sounded more like English in its degree of harshness though it could not be called harsh neither. They almost continually made use of the word *chircau*, which we conceived to be a term of admiration as they still used it whenever they saw anything new; also *cherr, tut tut tut tut tut*, which probably have the same signification.

Their canoe was not above ten feet long and very narrow built, with an outrigger fitted much like those at the islands only far inferior; they in shallow waters set her on with poles, in deep paddled her with paddles about four feet long; she just carried four people so that the six who visited us today were obliged to make two embarkations. Their lances were much like those we had seen in Botany Bay, only they were all of them single-pointed, and some pointed with the stings of stingrays and bearded with two or three beards of the same, which made them indeed a terrible weapon; the board or stick with which they flung them was also made in a neater manner.

After having stayed with us the greatest part of the morning they went away as they came. While they stayed two more and a young woman made their appearance upon the beach; she was to the utmost that we could see with our glasses as naked as the men...

14 July—Our second lieutenant who was a shooting today had the good fortune to kill the animal that had so long been the subject of our speculations. To compare it to any European animal would be impossible as it has not the least resemblance to any one I have seen. Its forelegs are extremely short and of no use to it in walking, its hind again as disproportionally long; with these it hops seven or eight feet at each hop in the same manner as the jerboa, to which animal it bears much resemblance except in size, this being in weight thirty-eight pounds and the jerboa no larger than a common rat.

15 July—The beast which was killed yesterday was today dressed for our dinners and proved excellent meat...

18 July—Indians were over with us today and seemed to have lost all fear of us and became quite familiar; one of them at our desire threw his lance which was about eight feet in length—it flew with a degree of swiftness and steadiness that really surprised me, never being above four feet from the ground and stuck deep in at the distance of fifty paces. After this they ventured on board the ship and soon became our very good friends, so the captain and me left them to the care of those

who stayed on board and went to a high hill about six miles from the ship. Here we overlooked a great deal of sea to leeward, which afforded a melancholy prospect of the difficulties we were to encounter when we came out of our present harbour. In whichever direction we turned our eyes shoals innumerable were to be seen and no such thing as any passage to sea but through the winding channels between them, dangerous to the last degree.

ARTHUR PHILLIP
One of the Finest Harbours in the World, 1788

Soon after the arrival of the First Fleet, Governor Phillip realised that its original destination, Botany Bay, was an unsuitable site for settlement. He set out to explore Port Jackson which Cook had sailed past eighteen years earlier. One can imagine the virginal cove which caught Phillip's attention: the small sandy beach, the brook running through Port Jackson figs, ferns and rock orchids, and the slopes behind with their massive pink-barked angophoras growing straight from the stone. Its deflowering was a distressing business and it began when Phillip, in an irksome exercise in sycophancy, named the cove for the incompetent and forgettable Lord Sydney. If he had simply asked the 'chief of the tribe' what the place was called, Australia's first city might today be known as Werrong.

Phillip's published account of the founding of the settlement at Port Jackson was compiled from various sources. We join the narrative at Phillip's first meeting with the Eora people, then at the discovery of Sydney Cove.

18 January—At the very first landing of Governor Phillip on the shore of Botany Bay, an interview with the natives took place. They were all armed, but on seeing the governor approach with signs of friendship, alone and unarmed, they readily returned

his confidence by laying down their weapons. They were perfectly devoid of clothing, yet seemed fond of ornaments, putting the beads and red baize that were given them on their heads or necks, and appearing pleased to wear them. The presents offered by their new visitors were all readily accepted, nor did any kind of disagreement arise while the ships remained in Botany Bay.

This very pleasing effect was produced in no small degree by the personal address, as well as by the great care and attention of the governor. Nor were the orders which enforced a conduct so humane more honourable to the persons from whom they originated than the punctual execution of them was to the officers sent out: it was evident that their wishes coincided with their duty, and that a sanguinary temper was no longer to disgrace the European settlers in countries newly discovered.

The next care after landing was the examination of the bay itself, from which it appeared that, though extensive, it did not afford a shelter from the easterly winds; and that, in consequence of its shallowness, ships even of a moderate draught would always be obliged to anchor with the entrance of the bay open, where they must be exposed to a heavy sea that rolls in whenever it blows hard from the eastward.

Several runs of fresh water were found in different parts of the bay, but there did not appear to be any situation to which there was not some very strong objection. In the northern part of it is a small creek, which runs a considerable way into the country, but it has water only for a boat, the sides of it are frequently overflowed, and the low lands near it are a perfect swamp. The western branch of the bay is continued to a great extent, but the officers sent to examine it could not find there any supply of fresh water, except in very small drains.

Point Sutherland offered the most eligible situation, having a run of good water, though not in very great abundance. But to this part of the harbour the ships could not approach, and the ground near it, even in the higher parts, was in general damp and spongy. Smaller numbers might indeed in several spots have found a comfortable residence, but no place was found in the whole circuit of Botany Bay which seemed at all calculated for the reception of so large a settlement.

While this examination was carried on, the whole fleet had arrived. The *Supply* had not so much outsailed the other ships as to give Governor Phillip the advantage he had expected in point of time. On the 19th of January, the *Alexander*, *Scarborough* and *Friendship* cast anchor in Botany Bay; and on the 20th the *Sirius*, with the remainder of the convoy. These ships had all continued very healthy; they had not, however, yet arrived at their final station.

The openness of this bay, and the dampness of the soil, by which the people would probably be rendered unhealthy, had already determined the governor to seek another situation. He resolved, therefore, to examine Port Jackson, a bay mentioned by Captain Cook as immediately to the north of this. There he hoped to find not only a better harbour, but a fitter place for the establishment of his new government. But that no time might be lost, in case of a disappointment in these particulars, the ground near Point Sutherland was ordered immediately to be cleared, and preparations to be made for landing, under the direction of the lieutenant-governor.

These arrangements having been settled, Governor Phillip prepared to proceed to the examination of Port Jackson; and as the time of his absence, had he gone in the *Supply*, must have been very uncertain, he went round with three boats, taking with him Captain Hunter and several other officers, that by examining several parts of the harbour at once the greater dispatch might be made. On the 22nd of January they set out upon this expedition, and early in the afternoon arrived at Port Jackson, which is distant about three leagues. Here all regret arising from the former disappointments was at once obliterated; and Governor Phillip had the satisfaction to find one of the finest harbours in the world, in which a thousand sail of the line might ride in perfect security.

The different coves of this harbour were examined with all possible expedition, and the preference was given to one which had the finest spring of water, and in which ships can anchor so close to the shore that at a very small expense quays may be constructed at which the largest vessels may unload. This cove is about half a mile in length, and a quarter of a mile across at the entrance. In honour of Lord Sydney the governor distinguished it by the name of Sydney Cove.

On the arrival of the boats at Port Jackson, a second party of the natives made its appearance near the place of landing. These also were armed with lances, and at first were very vociferous; but the same gentle means used towards the others easily persuaded these also to discard their suspicions and to accept whatsoever was offered. One man in particular, who appeared to be the chief of this tribe, showed very singular marks both of confidence in his new friends and of determined resolution. Under the guidance of Governor Phillip, to whom he voluntarily entrusted himself, he went to a part of the beach where the men belonging to the boats were then boiling their meat; when he approached the marines, who were drawn up near that place, and saw that by proceeding he should be separated from his companions, who remained with several of the officers at some distance, he stopped, and with great firmness seemed by words and gestures to threaten revenge if any advantage should be taken of his situation. He then went on with perfect calmness to examine what was boiling in the pot and, by the manner in which he expressed his admiration, made it evident that he intended to profit by what he saw.

Governor Phillip contrived to make him understand that large shells might conveniently be used for the same purpose, and it is probable that by these hints, added to his own observation, he will be enabled to introduce the art of boiling among his countrymen. Hitherto they appear to have known no other way of dressing food than broiling. Their methods of kindling fire are probably very imperfect and laborious, for it is observed that they usually keep it burning, and are very rarely seen without either a fire actually made, or a piece of lighted wood, which they carry with them from place to place, and even in their canoes. The perpetual fires, which in some countries formed a part of the national religion, had perhaps no other origin than a similar inability to produce it at pleasure; and if we suppose the original flame to have been kindled by lightning, the fiction of its coming down from heaven will be found to deviate very little from the truth.

In passing near a point of land in this harbour, the boats were perceived by a number of the natives, twenty of whom waded into the water unarmed, received what was offered them, and examined the boat with a curiosity which impressed a higher idea of them than any former accounts of their manners had suggested. This confidence and manly behaviour induced Governor Phillip, who was highly pleased with it, to give the place the name of Manly Cove.

The same people afterwards joined the party at the place where they had landed to dine. They were then armed, two of them with shields and swords, the rest with lances only. The swords were made of wood, small in the grip, and apparently less formidable than a good stick. One of these men had a kind of white clay rubbed upon the upper part of his face, so as to have the appearance of a mask. This ornament, if it can be called such, is not common among them, and is probably assumed only on particular occasions or as a distinction to a few individuals. One woman had been seen on the rocks as the boats passed, with her face, neck and breasts thus painted, and to our people appeared the most disgusting figure imaginable. Her own countrymen were perhaps delighted by the beauty of the effect.

During the preparation for dinner the curiosity of these visitors rendered them very troublesome, but an innocent contrivance altogether removed the inconvenience. Governor Phillip drew a circle round the place where the English were, and without much difficulty made the natives understand that they were not to pass that line; after which they sat down in perfect quietness. Another proof how tractable these people are, when no insult or injury is offered, and when proper means are to influence the simplicity of their minds.

On the 24th of January, Governor Phillip, having sufficiently explored Port Jackson and found it in all respects highly calculated to receive such a settlement as he was appointed to establish, returned to Botany Bay. On his arrival there, the reports made to him, both of the ground which the people were clearing, and of the upper parts of the bay, which in this interval had been more particularly examined, were in the greatest degree unfavourable. It was impossible after this to hesitate concerning the choice of a situation; and orders were accordingly issued for the removal of the whole fleet to Port Jackson.

ARTHUR BOWES SMYTH
The Golden Age, 1788

Of all the parts of Australia, just two tiny specks were truly virgin lands in 1788. Christmas Island in the Indian Ocean would remain unsettled until the last quarter of the nineteenth century, while people first stepped onto Lord Howe Island four months after the Europeans settled at Sydney Cove. Lord Howe Island was discovered by ships of the First Fleet, drawn there after hearing that the French mariner La Perouse had seen great flocks of seabirds in the area.

The infant colony was desperately short of food, and Lord Howe proved to be an extraordinarily well-stocked larder. The birds were superabundant and entirely tame. Some species had lost the ability to fly. Smyth's account gives us a glimpse of how the animals of Australia might have behaved on the day the ancestors of the first Aborigines set foot on the continent.

16th May 1788—This forenoon I went shore with Captain Sever and Mr Watts in the pinnace; we went through an opening in the reef over which the sea broke with a tremendous noise and swell. We landed in Hunter's Bay and saw great numbers of boobies, pigeons and many other birds. The captain and Mr

Watts returned to dinner but as Mr Anstis was coming on shore after dinner I continued there hunting birds etc. in the woods. Mr Anstis and the steward with several of the ship's company came in the afternoon and stayed on shore all night. The sport we had in knocking down birds etc. was great indeed, though at the expense of tearing most of the clothes off our backs. We made a fire under the trees and supped upon part of our game broiled, which was very sweet and good—the pigeons were the largest I ever saw. We afterwards slept in thick greatcoats carried on shore for that purpose, covered over with the leaves of the cabbage tree, which are here innumerable and many of them so small and tender that you may cut them down with a pocket knife.

When I was in the woods amongst the birds I could not help picturing to myself the Golden Age as described by Ovid to see the fowls or coots, some white, some blue and white, others all blue with large red bills and a patch of red on the top of their heads, and the boobies in thousands, together with a curious brown bird about the size of the landrail in England, walking totally fearless and unconcerned in all part around us, so that we had nothing more to do than to stand still a minute or two and knock down as many as we pleased with a short stick—if you throwed at them and missed them, or even hit them without killing them, they never made the least attempt to fly away and indeed they would only run a few yards from you and be as quiet and unconcerned as if nothing had happened.

The pigeons also were tame as those already described and would sit upon the branches of the trees till you might go and take them off with your hand, or if the branch was so high on which they sat, they would at all times sit till you might knock them down with a short stick—many hundreds of all the sorts mentioned above, together with many parrots and parakeets, magpies and other birds were caught and carried on board our ship and the *Charlotte*.

There has never been any quadruped or reptile seen on the island, which is five or six miles in length and one mile broad at the broadest part and in some parts not so much. The trees on it are chiefly mangroves, cabbage trees, bamboo canes, a species of large aloes plants.

After describing the number and tameness of the feathered inhabitants of this island, I must take notice that our surprise was no less in the morning upon going into the pinnace to fish with hooks and lines in the bay within side the reef. The water in many parts not more than four or five feet deep with a fine white sandy bottom with coral, brainstones and many other marine plants growing at the bottom, with the sun shining bright upon them, and the innumerable quantities and varieties of fish swimming amongst this coral grove (if I may be allowed the expression) exhibited such a novel and beautiful a scene as but few places in the world I believe will afford. The fish bit so very fast that in about two or three hours we had caught some hundredweight—and the pinnace was half loaded...The fish we caught in the space of three hours served the whole ship's company three days.

Watkin Tench
Gonin-Patta!, 1791

 In 1791 almost everything west of Rose Hill (Parramatta) was terra incognita. The First Fleeters mounted several expeditions to fill in the blanks on the map. Here we accompany Captain Watkin Tench, his friend Lieutenant Dawes, Governor Phillip and others into the wilds lying north and west of Sydney Cove, a region which today is rapidly disappearing under the city's vast sprawl. They wanted to discover if the Nepean and Hawkesbury rivers formed one stream.

Tench was a great wit, always ready to enjoy a joke at his own expense. His account of the expedition quickly turns into a comedy. He describes how the Aboriginal 'guides' Colbee and

Boladeree would relive every fall and mishap the Europeans have experienced. Tench's *ultima Thule* is 'that pile of desolation' the governor was pleased to name Tench's Prospect Mount.

Tench's explorations revealed little in the way of new territory, but they have left us some extraordinary insights into the language and life of the Aborigines of the Sydney area. They also remind us of the good relations which existed between black and white at the very beginning of European settlement.

Monday, April 11th, 1791. At twenty minutes before seven o'clock we started from the governor's house at Rose Hill and steered for a short time nearly in a north-east direction, after which we turned to north 34° west, and steadily pursued that course until a quarter before four o'clock, when we halted for the night.* The country for the first two miles, while we walked to the north-east, was good, full of grass and without rock or underwood. Afterwards it grew very bad, being full of steep, barren rocks, over which we were compelled to clamber for seven miles, when it changed to a plain country apparently very sterile, and with very little grass in it, which rendered walking easy. Our fatigue in the morning had, however, been so oppressive that one of the party knocked up. And had not a soldier, as strong as a pack-horse, undertaken to carry his knapsack in addition to his own, we must either have sent him back, or have stopped at a place for the night which did not afford water.

---

* Our method, on these expeditions, was to steer by compass, noting the different courses as we proceeded; and, counting the number of paces, of which two thousand two hundred, on good ground, were allowed to be a mile. At night when we halted, all these courses were separately cast up, and worked by a traverse table, in the manner a ship's reckoning is kept, so that by observing this precaution we always knew exactly where we were, and how far from home: an unspeakable advantage in a new country, where one hill, and one tree, is so like another that fatal wanderings would ensue without it. This arduous task was always allotted to Mr Dawes who, from habit and superior skill, performed it almost without a stop, or an interruption of conversation: to any other man, on such terms, it would have been impracticable.

Our two natives carried each his pack, but its weight was inconsiderable, most of their provisions being in the knapsacks of the soldiers and gamekeepers. We expected to have derived from them much information relating to the country, as no one doubted that they were acquainted with every part of it between the sea coast and the river Hawkesbury. We hoped also to have witnessed their manner of living in the woods, and the resources they rely upon in their journeys. Nothing, however, of this sort had yet occurred, except their examining some trees to see if they could discover on the bark any marks of the claws of squirrels and opossums, which they said would show whether any of those animals were hidden among the leaves and branches.[†] They walked stoutly, appeared but little fatigued, and maintained their spirits admirably, laughing to excess when any of us either tripped or stumbled, misfortunes which much seldomer fell to their lot than to ours.

At a very short distance from Rose Hill, we found that they were in a country unknown to them, so that the farther they went the more dependent on us they became, being absolute strangers inland. To convey to their understandings the intention of our journey was impossible. For, perhaps, no words could unfold to an Indian the motives of curiosity which induce men to encounter labour, fatigue and pain, when they might remain in repose at home, with a sufficiency of food. We asked Colbee the name of the people who live inland, and he called them Boòrooberongal; and said they were bad, whence we conjectured that they sometimes war with those on the sea coast, by whom they were undoubtedly driven up the country from the fishing ground, that it might not be overstocked; the weaker here, as in every other country, giving way to the stronger.

We asked how they lived. He said, on birds and animals, having no fish. Their laziness appeared strongly when we halted, for they refused to draw water or to cleave wood to make a fire;

---

† Sugar-gliders, and ringtail and brushtail possums.

but as soon as it was kindled (having first well stuffed themselves), they lay down before it and fell asleep. About an hour after sunset, as we were chatting by the fireside and preparing to go to rest, we heard voices at a little distance in the wood. Our natives catched the sound instantaneously and, bidding us be silent, listened attentively to the quarter whence it had proceeded. In a few minutes we heard the voices plainly; and, wishing exceedingly to open a communication with this tribe, we begged our natives to call to them, and bid them to come to us, to assure them of good treatment, and that they should have something given them to eat.

Colbee no longer hesitated, but gave them the signal of invitation, in a loud hollow cry. After some whooping and shouting on both sides, a man with a lighted stick in his hand advanced near enough to converse with us. The first words which we could distinctly understand were, 'I am Colbee, of the tribe of Càdigal.' The stranger replied, 'I am Bèreewan, of the tribe of Boòrooberongal.' Boladeree informed him also of his name and that we were white men and friends, who would give him something to eat. Still he seemed irresolute. Colbee therefore advanced to him, took him by the hand and led him to us. By the light of the moon, we were introduced to this gentleman, all our names being repeated in form by our two masters of the ceremonies, who said that we were Englishmen and *budyeree* (good), that we came from the sea coast, and that we were travelling inland.

Bèreewan seemed to be a man about thirty years old, differing in no respect from his countrymen with whom we were acquainted. He came to us unarmed, having left his spears at a little distance. After a long conversation with his countrymen, and having received some provisions, he departed highly satisfied.

Tuesday, April 12th, 1791. Started this morning at half past six o'clock, and in two hours reached the river. The whole of the country we passed was poor, and the soil within a mile of the river changed to a coarse deep sand, which I have invariably found to compose its banks in every part without exception that

I ever saw. The stream at this place is about 350 feet wide; the water pure and excellent to the taste. The banks are about twenty feet high and covered with trees, many of which had been evidently bent by the force of the current in the direction which it runs, and some of them contained rubbish and driftwood in their branches at least forty-five feet above the level of the stream. We saw many ducks, and killed one, which Colbee swam for. No new production among the shrubs growing here was found. We were acquainted with them all.

Our natives had evidently never seen this river before. They started at it with surprise, and talked to each other. Their total ignorance of the country, and of the direction in which they had walked, appeared when they asked which way Rose Hill lay; for they pointed almost oppositely to it. Of our compass they had taken early notice, and had talked much to each other about it. They comprehended its use, and called it *naa-mòro*, literally, 'to see the way': a more significant or expressive term cannot be found.

Supposing ourselves to be higher on the stream than Richmond Hill, we agreed to trace downward, or to the right hand. In tracing, we kept as close to the bank of the river as the innumerable impediments to walking which grow upon it would allow. We found the country low and swampy; came to a native fireplace, at which were some small fish bones; soon after we saw a native, but he ran away immediately. Having walked nearly three miles we were stopped by a creek which we could neither ford or fall a tree across. We were therefore obliged to coast it, in hope to find a passing place or to reach its head. At four o'clock we halted for the night on the bank of the creek. Our natives continued to hold out stoutly. The hindrances to walking by the river side which plagued and entangled us so much seemed not to be heeded by them, and they wound through them with ease; but to us they were intolerably tiresome. Our perplexities afforded them an inexhaustible fund of merriment and derision. Did the sufferer, stung at once with nettles and ridicule, and shaken nigh to death by his fall, use any angry expression to them, they retorted in a moment by calling him by every opprobrious name[*] which their language affords.

Boladeree destroyed a native hut today very wantonly before we could prevent him. On being asked why he did so, he answered that the inhabitants inland were bad; though no longer since than last night, when Bèreewan had departed, they were loud in their praise. But now they had reverted to their first opinion; so fickle and transient are their motives of love and hatred.

Wednesday, April 13th, 1791. We did not set out this morning until past seven o'clock, when we continued to trace the creek. The country which we passed through yesterday was good and desirable to what was now presented to us. It was in general high and universally rocky. 'Toiling our uncouth way', we mounted a hill, and surveyed the contiguous country. To the northward and eastward, the ground was still higher than that we were upon; but in a south-west direction we saw about four miles. The view consisted of nothing but trees growing on precipices; not an acre of it could be cultivated. Saw a tree on fire here, and several other vestiges of the natives. To comprehend the reasons which induce an Indian to perform many of the offices of life is difficult; to pronounce that which could lead him to wander amidst these dreary wilds baffles penetration.

About two o'clock we reached the head of the creek, passed it and scrambled with infinite toil and difficulty to the top of a neighbouring mountain, whence we saw the adjacent country in almost every direction, for many miles. I record with regret that this extended view presented not a single gleam of change which could encourage hope or stimulate industry to attempt its culture. We had, however, the satisfaction to discover plainly the object of our pursuit, Richmond Hill, distant about eight miles, in a *contrary* direction from what we had been proceeding upon. It

---

[*] Their general favourite term of reproach is *gonin-patta*, which signifies, 'an eater of human excrement'. Our language would admit a very concise and familiar translation. They have, besides this, innumerable others which they often salute their enemies with.

was readily known to those who had been up the Hawkesbury in the boats, by a remarkable cleft or notch which distinguishes it. It was now determined that we should go back to the head of the creek and pass the night there; and in the morning cut across the country to that part of the river which we had first hit upon yesterday, and thence to trace upward, or to the left. But before I descend, I must not forget to relate that to this pile of desolation on which, like the fallen angel on the top of Niphates, we stood contemplating our nether Eden, His Excellency was pleased to give the name of *Tench's Prospect Mount.*

Our fatigue today had been excessive; but our two sable companions seemed rather enlivened than exhausted by it. We had not sooner halted and given them something to eat than they began to play ten thousand tricks and gambols. They imitated the leaping of the kangaroo; sang, danced, poised the spear and met in mock encounter. But their principal source of merriment was again derived from our misfortunes, in tumbling amidst nettles and sliding down precipices, which they mimicked with inimitable drollery. They had become, however, very urgent in their inquiries about the time of our return, and we pacified them as well as we could by saying it would be soon, but avoided naming how many days.

Their method of testifying dislike to any place is singular: they point to the spot they are upon, and all around it, crying *weèree, weèree* (bad), and immediately after mention the name of any other place to which they are attached (Rose Hill or Sydney, for instance), adding to it, *budyeree, budyeree* (good). Nor was their preference in the present case the result of caprice, for they assigned very substantial reasons for such predilection. 'At Rose Hill,' said they, 'are potatoes, cabbages, pumpkins, turnips, fish and wine; here are nothing but rocks and water.' These comparisons constantly ended with the question of 'Where's Rose Hill? Where?' on which they would throw up their hands and utter a sound to denote distance, which it is impossible to convey an idea of upon paper.

Thursday, April 14th, 1791. We started early and reached the river in about two hours and a half. The intermediate country, except for the last half mile, was a continued bed of stones, which were in some places so thick and close together that they looked like a pavement formed by art. When we got off the stones, we came upon the coarse river sand beforementioned.

Here we began to trace upward. We had not proceeded far when we saw several canoes on the river. Our natives made us immediately lie down among the reeds, while they gave their countrymen the signal of approach. After much calling, finding that they did not come, we continued our progress until it was again interrupted by a creek, over which we threw a tree and passed upon it. While this was doing, a native, from his canoe, entered into conversation with us, and immediately after paddled to us with a frankness and confidence which surprised everyone. He was a man of middle age, with an open cheerful countenance, marked with the smallpox, and distinguished by a nose of uncommon magnitude and dignity.[†] He seemed to be neither astonished or terrified at our appearance and number. Two stone hatchets and two spears he took from his canoe, and presented to the governor, who in return for his courteous generosity, gave him two of our hatchets and some bread, which was new to him, for he knew not its use, but kept looking at it, until Colbee showed him what to do, when he ate it without hesitation.

We pursued our course and, to accommodate us, our new acquaintance pointed out a path and walked at the head of us. A canoe, also with a man and a boy in it, kept gently paddling up abreast of us. We halted for the night at our usual hour, on the bank of the river. Immediately that we had stopped, our friend (who had already told us his name) Gombeèree introduced the man and the boy from the canoe to us. The former was named Yèllomundee, the latter Dèeimba. The ease with which these people behaved among strangers was as conspicuous as

---

† An epidemic, apparently of smallpox, had swept through the Aboriginal population in April 1789.

unexpected. They seated themselves at our fire, partook of our biscuit and pork, drank from our canteens, and heard our guns going off around them without betraying any symptom of fear, distrust or surprise. On the opposite bank of the river they had left their wives and several children, with whom they frequently discoursed; and we observed that these last manifested neither suspicion or uneasiness of our designs towards their friends.

Having refreshed ourselves, we found leisure to enter into conversation with them. It could not be expected that they should differ materially from the tribes with whom we were acquainted. The same manners and pursuits, the same amusements, the same levity and fickleness, undoubtedly characterised them. What we were able to learn from them was that they depend but little on fish, as the river yields only mullets, and that their principal support is derived from small animals which they kill, and some roots (a species of wild yam chiefly) which they dig out of the earth. If we rightly understood them, each man possesses two wives. Whence can arise this superabundance of females?

Neither of the men had suffered the extraction of a front tooth. We were eager to know whether or not this custom obtained among them. But neither Colbee nor Boladeree would put the question for us; and, on the contrary, showed every desire to waive the subject. The uneasiness which they testified, whenever we renewed it, rather served to confirm a suspicion which we had long entertained, that this is a mark of subjection imposed by the tribe of Cameragal (who are certainly the most powerful community in the country) on the weaker tribes around them.[†]

Whether the women cut off a joint of one of the little fingers, like those on the sea coast, we had no opportunity of observing. These are petty remarks. But one variety struck us more forcibly. Although our natives and the strangers conversed on a par and

† Tooth evulsion is part of some Aboriginal initiation ceremonies, whose secret nature may have made Colbee and Boladeree reluctant to discuss the practice. It is also interesting to note that Governor Phillip was missing a foretooth. Did this predispose the Aborigines to accept him?

understood each other perfectly, yet they spoke different dialects of the same language; many of the most common and necessary words used in life bearing no similitude, and others being slightly different.

English	Name on the sea coast	Name at the Hawkesbury
The Moon	Yèn-ee-da	Con-dò-en
The Ear	Goo-reè	Bèn-na
The Forehead	Nùl-lo	Nar-ràn
The Belly	Bar-an`g	Bin`-dee
The Navel	Mùn-ee-ro	Boom-bon`g
The Buttocks	Boong	Bay-leè
The Neck	Càl-ang	Gan-gà
The Thigh	Tàr-a	Dàr-a
The Hair	Deè-war-a	Kee-war-a

That these diversities arise from want of intercourse with the people on the coast can hardly be imagined, as the distance inland is but thirty-eight miles; and from Rose Hill not more than twenty, where the dialect of the sea coast is spoken. It deserves notice that all the different terms seemed to be familiar to both parties, though each in speaking preferred its own.*

---

* How easily people, unused to speak the same language, mistake each other, everyone knows. We had lived almost three years at Port Jackson (for more than half of which period natives had resided with us) before we knew that the word *bèeal* signified 'no', and not 'good', in which latter sense we had always used it without suspecting that we were wrong; and even without being corrected by those with whom we talked daily. The cause of our error was this. The epithet *weeree*, signifying 'bad', we knew; and as the use of this word and its opposite afford the most simple form of denoting consent or disapprobation to uninstructed Indians, in order to find out their word for 'good', when Arabanoo was first brought among us, we used jokingly to say that any thing which he liked was *weeree*, in order to provoke him to tell us that it was good. When we said *weeree*, he answered *bèeal*, which we translated and adopted for 'good'; whereas he meant no more than simply to deny our inference, and say, 'no—it is not

Stretched out at ease before our fire, all sides continued to chat and entertain each other. Gombeèree showed us the mark of a wound which he had received in his side from a spear. It was large, appeared to have passed to a considerable depth, and must certainly have been attended with imminent danger. By whom it had been inflicted, and on what occasion, he explained to Colbee; and afterwards (as we understood) he entered into a detail of the wars and, as effects lead to causes, probably of the gallantries of the district, for the word which signifies a woman was often repeated. Colbee, in return for his communication, informed him who we were; of our numbers at Sydney and Rose Hill, of the stores we possessed and, above all, of the good things which were to be found among us, enumerating potatoes, cabbages, turnips, pumpkins and many other names which were perfectly unintelligible to the person who heard them, but which he nevertheless listened to with profound attention.

Perhaps the relation given by Gombeèree, of the cure of his wound, now gave rise to the following superstitious ceremony. While they were talking, Colbee turned suddenly round and asked for some water. I gave him a cupful, which he presented with great seriousness to Yèllomundee, as I supposed to drink. This last indeed took the cup and filled his mouth with water but, instead of swallowing it, threw his head into Colbee's bosom, spit the water upon him and, immediately after, began to suck strongly at his breast, just below the nipple. I concluded that the man was sick; and called to the governor to observe the strange place which he had chosen to exonerate his stomach.

The silent attention observed by the other natives, however, soon convinced us that something more than merely the accommodation of Yèllomundee was intended. The ceremony

---

bad'. After this, it cannot be thought extraordinary that the little vocabulary inserted in Mr Cook's account of this part of the world should appear defective—even were we not to take in the great probability of the dialects at Endeavour River and Van Diemen's Land differing from that spoken at Port Jackson. And it remains to be proved that the animal called here *Patagaram* is not there called *Kangaroo*.

was again performed; and, after having sucked the part for a considerable time, the operator pretended to receive something in his mouth, which was drawn from the breast. With this he retired a few paces, put his hand to his lips and threw into the river a stone, which I had observed him to pick up slyly and secrete. When he returned to the fireside, Colbee assured us that he had received signal benefit from the operation; and that this second Machaon had extracted from his breast two splinters of a spear by which he had been formerly wounded.† We examined the part, but it was smooth and whole, so that to the force of imagination alone must be imputed both the wound and its cure. Colbee himself seemed nevertheless firmly persuaded that he had received relief, and assured us that Yèllomundee was a *cáradyee*, or 'doctor of renown'. And Boladeree added that not only he but all the rest of his tribe were *cáradyee* of especial note and skill.

The doctors remained with us all night, sleeping before the fire in the fullness of good faith and security. The little boy slept in his father's arms, and we observed that, whenever the man was inclined to shift his position, he first put over the child, with great care, and then turned round to him.

Friday, April 15th, 1791. The return of light aroused us to the repetition of toil. Our friends breakfasted with us, and previous to starting Gombeeree gave a specimen of their manner of climbing trees in quest of animals. He asked for a hatchet and one of ours was offered to him, but he preferred one of their own making. With this tool he cut a small notch in the tree he intended to climb, about two feet and a half above the ground, in which he fixed the great toe of his left foot, and sprung upwards, at the same time embracing the tree with his left arm. In an instant he had cut a second notch for his right toe on the other side of the tree, into which he sprung, and thus, alternately cutting on each side, he mounted to the height of twenty feet in nearly as short a space as if he had ascended by a ladder, although

† Machaon: A doctor to the Greeks in the Trojan War.

the bark of the tree was quite smooth and slippery and the trunk four feet in diameter and perfectly straight. To us it was a matter of astonishment, but to him it was sport; for while employed thus he kept talking to those below and laughing immoderately. He descended with as much ease and agility as he had raised himself. Even our natives allowed that he was a capital performer, against whom they dared not enter the lists; for as they subsist chiefly by fishing they are less expert at climbing on the coast than those who daily practise it.

Soon after they bade us adieu, in unabated friendship and good humour. Colbee and Boladeree parted from them with a slight nod of the head, the usual salutation of the country; and we shook them by the hand, which they returned lustily.

John Price
Whom-Batts and Cullawines, 1798

 From the very beginning, the Irish convicts were the most troublesome, for many were freedom fighters who considered themselves political prisoners. They had no idea how Port Jackson stood in relation to the world, so constantly broke out, hoping to walk to China or to find some fanciful European settlement which was rumoured to exist in Australia.

Governor Hunter suffered constant thefts and irritation from such breakouts. In an effort to stem them and, as he said, 'save worthless lives', Hunter sent a few of the more persistent questers on an expedition to illustrate the nature of the country beyond the bounds of settlement. They were led by John Wilson, known as the wild white man by the colonists, and called Bunboe by his Aboriginal friends. Wilson was a convict who, after serving his time, left European society and joined the Aborigines.

Records of the travels were kept by John Price, Hunter's

servant. They are important because they contain the first recorded account of the lyre bird (shot on what was to become Australia Day), and mention of a mysterious animal, the cullawine, later identified as the koala. Here we join the party on its way to the Wollondilly River.

January 24th, 1798—Course, SSW. Left Mount Hunter for about twelve miles, till we fell in with the Nepean River, where the rocks run so steep it was with great difficulty we crossed them; the rest of the ground run very scrubby. We saw nothing strange except a few rock kangaroos with long black brush tails, and two pheasants which we could not get a shot at. Distance, eighteen miles.

January 25th—Course, SSW. The country runs very open; good black soil. We saw a great many kangaroos and emus, and we fell in with a party of natives which gave a very good account of the place we were in search of, that there was a great deal of corn and potatoes and that the people were very friendly.

We hearkened to their advice; we altered our course according to their directions. One of them promised that he would take us to a party of natives which had been there; but he not coming according to his promise, we proceeded on our journey as he had directed us. In the course of this day we found a great deal of salt. Distance, six miles.

January 26th—Course, WSW. The ground run very rocky and brushy, so that we could scarce pass. We crossed one small river, the banks of which were so rocky and steep that we could scarce pass it. We saw no signs of any natives about it, but we saw several sorts of dung of different animals, one of which Wilson called a whom-batt, which is an animal about twenty inches high, with short legs and a thick body forwards, with a large head, round ears and very small eyes; is very fat, and has much the appearance of a badger.

There is another animal which the natives call a cullawine, which much resembles the stoths in America. Here I shot a bird about the size of a pheasant, but the tail of it very much resembles a peacock, with two large long feathers, which are white, orange, and lead colour, and black at the ends; its body betwixt a brown and green; brown under his neck and black upon his head; black legs and very long claws. Distance, sixteen miles...

January 28th—Course, WSW. The land runs much the same, the timber thin, with a good many stringybark trees; and a little further we saw a number of meadows and 100 acres of land without a tree upon it. Here we saw a party of natives. Wilson run and caught one of them, a girl, thinking to learn something from them, but her language was so different from that one which we had with us that we could not understand her. We kept her all night, but she cried and fretted so much that the next morning we gave her a tomahawk and sent her to the rest of the natives, which were covered with large skins which reached down to their heels...

January 29th—Course, WSW. We steered our course for about four miles, but the country did not turn out to our expectation...We altered our course to the north for about twelve miles...We here saw in the creeks many pheasants and rock kangaroos, likewise dung of animals as large as horse-dung, but could not see any of them. We had nothing to eat for two days but one rat about the size of a small kitten. I myself was very sick, and wished myself at home again; the other man was sick like me, for he had hurt his leg and was not able to walk. Wilson was well and hearty. Distance, twenty-four miles.

January 30th—Course, WSW. The country still rocky and scrubby. We fell in with the head of a river very near as large as the Hawkesbury River, which seemed to run from NW to SE. The banks were so steep we could not get down them. The other side seemed open, but the banks very steep. Wilson proposed making a canoe; but the other man and myself were so faint and tired, having nothing to eat but two small birds each, we were afraid to venture on the other side of the river for fear we should not be able to procure anything to subsist on; likewise our shoes was gone and our feet were very much bruised with the rocks, so that we asked Wilson to return. Distance, sixteen miles...

February 2nd—Course, ENE...In the latter part of the day, after we had got over the first ridge of mountains, we fell in with a vast number of kangaroos. Here we were fortunate again, for Wilson killed one of them, which was a great refreshment to us.

The next morning, about sunrise, I myself heard two guns fire, which sounded to the SE. I was not certain that it was a gun until Wilson said, 'Do you hear that gun fire?' I said I did. I then took up my gun and fired again, but we could get no answer, although we fired five different times.

We here come to a resolution of returning, for Wilson here came to a part of the country which he knew, and a very barren one, for we could not get anything to eat but a few roots and grubs, and they very scarce. Indeed I thought that we must all have perished with hunger, which certainly would have been the case had it not been for the indefatigable zeal of Wilson to supply us with as much as would support life; for we travelled six days successively over hills and valleys full of rocks, and no appearance of any animals or birds of any size, so that we had no hopes of ever reaching back again, being so weak that Roe and myself were scarce able to travel; but on the sixth day we got through the rocks, and made the forest land about ten miles from Prospect, which very much enlivened our spirits, for we were all but starved, and were obliged to cut up all our clothing to cover our feet, which was cut with the rocks.

Enlivened as were at getting good ground to travel on, and being cheered up by Wilson who said we should soon make Prospect, we then proceeded on our journey with all the spirit and strength we were master of, and to our great joy we reached the desired place a little before sundown. Distance, sixteen miles.

MATTHEW FLINDERS
The Great Circumnavigator, 1802–3

 Few explorers were as admirable, and as ill-starred, as Matthew Flinders. A man of immense humanity and literary ability, he sailed to Westernport Bay with George Bass in 1797–98; the pair then circumnavigated Tasmania in 1798–99, proving the existence of Bass Strait. Between 1801 and 1803 he completed the first circumnavigation of Australia, making many discoveries, and beating the Frenchman Nicolas Baudin to mapping much of the coast. On his way back to England his leaking vessel was forced to sail to Mauritius for repairs. There Flinders was incarcerated by the French for six years, during which time the Baudin expedition results were published, falsely claiming for France many discoveries actually made by Flinders.

Physically broken by the hardships of his exploration and captivity, Flinders returned to England and his beloved wife in 1810, after an absence of thirteen years. He began preparing the book from which these passages are taken, and on 18 July 1814 the first copy was rushed to his tiny house in London. But it was too late. The volume was placed in the hands of the already unconscious explorer, who died the next day.

We join Flinders at the discovery of Kangaroo Island, a place which remained uninhabited after the Aborigines who once lived on the island died out 3,500 years ago. As Flinders observes, the kangaroos there are enormous, the largest recorded anywhere. We rejoin the expedition nearly a year later, in February 1803, off the north-eastern tip of Arnhem Land, where Flinders encounters explorers of a different ilk; the Macassans, who had come from distant Sulawesi. A week later Flinders describes how Bungaree, an Eora man and the first Aborigine to circumnavigate Australia, procured fish for the starving expeditioners.

21 March 1802—Neither smokes nor other marks of inhabitants had as yet been perceived upon the southern land, although we had passed along seventy miles of its coast. It was too late to go on shore this evening; but every glass in the ship was pointed there to see what could be discovered. Several black lumps, like rocks, were pretended to have been seen in motion by some of the young gentlemen, which caused the force of their imaginations to be much admired.

Next morning, however, on going toward the shore, a number of dark-brown kangaroos were seen feeding upon a grass plat by the side of the wood; and our landing gave them no disturbance. I had with me a double-barrelled gun, fitted with a bayonet, and the gentlemen my companions had muskets. It would be difficult to guess how many kangaroos were seen; but I killed ten, and the rest of the party made up the number to thirty-one taken on board in the course of the day; the least of them weighing sixty-nine, and the largest 125 pounds. These kangaroos had much resemblance to the large species found in the forest lands of New South Wales, except that their colour was darker, and they were not wholly destitute of fat.

After this butchery, for the poor animals suffered themselves to be shot in the eyes with small shot, and in some cases to be knocked on the head with sticks, I scrambled with difficulty through the brush wood and over fallen trees to reach the higher land with the surveying instruments; but the thickness and height of the wood prevented anything else from being distinguished. There was little doubt, however, that this extensive piece of land was separated from the continent; for the extraordinary tameness of the kangaroos and the presence of seals upon the shore concurred with the absence of all traces of men to show that it was not inhabited.

The whole ship's company was employed this afternoon in skinning and cleaning the kangaroos; and a delightful regale they afforded after four months privation from almost any fresh provisions. Half a hundredweight of heads, forequarters and tails were stewed down into soup for dinner on this and the succeeding days; and as much steaks given, moreover, to both officers and men as they could consume by day and by night. In gratitude for so seasonable a supply, I named this southern land Kangaroo Island...

17 February 1803—After clearing the narrow passage between Cape Wilberforce and Bromby's Isles, we followed the main coast to the SW; having on the starboard hand some high and large islands, which closed in towards the coast ahead so as to make it doubtful whether there were any passage between them. Under the nearest island was perceived a canoe full of men; and in a sort of roadstead, at the south end of the same island, there were six vessels covered over like hulks, as if laid up for the bad season.

Our conjectures were various as to who those people could be, and what their business here; but we had little doubt of their being the same whose traces had been found so abundantly in the Gulf. I had inclined to the opinion that these traces had been left by Chinese, and the report of the natives in Caledon Bay that they had firearms strengthened the supposition; and combining this with the appearance of the vessels I set them down for piratical ladrones who secreted themselves here from pursuit, and issued out as the season permitted, or prey invited them.[†]

Impressed with this idea, we tacked to work up for the road and, our pendant and ensign being hoisted, each of them hung out a small white flag. On approaching, I sent Lieutenant Flinders in an armed boat to learn who they were; and soon afterward we came to an anchor in twelve fathoms, within musket shot, having a spring on the cable, and all hands at quarters.[††]

Every motion in the whale boat, and in the vessel alongside which she was lying, was closely watched with our glasses, but

† Ladrones: outlaws.
†† This is Lieutenant Samuel Flinders who served under his captain, Matthew.

all seemed to pass quietly; and on the return of Lieutenant Flinders we learned that they were prows from Macassar, and the six Malay commanders shortly afterwards came on board in a canoe. It happened fortunately that my cook was a Malay, and through his means I was able to communicate with them. The chief of the six prows was a short, elderly man named Pobassoo; he said there were upon the coast, in different divisions, sixty prows, and that Salloo was the commander-in-chief. These people were Mahometans, and on looking into the launch expressed great horror to see hogs there; nevertheless they had no objection to port wine, and even requested a bottle to carry away with them at sunset...

My desire to learn everything concerning these people, and the strict look-out which it had been necessary to keep upon them, prevented me attending to any other business during their stay. According to Pobassoo, from whom my information was principally obtained, sixty prows belonging to the Rajah of Boni, and carrying one thousand men, had left Macassar with the north-west monsoon, two months before, upon an expedition to this coast; and the fleet was then lying in different places to the westward, five or six together, Pobassoo's division being the foremost. These prows seemed to be about twenty-five tons, and to have twenty or twenty-five men in each; that of Pobassoo carried two small brass guns, obtained from the Dutch, but the others had only muskets; besides which, every Malay wears a cress or dagger, either secretly or openly. I inquired after bows and arrows, and the *ippo* poison, but they had none of them; and it was with difficulty they could understand what was meant by the *ippo*.

The object of their expedition was a certain marine animal, called *trepang*. Of this they gave me two dried specimens; and it proved to be the *bêche-de-mer* or sea cucumber which we had first seen on the reefs of the east coast, and had afterwards hauled on shore so plentifully with the seine, especially in Caledon Bay. They get the *trepang* by diving in from three to eight fathoms water; and where it is abundant a man will bring up eight or ten at a time. The mode of preserving it is this: the animal is split down one side, boiled and pressed with a weight of stones, then stretched open by slips of bamboo, dried in the sun and afterwards in smoke, when it is fit to be put away in bags, but requires frequent exposure to the sun. A thousand *trepang* make a *picol*, of about 125 Dutch pounds; and one hundred *picols* are a cargo for a prow. It is carried to Timor and sold to the Chinese, who meet them there; and when all the prows are assembled the fleet returns to Macassar. By Timor seemed to be meant Timor-laoet; for when I inquired concerning the English, Dutch and Portuguese there, Pobassoo knew nothing of them: he had heard of Coepang, a Dutch settlement, but said it was upon another island...[†]

Pobassoo had made six or seven voyages from Macassar to this coast within the preceding twenty years, and he was one of the first who came; but had never seen any ship here before. This road was the first rendezvous for his division, to take in water previously to going into the Gulf. One of their prows had been lost the year before, and much inquiry was made concerning the pieces of wreck we had seen; and, a canoe's rudder being produced, it was recognised as having belonged to her.

They sometimes had skirmishes with the native inhabitants of the coast; Pobassoo himself had been formerly speared in the knee, and a man had been slightly wounded since their arrival in this road: they cautioned us much to beware of the natives.[*]

They had no knowledge of any European settlement in this country and, on learning the name Port Jackson, the son of Pobassoo made a memorandum of it as thus, ﺟﺎﻛﺴﻮﻥ, writing from left to right. Until this time, that some nutmegs were shown to them, they did not know of their being produced

---

[†] Timor-laoet: an island off Ceram.
[*] A question suggests itself here: could the natives of the west side of the Gulf of Carpentaria have learned the rite of circumcision from these Malay Mahometans? From the short period that the latter had frequented the coast, and the nature of the intercourse between the two people, it seems to me very little probable.

here, nor had they ever met with coconuts; bananas or other edible fruits or vegetables, fish and sometimes turtle being all they procured.

I inquired after if they knew of any rivers or openings leading far inland, if they made charts of what they saw, or used any charts. To all of which Pobassoo answered in the negative...I could find no other nautical instrument amongst them than a very small pocket compass, apparently of Dutch manufacture; by this their course is directed at sea without the aid of any chart or astronomical observation...

My numberless questions were answered patiently, and with apparent sincerity; Pobassoo even stopped one day longer, at my desire, than he had intended, for the north-west monsoon, he said, would not blow quite a month longer, and he was rather late. I rewarded his trouble and that of his companions with several presents, principally iron tools, which they seemed anxious to possess; and he begged of me an English jack, which he afterwards carried at the head of his squadron. He also expressed a desire for a letter, to show to any other ship he might meet; and I accordingly wrote him a note to Captain Baudin, whom it seemed probable he might encounter in the Gulf, either going or returning.

25 February 1803—At daylight, I took bearings from the low south-west point whilst Bongaree speared a few fish...Bongaree was busily employed preparing his fish when my bearings were concluded. The natives of Port Jackson have a prejudice against all fish of the ray kind, as well as against sharks and, whilst they devour with eager avidity the blubber of a whale or porpoise, a piece of skate would excite disgust.

Our good-natured Indian had been ridiculed by the sailors for this unaccountable whim, but he had not been cured; and it so happened that the fish he had speared this morning were three small rays and a mullet. This last, being the most delicate, he presented to Mr Westall and me, so soon as it was cooked; and then went to saunter by the water side, whilst the boats' crew should cook and eat the rays, although, having had nothing since the morning before, it may be supposed he did not want appetite.

I noticed this in silence till the whole were prepared, and then had him called up to take his portion of the mullet; but it was with much difficulty that his modesty and forbearance could be overcome, for these qualities, so seldom expected in a savage, formed leading features in the character of my humble friend. But there was one of the sailors also, who preferred hunger to ray-eating! It might be supposed he had an eye to the mullet; but this was not the case. He had been seven or eight years with me, mostly in New South Wales, had learned many of the native habits, and even imbibed this ridiculous notion respecting rays and sharks; though he could not allege, as Bongaree did, that 'they might be very good for white men, but would kill him'.

The mullet accordingly underwent a further division; and Mr Westall and myself, having no prejudice against rays, made up our proportion of this scanty repast from one of them.

FRANÇOIS PÉRON
Terre Napoleon, 1802

Napoleon Bonaparte had a special fascination with Australia. In 1801 he equipped and des-patched the Baudin expedition, probably the most magnificent scientific expedition ever to visit the region. For three years the French scientists probed, measured and charted every aspect of the new continent, naming its southern coast *Terre Napoleon* in honour of their emperor.

Following many deaths and desertions François Péron was to become scientific leader of the expedition. He was the first person ever to revel in the title of Field Anthropologist. He was also an experienced soldier, who knew that peace between the French and English was fragile. In April and May of 1802 Péron saw Sydney, somewhat improbably, as a model city, inhabited by model citizens universally improving their morals and manners in their new land. His careful observations of the nascent city and of its fortifications suggest that Péron felt that one day he might return to Port Jackson—this time to fight a war.

Our arrival at Port Jackson did not excite so much surprise amongst the colonists as might have been expected; but for ourselves, we were completely astonished at the flourishing state in which we found this singular and distant establishment. The beauty of the port at first attracted our whole attention. From an entrance, says Commodore Phillip (whose description is not in the least exaggerated), of not more than two miles across, Port Jackson gradually opens till it forms a spacious harbour, with sufficient depth of water for the largest ships, and room enough to contain, in perfect safety, all that could on any occasion be collected. Even a thousand ships of the line might manœuvre here with ease. The bay takes a western direction, extends to the distance of thirteen miles inland, and has at least a hundred little creeks, formed by very narrow tongues of land, which afford excellent shelter against winds, from any point of the compass.

Towards the middle of this magnificent port, and on its southern bank, in one of the principal creeks, rises Sydney Town, the capital of the county of Cumberland, and of all the English colonies in this part of the world. Seated at the base of two hills—they are contiguous to each other—and having the advantage of a rivulet which runs completely through it, this infant town affords a view at once agreeable and picturesque.

To the right, and at the north point of Sydney Cove, you perceive the signal battery, which is built upon a rock difficult of access: six pieces of cannon, protected by a turf entrenchment, cross their fire with that of another battery, which I shall presently mention, and thus defend, in the most effectual manner, the approach to the harbour and the town. Farther on appear the large buildings that form the hospital and which are capable of containing two or three hundred sick. Amongst these buildings there is one particularly worthy of notice, as all the parts of it were prepared in Europe and brought out in Commodore Phillip's squadron, so that, in a few days after its arrival, there was an hospital ready to receive such of the crews as were sick.

On the same side of the town, at the seashore, you observe a very fine magazine to which the largest ships can come up and discharge their cargoes. In the same direction are several private docks in which are built brigs and cutters, of different sizes, for the purpose of trading, either inland or beyond the colony. These vessels, which are from fifty to three hundred tons burthen, are built entirely with the native wood; even their masts are obtained from the forests of the colony.

The discovery of the strait which separates New Holland from Van Diemen's Land was made in a simple whale sloop commanded by Mr Bass, the surgeon of the *Reliance*. This vessel may be said to have been consecrated to that great discovery and hazardous navigation, for it is preserved in the harbour, with a sort of religious veneration. Some snuff boxes have been made out of its keel, of which the possessors are both proud and jealous; and the governor himself thought he could not make a more acceptable present to our chief than a piece of the wood of this sloop, encased in a large silver toothpick box, round which were engraved the principal particulars of the discovery of Bass's Straits.

It is at the spot called Hospital Creek that the ships of individuals unload their cargoes. Beyond the hospital, in the same line, is the prison, which has several dungeons capable of holding from an hundred and fifty to two hundred prisoners; it is surrounded by a high and strong wall and has a numerous guard on duty, both by day and night. A short distance from the prison is the storehouse, for the reception of wines, spirituous liquors, salt provisions etc. In the front of it is the armoury, where the garrison is drawn up every morning, accompanied by a numerous and well-composed band, belonging to the New South Wales regiment. The whole western part of this spot is occupied by the house of the lieutenant-governor-general, behind which is a vast garden which is worth the attention both of the philosopher and the naturalist, on account of the great number of useful vegetables which are cultivated in it, and which have been procured from every part of the world by its present respectable possessor, Mr Paterson, a distinguished traveller, and member of the Royal Society of London.

Between the house and the magazine, just mentioned, is the public school: here are educated, in those principles of religion, morality and virtue, those young females who are the hope of the rising colony but whose parents are either too degenerate or too poor to give them proper instruction. In the public school, however, under respectable matrons, they are taught, from their earliest years, all the duties of a good mother of a family. Such is one great advantage of the excellent colonial system established in these distant regions.

Behind the house of the lieutenant-governor-general, in a large magazine, are deposited all the dried pulse and corn belonging to the state. It is a sort of public granary, intended for the support of the troops and the people who receive their subsistence from the government. The barracks occupy a considerable square, and have in front several fieldpieces; the edifices, for the accommodation of the officers, form the lateral parts or ends of the building, and the powder magazine is in the middle. Near this, in a small private house, the principal civil and military officers assemble. It is a sort of coffee-house, maintained by subscription, in which there are several amuse-ments, but particularly billiards, at which any person may play, free of expense.

Behind the armoury is a large square tower, which serves for an observatory to those English officers who study astronomy. At the base of this tower the foundation of a church has been laid of which the building, just mentioned, is intended to form the steeple; but a structure of this kind, requiring considerable time, labour, and expense, the governors have hitherto neglected to carry it into execution, preferring the formation of such establishments as are more immediately necessary for the preservation of the colony. While waiting, however, for the erection of a church, divine service is performed in one of the apartments of the great corn magazine. Two fine windmills terminate on this side the series of the principal public edifices.

Over the rivulet that intersects the town, there was a wooden bridge which, together with a strong causeway, may be said to occupy all the bottom of the valley. We passed over this bridge in order to take a rapid view of the eastern part of Sydney Town. Before our departure the wooden bridge was destroyed to make way for one which they were about to build of stone; at the same time, a watermill was built here by the government, and strong locks had been formed, either to keep in the water of the rivulet, or to stop that of the marshes, which runs to a considerable distance into the valley and might be advantageously employed in turning the mill.

At the east point of the creek is a second battery, the fire of which crosses that of the signal station. The one of which I am now speaking was dismantled at the time of our arrival at Port Jackson, but it has been put in order since our departure. On the shore, as you approach the town, is a small salt-pit, where the Americans, who were allowed to settle for the purpose at Port Jackson in 1795, prepared most of the salt used in the colony. Farther on, and towards the bottom of the harbour, is the part called Government Creek, because it is reserved for the agents and vessels of the state. Between this creek and the salt-pit is the place for docking and careening the ships. The natural quays are so perpendicular and well formed that, without any kind of labour or expense on the part of the English, the largest ships might be laid along them in perfect security.

Near the Government Creek are three public magazines. One of them contains all the articles necessary for the various purposes of domestic life, such as earthenware, household furniture, culinary utensils, instruments of agriculture etc. The number of these articles that is here amassed is truly astonishing, and the mode in which they are delivered out is wise and salutary. In this distant country, the merchandises of Europe bear so high a price that it would have been next to impossible for the population to procure such as are indispensable to the common wants of life. The English government has therefore anticipated these wants by filling large storehouses with every article that can be required, all of which are delivered to the colonists at fixed prices that are extremely moderate, sometimes even below what they cost in Europe. But in order to prevent avaricious speculations, or waste, no one is admitted into these depots without a written order from the governor in which are specified the articles that the bearer is in need of. In another house are preserved the different uniforms and clothing for the troops and convicts, as well as vast quantities of sailcloth and cordage for the government ships. The last of the three buildings just mentioned is a kind of public manufactory in which are employed female convicts.

Behind these magazines is the governor's house, which is built in the Italian style, surrounded by a colonnade, as simple as it is elegant, and in front of which is a fine garden that descends to the seashore. Already in this garden may be seen the Norfolk Island pine, the superb Columbia, growing by the side of the bamboo of Asia; farther on is the Portugal orange and Canary fig, ripening beneath the shade of the French apple tree; the cherry, peach, pear, and apricot, are interspersed amongst the *Banksia, Metrosideros, Correa, Melaleuca, Casuarina, Eucalyptus* and a great number of other indigenous trees.

Beyond the government garden, on the other side of a neighbouring hill, is the windmill, the bakehouse and the state ovens that are used for making ship biscuit: these are capable of furnishing from fifteen to eighteen hundred pounds per day. Not far from a contiguous creek, at a spot which the natives call *Wallamoula*, is the charming habitation of Mr Palmer, the commissary general.[†] A rivulet of fresh water runs before it, and empties itself into the creek which here forms a safe and

† Wallamoula: Woolloomooloo.

convenient basin. Here, Mr Palmer has built several small vessels which he employs in whale fishing, and catching Phocae, or sea elephants, either at New Zealand or in Bass's Straits. The neighbouring brick-fields furnish a considerable quantity of bricks and tiles for the public and private buildings of the colony.

A short distance to the southward of Sydney Town, to the left of the great road that leads to Parramatta, you observe the remains of the first gibbet that was erected on the continent of New Holland. The increase of habitations having caused it to be, as it were, surrounded, it has been succeeded by another that has been erected farther off, in the same direction, and near the village of Brick-field.[†] This village, which consists of about two score of houses, contains several manufactories of tiles, earthenware, crockery etc. Its site is agreeable, and the soil, less sterile than that of Sydney, is better adapted to the different kinds of cultivation that have been introduced into these distant regions.

The great road just mentioned passes through the middle of Brick-field; while a small rivulet intersects it in an opposite direction. Between this village and Sydney Town is the public burying-ground, which is already rendered an object of interest and curiosity by several striking monuments that have been erected in it; and the execution of which is much better than could reasonably have been expected from the state of the arts in so young a colony.[††]

A crowd of objects, equally interesting, demanded our notice in every direction. In the port we saw, drawn up together, a number of vessels that had arrived from different parts of the world, and most of which were destined to perform new and difficult voyages. Some of them had come from the banks of the Thames or the Shannon to pursue whale-fishing on the frigid shores of New Zealand. Others, bound to China after depositing

[†] Brick-field was near the site of what is now the University of Sydney.
[††] The cemetery with its striking monuments was near the present Town Hall.

the freight which they had received from the English government for this colony, were preparing to sail for the mouth of the Yellow River; while some, laden with pit-coal, were about to convey that precious combustible to India, and the Cape of Good Hope. Several smaller vessels were on their way to Bass's Straits to receive skins, collected by a few individuals who had established themselves on the isles of those straits to catch the marine animals that resort to them.

Other ships, stronger built than those just alluded to and manned by more numerous and daring crews who were provided with all kinds of arms, were on the point of sailing for the western coast of America. Laden with various sorts of merchandise, these vessels were intended to carry on, by force of arms, a contraband trade on the Peruvian shores, which could not fail to prove extremely advantageous to the adventurers. Here they were preparing an expedition to carry on a skin trade with the people of the north-west shores of America; there all hands were engaged in sending off a fleet of provision ships to the Navigators', the Friendly, and the Society Islands, to procure for the colony a stock of salt provisions.[†]

At the same time the intrepid Captain Flinders, after effecting a junction with his companion ship, the *Lady Nelson*, was getting ready to continue his grand voyage round New Holland, a voyage which was soon afterwards terminated by the greatest misfortunes.[††] In short, at this period, the harbour of Port Jackson had become familiar to the American navigators, and their flag was continually flying in it during our residence.

All these great maritime operations gave to the place a character of importance and activity far beyond what we expected to meet with on shores scarcely known to Europeans, even by name, and the interest we took in the scene was only equalled by our admiration.

---

† Samoa, Tonga and Tahiti respectively.
†† Matthew Flinders' vessel was wrecked off the Queensland coast.

The population of the colony was to us a new subject of astonishment and contemplation. Perhaps there never was a more
worthy object of study presented to the philosopher—never was
the influence of social institutions proved in a manner more striking
and honourable to the distant country in question. Here we found
united, like one family, those banditti who had so long been the
terror of their mother country. Repelled from European society,
and sent off to the extremity of the globe, placed from the very
hour of their exile in a state between the certainty of chastisement
and the hope of a better fate, incessantly subjected to an inspection
as inflexible as it is active, they have been compelled to abandon
their anti-social manners; and the majority of them, having
expiated their crimes by a hard period of slavery, have been
restored to the rank which they held amongst their fellow men.
Obliged to interest themselves in the maintenance of order and
justice, for the purpose of preserving the property which they have
acquired, while they behold themselves in the situation of husbands
and fathers, they have the most interesting and powerful motives
for becoming good members of the community in which they exist.

The same revolution, effected by the same means, has taken
place amongst the women, and those who were wretched
prostitutes have imperceptibly been brought to a regular mode
of life and now form intelligent and laborious mothers of families.
But it is not merely in the moral character of the women that
these important alterations are discoverable, but also in their
physical condition, the results of which are worthy the consideration both of the legislator and the philosopher. For example,
everybody knows that the common women of great capitals are
in general unfruitful: at Petersburgh and Madrid, at Paris and
London, pregnancy is a sort of phenomenon amongst persons of
that description, though we are unable to assign any other cause
than a sort of insusceptibility of conception. The difficulty of
researches, as to this subject, has prevented philosophers from
determining how far this sterility ought to be attributed to the
mode of life of such women, and to what degree it may be
modified or altered by a change of condition and manners.

But both these problems are resolved by what takes place in the singular establishment that we are describing. After residing a year or two at Port Jackson most of the English prostitutes become remarkably fruitful; and what, in my opinion, clearly proves that the effect arises much less from the climate than from the change of manners amongst the women is that those prostitutes in the colony, who are permitted by the police to continue in their immoral way of life, remain barren the same as in Europe. Hence we may be permitted to deduce the important physiological result that an excess of sexual intercourse destroys the sensibility of the female organs to such a degree as to render them incapable of conception; while to restore the frame to its pristine activity nothing is necessary but to renounce those fatal excesses.

FRANCIS BARRALLIER
Portions of a Monkey, 1802

 In November 1802, Francis Barrallier, French-speaking ensign of the New South Wales Corps, came within a whisker of crossing the Blue Mountains. Although Barrallier turned back too soon, he brought with him the first evidence of the koala, an animal which the colonists knew about only by rumour. The creature's feet, pickled in rum, at first confused and then amazed Europe's savants. Was it a monkey—or an arboreal wombat?

7 November—After having walked for a little while, I perceived two natives seated under a bush, one of whom seemed as if he were anxious to run away, while the other one remained seated and appeared to be trying to persuade the former to stay.

Gogy, the native I had in my service, started running, and went and sat with them, where he remained until we arrived. He came and told me that one of these natives was a mountaineer called Bungin, and the other knew the white men and was called Wooglemai.*

I went to the mountaineer to examine a mantle with which he was covered. This mantle was made of skins of various animals sewn together. It was a very great curiosity and, as I was desirous of obtaining it, I proposed to him to exchange it for a new axe, but he would not part with it, and told me that the nights were very cold and his mantle was his only covering. I was compelled to abandon my proposal, and in order to attach to me this mountaineer, who would be very useful to me in the country I was in, I had the head of the kangaroo given to him to appease his hunger, after which he came and proposed, as a token of friendship, to exchange his old axe for the new one I had offered him for his mantle. I filled him with joy by complying with his request.

I resumed my journey at half past five o'clock, and arrived with my party and baggage on the border of a small creek...The place where I decided to spend the night was on the territory of the mountaineer Bungin. He gave a proof of his friendship and gratefulness for my good treatment by building a hut for me, and I was very thankful for his kind attention.

I was then at about two miles from a chain of mountains, the direction of which is westerly, inclining towards the south; southerly there is a range of hills stretching in various directions...

On the 8th November I crossed the creek, the banks of which are nearly perpendicular; but the bullocks succeeded in making a wide passage, quite practicable for men on foot, but too steep for a carriage to pass, and I was obliged to have the waggon carried by hand to the other side. I walked until noon, when I stopped near another creek in order to rest ourselves until four o'clock. A soup

---

* Wooglemai, in the natives' language, signifies 'one-eyed'. This native knew Gogy, as he used to go from time to time to Parramatta and Prospect Hill. The mountaineer called Bungin was an inhabitant of the south and had left the Canambaigle tribe because they wanted to kill him. He was the brother of a famous chief who had accidentally killed himself in falling from a tree. That chief was called Goonboole. He inhabited the mountains near Jervis Bay and was the terror of the neighbourhood.

made of boiled rice, with pickled pork, composed our repast, and I saw that the two natives had their share; but whilst one of the newly arrived mountaineers would not partake of this food the other ate it with avidity. The former, having caught a lizard, roasted it and devoured it. I tasted some of it and preferred it to the opossum...

I resumed my journey at four, and at six o'clock crossed another creek. After having travelled over a plain, I perceived fires in several places, and Bungin told me that it was a chief called Canambaigle with his tribe, who were hunting and had on that very day set the country on fire. He showed me the imprints of various feet, both of males and females, scattered here and there...

On the 9th November, at six in the morning when I was preparing to start, Bungin, one of the mountaineer natives, told me that he heard the voice of a native at some distance from us and, after having spoken to Gogy, they went together towards the spot whence the sound of the voice had appeared to come. I heard them repeat, several times, the word *coo-ee*, shouting with all their strength; and a quarter of an hour later after I had lost sight of them they came back, bringing two other mountaineers with them. One was called Bulgin and the other Wallarra. The latter had never seen a white man, but the former had seen several whilst kangaroo hunting.

Wallarra was seized with a great fright when I stepped forward to shake hands with him, and I was obliged to withdraw and leave him with the other natives, who tried to reassure him and give him confidence, telling him that I did not do them any harm, that I had come to gather some pebbles and plants and that I had the animals skinned to preserve their fur.[*]

---

[*] I had some boiled rice and sugar given to them. Bulgin ate it with greediness, but Wallarra ate only the sugar which I had to put on top. It would be difficult to describe his fright. He was standing with crossed arms and his eyes riveted on the ground. I had a second handful of sugar given to him which he ate; but when I again went near him his whole frame began to tremble.

The forenoon was already far advanced. I gave orders to yoke the bullocks to the waggon, and to place in it my utensils for my journey to Nattai, which I reached at 11 a.m., after having gone over a very difficult country, all covered with stones and bush, the soil of which is very arid...[†]

I told some of my people to cut some trees to make a hut large enough for the whole of my party, and to procure a good supply of water, as the nearest creek was almost one mile from us. Whilst my orders were being carried out, and the other portion of my people were preparing our dinner, I went to explore the neighbourhood and there gathered various plants.

After dinner I took two men with me and went down the creek, which I followed until dusk, gathering flowers and fragments of a rather peculiar sandstone. I returned to the depot at sunset, and about the same time Bulgin (one of the mountaineer newcomers), with Bungin, arrived with their wives and two children; but Wallarra, the other mountaineer, was not with them.

Gogy told me that they had brought portions of a monkey (in the native language *colo*) but they had cut it in pieces, and the head, which I should have liked to secure, had disappeared. I could only get two feet through an exchange which Gogy made for two spears and one tomahawk. I sent these two feet to the governor in a bottle of spirits.

NICHOLAS PATESHALL
The King of Port Phillip, 1803

 Young Nicholas Pateshall, third lieutenant on HMS *Calcutta*, wrote an intriguing account of the first attempt, in October 1803, to establish a European settlement on the shores of Port Phillip

[†] Nattai: south-west of Camden.

Bay. After the Baudin expedition the English suspected the French had designs on Australia. HMS *Calcutta* had been dispatched from England, with her cargo of convicts, to cut timber for the navy and to establish a settlement in Bass Strait before the French could. Pateshall provides tantalising evidence about Victoria's Aborigines when he records seeing a distinctively robed individual, whom he calls 'their king', being carried on the shoulders of other men. Early accounts of western Victoria also mention similar 'chiefs'. Is it possible that some Aboriginal societies of Victoria were more stratified than those of the rest of the continent? Unfortunately, they were so quickly destroyed that we will probably never know.

On the 8th of October birds were seen about the ship, and the air was fumigated with a sweet scent, so that we assured ourselves of our approach to land. Every person seemed enlivened after running 6,893 miles and being forty-five days without seeing land.

King's Island in Bass's Straits, New Holland was now seen right ahead which we stood very close to and then tacked in. A short time after, a hurricane of wind, with a tremendous sea making a clean breach over the ship's poop, suddenly split or blew away every sail from the yards. In this situation did we remain during a long and awful night in the unexplored sea until morning, when an opening in the land on the main gave us hopes as to its being our port of destination. The weather being now more moderate we stood in towards it. When we were within a mile of the entrance we observed the sea to break all across. Our situation now became most serious with the wind and sea dead upon the land. We attempted to tack the ship but she refused stays. This brought us still nearer the danger; our anchors now seemed to be our only dependence.

At length we observed a small opening in the breakers through or on which it was evident the ship must go. Our sails were scarcely trimmed for the purpose when a cry from the look-out men aloft that a ship's masts were seen over the land again animated every heart, as it assured us of its being Port Phillip and the ship at anchor to be our consort the *Ocean*. All sail was now crowded upon the ship and the supposed reef of rocks proved to be an immensely strong ebb tide against the wind which caused the great sea at the entrance.

On the 9th of October 1803 we came to an anchor under the southern shore, the *Ocean* being half a mile from us. Upon entering this spacious harbour nothing could be more pleasing to the eye than the beautiful green plains with lofty trees which surrounded us. In short the country appeared more like pleasure grounds than a wild savage continent...

On the following morning we hoisted out all the boats. Captain Woodriff, Governor Collins and Lieutenant Tuckey went on shore in the barge and in a short time afterwards returned with a very unfavourable account of the place, not having been able to find fresh water, and soil they found to be little better than sand. Upon their approaching the shore two natives appeared brandishing their spears and making signs of hostile motion but, a musket being fired over their heads, they ran into the woods with a hideous yell leaving their war weapons behind. Again all the boats went in search of fresh water and returned with the same ill success. Vast quantities of wild fowl, black swans, pelicans, ducks and an innumerable number of parrots were seen, and likewise the prints and other marks of the kangaroo.

It was now proposed and determined to fit the launch and another boat for the purpose of surveying the harbour and if possible to find an eligible situation for establishing the colony. We next began to make wells for the daily supply of water by boring holes in casks and sinking them in the low grounds even with the surface. This plan answered our purpose as well as could be expected but the water was brackish.

On the 11th the captain, governor and some others visited part of the bay called Arthur's Seat. Lieutenant Dowers, the Reverend Mr Knopwood and myself went to an island five miles from the ship where we found excellent shooting and returned to the ship before night, bringing with us large swans, two couple of redbills and six pelicans, besides many other small birds and as many eggs as we could conveniently carry.[†] Upon this island I got a young eagle of the golden species. Other parties were equally successful having killed quail, parrots, snakes and pigeons.

Captain Woodriff and party returned with no better opinion of the place than before, but had determined upon landing the convicts in a bay which we called Sullivan.[††] The two boats before mentioned, under the command of Lieutenant Tuckey and some civil officers belonging to the colony establishment, well armed and fitted out in every respect for fourteen days, proceeded upon the intended survey. Arming the boats was thought prudent for, although as yet few of the natives had appeared, there could be no doubt that the place was swarming with them from the constant fires round the bay. In the evening we hauled out nets for fish but not with any great success: most of those we caught were of one sort to which we gave the name of aldermen from their delicious eating and from finding fish in them half as big as themselves...[†††]

The natives in general were very friendly and proud of everything given them, but seemed quite ignorant of the use of firearms or anything else, although they stole from us axes and saws. Both sexes go entirely naked excepting their chiefs or kings who wear cloaks on their backs of small skins sewn very neatly together with grass. The men seldom approach you without their instruments of war, which are spears pointed with sharp bones and shields neatly carved and ingeniously made. The women carry fish-gigs, nets etc. They are a robust race of people fond of adorning themselves with scars, white and red paint, and long necklaces made of reeds. Their chief's head-dress is composed of feathers of the cockatoo and parrot, and kangaroo teeth. The

[†] The island was Mud Island.
[††] John Sullivan was Undersecretary of State for War and the Colonies.
[†††] The aldermen were possibly gummy sharks.

women appear very shy, always keeping in the rear, are well made, but very dirty; their heads are likewise dressed with feathers etc. When the men approach you with hostile intention their chiefs are carried upon the shoulders of four men and are otherwise distinguished by having a bone or reed from ten to twelve inches long run through their noses which, added to the painting of their faces, makes them curious figures.

On the 22nd Lieutenant Tuckey and the former party again proceeded in two boats armed to finish the survey of the NW part of the harbour and did not return till the 28th when he gave us the following report: that he had found two or three freshwater rivers at a distance from the ship, that the navigation was exceedingly difficult and that it would be impossible for a colony to flourish there, as the soil was little better than sand.

On the evening previous to his return he had had a serious skirmish with the natives, which proceeded from their wishing to steal or take by force everything he had on shore in a tent, or even in the boats. From the account he gave it is evident that they are brave and clever as to their mode of attack. A small party of them came down first, with every sign of friendship, and received several presents. Lieutenant Tuckey then left the shore in one of the boats to survey a small spot while dinner was preparing; this the look-out party of the natives observing, they stole off from about the tent without giving the least suspicion of anything improper. In less than half an hour a large body was seen advancing on the right, carrying their chiefs as before described, and another party on the left equally large.

Mr Gammon, a midshipman who was commander of the small party left by Lieutenant Tuckey, ordered them immediately to seize their arms but on looking round saw they were completely encircled by another party which had advanced in the rear through the woods. Lieutenant Tuckey very fortunately had observed them in their first approach and had used all possible exertion to get on shore, as he happily did just as they had begun to brandish their weapons and to sing their war songs. He immediately commenced a firing over their heads, which for the moment made them retreat, but in a short time afterwards they advanced again, seemingly with double resolution.

Our party then took to their boats and began a firing of ball and swan shot. This, after a short skirmish, made them retreat hastily, leaving one dead and having several others wounded.

Their king, who was with the centre party, wore a beautiful turban of feathers and a very large cloak. He was a man of two or three and twenty, remarkably handsome, well made and of a much fairer complexion than the rest. Those of our party who wore fur caps were supposed by them to be females. Except the chiefs as before mentioned, all the natives were entirely naked, but had much disfigured themselves by painting their bodies with a red and white clay. Before they fight they make all the horrid faces imaginable, by way of defiance, which no doubt in many instances have great effect.

When in a good humour they are constantly laughing. At first we found them very curious in opening our shirts and taking off our hats etc. Their language is far from harsh and differs from that spoken in many parts of the same continent: the words *warree! warree! mallo! mallo!* they are constantly repeating, which words I rather think express astonishment.

A party of them one day followed me along the beach shouting. A pelican being within shot, I made signs to them to keep behind, and they immediately ran into the bushes. I then fired and killed the bird. This alarmed them so much that they could not be prevailed on to come near me for a considerable time and then they would not upon any account touch the bird, but kept at a great distance from the person who carried it. They have in general many dogs with them large and swift enough to catch the kangaroo; but they are if possible wilder than their masters.

On the 25th of October we fired a royal salute in commemoration of His Majesty's accession to the throne.[†] Everything

† George III.

now appeared to wear a new aspect. The place, which upon our first arrival seemed to afford everything that could be wished, now proved the most deplorable, without water or soil sufficient to produce the common necessaries of life. It was therefore thought prudent to equip a boat with Mr Collins (a colonial officer) and seven men to be dispatched to the governor of Port Jackson to inform him of our arrival, proceedings, and to give him an account of the place.

TE PAHI
Trans-Tasman Explorer, 1805–6

 Te Pahi, leading chief of the Rangihoua on New Zealand's northern Bay of Islands, had long nurtured a desire to visit the strange new English colony. In late November 1805 the great chief got his chance, travelling by whaler first to Norfolk Island and then on to Sydney.

Te Pahi was feted in Sydney society, and must have cut a fine if rather terrifying figure, his deeply carved tattoos transforming his face into a largely immobile mask. His interactions with the Eora people give us an inkling of how different Maori and Aborigines were, and of how they regarded each other.

Te Pahi formed emphatic views about the society he was exploring, and he certainly impressed Governor King who made these notes about him.

Soon after the *Buffalo* anchored, Captain Houstoun waited on me with his guest, who was clad in the costume of his country. On being introduced he took up a number of his mats, laying them at my feet, and disposed of a stone *patoo patoo* in the same manner, after which he performed the ceremony of *etongi* or joining of noses.

After many exclamations of surprise at the house and other

objects that attracted his passing attention, he gave me to understand that he had long desired the visit he had now accomplished, to which he had been encouraged by the reports of my two visitors at Norfolk Island in 1793, the request of his father, and the prospect of his country being benefited by his visit, as it had been for the great blessing bestowed on it by the introduction of potatoes at Tookee and Woodoo's return from Norfolk Island. He also added that leaving New Zealand was much against the wishes of his dependants, but that objection was much outweighed by the probable advantages they would derive from his visit, and concluded by saying that he considered himself under my protection. If I wished him to remain here, go to Europe, or return to his own country, he was resigned to either, and in the most manly confidence submitted himself and his sons to my directions. All this was said in such an imposing manner that no doubt could be entertained of his sincerity.

As I was anxious that no kindness should be wanting to impress him with a full sense of the hospitality I wished to make him sensible of, he with his eldest son, named Tookey, lived with me and eat at the table, whilst a very good room was allotted for his lodgings and that of his sons.

Tip-a-he is five feet eleven inches high, stout, and extremely well made. His age appears about forty-six or forty-eight. His face is completely tattooed with the spiral marks shown in *Hawkesworth's and Cook's Second Voyage*, which, with similar marks on his hips and other parts of his body, point him out as a considerable chief or *etangatida etikitia* of the first class. To say that he was nearly civilised falls far short of his character, as every action and observation shows an uncommon attention to the rules of decency and propriety in his every action, and has much of the airs and manners of a man conversant with the world he lives in. In conversation he is extremely facetious and jocose and, as he never reflected on any person, so Tip-a-he was alive to the least appearance of slight or inattention in others.

He never missed any opportunity of gaining the most particular information respecting the cause and use of everything that struck his notice, and but few things there were of real utility that did not entirely engross his most serious attention. In communicating observations on his own country he was always very anxious to make himself understood, and spared no pains to convince us that the customs of his country were in several instances better than ours, many of which he looked upon with the greatest contempt, and some with the most violent and abusive disapprobation, of which the following is an instance:

Two soldiers and a convict were sent prisoners from Port Dalrymple to be tried by a criminal court for stealing some pork from the king's stores at that place. Tip-a-he attended their trial on the Friday, and one of them was ordered for execution on the following Monday. As is usual, they attended divine service on the Sunday. As everyone was much affected by their situation Tip-a-he was not wanting in commiseration; but the instant the service was ended he went to the criminals and embracing them accompanied them back to the jail, where it appeared they gave Tip-a-he a petition to present to me.

On returning to Government House he came into the room where I was writing, and in a very earnest manner, and I believe from the full force of conviction, he endeavoured to reason with me on the injustice of slaying men for stealing pork, and at the same time showing the severest sorrow and grief for their fate, which he concluded by taking the petition out of his pocket and giving it to me, at the same time shedding tears. He threw himself prostrate on the ground, sobbing most bitterly.

Observing that I did not give him any answer or hopes than by saying I should consider of it, he left the room and did not make his reappearance until the hour of dinner, having taken off the dress he had made here, and appeared very violent, exclaiming in most furious manner against the severity of our laws in sentencing a man to die for stealing pork, although he admitted that a man might very justly be put to death for stealing a piece of iron, as that was of a permanent use; but stealing a piece of pork which, to use his own expression, was eat and passed off, he considered as sanguine in the extreme. With much earnestness he urged his being allowed to take them to New Zealand, where taking provisions was not accounted a crime; and so earnest was he on this expedient that he went to the master of an American vessel, then lying here, to request he would take them to New Zealand, where his ship would be loaded with potatoes as a recompense for their passage.

During the three days that the fate of those criminals was pending Tip-a-he would take no nourishment whatever, and in several instances was inclined to be furious. However, on its being signified that two were forgiven and that neither of the others would be executed at Sydney, he came about by degrees, but would never be reconciled to the idea of men suffering death for taking wherewithal to eat—a natural reasoning for one who inhabits a country where everything of that kind is common, and where their other wants are but few.

A material object of Tip-a-he's visit here was to know if the ships that touched at the bay all belonged to King George, and whether the refreshments and assistance he and his people gave them were right and agreeable to me. On this subject I explained to him the difference between the English and American colours, and that both were equally entitled to his kindness. He complained that in one instance a New Zealander had been flogged by the captain of a whaler and hoped that I would give orders that no such act should be committed in future, and very liberally observed that he supposed the captain must have been a very bad man in his own country to commit such violence on a stranger who he had nothing to do with.

As all the whalers and other vessels which have visited Tip-a-he's residence have expressed the great convenience, hospitality and assistance they have uniformly received from this worthy chief and his people, I told him that I should impress on those who might visit him the necessity of their conducting themselves and people in a peaceable manner, and to give them articles in exchange for their potatoes and what stock he may in future have to spare—which the supplies of breeding swine and goats, with fowl etc., sent from Norfolk Island, will soon enable him to do.

To give him some proof of the estimation he was held in by me and the inhabitants of this place, I caused a medal to be made of silver with the following engraving: 'Presented by Governor King to Tip-a-he, a Chief of New Zealand, during his visit at Port Jackson, in January, 1806'; and on the reverse: 'In the reign of George the Third, by the Grace of God King of the United Kingdom of Great Britain and Ireland.' This medal was suspended by a strong silver chain round his neck.

With this and his other presents he was pleased and gratified— particularly with the numerous tools and other articles of iron given him from the public stores and by every class of individuals. As several New Zealanders of the lower class had come here by different vessels, it was a desirable and useful object to endeavour to get a number of people sent from that country to distribute about as shepherds. On communicating this wish to Tip-a-he he appeared to give very readily into the idea, but insisted on sending the middling order of people, who would be more expert at labour and tractable than the *emokis* or lower class, who were too idle and vicious to send here and from whom no good could be got.

Hence it appears, as well as from his general conversation, that the *emokis* are made to labour by the authority of the chiefs. How far our friend will be able to comply with his promise of sending some of his subjects here must depend on the degree of authority he possesses. From what I was able to learn, Tip-a-he's authority is very extensive. His residence we know to be on the north side of the Bay Islands, just within Point Pococke, where he has a considerable hippah, or fortified place. The district extending to the northward is called Why-po-poo; but he claims the whole country from Moodee Whenua across the island, which must be very extensive; and, as a proof of the accuracy of his assertions, he admits that Mowpah, who is chief about the River Thames, is his rival on the south and Moodee Whenua on the north.

On the subject of cannibalism we could get but little certain information, as Tip-a-he decidedly denied the existence of such a practice in his dominions, but said it was common in Mowpah's district. Ti-a-pe, a native of Moodee Whenua, also said it was a practice with Tip-a-he and his subjects. Where truth lies I am undecided; but I am of opinion, from everything I have heard and observed, that this practice most certainly prevails in New Zealand.

As our visitor was constant in his attendance at divine service, his ideas on the existence of a God and matters of religion were often conversed upon. The existence of a God who resides above they believe, and that his shadow frequently visits the earth; that it is in the power of the priests to invoke the appearance of this shadow (which is perceptible to them only) either for the purpose of succouring the sick or on any other exigency. The presence of the deity is made known by a gentle whistling. The rest of the cure or other benefit depends on the charms or incantations of the priests, in whose efficacy they have an implicit belief. The dead are buried, and they believe that the spirit ascends; but if it enjoys a new state, or this 'death is an eternal sleep', we could not ascertain. But that there are future rewards and punishments they consider as certain; as well as the existence of an evil spirit as opposed to the deity, which they distinguish by the Otaheitian name of *Eatooa*; but they have no image to represent it, as have the Otaheitians.

Polygamy exists. Tip-a-he told us of several wives he has had, one of whom he killed for having a troublesome tongue; nor could he help testifying his surprise that many of the women here did not suffer the same fate. He has fifty-two children living, but he now attaches himself to only one young woman, by whom he has a son now eight years old, who accompanies him on his visit and of whom he is very fond.

Of the natives of this country he had the most contemptible opinion, which both he and Tookey did not fail to manifest by discovering the utmost abhorrence at their going naked, and their want of ingenuity or inclination to procure food and make themselves comfortable, on which subject Tip-a-he on every occasion reproached them very severely. Their battles he treated as the most trifling mode of warfare, and was astonished that when they had their adversary down they did not kill him, which it seems is a custom among the New Zealanders and is carried to the most unrelenting pitch; indeed, no race of men could be treated with a more marked contempt than the natives of this country were by our visitors, who, it must be confessed, were infinitely their superiors in every respect.

Of Tip-a-he's independent and high spirits a better proof cannot be given than the following circumstance that occurred a week previous to his departure. Every person, particularly the officers and their wives, had made him presents of some baubles, as well as the greater part being of great use to him, which was clothing and iron tools of most description. An officer's wife had given him, among other things, a pair of earrings, which he very inconsiderately bestowed on a young woman. The donation was soon after discovered, and the earrings taken from the girl, on which Tip-a-he was reproached for his want of respect for the original donor who, before this unlucky event, was very much respected by him.

However, the instant he found that the earrings had been taken away, he packed every article up which he had received from that person (and among which were some very useful things) and sent them by one of his sons; nor could he ever be persuaded to speak or see the lady who gave him the things, and constantly expressed his disgust at hearing of the presents he had received being in any way mentioned except by himself; and, to do him justice, he always took every opportunity of speaking of the donors with the most grateful respect.

A few weeks after he arrived Te Pahi witnessed a skirmish near the Brickfields between two groups of Aborigines, in which a young warrior named Blewit was encircled. On 22 December 1805 the *Sydney Gazette* published an account of Blewit's predicament.

The animosity of his assailants was uncommonly remarkable; their party was far the most powerful and, confident of their superiority, took every advantage of their numbers. The flights of spears were seldom less than six, and managed with a precision that seemed to promise certain fatality. After 170 had been thus thrown, ten of the most powerful stationed themselves so as nearly to encircle the culprit, and front and rear darted their weapons at the same instant. His activity and strong presence of mind increased with the danger, and five he dexterously caught with his feeble target. The others he miraculously managed to escape.

One of his friends, enraged at the proceeding, threw a spear and received ten in return. Blewit turned one of the assailants' spears upon themselves and passed it through the body of old Whitaker: the affray then became general, but terminated without further mischief.

Tip-pa-he, who with several of his sons was present, regarded with contempt their warfare. He frequently discovered much impatience at the length of interval between the flights, and by signs exhorted them to dispatch. He considered the heel-a-man or shield an unnecessary appendage, as the hand was sufficient to put aside and alter the direction of any number of spears. He nevertheless praised highly the woomera or throwing stick, as from its elasticity he acknowledged the weapon to receive much additional velocity.

He was visibly chagrined when he saw the old man wounded through the body and would certainly have executed vengeance upon its author had he not been restrained by the solicitations of the spectators.

The natives have formed some extravagant notions of this stranger: they dread to approach him and as much as possible avoid him; but whether from a deference to his rank presumed from the very great attention shown him or from superstitious apprehensions excited by his appearance is indeterminable, though the latter by far the more probable conjecture.

One of his eldest sons, communing familiarly with a large group on the use of the spear, was very politely and generally acquiesced with. He requested the loan of one of their weapons, which was immediately presented; but as soon as he took it in his hand they all took to their heels, men, women and children, and could not by all his most friendly assurances be prevailed upon to return until he had lain it aside.

Páloo Máta Môigna
What Is Money Made of?, 1806

Two indigenous proto-empires had developed in the Pacific by the time of European contact: the Hawaiian Islands and Tonga (now the only surviving Pacific Islands kingdom). In late May 1806 two Tongan royals arrived in Sydney on an extended visit. Their painful story was later heard by William Mariner, a cabin boy who had been shipwrecked on Tonga in 1806 and adopted by the king, Finau. By 1811 Mariner was back in England, where he dictated his recollections of Tonga to one Dr Martin, a man fascinated by the variety of human societies.

Stories of deprivation and death in the hinterlands are central to Australian exploration. For their part, the Tongan expeditioners nearly succumbed in the heart of Sydney Town. Their nobility was not recognised, and they were considered a mere nusiance by governors King and later Bligh, who grudgingly gave them shelter. Part of the problem was money. The idea of it seemed completely weird to the Tongans, no less weird than the landscape and the Aborigines seemed to many Europeans. At precisely the same time that the Royal Society in London was sponsoring explorers to deliver learned papers on the savages of the south seas, the Tongans were discussing money and morality with a sharpness worthy of Adam Smith.

Whilst Finow was yet at the Hapai Islands, he often held conversations at his kava parties with Filimóëátoo, respecting the state of affairs at Tonga.[†] Among other things, this chief related, that a ship from Botany Bay had touched there about a week before he arrived, on board of which there was a Tonga chief, Páloo Máta Môigna, and his wife, Fatafehi, both of whom had left Tonga before the death of Toogoo Ahoo, and had resided some years at the Fiji Islands, from which place they afterwards went along with one Selly (as they pronounced it) or, probably, Selby, an Englishman, in a vessel belonging to Botany Bay, to reside there.[††] At this latter place he and his wife remained about two years, and now, on their return to Tonga, finding the island in such an unsettled state, they chose rather (notwithstanding the earnest entreaties of their friends) to go back again to Botany Bay.

The account they gave of the English customs at this place, and the treatment they at first met with, it may be worthwhile to relate. The first thing that he and his wife had to do, when they arrived at the governor's house, where they went to reside, was to sweep out a large courtyard and clean down a great pair of stairs. In vain they endeavoured to explain that in their own country they were chiefs and, being accustomed to be waited on, were quite unused to such employments.

Their expostulations were taken no notice of, and work they must. At first their life was so uncomfortable that they wished to die. No one seemed to protect them; all the houses were shut against them; if they saw anybody eating they were not invited to partake. Nothing was to be got without money, of which they could not comprehend the value, nor how this same money was to be obtained in any quantity. If they asked for it, nobody would give them any, unless they worked for it; and then it was so small in quantity that they could not get with it one-tenth part of what they wanted.

[†] Filimóëátoo: a relative of King Finau.
[††] Selly was in fact an American sailor, Captain Peter Chase, who berthed his vessel the *Criterion* at Port Jackson on 26 May 1806.

One day, whilst sauntering about, the chief fixed his eyes upon a cook's shop and, seeing several people enter and others again coming out with victuals, he made sure that they were sharing out food, according to the old Tonga fashion; and in he went, glad enough of the occasion. After waiting some time with anxiety to be helped to his share, the master of the shop asked him what he wanted and, being answered in an unknown language, straightway kicked him out, taking him for a thief that only wanted an opportunity to steal.

Thus, he said, even being a chief did not prevent him being used ill, for when he told them he was chief they gave him to understand that *money* made a man a chief.

After a time, however, he acknowledged that he got better used, in proportion as he became acquainted with the customs and language. He expressed his astonishment at the perseverance with which white people worked from morning till night to get money; nor could he conceive how they were able to endure so much labour.

After having heard this account, Finow asked several questions respecting the nature of money. What is it made of? Is it like iron? Can it be fashioned like iron into various useful instruments? If not, why cannot people procure what they want in the way of barter? But where is money to be got? If it be made, then every man ought to spend his time in making money, that when he has got plenty he may be able afterwards to obtain whatever else he wants.

In answer to the last observation, Mr Mariner replied that the material of which money was made was very scarce and difficult to be got and that only chiefs and great men could procure readily a large quantity of it; and this either by being inheritors of plantations or houses which they allowed others to have, for paying them so much tribute in money every year; or by their public services; or by paying small sums of money for things when they were in plenty and afterwards letting others have them for larger sums when they were scarce; and, as to the lower classes of people, they worked hard and got paid by their employers in small quantities of money as the reward of their labour etc. That the king was the only person that was allowed to make (to coin) money, and that he put his mark upon all he made, that it might be known to be true; that no person could readily procure the material of which it was made without paying money for it; and if, contrary to the *taboo* of the king, he turned this material into money he would scarcely have made as much as he had given for it.

Mr Mariner was then going on to show the convenience of money as a medium of exchange, when Filimóëátoo interrupted him, saying to Finow, I understand how it is: money is less cumbersome than goods and it is very convenient for a man to exchange away his goods for money which, at any other time, he can exchange again for the same or any other goods that he may want; whereas the goods themselves may perhaps spoil by keeping (particularly if provisions), but the money, he supposed, would not spoil; and although it was of no true value itself, yet being scarce and difficult to be got without giving something useful and really valuable for it, it was imagined to be of value; and if everybody considered it so and would readily give their goods for it, he did not see but what it was of a sort of real value to all who possessed it, as long as their neighbours chose to take it in the same way.

Mr Mariner found he could not give a better explanation; he therefore told Filimóëátoo that his notion of the nature of money was a just one.

After a pause of some length, Finow replied that the explanation did not satisfy him. He still thought it a foolish thing that people should place a value on money when they either could not or would not apply it to any useful (physical) purpose. 'If,' said he, 'it were made of iron and could be converted into knives, axes and chisels, there would be some sense in placing a value on it; but as it is I see none. If a man,' he added, 'has more yams than he wants, let him exchange some of them away for pork or *gnatoo*.[†] Certainly money is much handier, and more convenient,

---

[†] Gnatoo: tapa, a bark cloth.

but then, as it will not spoil by being kept, people will store it up, instead of sharing it out, as a chief ought to do, and thus become selfish; whereas, if provisions were the principal property of a man, and it ought to be, as being both the most useful and the most necessary, he could not store it up, for it would spoil, and so he would be obliged either to exchange it away for something else useful or share it out to his neighbours, and inferior chiefs and dependants, for nothing.'

He concluded by saying, 'I understand now very well what it is that makes the Papalangis so selfish—it is this money!'[†]

GREGORY BLAXLAND
Blaxland, Wentworth and Lawson
Breach the Barrier, 1813

 A modest man, Gregory Blaxland wrote his official account of the first crossing of the Blue Mountains in the third person, and referred to it in his title as 'a tour'. And the crossing itself, after so many frustrated attempts by others, seems to have been ridiculously easy. Aboriginal trails may have aided the explorers in finding their way through the maze of canyons, cliffs and isolated pinnacles that form the Blue Mountains, but the key was to stick to the ridges. Whatever the case, this defining moment in European Australian exploration seems like an anticlimax.

On Tuesday, May 11, 1813, Mr Gregory Blaxland, Mr William Wentworth and Lieutenant Lawson, attended by four servants, with five dogs, and four horses laden with provisions, ammunition and other necessaries, left Mr Blaxland's farm at the South Creek for the purpose of endeavouring to effect a passage over the

† Papalangis: Europeans.

Blue Mountains, between the Western River and the River Grose. They crossed the Nepean, or Hawkesbury River, at the ford, on to Emu Island, at four o'clock, p.m., and having proceeded, according to their calculation, two miles in a south-west direction, through forest land and good pasture, encamped at five o'clock at the foot of the first ridge. The distance travelled on this and on the subsequent days was computed by time; the rate being estimated at about two miles per hour...

On Monday the 17th, having laden the horses with as much grass as could be put on them, in addition to their other burdens, they moved forward along the path which they had cleared and marked, about six miles and a half. The bearing of the route they had been obliged to keep along the ridge varied exceedingly; it ran sometimes in a north-north-west direction, sometimes south-east, or due south, but generally south-west or south-south-west. They encamped in the afternoon between two very deep gullies, on a narrow ridge, Grose Head bearing north-east by north, and Mount Banks north-west by west. They had to fetch water up the side of the precipice, about six hundred feet high, and could get scarcely enough for the party. The horses had none this night: they performed the journey well, not having to stand under their loads.

The following day was spent in cutting a passage through the brushwood, for a mile and a half farther. They returned to their camp at five o'clock, very much tired and dispirited. The ridge, which was not more than fifteen or twenty yards over, with deep precipices on each side, was rendered almost impassable by a perpendicular mass of rock, nearly thirty feet high, extending across the whole breadth, with the exception of a small broken rugged track in the centre. By removing a few large stones, they were enabled to pass.

On Wednesday the 19th, the party moved forward along this path, bearing chiefly west and west-south-west. They now began to ascend the second ridge of the mountains and, from this elevation, they obtained for the first time an extensive view of the settlements below. Mount Banks bore north-east; Grose

Head, north-east; Prospect Hill, east by south; the Seven Hills, east-north-east; Windsor, north-east by east.

At a little distance from the spot at which they began the ascent, they found a pyramidical heap of stones, the work, evidently, of some European, one side of which the natives had opened, probably in the expectation of finding some treasure deposited in it. This pile they concluded to be the one erected by Mr Bass to mark the end of his journey.[†] That gentleman attempted, some time ago, to pass the mountains, and to penetrate into the interior; but having got thus far, he gave up the undertaking as impracticable; reporting, on his return, that it was impossible to find a passage even for a person on foot. Here, therefore, the party had the satisfaction of believing that they had penetrated as far as any European had been before them...

On Saturday the 22nd instant, they proceeded in the track marked the preceding day rather more than three miles in a south-westerly direction, when they reached the summit of the third and highest ridge of the mountains southward of Mount Banks. From the bearing of Prospect Hill, and Grose Head, they computed this spot to be eighteen miles in a straight line from the River Nepean, at the point at which they crossed it. On the top of this ridge, they found about two thousand acres of land clear of trees, covered with loose stones and short coarse grass, such as grows on some of the commons in England. Over this heath they proceeded for about a mile and a half, in a south-westerly direction, and encamped by the side of a fine stream of water, with just wood enough on the banks to serve for firewood. From the summit, they had a fine view of all the settlements and country eastward, and of a great extent of country to the westward and south-west. But their progress in both the latter directions was stopped by an impassable barrier of rock, which appeared to divide the interior from the coast, as with a stone

---

† George Bass attempted to cross the mountains in 1796, equipped with scaling irons, hooks and long ropes.

wall rising perpendicularly out of the side of the mountain.

In the afternoon, they left their little camp in the charge of three of the men, and made an attempt to descend the precipice by following some of the streams of water, or by getting down at some of the projecting points where the rocks had fallen in; but they were baffled in every instance. In some places, the perpendicular height of the rocks above the earth below could not be less than four hundred feet. Could they have accomplished a descent, they hoped to procure mineral specimens which might throw light on the geological character of the country, as the strata appeared to be exposed for many hundred feet, from the top of the rock to the beds of the several rivers beneath.

The broken rocky country on the western side of the cow pasture has the appearance of having acquired its present form from an earthquake, or some other dreadful convulsion of nature, at a much later period than the mountains northward, of which Mount Banks forms the southern extremity. The aspect of the country which lay beneath them much disappointed the travellers: it appeared to consist of sand and small scrubby brushwood, intersected with broken rocky mountains, with streams of water running between them to the eastward towards one point where they probably form the Western River and enter the mountains.

They now flattered themselves that they had surmounted half the difficulties of their undertaking, expecting to find a passage down the mountain more to the northward...

On the 28th, they proceeded about five miles and three-quarters. Not being able to find water, they did not halt till five o'clock when they took up their station on the edge of the precipice. To their great satisfaction, they discovered that what they had supposed to be sandy barren land below the mountain was forest land, covered with good grass and with timber of an inferior quality. In the evening, they contrived to get their horses down the mountain by cutting a small trench with a hoe, which kept them from slipping, where they again tasted fresh grass for the first time since they left the forest land on the other side of the mountain. They were getting into miserable condition...

On the 29th, having got up the horses, and laden them, they began to descend the mountain at seven o'clock, through a pass in the rock about thirty feet wide, which they had discovered the day before when the want of water put them on the alert. Part of the descent was so steep that the horses could but just keep their footing without a load, so that, for some way, the party were obliged to carry the packages themselves. A cart road might, however, easily be made by cutting a slanting trench along the side of the mountain, which is here covered with earth.

This pass is, according to their computation, about twenty miles north-west in a straight line from the point at which they ascended the summit of the mountain. They reached the foot at nine o'clock, a.m., and proceeded two miles, north-north-west, mostly through open meadow land, clear of trees, the grass from two to three feet high. They encamped on the bank of a fine stream of water. The natives, as observed by the smoke of their fires, moved before them as yesterday. The dogs killed a kangaroo, which was very acceptable, as the party had lived on salt meat since they caught the last. The timber seen this day appeared rotten and unfit for building.

Sunday the 30th, they rested in their encampment. One of the party shot a kangaroo with his rifle at a great distance across a wide valley. The climate here was found very much colder than that of the mountain, or of the settlements on the east side, where no signs of frost had made its appearance when the party set out. During the night, the ground was covered with a thick frost and a leg of the kangaroo was quite frozen. From the dead and brown appearance of the grass, it was evident that the weather had been severe for some time past. We were all much surprised at this degree of cold and frost, in the latitude of about 34. The track of the emu was noticed at several places near the camp.

On the Monday, they proceeded about six miles, south-west and west, through forest land, remarkably well watered, and several open meadows, clear of trees and covered with high good grass. They crossed two fine streams of water...

The party encamped by the side of a fine stream of water, at a short distance from a high hill in the shape of a sugar loaf. In the afternoon they ascended its summit, from whence they descried all around forest or grass land, sufficient in extent, in their opinion, to support the stock of the colony for the next thirty years.

This was the extreme point of their journey. The distance they had travelled, they computed, at about fifty-eight miles nearly north-west; that is, fifty miles through the mountain (the greater part of which they had walked over three times) and eight miles through the forest land beyond it, reckoning the descent of the mountain to be half a mile to the foot...

They now conceived that they had sufficiently accomplished the design of their undertaking, having surmounted all the difficulties 0which had hitherto prevented the interior of the country from being explored, and the colony from being extended. They had partly cleared, or at least marked out, a road by which the passage of the mountain might easily be effected. Their provisions were nearly expended, their clothes and shoes were in very bad condition, and the whole party were ill with bowel complaints.

These considerations determined them, therefore, to return home by the track they came...On Sunday the 6th of June, they crossed the river after breakfast, and reached their homes, all in good health. The winter had not set in on this side of the mountain, nor had there been any frost.

GEORGE EVANS
They Began to Laugh, 1814

George William Evans arrived in Australia in 1804 and managed the government grain store at Parramatta. He went on to become acting surveyor-general, a farmer, an artist and a resolute explorer. In November 1813, in the wake of Blaxland, Wentworth and Lawson, he became the first

European to roam the lush plains to the west of the Blue Mountains. For this work he was awarded the sum of £100 and a thousand acres of land in Tasmania. He was to join other expeditions in both New South Wales and Tasmania.

In his later years, Evans opened a bookshop in Sydney. I wonder how many people dropped in just to chat with the old explorer. He loved children, for he had at least twelve of them himself, and seems to have delighted in their company, regardless of whether they were black or white. We join him in April 1814 near Bathurst.

Tuesday, 21st—Fine weather very warm; halted at the commencement of Bathurst Plains early, as I was desirous to examine this part. I ascended Mount Pleasant: the west end led me on a ridge of beautiful hills, along which I travelled about three miles; a small stream of water forming ponds run at their foot. I was gratified with a pleasant sight of an open country to the SW of them; at the space of seven or eight miles I could discern the course of a river winding to the west. I saw three or four large plains; the first of them I was on, the chain of ponds before mentioned running through it.

I feel much regret I am not able to travel a week or more in that direction. I imagine the flat open country extends thirty or forty miles; at the termination I can only discern one mountain quite pale with three peaks. I suspect an open country lay about the SW point; as I passed, the range of hills then obscured it from me, nor had I time to examine it.

I cannot speak too much of the country. The increase of stock for some 100 years cannot overrun it, the grass is so good and intermixed with variety of herbs. Emus and geese are numerous, but cannot get any.† We counted forty-one emus this day: our dogs will not follow them.

Returning we saw smoke on the north side of the river. At

† The geese were probably magpie geese.

sunset as we were fishing I saw some natives coming down the plain. They did not see us until we surprised them: there were only two women and four children. The poor creatures trembled and fell down with fright; I think they were coming for water. I gave them what fish we had; some fish hooks, twine and a tomahawk they appeared glad to get from us. Two boys ran away; the other small children cried much at first. A little while after I played with them they began to be good-humoured and laugh. Both of the women were blind of their right eye.

JOHN OXLEY
An Oval Grave, 1817

 An Englishman who initially pursued a career in the navy, John Oxley was the first of the great overland explorers. His expeditions into the country west and north of the Blue Mountains, with George Evans and others, can be said to mark the beginning of the classic phase of Australian exploration.

Explorers are naturally curious. But here, on the banks of the Lachlan River in 1817, did Oxley go too far?

July 29—The stream where we stopped was about four feet from the banks, running with much rapidity; and I think the flood in it has rather increased than abated.

Almost directly under the hill near our halting-place, we saw a tumulus which was apparently of recent construction (within a year at most). It would seem that some person of consideration among the natives had been buried in it, from the exterior marks of a form which had certainly been observed in the construction of the tomb and surrounding seats. The form of the whole was semi-circular. Three rows of seats occupied one half, the grave and an outer row of seats the other; the seats formed segments of circles of fifty, forty-five and forty feet each, and were formed by the soil being trenched up from between them. The centre part of the grave was about five feet high, and about nine long, forming an oblong pointed cone.

I hope I shall not be considered as either wantonly disturbing the remains of the dead, or needlessly violating the religious rites of an harmless people, in having caused the tomb to be opened that we might examine its interior construction. The whole outward form and appearance of the place was so totally different from that of any custom or ceremony in use by the natives on the eastern coast, where the body is merely covered with a piece of bark and buried in a grave about four feet deep, that we were induced to think that the manner of interring the body might also be different.

On removing the soil from one end of the tumulus, and about two feet beneath the solid surface of the ground, we came to three or four layers of wood, lying across the grave, serving as an arch to bear the weight of the earthy cone or tomb above. On removing one end of those layers, sheet after sheet of dry bark was taken out, then dry grass and leaves in a perfect state of preservation, the wet or damp having apparently never penetrated even to the first covering of wood. We were obliged to suspend our operation for the night, as the corpse became extremely offensive to the smell, resolving to remove on the morrow all the earth from the top of the grave, and expose it for some time to the external air before we searched farther...

July 30—The rain continued throughout the day without intermission...This morning we removed all the earth from the tomb and grave, and found the body deposited about four feet deep in an oval grave, four feet long and from eighteen inches to two feet wide. The feet were bent quite up to the head, the arms having been placed between the thighs. The face was downwards, the body being placed east and west, the head to the east.

It had been very carefully wrapped in a great number of opossum skins, the head bound round with the net usually worn by the natives, and also the girdle. It appeared, after being enclosed in those skins, to have been placed in a larger net, and then deposited in the manner before mentioned. The bones and head showed that they were the remains of a powerful tall man. The hair on the head was perfect, being long and black; the under part of the body was not totally decayed, giving us reason to think that he could not have been interred above six to eight months. Judging from his hair and teeth, he might have been between thirty and forty years of age.[†] To the west and north of the grave were two cypress trees distant between fifty and sixty feet. The sides towards the tomb were barked, and curious characters deeply cut upon them, in a manner which, considering the tools they possess, must have been a work of great labour and time. Having satisfied our curiosity, the whole was carefully re-interred, and restored as near as possible to the station in which it was found. The river fell in the course of the day near two feet.

JOHN OXLEY
The Finest Park Imaginable, 1818

 On a second expedition in 1818, Oxley encountered a land of plenty. His description of the fertile hills and beautiful, spacious valleys of the New England region helped to draw settlers over the ranges by the score. Soon the idyllic scenes of clear-flowing rivers, of plains full of kangaroos and emus, of Aborigines and their intricate cultures, were all to be things of the past.

September 7—The morning clear and fine. At half past seven o'clock we proceeded on our journey: in the whole course of it we never experienced more precipitous travelling than during

[†] Allan Cunningham, who was on this expedition, mentions in his diary that Oxley intended to remove the skull for studies in craniometry.

the first six miles. Travellers less accustomed to meet difficulties might perhaps have been a little alarmed at traversing such steep and shelving hills, the loose stones on which added to the insecurity of our footing. Nevertheless we found it extremely pleasant from the romantic beauty of the scenery and the freshness of the verdure.

We had been ascending an extremely elevated country for the last thirty miles; and I was in great hopes of soon reaching the point of division between the eastern and western waters. By a tolerably easy acclivity, we gained that which I took to be the highest of these congregated hills, in hopes it might possibly lead into a main range. From its summit we had a very extensive prospect over the country we had left, and also to the southward, in which direction the land appeared broken and hilly, and but thinly clothed with timber. To the east and north-east it appeared far less broken, and certainly less elevated than the ridge we were on. This ridge soon expanded to a broad surface of open forest land, and proceeding on it to the east about a mile we perceived in the valley beneath us a considerable and rapid stream running to the north, and afterwards apparently taking a more easterly direction.

A more remarkable change in the outward appearance of a country was perhaps never before witnessed. In less than a mile the timber had entirely changed from the bastard box to another kind of eucalyptus called common blue gum which grew in great luxuriance in the country before us. Until now this species had never been seen except on the immediate banks of running streams. In the course of the day, great quantities of fine stringybark were also seen. The soil, instead of the light black mould which had been the general covering of the country, was now changed to a stiff tenacious clay; and although well clothed with grass its less luxuriant growth evidently showed the difference of soil not to be favourable.

From this hill or range we descended very gradually for nearly two miles to the river before seen, and up the banks of which we proceeded about a mile farther, when we halted for the evening. The country was perfectly open, though much covered with fallen timber; the banks of the river sloping and quite clear of timber; and, being within one hundred miles of the sea coast, I had a strong belief that we had descended from the highest land, and that we should meet with no dividing ranges in the course of our future progress. It is impossible to form any certain conclusion at present as to the course taken by this stream. Whether it finds its way to the coast, or is lost like the other streams of this country, will, I think, in a great measure depend upon the fact of our having crossed the highest ranges of the country.

One of the men who had taken the dogs out after kangaroos fell in with a party of natives, among whom were some women and children. Two of the men accompanied him to the tent. It was evident from the whole tenor of their behaviour that they had previously heard of white people (most probably from the settlement at Newcastle). Their appearance was most miserable, their features approached deformity and their persons were disgustingly filthy. Their small attenuated limbs seemed scarcely able to support their bodies and their entire person formed a marked contrast to the fine and manly figures of their brethren in the interior. We gave them a small turtle which we had just caught in the river, and they sat down to dress it instantly. In fact, their cooking was very simple; the fire soon separated the shell from the meat, which with the entrails was devoured in a few minutes. Some of the people went to visit their camp, where they found eight or ten men, but the women and children were sent away. The same jealousy of women exists throughout the interior.

The great number of fallen trees was in some measure accounted for by the men observing about a dozen trees on fire near this camp, no doubt the more easily to expel the opossums, rats and other vermin which inhabit their hollows. We were not successful with our lines, though the depth and breadth of the river had made us a little sanguine. There did not appear any great marks of flood; none was seen exceeding five feet in height, which led us to conclude its source was not very distant. This river was named Sydney, as we this day crossed the meridian of that town.[†]

September 8—We proceeded up Sydney River to the south-east about three miles before we could find a convenient place to cross, as the stream ran with great rapidity over a rocky bottom. The country on either side sloped to the river with gradual declension and was an open forest country. On crossing the river, we passed through some noble forests of stringybark, growing generally on the sides and ridges of stony barren hills. These forests extended above two miles from the east of the river, after which the country became perfectly open, and of a level or rather alternately rising surface.

To the north and north-east the river was beautiful, the same description of country extending as far as the eye could reach, with no elevated points or ridges to obstruct it. Indeed I am clearly of opinion that if we had kept a more northerly course from Lushington Valley we should have avoided the rugged though fine country we have passed through for the last two days. The determination of all the hills and slopes is northerly, and the rivers which we have crossed have also taken the same direction.

We proceeded about nine miles farther through the finest open country, or rather park, imaginable; the general quality of the soil excellent, though of a stronger and more tenacious description than farther westerly. We halted in a fine and spacious valley, where art, so far as it is an auxiliary of beauty, would have been detrimental to the fresher and simpler garb of nature. This valley was watered by a fine brook, and at a distance of a mile we saw several fires, at which appeared many natives. Upon discovering us, however, they immediately departed.

I think that the most fastidious sportsman would have derived ample amusement during our day's journey. He might without moving have seen the finest coursing, from the commencement of the chase to the death of the game; and when tired of killing

† Sydney River: now the MacDonald River.

kangaroos, he might have seen emus hunted with equal success. We numbered swans and ducks among our acquisitions, which in truth were caught without much exertion on our part, or deviating in the least from our course. Granite and a hard whinstone were the most predominant among the stones. Small pieces of quartz and loose rotten slates covered the tracks, on which grew some of the finest stringybark trees I ever saw.

HAMILTON HUME
They Quarrelled about the Frying-Pan, 1824

 The names Hume and Hovell have been inextricably linked in the minds of countless Australian schoolchildren. In my case, it was some time before I could comprehend precisely what this 'human hovel' was or had achieved; and how their exploration was linked to the Hume Highway which our family travelled each Christmas holidays on visits to country relatives.

Hume and Hovell started just south of Sydney at Hume's farm on 17 October 1824 and ten weeks later looked out on the waters of Corio Bay. It appears from this passage—taken from the third edition of Hume's account, published posthumously fifty years after their journey—that the explorer would turn in his grave if he knew that posterity had linked his name so closely with that of William Hovell. We join the pair on 22 October 1824 as they attempt to cross the Murrumbidgee River.

Returning to the camp, I immediately set to work, took the wheels off my cart, covered the body of it with my tarpaulin and made of it a very excellent and serviceable punt. This expedient I had seen adopted by Mr Surveyor Meehan, in the year 1817, when crossing Bong-Bong River while flooded.

Thomas Boyd, who is an excellent swimmer, and myself,

swam across the river with a line in our teeth, and thus established a communication between either bank; when, with much trouble and not a little danger, the whole party, with the cattle and stores, were safely landed on the other side...

Thomas Boyd states his recollection of our crossing the Murrumbidgee as follows: 'When we came to the Murrumbidgee we found it very high. Captain Hovell was discouraged at this and wished to turn back. I heard him say to Mr Hume, "We shall never get on with our expedition, we cannot cross those rivers."

'Mr Hume replied, "If you think you can't you may go back, for I mean to go on."

'Mr Hovell then asked, "How do you mean to get across this river?"

'Mr Hume answered, "That's best known to myself; I'll soon get over. Boyd, you get a tomahawk."

'I then went with Mr Hume and we cut a canoe, but it would not answer: the bark cracked. When we returned to the camp Mr Hovell was doing nothing. Mr Hume then took his cart to pieces, made a punt of it with the tarpaulin, with which we crossed the men and the supplies. Our method was this. Mr Hume and I had stout fishing lines made fast to us, which were attached to the punt, and we swam and dragged the punt to and fro. Mr Hovell could swim, but gave us little or no assistance in getting across...'

James Fitzpatrick says, 'We crossed the Murrumbidgee, near Yass, by making Mr Hume's cart into a punt, taking it off the wheels, and covering the body of it with his tarpaulin. Mr Hovell had no hand in this, neither doing nor suggesting it. It was Mr Hume did it. Mr Hovell's cart was taken across the Murrumbidgee in Mr Hume's.'

From these statements it will be evident that my associate, had he been dependent on his own resources and left to his own shifts, would not, under the circumstances, have crossed the Murrumbidgee, though he might have proceeded to trace it downwards, and by so doing, he would have acted, so far, according to the instructions furnished for our guidance.

After crossing the river and advancing a day's journey or more, we found ourselves hemmed in by the mountains, and camped for two nights on the Narrengullen Meadows. In order to find an outlet Mr Hovell took one direction and I took another. I was fortunate enough to hit upon an outlet, and through it we were able to extricate ourselves, though with no small difficulty and toil.

On this occasion Mr Hovell lost himself for part of two days and, when I found him, he was actually, but unsuspectingly, travelling back in the direction of Yass or Bowning...He lost himself and his road. I did not.

Thomas Boyd relates: 'While camped at Narrengullen, Mr Hume went in one direction and Mr Hovell in another to seek for an outlet. I accompanied Mr Hovell; we two got lost, and were out all night, away from the camp and the rest of the party. About seven or eight o'clock next morning I heard Mr Hume firing guns for us, on which I remarked to Mr Hovell that we were out of our latitude altogether. He asked me, how? I replied that I judged from the direction from which the guns sounded. We made in that direction and shortly met Mr Hume looking for us. We returned with him to the camp.

'I remarked to Captain Hovell in the night, when we were out, that I would not be out another night with him—no more was I. In fact he never put himself forward in any single thing afterwards. This was his first and last expedition by himself. He never slept all night.'

'I recollect,' says Angel, 'of Mr Hovell and some of his men losing themselves, and Mr Hume being out looking for them and firing guns until he met in with them. I know well, from our own talk among ourselves, that none of the men had any confidence in Captain Hovell. We had no dependence on his taking us through. In fact, he was the worst man in the party, excepting Claude.'

On Tuesday, the 26th, we were engaged in sending the carts and supplies across the Cooradigby River, and finding ourselves in a difficulty country we were compelled to leave the carts, harness, and part of our supplies. I took my tarpaulin with me. Mr Hovell left his. We had then to use the pack saddles and, owing to the cattle not being accustomed to them, they gave us great trouble, as well as occasioning great delay.

It may be asked why such a seemingly trivial matter as the leaving of Mr Hovell's tarpaulin, and the taking of mine forward, should be so pointedly mentioned. The reason is very obvious when its use at the crossing of the Murrumbidgee is remembered. I calculated ('accidentally' or not) that we would encounter other rivers as formidable as the Murrumbidgee and that the tarpaulin being at hand would serve us a good turn again. My readers will judge whether my fellow traveller displayed the smallest foresight when he left his tarpaulin after he had both witnessed and experienced the usefulness of such an article so shortly before. Had I not taken mine, as will be seen, the expedition must have returned. One cause of our success, simple as it may appear, was my sticking to my tarpaulin, and lugging it along through all our weary journey.

A few days afterwards we crossed the Tumut River. As we advanced I found we were getting into too high a country, for the Snowy Mountains (the Australian Alps) were observed crossing our course. I proposed that we should take a direction more westerly, in order to avoid the formidable barrier which threatened to intercept our way—but Mr Hovell dissented from my proposal.

After some wrangling and disputing, each being positive of the correctness of his own opinion, we resolved to part company and follow each his own course. Accordingly we did separate. Mr Hovell held his course south; I steered mine west. However, when my party turned into camp and lighted the fire for the night, great, indeed, was my surprise to hear one of my men call out, 'Here comes Mr Hovell.'

And, sure enough, there he was with his man Boyd running down our tracks. If my fellow traveller had had any confidence in himself, would he, after a lapse of a few hours, have deserted his determination to go south, returned upon my footsteps, and adopted for the future my westerly course?

Thomas Boyd says of the separation and its result at this time: 'Nothing worthy of notice occurred until two or three days after we came in sight of the Snowy Mountains, after having crossed the Tumut, when Mr Hume and Mr Hovell had a great difference about the course they should go. After quarrelling over it they parted, each going his own way. I had to go with Mr Hovell. After travelling some distance I represented to him that the course we were steering led us right among the Snowy Mountains, and that if we once got among them we could never get out, and must be all lost. He agreed with me; and at his desire I sought and found Mr Hume's track, ran it down, and we joined him and his party about dusk the same evening, just as they had camped for the night.'

Angel says: 'I recollect Mr Hume and Mr Hovell having a dispute about which course we were to travel after we came in sight of the Snowy Mountains. After some wrangling they separated, each going his own course. Before they parted they had a row about who was to have the tent; they were going to cut it in two, but Mr Hume let Mr Hovell have it. Then they quarrelled about the frying-pan* and broke it in pulling at it. It was not long, however, before Mr Hovell came after us, a few hours or half a day...'

After the rupture we again joined forces in the manner described, and travelled together to the Hume River, which we reached early on the 16th of November. I named it the Hume in compliment to my father. We crossed it above its junction with the Mitta Mitta. On the 20th, and after travelling four or five miles, we came upon the latter river. On my getting ready to cross the Mitta Mitta, to my surprise Mr Hovell objected, and volunteered an address to the men, in which he pointed out, as well as he could, the hazards existing in the rear, suggesting the probability of others ahead, and appealed to their sense of personal safety, in conclusion asking whether it would

---

* Mr Hovell left his pan at Cooradigby.

not be the most prudent step to turn back, recross the Hume, and trace down its nearest bank, according to part of our instructions. Mr Hovell appealed to Claude Bossawa, a man of mine, and asked his opinion; of course he agreed with Mr Hovell.

On this I got angry and told Mr Hovell that I would prefer being rid of him altogether rather than have one in his position setting such a bad example. I gave him to understand very plainly that for me, or all I cared, he might just remain on the side of the river he was standing on, but I was determined to pursue the journey as originally intended.

I also threatened to put Claude *in* the river if he did not cross it with me, at the same time seizing him by the throat, as if to make good my threat; in fact, I frightened the fellow into crossing along with me.

I then rigged out my tarpaulin boat[*] and crossed with my men and my cattle. Mr Hovell, with his men, remained on the near side of the river, with the asserted purpose of recrossing the Hume and following down its northern bank.

After I had crossed the Mitta Mitta, taken my wattle-boat to pieces, and made a start onwards, Mr Hovell called after me, pressing me to stop and assist him over, and that he would accompany me. I did so. To his horror, on the very same afternoon, we made the Kiewa River (Little River), bank high; but were saved the trouble of using the boat, as a fallen tree assisted our crossing. We then passed over the present Ovens goldfields...

Had I, at this time, become in any way discouraged, or had I yielded in the least to the reluctance of Mr Hovell at crossing the Hume, and his refusal to cross the Mitta Mitta with me, our expedition must have ended on the north bank of the Hume. I

---

[*] The boat was made out of wattles, in this manner: the bottom was formed of three pieces of stout saplings, bound across the end and middle by similar transverse pieces; through these we laced wattles, which we bent up to form the sides, binding them across from the opposite heads to keep them from springing outwards. This formed a square body, like a cart body, on the outside of which we stretched the tarpaulin.

can here safely affirm that, only for my own fixed determination
to go on at this point, Bass's Straits would never have been
reached by any of our party.

JULES DUMONT D'URVILLE
Faculties Peculiar to Man, 1826

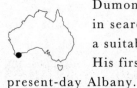 Dumont d'Urville sailed into Australian waters
in search of safe anchorages for French ships and
a suitable location for a possible penal settlement.
His first port of call was King George Sound near
present-day Albany.

Dumont d'Urville led an extraordinary life. In 1810 he
purchased the *Venus de Milo* from a Greek peasant—it had
arms then, but these were broken off in a tussle for the
priceless object between the French and Turkish soldiers. He
later explored in Australia, the subantarctic and elsewhere.
He died in a train crash in Versailles in 1842.

In King George Sound in October 1826, the expedition
scientists Jean René Quoy and Joseph Paul Gaimard wrote
detailed notes on the Aborigines they encountered there
which formed part of Dumont d'Urville's original expedition
report.

The natives of King George Sound are generally below average
height; however, there were some quite tall ones among the
twenty-five to thirty of them that we were able to see. At first
sight one is struck by their thinness and the diminutiveness of
their lower limbs, but this tendency does not appear to be
peculiar to these people; it is due to the miserable state in which
they live and lack of sufficient nourishment to develop those
parts. What we have seen in these regions seems to bear this
out. Some women from a New Holland tribe that lives on the
mainland opposite Kangaroo Island, and others from Port

Dalrymple in Van Diemen's Land and abducted by English sealers in this emaciated condition, after living with them and eating meat in abundance, had very well developed, even obese, extremities. The same condition applied to several tribes in New South Wales. Whatever the cause, this characteristic emaciation is so marked among the men we are concerned with here, that it seems peculiar and quite extraordinary at first sight and the drawing that M. Sainson made of a child looks like a real caricature; one would say that his lower limbs are nothing but a femur and tibia covered with skin.

If the torso seems more developed and compact, one can only attribute this to the spindliness of their legs, because it is usually thin. The arms too are the same but slightly less so. However, the stomach is rounded with a tendency to enlarge; which can easily be explained by the habit these savages have; as they are exposed to long periods of abstinence, they overeat when they get the opportunity.

The head is quite large, the face broad, the brow ridges very prominent, the more so perhaps because their eyes, the whites of which are a yellowish white, are very deepset. They have fairly wide and flat nostrils, their lips are moderately thick, the gums are pale, a big wide mouth is filled with beautiful regular teeth, the whole set resembling those artificial jaws that one sees in Paris in the Palais-Royal. They have quite ordinary ears; their hair is wavy without being frizzy, but it is hard to recognise the colour because it is always covered with a layer of ochre, except in the children, who have brown or black hair. Their beards are sparse as are their moustaches.

Their usual colour varies between a light black and a reddish black. Their emaciation is so pronounced that some of them look like spectres. This is not surprising when you consider that the earth provides practically no food for these people whose only weapon is a primitive spear, and who have to cover large areas in search of small prey like snakes, lizards, skinks and sometimes phalangers and bandicoots, which they eat without cooking after merely scorching them in the fire. We have occasionally seen them devour with the same relish the fish intestines that our sailors threw away...

The wretched state in which these tribes seem to live has not destroyed, as one might think likely, certain of the faculties peculiar to man. Thus, for example, one cannot say that the inhabitants of King George Sound are stupid, although their existence is spent almost entirely in sleeping or searching for food. Our presence put them in high spirits, and they tried to communicate their feelings to us with a loquacity to which we could not respond because we did not know their language. On meeting, they approached us first, talking and gesticulating a great deal; they would give loud shouts, and if we responded in the same tone, their delight knew no bounds. Soon there would be an exchange of names, and it was not long before they would ask for food by patting their stomachs. During a night spent among them on shore, we quite easily picked up their words for everyday things, and they were unfailingly very kindly disposed towards us. They sometimes followed us as we went about our work; however, it must be said that they continually displayed a lack of industry and a laziness which never moved them to offer to help with certain work that other men would have been eager to lighten for us, such as, for example, carrying our collection of specimens, looking for shells and so on.

If the need for food or some other reason obliges them to leave the settlements where they have their huts, they can be seen wandering about in small groups of two, three or four, rarely seven or eight, and they are not afraid to camp out in the open without any shelter. They merely light a fire beside which they never stop shivering with cold. And this was in spring in the southern hemisphere. What must it be like in winter?...These children of nature, of whom such a brilliant picture has been painted, sometimes seem to us very much to be pitied. If they intend spending a night somewhere, they promptly build a small hut hardly adequate to protect them from the rain.

When they are distressed they cry easily; this happened to an old man who was involuntarily kept on board a little longer than he wanted to be. They sometimes sing, or rather they chant. Paternal love seems fairly well developed among them, as we saw from our friend Patêt; this good Australian took great care of his son Yalepouol, who accompanied him everywhere and came aboard *Astrolabe* with him.

CHARLES STURT
On the Importance of a Good Introduction, 1830

 Charles Sturt was as gifted with the pen as he was with the compass. We join him here in a boat on the Murray in January 1830, between the Murrumbidgee and the Darling. In contrast with most other explorers, he encountered vast numbers of Aborigines in this heavily populated region. Clearly, tribal boundaries were fiercely defended, and the use of emissaries to provide an introduction for travelling groups was essential if conflict was to be avoided. All goes well for Sturt—until his boat outsails his Aboriginal heralds.

Of all expeditionary turning points, I like this one best. Sturt's progress is stopped by a vast fishing net strung across the Darling. Out of consideration for the Aborigines who depend upon it for survival, Sturt decides not to breach the net. Instead he raises the Union Jack, gives three cheers and returns whence he came.

We had not seen any natives since falling in with the last tribe on the Murrumbidgee. A cessation had, therefore, taken place in our communication with them, in re-establishing which I anticipated considerable difficulty. It appeared singular that we should not have fallen in with any for several successive days, more especially at the junction of the two rivers, as in similar situations they generally have an establishment. In examining the country back from the stream, I did not observe any large

CHARLES STURT

paths, but it was evident that fires had made extensive ravages in the neighbourhood, so that the country was, perhaps, only temporarily deserted. Macnamee, who had wandered a little from the tents, declared that he had seen about a dozen natives round a fire, from whom (if he really did see them) he very precipitately fled, but I was inclined to discredit his story, because in our journey on the following day we did not see even a casual wanderer.[†]

The river maintained its character, and raised our hopes to the highest pitch. Its breadth varied from 150 to 200 yards; and only in one place, where a reef of ironstone stretched nearly across from the left bank, so as to contract the channel near the right and to form a considerable rapid, was there any apparent obstruction to our navigation. I was sorry, however, to remark that the breadth of alluvial soil between its outer and inner banks was very inconsiderable, and that the upper levels were poor and sandy. Blue gum generally occupied the former, while the usual productions of the plains still predominated upon the latter, and showed that the distant interior had not yet undergone any favourable change. We experienced strong breezes from the north, but the range of the thermometer was high, and the weather rather oppressive than otherwise. On the night of the 16th, we had a strong wind from the NW, but it moderated with daylight, and shifted to the ENE, and the day was favourable and cool...

About 4 p.m. some natives were observed running by the river side behind us, but on our turning the boat's head towards the shore they ran away. It was evident that they had no idea what we were and, from their timidity, feeling assured that it would be impossible to bring them to a parley, we continued onwards till our usual hour of stopping, when we pitched our tents on the left bank for the night, it being the one opposite to that on which the natives had appeared. We conjectured that

[†] Macnamee was a convict travelling with Sturt.

134

their curiosity would lead them to follow us, which they very shortly did; for we had scarcely made ourselves comfortable when we heard their wild notes through the woods as they advanced towards the river; and their breaking into view with their spears and shields, and painted and prepared as they were for battle, was extremely fine. They stood threatening us and making a great noise for a considerable time but, finding that we took no notice of them, they, at length, became quiet.

I then walked to some little distance from the party and, taking a branch in my hand as a sign of peace, beckoned them to swim to our side of the river, which, after some time, two or three of them did. But they approached me with great caution, hesitating at every step. They soon, however, gained confidence, and were ultimately joined by all the males of their tribe. I gave the first who swam the river a tomahawk (making this a rule in order to encourage them) with which he was highly delighted. I shortly afterwards placed them all in a row and fired a gun before them: they were quite unprepared for such an explosion, and after standing stupified and motionless for a moment or two they simultaneously took to their heels, to our great amusement. I succeeded, however, in calling them back, and they regained their confidence so much that sixteen of them remained with us all night, but the greater number retired at sunset.

On the following morning, they accompanied us down the river, where we fell in with their tribe who were stationed on an elevated bank a short distance below—to the number of eighty-three men, women and children. Their appearance was extremely picturesque and singular. They wanted us to land, but time was too precious for such delays. Some of the boldest of the natives swam round and round the boat so as to impede the use of the oars, and the women on the bank evinced their astonishment by mingled yells and cries. They entreated us, by signs, to remain with them but, as I foresaw a compliance on this occasion would hereafter be attended with inconvenience, I thought it better to proceed on our journey, and the natives soon ceased their importunities and, indeed, did not follow or molest us.

The river improved upon us at every mile. Its reaches were of noble breadth and splendid appearance. Its current was stronger and it was fed by numerous springs. Rocks, however, were more frequent in its bed, and in two places almost formed a barrier across the channel, leaving but a narrow space for the boats to go down. We passed several elevations of from seventy to ninety feet in height, at the base of which the stream swept along. The soil of these elevations was a mixture of clay (marl) and sand, upon coarse sandstone. Their appearance and the manner in which they had been acted upon by water was singular, and afforded a proof of the violence of the rains in this part of the interior. From the highest of these, I observed that the country to the SE was gently undulated, and so far changed in character from that through which we had been travelling; still, however, it was covered with a low scrub, and was barren and unpromising...

On the 19th, as we were about to conclude our journey for the day, we saw a large body of natives before us. On approaching them, they showed every disposition for combat, and ran along the bank with spears in rests, as if only waiting for an opportunity to throw them at us. They were upon the right, and as the river was broad enough to enable me to steer wide of them I did not care much for their threats; but upon another party appearing upon the left bank, I thought it high time to disperse one or the other of them, as the channel was not wide enough to enable me to keep clear of danger, if assailed by both, as I might be while keeping amid the channel.

I found, however, that they did not know how to use the advantage they possessed, as the two divisions formed a junction; those on the left swimming over to the stronger body upon the right bank. This, fortunately, prevented the necessity of any hostile measure on my part, and we were suffered to proceed unmolested for the present. The whole then followed us without any symptom of fear, but making a dreadful shouting, and beating their spears and shields together, by way of intimidation.

It is but justice to my men to say that in this critical situation they evinced the greatest coolness, though it was impossible for anyone to witness such a scene with indifference. As I did not intend to fatigue the men by continuing to pull farther than we were in the habit of doing, we landed at our usual time on the left bank, and while the people were pitching the tents I walked down the bank with M'Leay to treat with these desperadoes in the best way we could, across the water, a measure to which my men showed great reluctance, declaring that if during our absence the natives approached them they would undoubtedly fire upon them. I assured them it was not my intention to go out of their sight. We took our guns with us, but determined not to use them until the last extremity, both from a reluctance to shed blood and with a view to our future security.

I held a long pantomimical dialogue with them, across the water, and held out the olive branch in token of amity. They at length laid aside their spears, and a long consultation took place among them, which ended in two or three wading into the river, contrary, as it appeared, to the earnest remonstrances of the majority who, finding that their entreaties had no effect, wept aloud and followed them with a determination, I am sure, of sharing their fate, whatever it might have been.

As soon as they landed, M'Leay and I retired to a little distance from the bank, and sat down; that being the usual way among the natives of the interior to invite to an interview. When they saw us act thus, they approached, and sat down by us, but without looking up, from a kind of diffidence peculiar to them, and which exists even among the nearest relatives, as I have already had occasion to observe. As they gained confidence, however, they showed an excessive curiosity, and stared at us in the most earnest manner. We now led them to the camp, and I gave, as was my custom, the first who had approached, a tomahawk; and to the others some pieces of iron hoop. Those who had crossed the river amounted to about thirty-five in number. At sunset, the majority of them left us; but three old men remained at the fireside all night.

I observed that few of them had either lost their front teeth or lacerated their bodies, as the more westerly tribes do. The most loathsome diseases prevailed among them. Several were disabled by leprosy, or some similar disorder, and two or three had entirely lost their sight. They are, undoubtedly, a brave and a confiding people, and are by no means wanting in natural affection. In person, they resemble the mountain tribes. They had the thick lip, the sunken eye, the extended nostril, and long beards, and both smooth and curly hair are common among them. Their lower extremities appear to bear no proportion to their bust in point of muscular strength; but the facility with which they ascend trees of the largest growth, and the activity with which they move upon all occasions, together with their singularly erect stature, argue that such appearance is entirely deceptive.

The old men slept very soundly by the fire, and were the last to get up in the morning. M'Leay's extreme good humour had made a most favourable impression upon them, and I can picture him, even now, joining in their wild song. Whether it was from his entering so readily into their mirth, or from anything peculiar that struck them, the impression upon the whole of us was that they took him to have been originally a black, in consequence of which they gave him the name of Rundi. Certain it is, they pressed him to show his side, and asked if he had not received a wound there—evidently as if the original Rundi had met with a violent death from a spear wound in that place.

The whole tribe, amounting in number to upwards of 150, assembled to see us take our departure. Four of them accompanied us, among whom there was one remarkable for personal strength and stature. The 21st passed without our falling in with any new tribe, and the night of the 22nd saw us still wandering in that lonely desert together. There was something unusual in our going through such an extent of country without meeting another tribe, but our companions appeared to be perfectly aware of the absence of inhabitants, as they never left our side.

Although the banks of the river had been of general equality of height, sandy elevations still occasionally formed a part of them, and their summits were considerably higher than the alluvial flats.

It was upon the crest of one of these steep and lofty banks that, on the morning of the 22nd, the natives who were ahead of the boat suddenly stopped to watch our proceedings down a foaming rapid that ran beneath. We were not aware of the danger to which we were approaching until we turned an angle of the river, and found ourselves too near to retreat. In such a moment, without knowing what was before them, the coolness of the men was strikingly exemplified. No one even spoke after they became aware that silence was necessary. The natives (probably anticipating misfortune) stood leaning upon their spears upon the lofty bank above us.

Desiring the men not to move from their seats, I stood up to survey the channel, and to steer the boat to that part of it which was least impeded by rocks. I was obliged to decide upon a hasty survey, as we were already at the head of the rapid. It appeared to me that there were two passages, the one down the centre of the river, the other immediately under its right bank. A considerable rock stood directly in our way to the latter, so that I had no alternative but to descend the former. About forty yards below the rock, I noticed that a line of rocks occupied the space between the two channels, whilst a reef, projecting from the left bank, made the central passage distinctly visible, and the rapidity of the current proportionally great.

I entertained hopes that the passage was clear, and that we should shoot down it without interruption; but in this I was disappointed. The boat struck with the fore-part of her keel on a sunken rock and, swinging round as it were on a pivot, presented her bow to the rapid, while the skiff floated away into the strength of it. We had every reason to anticipate the loss of our whaleboat, whose build was so light that, had her side struck the rock instead of her keel, she would have been laid open from stem to stern. As it was, however, she remained fixed in her position, and it only remained for us to get her off the best way we could.

I saw that this could only be done by sending two of the men with a rope to the upper rock, and getting the boat, by that means, into the still water between that and the lower one. We should then have time to examine the channels, and to decide as to that down which it would be safest to proceed. My only fear was that the loss of the weight of the two men would lighten the boat so much that she would be precipitated down the rapid without my having any command over her; but it happened otherwise. We succeeded in getting her into the still water, and ultimately took her down the channel under the right bank without her sustaining any injury. A few miles below this rapid the river took a singular bend, and we found, after pulling several miles, that we were within a stone's throw of a part of the stream we had already sailed down.

The four natives joined us in the camp, and assisted the men at their various occupations. The consequence was that they were treated with more than ordinary kindness; and Fraser, for his part, in order to gratify these favoured guests, made great havoc among the feathered race. He returned after a short ramble with a variety of game, among which were a crow, a kite and a laughing jackass (*Alcedo gigantea*), a species of king's-fisher, a singular bird, found in every part of Australia.[†] Its cry, which resembles a chorus of wild spirits, is apt to startle the traveller who may be in jeopardy, as if laughing and mocking at his misfortune. It is a harmless bird, and I seldom allowed them to be destroyed, as they were sure to rouse us with the earliest dawn. To this list of Fraser's spoils a duck and a tough old cockatoo must be added. The whole of these our friends threw on the fire without the delay of plucking, and snatched them from that consuming element ere they were well singed, and devoured them with uncommon relish.

We pitched our tents upon a flat of good and tenacious soil. A brush, in which there was a new species of melaleuca, backed

---

† Fraser shot a kookaburra.

it, in the thickest part of which we found a deserted native village. The spot was evidently chosen for shelter. The huts were large and long, all facing the same point of the compass, and in every way resembling the huts occupied by the natives of the Darling. Large flocks of whistling ducks, and other wild fowl, flew over our heads to the NW, as if making their way to some large or favourite waters. My observations placed us in latitude 34° 8' 15" south, and in east longitude 141° 9' 42" or nearly so; and I was at a loss to conceive what direction the river would ultimately take. We were considerably to the NW of the point at which we had entered it, and in referring to the chart it appeared that if the Darling had kept a SW course from where the last expedition left its banks, we ought ere this to have struck upon it, or have arrived at its junction with the stream on which we were journeying.

The natives, in attempting to answer my interrogatories, only perplexed me more and more. They evidently wished to explain something, by placing a number of sticks across each other as a kind of diagram of the country. It was, however, impossible to arrive at their meaning. They undoubtedly pointed to the westward, or rather to the south of that point, as the future course of the river; but there was something more that they were anxious to explain, which I could not comprehend. The poor fellows seemed quite disappointed, and endeavoured to beat it into Fraser's head with as little success. I then desired Macnamee to get up into a tree. From the upper branches of it he said he could see hills, but his account of their appearance was such that I doubted his story; nevertheless it might have been correct. He certainly called our attention to a large fire, as if the country to the NW was in flames, so that it appeared we were approaching the haunts of the natives at last.

It happened that Fraser and Harris were for guard, and they sat up laughing and talking with the natives long after we retired to rest. Fraser, to beguile the hours, proposed shaving his sable companions, and performed that operation with admirable dexterity upon their chief, to his great delight. I got up at an

CHARLES STURT

early hour, and found to my surprise that the whole of them
had deserted us. Harris told me they had risen from the fire
about an hour before, and had crossed the river. I was a little
angry, but supposed they were aware that we were near some
tribe, and had gone on ahead to prepare and collect them.

After breakfast, we proceeded onwards as usual. The river
had increased so much in width that, the wind being fair, I
hoisted sail for the first time, to save the strength of my men as
much as possible. Our progress was consequently rapid. We
passed through a country that, from the nature of its soil and
other circumstances, appeared to be intersected by creeks and
lagoons. Vast flights of wild fowl passed over us, but always at
a considerable elevation, while, on the other hand, the paucity
of ducks on the river excited our surprise. Latterly, the trees
upon the river, and in its neighbourhood, had been a tortuous
kind of box. The flooded gum grew in groups on the spaces
subject to inundation, but not on the levels above the influence
of any ordinary rise of the stream. Still they were much smaller
than they were observed to be in the higher branches of the
river.

We had proceeded about nine miles, when we were surprised
by the appearance in view, at the termination of a reach, of a
long line of magnificent trees of green and dense foliage. As we
sailed down the reach, we observed a vast concourse of natives
under them and, on a nearer approach, we not only heard their
war song, if it might be so called, but remarked that they were
painted and armed, as they generally are prior to their engaging
in deadly conflict. Notwithstanding these outward signs of hostility,
fancying that our four friends were with them, I continued to
steer directly for the bank on which they were collected.

I found, however, when it was almost too late to turn into
the succeeding reach to our left, that an attempt to land would
only be attended with loss of life. The natives seemed determined
to resist it. We approached so near that they held their spears
quivering in their grasp ready to hurl. They were painted in
various ways. Some, who had marked their ribs and thighs and

142

faces with white pigment, looked like skeletons, others were daubed over with red and yellow ochre, and their bodies shone with the grease with which they had besmeared themselves. A dead silence prevailed among the front ranks, but those in the background, as well as the women, who carried supplies of darts and who appeared to have had a bucket of whitewash capsized over their heads, were extremely clamorous. As I did not wish a conflict with these people, I lowered my sail and, putting the helm to starboard, we passed quietly down the stream in mid-channel. Disappointed in their anticipations, the natives ran along the bank of the river, endeavouring to secure an aim at us; but, unable to throw with certainty, in consequence of the onward motion of the boat, they flung themselves into the most extravagant attitudes, and worked themselves into a state of frenzy by loud and vehement shouting.

It was with considerable apprehension that I observed the river to be shoaling fast, more especially as a huge sandbank, a little below us and on the same side on which the natives had gathered, projected nearly a third-way across the channel. To this sandbank they ran with tumultuous uproar, and covered it over in a dense mass. Some of the chiefs advanced to the water to be nearer their victims, and turned from time to time to direct their followers. With every pacific disposition, and an extreme reluctance to take away life, I foresaw that it would be impossible any longer to avoid an engagement, yet with such fearful numbers against us I was doubtful of the result.

The spectacle we had witnessed had been one of the most appalling kind, and sufficient to shake the firmness of most men; but at that trying moment my little band preserved their temper coolness, and if anything could be gleaned from their countenances it was that they had determined on an obstinate resistance. I now explained to them that their only chance of escape depended, or would depend, on their firmness. I desired that, after the first volley had been fired, M'Leay and three of the men would attend to the defence of the boat with bayonets only, while I, Hopkinson and Harris would keep up the fire as being more used to it. I ordered, however, that no shot was to be fired until after I had discharged both my barrels. I then delivered their arms to the men, which had as yet been kept in the place appropriated for them, and at the same time some rounds of loose cartridge. The men assured me they would follow my instructions, and thus prepared, having already lowered the sail, we drifted onwards with the current.

As we neared the sandbank, I stood up and made signs to the natives to desist, but without success. I took up my gun, therefore, and, cocking it, had already brought it down to a level. A few seconds more would have closed the life of the nearest of the savages. The distance was too trifling for me to doubt the fatal effects of the discharge; for I was determined to take deadly aim, in hopes that the fall of one man might save the lives of many. But at the very moment when my hand was on the trigger, and my eye was along the barrel, my purpose was checked by M'Leay, who called to me that another party of blacks had made their appearance upon the left bank of the river.

Turning round, I observed four men at the top of their speed. The foremost of them, as soon as he got ahead of the boat, threw himself from a considerable height into the water. He struggled across the channel to the sandbank, and in an incredibly short space of time stood in front of the savage against whom my aim had been directed. Seizing him by the throat, he pushed him backwards, and forcing all who were in the water upon the bank, he trod its margin with a vehemence and an agitation that were exceedingly striking. At one moment pointing to the boat, at another shaking his clenched hand in the faces of the most forward, and stamping with passion on the sand, his voice, that was at first distinct and clear, was lost in hoarse murmurs. Two of the four natives remained on the left bank of the river, but the third followed his leader (who proved to be the remarkable savage I have previously noticed) to the scene of action.

The reader will imagine our feelings on this occasion: it is impossible to describe them. We were so wholly lost in interest at the scene that was passing that the boat was allowed to drift at pleasure. For my own part I was overwhelmed with astonishment, and in truth stunned and confused; so singular, so unexpected and so strikingly providential had been our escape.

We were again roused to action by the boat suddenly striking upon a shoal, which reached from one side of the river to the other. To jump out and push her into deeper water was but the work of a moment with the men, and it was just as she floated again that our attention was withdrawn to a new and beautiful stream, coming apparently from the north.[†] The great body of the natives having posted themselves on the narrow tongue of land formed by the two rivers, the bold savage who had so unhesitatingly interfered on our account was still in hot dispute with them, and I really feared his generous warmth would have brought down upon him the vengeance of the tribes. I hesitated, therefore, whether or not to go to his assistance. It appeared, however, both to M'Leay and myself, that the tone of the natives had moderated and, the old and young men having listened to the remonstrances of our friend, the middle-aged warriors were alone holding out against him. A party of about seventy blacks were upon the right bank of the newly discovered river, and I thought that by landing among them we should make a diversion in favour of our late guest; and in this I succeeded. If even they had still meditated violence they would have to swim a good broad junction, and that, probably, would cool them, or we at least should have the advantage of position.

I therefore ran the boat ashore, and landed with M'Leay amidst the smaller party of natives, wholly unarmed, and having directed the men to keep at a little distance from the bank. Fortunately, what I anticipated was brought about by the stratagem to which I had had recourse. The blacks no sooner observed that we had landed than curiosity took place of anger. All wrangling ceased, and they came swimming over to us like

---

† The new river was the Darling.

a parcel of seals. Thus, in less than a quarter of an hour from the moment when it appeared that all human intervention was at an end, and we were on the point of commencing a bloody fray which, independently of its own disastrous consequences, would have blasted the success of the expedition, we were peacefully surrounded by the hundreds who had so lately threatened us with destruction; nor was it until after we had returned to the boat, and had surveyed the multitude upon the sloping bank above us, that we became fully aware of the extent of our danger, and of the almost miraculous intervention of providence in our favour. There could not have been less than six hundred natives upon that blackened sward.

But this was not the only occasion upon which the merciful superintendence of that providence to which we had humbly committed ourselves was strikingly manifested. If these pages fail to convey entertainment or information, sufficient may at least be gleaned from them to furnish matter for serious reflection; but to those who have been placed in situations of danger where human ingenuity availed them not, and where human foresight was baffled, I feel persuaded that these remarks are unnecessary.

It was my first care to call for our friend, and to express to him, as well as I could, how much we stood indebted to him, at the same time that I made him a suitable present; but to the chiefs of the tribes I positively refused all gifts, notwithstanding their earnest solicitations. We next prepared to examine the new river, and turning the boat's head towards it endeavoured to pull up the stream. Our larboard oars touched the right bank, and the current was too strong for us to conquer it with a pair only; we were, therefore, obliged to put a second upon her, a movement that excited the astonishment and admiration of the natives. One old woman seemed in absolute ecstasy, to whom M'Leay threw an old tin kettle, in recompense for the amusement she afforded us.

As soon as we got above the entrance of the new river, we found easier pulling, and proceeded up it for some miles, accompanied by the once more noisy multitude. The river preserved a breadth of one hundred yards and a depth of rather more than twelve feet. Its banks were sloping and grassy, and were overhung by trees of magnificent size. Indeed, its appearance was so different from the water-worn banks of the sister stream that the men exclaimed, on entering it, that we had got into an English river. Its appearance certainly almost justified the expression; for the greenness of its banks was as new to us as the size of its timber. Its waters, though sweet, were turbid and had a taste of vegetable decay, as well as a slight tinge of green.

Our progress was watched by the natives with evident anxiety. They kept abreast of us, and talked incessantly. At length, however, our course was checked by a net that stretched right across the stream. I say checked, because it would have been unfair to have passed over it with the chance of disappointing the numbers who apparently depended on it for subsistence that day. The moment was one of intense interest to me. As the men rested upon their oars, awaiting my further orders, a crowd of thoughts rushed upon me. The various conjectures I had formed of the course and importance of the Darling passed across my mind. Were they indeed realised? An irresistible conviction impressed me that we were now sailing on the bosom of that very stream from whose banks I had been twice forced to retire.

I directed the Union Jack to be hoisted, and giving way to our satisfaction we all stood up in the boat and gave three distinct cheers. It was an English feeling, an ebullition, an overflow, which I am ready to admit that our circumstances and situation will alone excuse. The eye of every native had been fixed upon that noble flag, at all times a beautiful object, and to them a novel one, as it waved over us in the heart of a desert. They had until that moment been particularly loquacious, but the sight of that flag and the sound of our voices hushed the tumult, and while they were still lost in astonishment the boat's head was speedily turned, the sail was sheeted home, both wind and current were in our favour, and we vanished from them with a rapidity that surprised even ourselves, and which precluded every hope of the most adventurous among them to keep up with us.

GEORGE AUGUSTUS ROBINSON
The Big River Tribe, 1831

 George Augustus Robinson was born the year Australia was settled. He emigrated to Tasmania in 1823, at a time when the war between settlers and Aborigines was escalating. A serious, religious man, Robinson believed that conciliation between black and white was possible. The opportunity to put his belief into practice came when he answered a government advertisement for a man of good character to 'effect an intercourse with natives'.

In September and October of 1830, Governor Arthur organised 2200 men into a massive line to sweep the Tasmanian bush free of Aborigines. The exercise was a dismal failure—just one man and one boy were captured. We join Robinson here a year later in October 1831 as he tracks the Big River Tribe through central Tasmania. The tribe, a pathetic remnant of twenty-six individuals, had fought a brilliant guerilla war that had held white Tasmania to ransom. A leader of the tribe had lost an arm—after being shot by a settlers' musket he had burnt the useless limb off in a fire.

By August 1834 the 'Aboriginal Problem', as the settlers called it, was ended. Robinson played a vital role in its resolution. It remains for the modern reader to decide whether his actions were for the best.

23 October—...This morning crossed a deep gully whose sides consisted of rocks, and on ascending to the opposite hills observed a junction of gullies. The whole of these hills are covered with thick forest and scrub. These gullies communicate with Little Swanport River. At this place Mannalargenna procured himself a spear, as did another of the natives (Timmy). At meridian caught a boomer kangaroo which the natives roasted. When the animal was opened the natives took the shavings of their spears and dipped them in the blood of the animal, probably with a view to act as a charm.

Whilst partaking of this repast the chief Mannalargenna said his spirit told him that the natives was on an adjacent hill looking at them. Though I felt convinced it was a delusion, yet in order to gratify his whim I sent two of the native men to see if there was any footmarks of natives. They shortly returned and had seen no signs of native footmarks or any indications whatever.

The strange native woman whom I had brought from the gaol and who belonged to the Big River tribe informed her husband Umurrah that she knew where there was plenty of guns and spears concealed. Tom and Umarrah informed me accordingly and it was agreed that the woman should conduct me to the place and that I should get them accordingly. This is another strong and striking proof of their confidence in me. These firearms had been taken by her countrymen in their attacks upon the whites and when she was present, and now she is desirous to make atonement by restoring them to the whites again.

One of the native women, Sall, found a bulbous plant called by the white people 'native bread', which they gave to me as a present.[†] At 4 p.m. came to the top of a hill and was informed by my natives that the white man's house was close by, and at the same time they showed me a tree which the white men had cut. I had not intended approaching so close to the whites lest my party should be discovered by stockkeepers, in which case I apprehended that some of my natives might get shot, as the practice of this class of individuals is to come upon them and to fire at them—a similar practice to the blacks in their attacks upon the whites—unless fear seizes the white and he seeks his safety by flight. I cautioned my natives and said if the whites saw them they would shoot them. They replied that they could see the whites first, and that they could not always shoot straight...

25 October—...Set off travelling in a south-east direction and with a view to procure the spears and guns which the native

---

† Native bread: a fungus.

woman of the Big River tribe had disclosed and which had been concealed by her and the Oyster Bay tribe. She said there was two places where they had those various death instruments concealed.

In our way the natives showed me a dead tree where there was native bread growing. I saw no signs myself; they smelt the wood and said the plant was a long way in the ground. The natives showed me a bird's nest built in a hole in the ground, with three small white eggs. The bird resembled the honey bird, but smaller. Crossed the head of Prosser River and decamped in a small meadow on its banks, the natives having assured me that no grass would be met with after leaving this place.

Leaving the baggage and some of the people at this encampment I set off with five black men and the native woman of the Big River tribe to procure the muskets and spears which she had previously divulged to having been concealed. This woman led us over several stony hills covered with thick forest and across gullies. On arriving at a small grass plot enclosed by a green copse, the female guide pointed out the embers of a fire and where she said her and her tribe had enjoyed a little hilarity by dancing. This woman had previously said that those weapons would be found near to where they had had a fire and had danced. On beholding this spot again the woman evinced much feeling and all the circumstances connected therewith burst on her mind and with which she agreeably entertained her sable friends.

On leaving this place she proceeded to the distance of about forty yards further and on reaching a large fallen tree pointed out that as the place where the things were concealed. They were soon sought out by her and the rest of the natives, and was presented to me as a token of their confidence in me. They consisted of several bundles of spears tied round with pieces of blankets and check shirts, and amounted to forty-five spears, six waddies, one fowling piece and one tower musket, a bag containing bullets, slugs, buck and small shot, and a bag which had contained powder and a newspaper. They were in tolerable condition; was placed under the tree.

On restoring those weapons of destruction they evinced much pleasure, and if any further proof was wanting of their confidence this alone would be sufficient. On our way from the place of encampment to this sequestered retreat the natives discovered a smoke, which they said was that of the natives. I loaded myself with the spears and one of the muskets and returned to the encampment with the native woman, who carried the fowling piece.

The men set off by a different route on an hunting excursion. Umarrah had selected from the spears one for himself, and two waddies. The rest would have followed his example but that I told them I purposed sending them to the governor, to which they agreed. I ascertained from this woman that these weapons had been placed there in concealment at the time of the Line and that some of the small spears belonged to the young lad that was taken at the time of the Line and the big ones to his father. She said that the embers of the fire I saw was where she and the other women, about eight in number, had *kar.ne.win.ne*, i.e., danced, and that there was two men with them, that the rest of the men was dancing at another fire down in the bottom. Said that Memermannalargenna had speared a woman near the Blue Hills.

The country in these parts consists of a succession of stony hills covered with forest and intersected by gullies, and is bounded by dense underwood, and affords as secure a retreat for the natives as can possibly be in any part of the colony. There is fine scope for reflection to consider that at this period last year the grand military operations was then in active service, that those spears had been manufactured by those very natives whom they was then in quest of and that when they took their departure they concealed those weapons, that the woman was then with them and now with me leading me in quest of her countrymen and telling me all the various schemes they adopted. The large spear that we found belonged to Montpelieratter and with which he had speared a white woman. The natives informed me that the white men about those parts had killed plenty of the natives,

that they used to shoot them in their huts in the winter time.
This night the place to find the natives was a subject of deliberation. Tom said Mannalargenna would ask his devil. Accordingly, he went to work, Tom and his wife asking him occasionally where the natives rendezvoused. He said they was about the banks of the river. When he had finished he got up (it being dark) and said that a dead man's devil that had been put in a tree was walking about and would tell him about it. He set off in the woods; Tom and another native trembling followed him; the women lay as still as mice. They said I should know if he was there by his whistling. By and by heard a whistle and several whistles. They returned. I asked Tom if he had seen the devil; he said he had only heard him whistle. Said that when there was a small fire he would come and look at us at night.

I told them I would go and make a small fire in the woods and see if the devil would come, that if he made his appearance I would lay hold of his ears and pull him along and put him in the fire. I did not treat their superstition with that contempt I should do had I not been engaged in this anxious enterprise. Was therefore willing to indulge them in their whims, hoping thereby to succeed, as for their own credit they would find them out. Umarrah pointed out the way this afternoon he took when he left the Line.

JOHN LHOTSKY
Decrepitation at Last, 1834

 John Lhotsky—he of mendacious memory, as Baron Von Hugel, his compatriot in exile, characterised him—was a German wanderer with some geological training and a most peculiar turn of phrase and mind. Representing him as an explorer is perhaps overly generous. But he did wander and recount what he saw. His 'aerial baths' and discomfort at being decrepitated upon between Sydney and Bargo are more memorable today than his hard-won geological insights. Indeed, decrepitation was his downfall for, as he reminds us, his geological specimens became so sodden that the packages were 'converted into mere dung'!

After a labour, which I may call immense, in order to compress into a narrow compass, and that at the least possible expense, the requisites of a long journey, I started from Sydney on the 10th of January, 1834. I had with me a cart with one horse, and four men. It matters not whether they were called free or assigned: as long as an assigned servant conducts himself properly I treat him as a free one, and I should wish to possess the discretion, as often as I should deem it expedient, of acting *vice versa*. I left behind me all bills of exchange, courts, summonses, attorneys, editors of newspapers, gaols and such like, and exulted in the feeling that, abandoning all these delights of ultra-civilised society, I should once again enjoy for some time a freedom nearly approaching the state of nature.

I left Sydney at 10 a.m., and determined to stop for dinner with my party in the bush opposite Grose Farm, as the heat was excessive and I was desirous of habituating my half-wild horse and town-fashioned servants by degrees to the change of life we were about to commence. We were all in the best possible spirits. At 3 p.m. the heat reached its highest degree, and there were only a few fine cirrho clouds standing in the zenith, at an immense altitude in the perfectly clear and serene firmament, while a rather fresh NE breeze was blowing intermittingly.

My health, which did not suffer during an eighteen months' residence in the hottest parts of the Brazils, had been much impaired since my arrival in New South Wales, and though I cannot call the climate of Sydney unhealthy, yet the sudden transitions of Australian temperature and the predominance of southerly gales, charged as they are with incredible quantities of the dust of our unpaved and unwatered streets, injure the lungs of the inhabitants more than might be believed. This day, however, I was induced to attempt a remedy, which under the necessary precautions and restrictions may be adopted by persons similarly circumstanced. I bared the upper part of my body, and in that state walked for half an hour in the currents of air among the trees. The effect was excessively beneficial, and I felt the muscles of my thorax so much invigorated that I repeated the experiment during my journey with the most beneficial result. To physicians at home, this aerial bath has been long known, and it would appear besides that the slender clothing of tropical nations rests on a deeper diatetical foundation than is generally supposed. I stopped the first night at J. Solomon's inn, on the Liverpool Road, where the accommodation as in many other country inns of the colony was not to be complained of...

At an early hour in the following morning (January 11) I resumed my journey along the Liverpool Road. The deep sand which surrounds the neighbourhood of the metropolis soon disappeared, small declivities of red loam were seen, and the land began to assume a more fertile character...The country near Liverpool is well cultivated, in fact so much so that this is one of the few places in the colony where a traveller may fancy himself in some parts of Europe, surrounded as he is by drays and teams, persons on horseback and in vehicles, combining the appearances of active agriculture and thriving village life. The public houses here, as in many other parts of the colony, are far too numerous, their number between Sydney and Parramatta being twenty-nine. Thus I arrived at Liverpool, an improving little town having some good public edifices.

We encamped at noon beside a pond of water, near the roadside at an open forest space, called 'the Long Bridge'. This was the first time I bivouaced with so large a party in Australia. During such intervals, my horse was walked about, a practice which I never allowed to be neglected when it was taken from the shafts, either at noon or night, and by this and some other means I was able to bring this animal (which, by some accident in its purchase, happened to be a very bad one) so far as Pass Britannia, where it died. To the little attention which travellers are usually able to pay to such apparent trifles in this wholesale country, the failure of many expeditions is to be attributed...

Several persons passed the road near us, asking the usual hospitalities of Australian camps: a drink of water and a light for their pipe. My people were ordered to give a bit of tobacco to all persons who appeared in need of such a present. In the afternoon I descended some slightly undulating hills, and passed Raby, one of the most famous farms in the colony. I stopped for the night at Mr Howell's farm, called Molle's Main, and situated a short distance to the left of the road. Mr H. had invited me previously at Sydney, and I could not fail to call upon a gentleman who, in conjunction with Mr Hamilton Hume, was the first traveller who saw the Australian Alps from a distance, and brought these giants to the notice of the world.[†] Both he and Mrs Howell received me very politely. I saw the chart of Mr Howell's journey, and was confirmed by this document and his information in my original plan to approach the Alps (as I did afterwards) by the eastern side. The soil of the farm is rather moist, and rich in grass, upon which a considerable dairy stock is kept. In the winter of 1831, ice was seen about this place.

On Sunday (12th January) I left Molle's Main, whence the land ascends towards Mr Scott's farm and commands a fine view over the land at the Cow Pasture River, towards which the country gently verges...At noon, I stopped at Cawdor, an old government station. This is one of the places which are called in the colony 'watering places'. In such the government men,[*] and other people who are desirous of practising economy, stop with their teams and cook their provisions; here the travelling stockmen remain with their herds for refreshment.

Here, therefore, you may be assured of meeting with large heaps of half-consumed timber, often still burning, and then

† Mr H. was of course William Hovell.
* This is one of the names by which the transported convicts are distinguished in the colony.

nothing is necessary but to put on pots of water for tea. In such places the Australian traveller who happens to have a few good servants may enjoy a state of the greatest independence and ease. Nothing but the sun and meteors (those rulers of nature herself) will influence his determination, he may fancy himself master of all that surrounds him, he can walk for hours or days under the dome of gigantic eucalyptus, repose on the down of ever-verdant herbage; he may stop or start as he pleases and, circumscribed by his own will to the moderate comforts conveyed in his cart (a sort of terrestrial vessel), he is always in that tranquil state where neither buying nor selling is wanted. In that way I greatly enjoyed my camps. One of my younger servants was strolling about to catch some insect, another to gather plants, whilst I was occupied in arranging and classifying such objects, and composing my journal.

In the afternoon I ascended a slight range, which lies before a higher one, called Razorback...The highest peak of the Blue Mountains bears here NNW forty miles distance. On the most elevated point of Razorback the view is still more extensive and majestic. But such and all similar sensations were damped by a feeling which darkened all my views in Australia, namely that the vivifying feature to all this scenery—the man—is no more. The Aborigines of all these extensive lands are gone, they have given room to another race of people, and what these will be, time alone can unveil!...

Monday (January 13) at half past five a.m., the thermometer ranged from 58 to 60, according to the force of the western breeze. I found afterwards that the thermometer is always affected by this circumstance. At 6 a.m. the rivulet, which is at the foot of the rock, showed 61. Here, as well as at Razorback, it was that I and my men began to collect specimens with more carefulness, and we stopped at this place until 3 p.m. All sorts of preparations were going on, of the product of which unfortunately I can give the reader little account, several of my boxes which I left in charge on the road (those from the Alps, I took back in my cart myself) having been maliciously spoiled or plundered. The discriminating reader will not blame me for the many apparently minor affairs I mingle with this work. In this spacious country the germ of a vast empire is laid...

After the heat of the day was over and our business transacted, we started and, passing different ridges of forest land, reached Stone Quarry Creek, whence we proceeded to Myrtle Creek to stop for the night. Between these two places is a remarkable stratum of limestone, and at the last one an interesting simple mineral of the same tribe—which at present I am unable to distinguish any further, two parcels containing my collections in this quarter, having been exposed for weeks in the heaviest rain at Sydney, and in consequence all the paper and straw which surrounded the stones was converted into mere dung, all labels were rotted etc. At the Travellers Arms I found a merry party dancing to the strains of a violin. Music is a thing seldom heard in our colony; I listened therefore with pleasure even to these monotonous tones. All passed very decently, and I enjoyed myself in my room seeing others to enjoy.

A crystalline dew the next morning (Jan. 14) covered all herbage along the way; such freshness and elasticity of the air may, I am sure, extract every germ of pulmonary affection from the discriminating European traveller's chest. We approached Bargo Brush, a range of little elevation, stretching from SW to NE. The heat was oppressive; we therefore encamped near Lupton's inn to divert the harassing way through the Bargo...

From Bargo we arrived at J. Keigron's inn, situated in a valley of good land, but closely encompassed by bushy hills, which give to the whole place a rather wild aspect. The continual anxiety of an Australian traveller is regarding the existence of some potable water. I was therefore much annoyed when I saw this day towards sunset the firmament getting covered with dark clouds, which decrepitated at last in a heavy southerly storm with lightning, whilst we had still five miles to go to the place where I had determined to stop. We therefore proceeded with some haste through a wood of gum trees, which were actuated and as it were swept by a heavy gale. After some time proceeding on a road not well settled, we perceived, quite in the darkness, lights which however were only belonging to some drays, the pitched tents of which looked rather strange in this perplexing obscurity. Upon inquiry we heard that houses were near and, after some straggling about, I fell into the house of——Chalker. This rather renowned pugilist received me with civility enough, and offered us every accommodation his little quasi inn offered.

GEORGE FRANKLAND
A Landscape beyond All Description, 1835

 The breathtaking beauty of Tasmania's central highlands remained unknown for decades after European settlement. The Aboriginal inhabitants had been largely exterminated or removed before George Frankland entered this fairy-tale landscape on an exploring expedition to the head of the Derwent River in February 1835. Frankland left the expedition two weeks before Lake Pedder was discovered by John Wedge on 11 March 1835. What would he have thought had he known that, little more than a century after European eyes first lighted on glorious Lake Pedder, the jewel in the south-west's crown would follow its first human inhabitants into oblivion?

10 February 1835—In the evening having advanced about six miles we reached the eastern extremity of an unusually extensive marsh—through which we found a considerable river took its course which I called the Humboldt in honor of the distinguished naturalist of that name. We encamped on the edge of a small streamlet which joined the river towards the western end of the marsh, and before night I reconnoitred the country to the extent of four or five miles around our ground. We found a great abundance of kangaroos but no wild cattle.

A very remarkable mountain here discovered itself to our

view towards the north-west. It appeared of immense height, and perpendicular on all sides. From its situation and features I conjectured that it must be the hill called Barn's Bluff which lies to the south of the Company's lands, and which I had formerly seen from that side—and in this belief we remained for several days afterwards. Its isolated and commanding position at once excited in us the desire of ascending to its summit, but the apparently inaccessible nature of its faces left us but slender hope of being able to accomplish the object.

11 February—The first portion of this day's march lay through the long plain before described. The Humboldt running to the south was crossed by a good ford—and we again entered tracts of open forests—with occasional intervals of beautiful marshes wearing the most luxuriant appearance. Continuing a west course and after advancing five miles we suddenly found ourselves on the edge of a beautiful lake in the heart of scenery of the most picturesque character.

I here halted the party to breakfast, and on climbing a tree I ascertained that the sheet of water on the border of which we then stood formed but a comparatively small proportion of the lake which, after winding round several tongues of land beautifully tufted with rich luxuriant foliage, extended for many miles to the north-west, washing the north-east bases of the lofty mountains which I have just mentioned. Judging from the appearances around us that a river probably discharged itself from the lake near the point we then occupied, I despatched Alexander Mackay to coast it to the westward for a mile or two while the party were breakfasting, and while I was engaged in making drawings of the romantic scenery around.

In the course of half an hour he returned, bringing the intelligence that his progress had soon been arrested by a large river falling out of the lake, and being to all appearance the Derwent. This conjecture—in which I entirely agreed so soon as I had reached its banks—was, as will be seen, subsequently verified by the result of our journey.

After breakfasting on this beautiful spot we anxiously pressed forward to explore the extent and features of the lake. The eastern bank being evidently very steep and woody—high tabular hills falling abruptly to the edge of the water—I determined on crossing the river and coasting the lake by its western shore. At a point a few hundred yards from where the water discharges itself we found a tree lying across the river, which served to us for a secure bridge and enabled us to cross the whole of our baggage—the horses being unladen and made to ford the lake a little above the commencement of the river.

Arrived on the other side, I found an extensive flat tract of land bounding Lake Saint Clair on the south and, leaving the reach which had first come under our notice, we traversed this marsh in a north-west direction; and after walking about a mile we again joined the lake and obtained a magnificent view of the greatest portion of this beautiful sheet of water—a deep bay stretched away to our left (south-west) and lay embosomed in sloping hills covered with the most varied foliage, but the main arm extended in a north-west direction in one unbroken sheet apparently ten miles long and three wide, washing the north-eastern base of that lofty basaltic mountain which I have before adverted to.

It was a fine summer's day and the air was so serene that the surface of the water was scarcely ruffled but the sandy beaches bore evidence of the lake being at times as rough as the sea. I will not here dilate on the extreme beauty of this scenery as it might be considered out of place in an official report, but I confess that while thus narrating the circumstances of the journey I feel it difficult to avoid expressing the impressions of delight which were inspired by the first discoverings of such a romantic country, impressions which are almost revived by retracing one's progress through it, even in cold narrative. I believe every man of the party felt more or less the calm influence of the scenery and, to all, this day's journey was a matter of recreation.

We sauntered along the south coast of the western bay for three miles, sometimes walking along the finest beaches of white gravel and sometimes ascending the banks—where an open forest opposed no obstacles to our travelling; at length, having reached the head of the bay and the clearer ground here closing in, we determined to halt and accordingly we pitched our blankets on the beach.

The point where we encamped commanded a good view of the upper portions of the great mountain and gave us the opportunity of reconnoitring its features at leisure. On every side it appeared scarped by perpendicular columns of basalt so as to be quite insurmountable but when the setting sun lit up in bold relief every pillar of this singular natural structure we conceived hopes of being able to find some fissure through which an ascent might be practicable, and as the position of the mountain rendered it probable that a most extensive view of the adjacent country would be commanded from its summit I resolved on attempting to scale it.

The base was computed to be seven miles from our encampment—and the intervening ground seemed thickly wooded. It was judged necessary therefore to provide ourselves with four days' provisions for this excursion, and on the morning of the 12th—leaving a party of men with the pack horses and baggage at our encampment on the little bay, which was named Cynthia's Cove—the remainder consisting of fourteen persons started in the direction of the mountain.

In the course of half an hour we reached a rapid torrent flowing towards the lake from the south-west. I named it the River Hügel in honour of Baron Charles Hügel of Vienna—and a few paces further we met another larger stream coming from the north-west and joining the Hügel close to the point of our crossing. This river I named Cuvier after the great naturalist who has by his genius and researches added so extensively to human knowledge.

The opposite bank of this river was steep but thinly wooded and small wet marshes were every here and there interspersed. These clear patches occurred more frequently as we advanced, and after proceeding about a mile we emerged into a long open valley—quite free from timber save a few ornamental clumps of small gum trees. This beautiful valley extended in a north-west direction beyond the great mountain, skirting its base; the Cuvier wound through its centre. On the south-west it was confined by a range of lofty hills apparently separating it from the Hügel. On the north-east it was bounded by the great mountain and its minor ridges.

The discovery of this valley, into which we were ushered so opportunely by chance, gave—as may be conceived—a high zest to the excursion, the more especially as we had been prepared to encounter nothing but the most embarrassing forests. We pushed on rapidly to the foot of the mountain, only halting occasionally to sketch the scenery, or map the country, and before eleven o'clock we found ourselves fairly at the foot of the object of our ambition, its stupendous groups of columns hanging over our heads in the most imposing manner.

We chose the most abrupt point of ascent, and were not disappointed in our hope of finding a crevice between the pillars through which we could clamber. In one hour and twenty minutes we reached the top—hands and feet bearing a pretty equal share in the process—and, on assembling the party at the summit, the little remaining breath was devoted to three hearty cheers and we named the mountain—Olympus.

The view from this point was beyond all description—the whole of Lake Saint Clair lay at our feet with its beautiful bays and its golden beaches, and in addition we could descry at least twenty other lakes of various dimensions in different parts of the panorama. Two in particular attracted our especial notice and admiration by their beauty. They were both situated near Saint Clair's and I named these lakes Petrarch and Laura. The former lay at the north-west extremity of Cuvier's valley and gave rise to the river of that name, the latter deeply embosomed in the woody hills on the north side of Saint Clair's. The whole of the country to the north was intersected by lofty alps; the north-eastern country was high and tabular, abounding in lakes. The west too exhibited many chains of mountains and the ocean beyond; the well-known mountain at Macquarie Harbour—-

162

called Frenchman's Cap—being a conspicuous object in that direction, but towards the south-east the eye ranged over extensive plains watered by the Derwent. We found no water on the top of Mount Olympus but after a long search we fortunately discovered a patch of snow, and mixing it with sugar and ginger in our tin cups it was converted into a most refreshing repast. We passed several hours on the summit of this mountain, making every observation which the object of the expedition prompted and it was with reluctance that I commenced the descent after the sun had sunk beneath the horizon of the western ocean.

JOHN BATMAN
Batmania, 1835

 John Batman, who sailed from Van Diemen's Land to explore the Port Phillip district, was not a modest man. He named Batman Creek 'after my good self', and I'm sure he would have been delighted if Melbourne had retained the name of its founder. Doubtless, the name of the city of Batman with its crowds of Batmanians would eventually have become commonplace—but the same colonial sycophancy that lumbered us with the name Sydney ensured that Melbourne would prevail.

What Batman thought he was doing by getting Bungett and Jagajaga to draw sacred designs on a tree, by way of concluding his purchase of 600,000 acres of tribal land in exchange for a barrow load of trinkets, God only knows.

Friday 29 May 1835—This morning as soon as daylight appeared saw the heads of Port Phillip about eight miles off. With a fair wind we got between the heads about nine o'clock a.m., the tide running out, nearly low water. A very heavy surf running at the entrance. The wind was light, and with some difficulty we got in; width about one mile and a quarter, the depth five-and-a-half to seven fathoms of water. We got well into the port about ten o'clock, where the water is very smooth, and one of the finest basins of water I ever saw, and most extensive. I would not recommend anyone to come in until the tide was running in, when the surf is smooth at the mouth.

As we were sailing up the port heard a dog on the shore howling. Cannot think what brought it there. Just called upon deck to see about one hundred geese flying near the vessel; they seemed very large, and flew up the port before us. We anchored in a small bay about twelve miles up the port, and went on shore. Before we got into the boat we saw a dog on the sand. We put off and came up to the dog, which proved to be a native dog of New Holland, which had surely left the natives within a day or so, as he came quite close to my natives, and did not appear at all afraid, but would not allow them to take hold of him. Our dogs, after some time, took after him, and ran him into the water, where we shot him. He was a large dog, and much the same I have seen in New South Wales. We fell in with the tracks of the natives, which was only a day or two old; also huts on the bay where they had been eating mussels...

Saturday 30 May 1835—...I went on shore to look at the land, which appeared beautiful, with scarcely any timber on. On my landing I found the hills of a most superior description— beyond my most sanguine expectations. The land excellent and very rich—and light black soil, covered with kangaroo grass two feet high, and as thick as it could stand. Good hay could be made, and in any quantity. The trees were not more than six to the acre, and those small she-oak and wattle. I never saw anything equal to the land in my life. I walked over a considerable extent, and all of the same description. This land forms an isthmus which is about twenty miles long by ten across it—upwards of 100,000 acres of good land or more. I could see five or six miles in every direction. Most of the high hills was covered with grass to the summit, and not a tree, although the land was as good as land could be. The whole appeared like land laid out in farms for some one hundred years back, and every tree transplanted. I was never so astonished in my life...We anchored in three fathoms water and, to my joy and delight, we saw at some distance the natives' fire. I intend to go off to them early in the morning and get, if possible, on a friendly footing with them in order to purchase land etc. from them...

Sunday 31 May 1835—...At daylight this morning we landed, to endeavour to meet the natives. We had not proceeded more than one and a half mile when we saw the smoke at seven large huts. My natives stripped off and went up to them quite naked. When they got to the huts, found that they had left this morning. Then, with the natives, went round, and found by their tracks the direction they went in. We followed on the tracks for ten miles or nearly, when Stomert, one of my natives, saw a black at the distance of a mile. We were at this time spread along. He made a sign to us, and all made in the same direction. He came up to the person (an old woman), quite cripple. She had no toes on one foot.

We then saw the remainder of the tribe about a mile further on. We made towards them, and got up to them about one o'clock p.m. They seemed quite pleased with my natives, who could partially understand them. They sang and danced for them. I found them to be only women and children: twenty of the former and twenty-four of the latter. The women were all of a small size, and every woman had a child at her back except one, who was quite a young woman and very good-looking. We understood that the men went up the river. They had four native dogs, and every woman had a load of sixty pounds or seventy pounds on her back, of one thing or another.[†] Each had two or three baskets, net-bags, native tomahawks, bones etc. I found in one of the net-bags a part of a strake of a cart-wheel, which had two nail holes in. They had ground it down to a sharp edge, and put it in a stick to cut with

---

† The very large loads the women are carrying suggest a more sedentary lifestyle for these Aborigines.

as a tomahawk. They had also several pieces of iron hoop, ground sharp to cut with; several wooden buckets to carry water in. They had some water with them, which was very bad.

They came back with us to where I had some blankets, looking-glasses, beads, handkerchiefs, sugar, apples. I gave them eight pair blankets, thirty handkerchiefs, one tomahawk, eighteen necklaces of beads, six pounds sugar, twelve looking-glasses, a quantity of apples, which they seemed well pleased with. They then went off again. I promised to see them again tomorrow. The young woman, who I have spoke of before, gave me a very handsome basket of her own make. Other women gave me two others; also some spears. I got a native bucket, which I brought on board with me...I never saw or could suppose there could be so extensive plains as I saw today. Five thousand sheep would be almost lost upon them. But the only thing I see at present is the want of water, but am sure it could be obtained by digging in almost any place. The children were good-looking, and of an healthy appearance; they were dreadfully affrighted by the discharge of a gun, and all of them dropped down immediately. I think they never heard the report or saw a gun before. We saw a great number of wild turkeys today, but could not shoot one. We could not have walked less than thirty miles today.

Monday 1 June 1835—We left the vessel this morning at daybreak, and went round a bay to look at and examine some plains and clear hills at a distance, which looked very well. We crossed the neck of land and came to a small river or creek, which we were obliged to follow up, as we could not cross, and I also expected to find at the head of it some fresh water. We followed this stream about ten miles. We saw great numbers of ducks and teal. The creek was about fifty to sixty yards wide, in some places less.

We saw several places on going up which the natives had made with stones across the creek, to take fish, I suppose, in summer time. The walls were built of stones about four feet high, and well done and well planned out; two or three of these places following each other down the stream with gates to them, which they appear to stop with a bundle of bushes. We saw those in about ten or twelve different places up this stream.

On this stream we also met with the bones of an animal or beast of some kind which I had never met with before, and cannot accurately describe it. I counted twenty-four joints in the backbone, which is at least three inches each, therefore the animal must have been upwards of six feet in length. It must have been killed some time, and part of the bones were burnt. There may have been a greater number of bones in the back than I have seen. I have brought on board part of the head, thigh bones, and some joints of the back for the learned gents to study over on my return to Van Diemen's Land.[†]

Saturday 6 June 1835—The wind blew hard all night with some rain. We started this morning at eight and went to find the natives. We travelled over as good a country as I have yet met with and if possible richer land, thinly timbered. The grass was mostly three and four feet high and as thick as it could lie on the ground. The land quite black. We walked about eight miles when we fell in with the tracks of the natives, and shortly after came up with a family: one chief, his wife and three children. I gave him a pair of blankets, handkerchiefs, beads and three knives. He then went on with us and crossed a freshwater creek. The land on each side excellent. He took us on, saying he would take us to the tribe and mentioned the names of chiefs.

We walked about eight miles when, to our great surprise, we heard several voices calling after us. On looking back we saw eight men all armed with spears etc. etc. When we stopped they threw aside their weapons and came very friendly up to us. After shaking hands, and my giving them tomahawks, knives etc., they took us with them about a mile back, where we found huts, women and children. After some time and full explanation, I found eight chiefs amongst them who possessed the whole of the territory near Port Phillip. Three brothers, all of the same name,

---

† The strange beast was probably a seal.

were the principal chiefs, and two of them men of six feet high and very good-looking; the other not so tall, but stouter. The other five chiefs were fine men. After a full explanation of what my object was, I purchased two large tracts of land from them—about 600,000 acres, more or less, and delivered over to them blankets, knives, looking-glasses, tomahawks, beads, scissors, flour etc. etc., as payment for the land; and also agreed to give them a tribute or rent yearly. The parchment the eight chiefs signed this afternoon, delivering to me some of the soil, each of them, as giving me full possession of the tracts of land. This took place alongside of a beautiful stream of water, and from whence my land commences, and where a tree is marked four ways to know the corner boundary. The country about here exceeds anything I ever saw, both for grass and richness of soil. The timber light, and consists of she-oak and small gum, with a few wattle. My natives gave the chiefs and their tribe a grand corroboree tonight. They seemed quite delighted with it. Each of the principal chiefs has two wives and several children each. In all, the tribe consists of forty-five—men, women and children.

Sunday 7 June 1835—Detained this morning some time drawing up triplicates of the deeds of the land I purchased, and delivering over to them more property on the banks of the river which I have named Batman Creek—after my good self. Just before leaving, the two principal chiefs came and brought their two cloaks, or royal mantles, and laid at my feet, wishing to accept the same. On my consenting to take them, they placed them round my neck and over my shoulders, and seemed quite pleased to see me walk about with them on. I asked them to accompany me to the vessels. They very properly pointed to the number of young children, and then at their feet, meaning that they could not walk but said they would come down in a few days.

I had no trouble to find out their sacred marks. One of my natives (Bungett) went to a tree, out of sight of the women, and made the Sydney natives' mark. After this was done, I took with me two or three of my natives to the principal chief and showed the marks on the tree. This he knew immediately, and pointed to the knocking out of the teeth. The mark is always made when the ceremony of knocking out the tooth in the front is done. However, after this I desired, through my natives, for him to make his mark; which, after looking about some time, and hesitating some few minutes, he took the tomahawk and cut out in the bark of the tree his mark, which is attached to the deed, and is the signature of their country and tribe.

Sunday 7 June 1835—About 10 a.m. I took my departure from those interesting people. I think the principal chief stands six feet four inches high, and his brother six feet two inches, and as fine looking men as ever I saw...

Monday 8 June 1835—The wind foul this morning for Indented Head. We tried, but could not get out of the river. The boat went up the large river I have spoken of, which comes from the east, and I am glad to state, about six miles up found the river all good water and very deep. This will be the place for a village—the natives on shore.[†]

Batman drew up two deeds, one for the Geelong area and the other for Melbourne. Here is the latter document.

Know all persons that three brothers, Jagajaga, Jagajaga, Jagajaga, being the principal chiefs, and also Cooloolock, Bungarie, Yanyan, Moowhip, Mommarmalar, being the chiefs of a certain native tribe called Dutigallar, situate at and near Port Phillip, called by us, the above mentioned chiefs Iramoo, being possessed of the tract of land hereinafter mentioned for and in consideration of twenty pair of blankets, thirty tomahawks, one hundred knives, fifty pair scissors, thirty looking glasses, two hundred handkerchiefs, and one hundred pounds of flour, and six shirts, delivered to us by John Batman, residing in Van Diemen's Land, Esquire, but at present sojourning with us and our tribe, do for ourselves our heirs and successors give grant enfeoff and confirm unto the said John

† Batman was on the Yarra River near where Queen Street now terminates.

Batman, his heirs and assigns, all that tract of country situate and being at Port Phillip, running from the branch of the river at the top of the port, about seven miles from the mouth of the river, forty miles north-east, and from thence—west, forty miles across Iramoo Downs or Plains and from thence south-south-west, across Mount Vilaumarnartar to Geelong Harbour at the head of the same, and containing about 500,000 more or less acres, as the same hath been before the execution of these presents delineated and marked out by us according to the custom of our tribe by certain marks made upon the trees growing along the boundaries of the said tract of land, to hold the said tract of land, with all advantages belonging thereto, unto and to the use of the said John Batman, his heirs and assigns for ever, to the intent that the said John Batman, his heirs, and assigns may occupy and possess the said tract of land and place thereon sheep and cattle. Yielding and delivering to us, and our heirs or successors the yearly rent or tribute of one hundred pair of blankets, one hundred knives, one hundred tomahawks, fifty suits of clothing, fifty looking glasses, fifty pair scissors and five tons flour.

In witness whereof we, Jagajaga, Jagajaga, Jagajaga, the before mentioned principal chiefs, and Cooloolock, Bungarie, Yanyan, Moowhip, and Mommarmalar, the chiefs of the said tribe, have hereunto affixed our seals to those presents and have signed the same. Dated according to the Christian era, this sixth day of June, 1835.

Signed sealed and delivered in the presence of us the same having been fully and properly interpreted and explained to the said chiefs	Jagajaga
	Jagajaga
	Jagajaga
	Cooloolock
James Gumm	Bungarie
Alexander Thompson	Yanyan
Willm. Todd	Moowhip
	Mommarmalar
	John Batman

Signed on the banks of Batman Creek 6th June 1835.

Sir Thomas Mitchell, surveyor-general, undertook four major expeditions in eastern Australia between 1831 and 1845. He was one of the very few explorers fated to discover rich pastoral land, and he called Victoria's Western District his 'Australia Felix'. Horses were still expensive in 1836, so Mitchell travelled by bullock dray.

Mitchell was a man of great natural parts. He patented the 'boomerang propellor for steamers' and later translated Camoens' sixteenth-century Portuguese epic, the *Lusiads*.

On 30 June 1836 Mitchell climbed Pyramid Hill, not far from where the town of Warrnambool now stands, and beheld a 'scene...different from anything I had ever before witnessed...As I stood, the first European intruder on the sublime solitude of these verdant plains, as yet untouched by flocks or herds, I felt conscious of being the harbinger of mighty changes.' Two months later he had the unusual explorer's experience of discovering a European settlement: the Hentys had arrived from across Bass Strait and established a secret station. The mighty changes were already at hand.

August 9—Once more in a state of forward movement, we crossed green hills and running brooks until, when we had travelled nearly six miles from Muddy Camp, and had crossed six fine streams or burns, we met with a more formidable impediment in the seventh. The sides of the ravine were so uncommonly steep that our new difficulty was how to move the vehicles down to the bank of the stream. In one place, where a narrow point of ground projected across, a passage seemed just possible; and after we had made it better with spades we attempted to take a light cart over. The acclivity was still, however, rather too much and over went the cart, carrying the shaft bullock with it and depositing all my instruments etc. under it in the bed of the stream.

171

With travellers *on roads*, this might have been thought a serious accident, but in our case we were prepared for joltings, and nothing was in the least degree injured; neither was the animal hurt, and we ascertained by the experiment, dangerous though it was, that still more was necessary to be done for the passage of the heavy carts and boats, which were still some way behind; and I encamped on the bank beyond that the men might set about this work. No time was lost in filling up the hollow with all the dead trees that lay about, and what others we could cut for the purpose; and thus, before sunset, the three carts and one wagon were got across. The rocks in the bed of this stream consisted of grey gneiss, and on the hills beyond it I found nodules of highly ferruginous sandstone.

August 10—By means of a block and tackle attached to a large tree, the remaining carts and the boat-carriage were safely lowered to the bed of the stream. To draw them up the opposite bank was practicable only by uniting the strength of several teams, yet this too was effected successfully, and the whole party were enabled to go forward in the morning.

At a mile and a half from the camp, a scene was displayed to our view which gladdened every heart. An open grassy country, extending as far as we could see—hills round and smooth as carpet, meadows broad, and either green as an emerald or of a rich golden colour from the abundance, as we soon afterwards found, of a little ranunculus-like flower. Down into that delightful vale our vehicles trundled over a gentle slope, the earth being covered with a thick matted turf, apparently superior to anything of the kind previously seen. That extensive valley was enlivened by a winding stream, the waters of which glittered through trees fringing each bank.

As we went on our way rejoicing, I perceived at length two figures at a distance who at first either did not see or did not mind us. They proved to be a gin with a little boy, and as soon as the female saw us she began to run. I presently overtook her, and with the few words I knew prevailed on her to stop until the two gins of our party could come up; for I had long been at a loss for the names of localities. This woman was not so much alarmed as might have been expected; and I was glad to find that she and the gins perfectly understood each other.

The difference in the costume on the banks of the Wándo immediately attracted the notice of the females from the Lachlan. The bag usually carried by gins was neatly wove in basketwork, and composed of a wiry kind of rush. She of Wándo carried this bag fastened to her back, having under it two circular mats of the same material, and beneath all a kangaroo cloak, so that her back at least was sufficiently clothed, although she wore no dress in front.

The boy was supported between the mats and cloak; and his pleased and youthful face, he being a very fine specimen of the native race, presented a striking contrast to the miserable looks of his whining mother. In the large bag she carried some pieces of firewood, and a few roots, apparently of taö, which she had just been digging from the earth.[†] Such was the only visible inhabitant of this splendid valley, resembling a nobleman's park on a gigantic scale. She stated that the main river was called Temiángandgeen, a name unfortunately too long to be introduced into maps. We also obtained the gratifying intelligence that the whole country to the eastward was similar to these delightful vales; and that, in the same direction, as Piper translated her statement, 'there was no more sticking in mud'.

A favourable change in the weather accompanied our fortunate transition from the land of watery soil and dark woody ravines to an open country. The day was beautiful; and the balmy air was sweetened with a perfume resembling hay, which arose from the thick and matted herbs and grass. Proceeding along the valley, the stream on our left vanished at an isolated, rocky hill; but, on closer examination, I found the apparent barrier cleft in two, and that the water passed through, roaring over rocks. This was rather a singular feature in an open valley, where the ground

† It wasn't taro she was digging, but the root of the yam daisy.

on each side of it was almost as low as the rocky bed of the stream itself...

Another rivulet approached this hill, flowing under its eastern side and joining the Wándo just below. According to my plan of following down the main river, it was necessary to cross both these tributaries. In the open part of the valley, the channels of these streams were deep and the banks soft; but at the base of the hill of Kingànyu (for such was its name) we found rock enough and, having effected a passage there of both streams that afternoon, we encamped, after travelling about three miles further, on the banks of the Glenelg once more. Our route lay straight across an open grassy valley at the foot of swelling hills of the same description. Each of these valleys presented peculiar and very romantic features, but I could not decide which looked most beautiful. All contained excellent soil and grass, surpassing in quality any I had seen in the present colony of New South Wales. The chase of the emu and kangaroo, which were both numerous, afforded us excellent sport on these fine downs.

When about to cross the Wándo, I took my leave of the native woman before mentioned, that she might not have the trouble of fording the river, and I presented her with a tomahawk, of which our females explained to her the use—although she seemed still at a loss to conceive the meaning of *a present*.[†] The use of the little hatchet would be well enough known, however, to her tribe, so, leaving her to return to it and assuring her at the same time of our friendly disposition towards the natives, we proceeded...

August 29—The groaning trees had afforded us shelter, without letting fall even a single branch upon our heads, but the morning was squally and unfavourable for the objects of the excursion, and we had still to ride some way before I could commence operations.

† Wándo River: now the Wannon River.

Proceeding along the skirts of the woody ridge on the left in order to avoid swamps, we at length saw through the trees the blue waters of the sea and heard the roar of the waves. My intended way towards the deepest part of the bay and the hills beyond it did not lead directly to the shore, and I continued to pursue a course through the woods, having the shore on our left. We thus met a deep and rapid little river, exactly resembling the Fitzroy, and coming also from the westward. Tracing this a short distance upwards, we came to a place set with a sort of trellis work of bushes by the natives, for the purpose, no doubt, of catching fish. Here we found the stream fordable, though deep, a brownish granular limestone appearing in the bank. We crossed and then continuing through a thick wood we came out at length on the shore of Portland Bay, at about four miles beyond the little river.

Straight before us lay Laurence's Island or, rather, islands, there being two small islets of rock in that situation; and, some way to the eastward, I perceived a much larger island which I concluded was one of Lady Julia Percy's Isles. At a quarter of a mile back from the beach, broad broom-topped *casuarinae* were the only trees we could see; these grew on long ridges, parallel to the beach, resembling those long breakers which, aided by winds, had probably thrown such ridges up. They were abundantly covered with excellent grass; and, as it wanted about an hour of noon, I halted that the cattle might feed, while I took some angles and endeavoured to obtain the sun's altitude during the intervals between heavy squalls, some of which were accompanied by hail and thunder.

On reaching the seashore at this beach, I turned to observe the face of Tommy Came-last, one of my followers, who being a native from the interior had never before seen the sea. I could not discover in the face of this young savage, even on his first view of the ocean, any expression of surprise; on the contrary, the placid and comprehensive gaze he cast over it seemed fully to embrace the grand expanse then for the first time opened to him.

I was much more astonished when he soon after came to tell me of the fresh tracks of cattle that he had found on the shore, and the shoe marks of a white man. He also brought me two portions of tobacco-pipes and a glass bottle without a neck. That whaling vessels occasionally touched there I was aware, as was indeed obvious from the carcases and bones of whales on the beach; but how cattle could have been brought there I did not understand.

Proceeding round the bay with the intention of examining the head of an inlet and continuing along shore as far as Cape Bridgewater, I was struck with the resemblances to houses that some supposed grey rocks under the grassy cliffs presented; and while I directed my glass towards them my servant Brown said he saw a brig at anchor, a fact of which I was soon convinced, and also that the grey rocks were in reality wooden houses. The most northern part of the shore of this bay was comparatively low, but the western consisted of bold cliffs rising to the height of 180 feet.

We ascended these cliffs near the wooden houses, which proved to be some deserted sheds of the whalers. One shot was heard as we drew near them, and another on our ascending the rocks. I then became somewhat apprehensive that the parties might either be, or suppose us to be, bushrangers, and to prevent if possible some such awkward mistake I ordered a man to fire a gun and the bugle to be sounded; but on reaching the higher ground we discovered not only a beaten path, but the track of two carts, and while we were following the latter a man came towards us from the face of the cliffs. He informed me in answer to my questions that the vessel at anchor was the *Elizabeth of Launceston*; and that just round the point there was a considerable farming establishment belonging to Messrs Henty, who were then at the house.

It then occurred to me that I might there procure a small additional supply of provisions, especially of flour, as my men were on very reduced rations. I, therefore, approached the house and was kindly received and entertained by the Messrs Henty, who as I learnt had been established there during upwards of two years. It was very obvious indeed from the magnitude and extent of the buildings, and the substantial fencing erected, that both time and labour had been expended in their construction. A good garden stocked with abundance of vegetables already smiled on Portland Bay; the soil was very rich on the overhanging cliffs, and the potatoes and turnips produced there surpassed in magnitude and quality any I had ever seen elsewhere.

I learnt that the bay was much resorted to by vessels engaged in the whale fishery, and that upwards of 700 tons of oil had been shipped that season. I was likewise informed that only a few days before my arrival five vessels lay at anchor together in that bay, and that a communication was regularly kept up with Van Diemen's Land by means of vessels from Launceston. Messrs Henty were importing sheep and cattle as fast as vessels could be found to bring them over, and the numerous whalers touching at or fishing on the coast were found to be good customers for farm produce and whatever else could be spared from the establishment...

August 30—I was accommodated with a small supply of flour by Messrs Henty, who having been themselves on short allowance were awaiting the arrival of a vessel then due two weeks. They also supplied us with as many vegetables as the men could carry away on their horses. Just as I was about to leave the place, a whale was announced, and instantly three boats well manned were seen cutting through the water, a harpooneer standing up at the stern of each with oar in hand, and assisting the rowers by a forward movement at each stroke.

It was not the least interesting scene in these my Australian travels, thus to witness from a verandah on a beautiful afternoon at Portland Bay the humours of the whale fishery, and all those wondrous perils of harpooneers and whale boats, of which I had delighted to read as scenes of 'the stormy north'. The object of the present pursuit was a 'hunchback' and, being likely to occupy the boats for some time, I proceeded homewards. I understood it frequently happened that several parties of fishermen, left by different whaling vessels, would engage in the pursuit of the same whale, and that in the struggle for possession the whale would occasionally escape from them all and run ashore, in which case it is of little value to whalers, as the removal, etc, would be too tedious, and they in such cases carry away part of the head matter only.

The natives never approach these whalers, nor had they ever shown themselves to the white people of Portland Bay; but as they have taken to eat the castaway whales it is their custom to send up a column of smoke when a whale appears in the bay, and the fishers understand the signal. This affords an instance of the sagacity of the natives, for they must have reflected that, by thus giving timely notice, a greater number will become competitors for the whale, and that consequently there will be a better chance of the whale running ashore, in which case a share must fall finally to them. The fishers whom I saw were fine able fellows; and with their large ships and courageous struggles with the whales they must seem terrible men of the sea to the natives. The neat trim of their boats, set up on stanchions on the beach, looked well, with oars and in perfect readiness to dash at a moment's notice into the 'angry surge'. Upon the whole, what with the perils they undergo and their incessant labour in boiling the oil, these men do not earn too cheaply the profits derived from that kind of speculation. I saw on the shore the wreck of a fine boat which had been cut in two by a single stroke of the tail of a whale.

JOHN GRAHAM
That Abject Captive Lady, 1836

The idea of a white woman living among the Aborigines provoked a powerful reaction in colonial Australia. She was a recurrent myth on the frontier, and searches for her were used more than once as an excuse for the massacre of Aborigines. There were, however, several actual instances of European women living with Aborigines. Perhaps the most famous is Eliza Fraser, whose story inspired Sidney Nolan to paint, and Patrick White to write *A Fringe of Leaves*. Shipwrecked with her husband on Swain Reef near present-day Rockhampton in May 1836, Fraser was lucky to survive. She was heavily pregnant and gave birth in a longboat to a baby who died. Eventually she fell in with the Kabi people on Fraser Island. The Aborigines believed that she was Mamba, a woman who had died some time previously, and that she had lost both colour and language during her time in the grave. Her husband was speared to death, but she lived with her captors until rescued, three months later, in August 1836.

This breathlessly idiomatic account is the verbal testimony of a convict, John Graham, who lived with the Aborigines for years before returning to Moreton Bay. He was known to them as Moilow, one of their clan who had returned from the dead. He was fluent in the Kabi language, and in his account of his expedition to rescue Eliza Fraser we gain a rare insight into what the Aborigines were thinking as they met the Europeans. Graham's account is addressed to Captain Foster Fyans, commandant at Moreton Bay.

Your Honour, to whom I here refer the difficulties I had to surmount, the horrors of death which to me seemed sure, and even prophesied by my comrades who were praying for my safety, vowed to have revenge for my blood, expecting to see me no more—I was determined to brave the worst of fates or finish a miserable existence to rescue that abject captive lady.

Though solicited by that gentleman Mr Otter to accompany me with all the arms he had, it was of no avail, for had we been able to assail them she must have fallen a sacrifice to their spears or be carried by hundreds further through the mountains. I must act on other plans though doomed to face hundreds of savages, amongst whom were the very men but a few days before I fired at. I depended on a tribe whose former friendship I had experienced, several of whom acknowledged me their father, or spirit thereof.

There were several resolutions of detaining hostages and sending word, to see if they would give her up. This would have caused lives on both sides, and certainly would have proved fatal to her and also shown a coward in me, I alone knowing where she was. I think it a pleasure in giving your Honour an account of this transaction and every minute detail, showing I was determined, or die the worst of deaths, or fulfil my promise.

Lieutenant Otter wishing to accompany me to whom I refer, and spoke these words: 'Sir, I am but one, my life I do not care for, it being of little use to me. If I do not return in two days then take hostages and revenge for my blood.' The sentiments of his mind were seen by me in not being a co-partner; he must risk his life and follow me. He took me to his tent giving me a glass of rum and water. I here gave him directions of the route. He was to follow me on the following morning by the mark of the broad arrow which I was to leave for his instruction, and to sit where it was, stop till I should come next day if living.

I strove much to get two of those blacks to come with me. I brought them to the tents, showed two blankets, two tomahawks and two axes to induce them to come. They told me their hearts failed them, they would be killed. I recollect telling Mr Otter at the time what they said when, taking a roasted bream and a small piece of bread, I took my departure, my comrades saying they would revenge my fate, expecting no more to see me. I soon crossed the hills and was out of sight on Tuesday at eleven o'clock August the 16th.

Lest my bread should be took from me, expecting to meet several natives, I eat it. I had trousers on, and continued my route making the mark as I went along. Drawing near sundown I thought of my supper, having none, nor time to look for any. Your Honour can here read ideas of my mind, and think the arm of God alone strengthened and assisted me in this virtuous act of humanity. Proceeding on, I found a snake seven feet long which showed me providence was assisting and protecting me. On getting back I retired to a gully, made a fire and roasted my snake which I hung up for morning. Of all my life this was the most disturbed night I ever spent, too tedious to mention here. The dawn of day called me forth, after taking God for my guide, and my breakfast which his mercies sent me.

I descended from my gully twenty-five miles from the tents and continued my route, making the mark. On coming where I was to turn, I put a stop with those words, 'Stop. Here you will find fresh water at the rock.' This was thirty miles in all. I saw no blacks ascending the hills and crossing the forest ground. About four miles you descend into a boggy ground or swamp ankle-deep for a mile, after which a lake about thirty miles in circumference, four miles where I crossed it, knee-deep at low water, after which a freshwater river.

Being about to swim across, a black man and his wife appeared in their canoe. Being horror-struck at my appearance and thinking I had more confederates, they were making away saying they would bring plenty of men. I standing on the brink of the river telling them I was alone, and showing two fish hooks, the woman induced him to return. Their approach was timid, and asking me what he would get, I tore the leg of my trousers off and gave it to him. The hooks for her. After inquiring the different tribes that were there, and particularly after my own kindred, and what part of the field they were in, I made enquiry after my wife [the woman who said I was her husband's spirit and died in 1827], if she had strayed amongst them.

They told me there was a female spirit, but a man by the name of Mothervane claimed her as his wife's sister. As they had heard of the skirmages we had, which I left to the stupid spirits that were along with me, as I came to do no harm but take my wife down to the beach and there live on my ground as I had done before. Promising him my trousers, and her as many hooks as she could carry, if she would go and tell the men, especially my friends, not to be cross as I came to live amongst them and make axes and fish hooks at Thaying (my ground), and I would show Mothervane that spirit was Mamba, whose sons was there visiting. Murrow Dooling and Caravanty—two young men who always claimed me as their father's spirit, who had a great connection in several tribes.

The woman said they were there and dispatched to tell them, while the man and I hurried on, telling me he would assist me.

On coming in sight of the camp, I watched the woman going to the south side where I supposed my friends were. I made there. She was telling them I was making onward but, surrounded by numbers, I was forced to stand. Black and savage as they were, no horror struck me as the sight of that unhappy lady, who caught my eye as it wandered round their huts.

Could I then have armed myself with vengeance would I have been detained from giving the cannibal race any account of my demands? Courage flushed to me and I feared no fate. Hearing the sound of Mamba, which the woman had told she was, and my sons amongst the crowd, to whom I said: 'Is your eyes blind, don't you know your mother?' upon whose neck I fell, fancying to cry. My father-in-law jumped to his knife, saying, 'No crying, go and take her.' (This man's name is Mootemu.)

Upwards of 400 blacks had seized their spears when Mothervane came forward, to whom I said, 'Do you claim a spirit? And she my wife. She can't speak to tell having lost her speech, and I who have got sense do tell the truth and here are her two sons and father,' pointing to the people above-named.

A dead silence was here and all eyes were on me whilst I told them how she was along with me in a canoe after turtle, and being cast away she swam amongst the north men, who gave her nothing to eat. She being a stranger could not tell who were her friends, having lost her tongue, and if Mothervane would [be] cross I would call a challenge. Here throwing off my trousers, to make fresh friends, I impeached them with being stupid in not knowing her.

All the coast blacks here stood on my side, and said I always told the truth. Saying, 'Give her,' 'She is his,' being now satisfied that she was Mamba. As they wanted me to go along with them

into the mountains as their friends had heard of that spirit and
their hearts would be glad at seeing her.

I here said, 'You see she is near dead with hunger, let your
friends wait till she is recovered and then I will go a season to
the mountains.'

Mothervane said it was a pity to let that spirit go, but here
Mootemu said, 'They are two ghosts and no men has any right
to separate them. Moilow* has good sense and knows how to live
as well as us, he must have his wife.'

The father of the child to whom I gave the skirt coming
forward, telling him what I had done for his girl, and where I
left her with a full belly, not as my wife was, starving among
them. He said in an angry voice, 'You people hear that, he is
coming with good fingers and why be cross?'

They began to retire to their respective huts, and a black man
sitting opposite her hut, and again I seen the face of a Christian
woman, and a black man sitting opposite her hut with a spear
in his hand as a sentinel. On looking I recognised him to be a
nephew of mine who has four wives, by name Dapen (left-handed
man)—and coming to me said, 'Come uncle, I was watching my
aunt, that the mountain blacks should not come near, whilst you
were talking. I fear none. I'll give her to you.'

On approaching to the hut, could I believe—I lost my sense
of surprise and joy, and a sense of gratitude to the most of those
savages who stood my friend. With a heartfelt sorrow for her
then before me, I sunk to the ground. When roused by the voice
of Dapen saying, 'The sun is going round uncle, you have far to
go.'

Roused to a sense of my situation I rose, reached my hand,
saying, 'Come with me. God has made me your deliverer.'

Fortitude was what I now called from heaven to assist me in
seeing a woman survive in the most distressed state than can be
painted, and one but a few months rolled in the affluence of

* My native name.

plenty, doomed to subsist on the husks of the earth, and forced to bear the wood on them sunburnt shoulders where the tender skin hung in scales, ordered to hop on lacerated feet to fetch them water, and for what reward? The entrails of a snake or that of a fish, the body being devoured in her absence, caused to come forth as a show in their mock fights and sports. What but heaven could have prolonged a life of such misery for a deliverance? Or what could have given a fortitude but a patience which Job never experienced?

This lady rising and taking my hand, I proceeded through a camp of some hundreds of blacks. On the most judicious plan I asked four of those men to come with me to Nemberthan. Taking my leave of my friends, Mootemu wanted me to take some *bungwal* (a root), which I refused. Having come to the canoes, two were brought—three in each we crossed the lake. On her head was a south-wester, the smell of paint kept the blacks from taking it. Around her loins were part of the legs and waistband of a pair of trousers, which covered part of her thighs, wound round with vines twentyfold as well for delicacy as the preservation of her marriage and earrings which she concealed under the vines, and the only articles that were saved from those savage hands.

In ascending the forest ground I caused the blacks to follow my example which they did to the rocks, where arriving I saw that relief was come. Leaving the lady at the waterhole telling her to remain a few minutes, I took the blacks with me to the beach where was Lieutenant Otter, who came to meet me in such haste that almost frightened the blacks, enquiring where she was. I told him all was right, asking him for some clothes for her, at which he clasped his hands and thanked his God, going to his bag.

I seated the blacks along with corporals McGuire and Campbell of the 4th Regiment and Nathaniel Mitchell who came with Mr Otter, to whom I went and got a boat cloak and some other articles of dress and returned to prepare the lady for his reception, and for the first time them vines were pulled off which the hands of her dear and much lamented husband had put on.

I beg leave to omit several distressing incidents in regard to this surprising unhappy lady whose history of woes is unparalleled as also in passing any encomiums in behalf of myself through the many acts I was destined to fulfil under the providence of God.

Your Honour best can judge the situation of her mind, being about to enter into society, and the distress which attended this meeting when, assisting her forth, I gave her hand to that gentleman Mr Otter about one o'clock on Wednesday the 17th of August.

GEORGE GREY
A Horrid Dream, 1838

 Sir George Grey: now there was a man destined for greatness. One day he would be governor of South Australia, then of New Zealand, then of the Cape. But here we see a younger George Grey at the beginning of his career: an English officer of twenty-five who disliked military life, still wet behind the ears, attempting to explore the Prince Regent River region in the Kimberley—some of the most difficult terrain in Australia.

The thing that I love most about Grey is that, despite incidents like the one related here, he had a gift for getting on with the Aborigines. He learned their language and understood them, and he never saw them as second-class. Later, he was to sum up the cause of their lack of progress in white society in one word: prejudice.

11 February—On quitting the camp in the morning, I and my two companions traversed for some time portions of the elevated sandstone plains which I had passed on a former occasion; and after an hour's walking through the gloomy stringybark forest which covered them we reached a stream of water running in a

shallow valley; and as there was a bad route down to this I halted to make a road which the ponies could traverse. There was plenty of water and forage hereabouts, and a fine level country for our proceedings, so that we were all in high hopes and spirits and, as I then believed, our principal difficulties were at an end.

Whilst at work at the road we all thought that we heard a native call and that others answered him; having listened for a repetition of these sounds, we again heard them, but they were so indistinct in character that none of us this time agreed as to what they were—I imagined that it was the call of a bird, and when I again heard the same sound very faintly in the distance, I felt convinced it was not a human voice, and proceeded on my way perfectly at ease.

My attention was soon occupied by other objects. I saw from a hill I ascended some remarkable blue peaks to the south. This gave us fresh hopes, and nothing occurred till about three-quarters of an hour after we had first heard the native call, when we arrived at a short descent covered with rocks, from which started a large kangaroo; I got a fair shot at and knocked it over, but it sprang up again and hopped away. We then tried to track it, but soon lost its footsteps in the scrubby vegetation of the gloomy forest.

It was the duty of the Cape man who accompanied me to mark a tree every here and there by chipping the bark, so that the party might the next day easily recognise the route which they had to pursue; upon looking back I now perceived that he had neglected a very remarkable tree about twenty or thirty yards behind us, and which stood close to the spot where I had fired at the kangaroo. I desired him to go back and chip it, and then to rejoin us; in the meantime I stood musing as to the best means of avoiding the little rocky ravine in our front.

Finding that the man remained absent longer than I had expected, I called loudly to him but received no answer, and therefore passed round some rocks which hid the tree from my view to look after him. Suddenly I saw him close to me, breathless and speechless with terror, and a native with his spear fixed in a throwing-stick, in full pursuit of him; immediately numbers of other natives burst upon my sight; each tree, each rock seemed to give forth its black denizen, as if by enchantment.

A moment before, the most solemn silence pervaded these woods, we deemed that not a human being moved within miles of us, and now they rang with savage and ferocious yells, and fierce armed men crowded round us on every side, bent on our destruction.

There was something very terrible in so complete and sudden a surprise. Certain death appeared to stare us in the face, and from the determined and resolute air of our opponents I immediately guessed that the man who had first seen them, instead of boldly standing his ground, and calling to Coles and myself for assistance, had at once, like a coward, run away; thus giving the natives confidence in themselves, and a contempt for us—and this conjecture I afterwards ascertained was perfectly true.

We were now fairly engaged for our lives; escape was impossible and surrender to such enemies out of the question.

As soon as I saw the natives around me, I fired one barrel of my gun over the head of him who was pursuing my dismayed attendant, hoping the report would have checked his further career. He proved to be the tall man seen at the camp, painted with white. My shot stopped him not; he still closed on us, and his spear whistled by my head but, whilst he was fixing another in his throwing stick, a ball from my second barrel struck him in the arm, and it fell powerless by his side. He now retired behind a rock, but the others still pressed on.

I now made the two men retire behind some neighbouring rocks which formed a kind of protecting parapet along our front and right flank, whilst I took post on the left. Both my barrels were now exhausted; and I desired the other two to fire separately whilst I was reloading; but to my horror Coles, who was armed with my rifle, reported hurriedly that the cloth case with which he had covered it for protection against rain had become entangled. His services were thus lost at a most critical moment, whilst trying to tear off the lock cover; and the other man was so paralysed with fear that he could do nothing but cry out, 'Oh, God! Sir, look at them; look at them!'

In the meantime, our opponents pressed more closely round; their spears kept whistling by us, and our fate seemed inevitable. The light-coloured man, spoken of at the camp, now appeared to direct their movements. He sprang forward to a rock not more than thirty yards from us and, posting himself behind it, threw a spear with such deadly force and aim that had I not drawn myself forward by a sudden jerk it must have gone through my body and, as it was, it touched my back in flying by. Another well-directed spear, from a different hand, would have pierced me in the breast but, in the motion I made to avoid it, it struck upon the stock of my gun, of which it carried away a portion by its force.

All this took place in a few seconds of time, and no shot had been fired but by me. I now recognized in the light-coloured man an old enemy who had led on the former attack against me on the 22nd of December. By his cries and gestures he now appeared to be urging the others to surround and press on us, which they were rapidly doing.

I saw now that but one thing could be done to save our lives, so I gave Coles my gun to complete the reloading, and took the rifle which he had not yet disengaged from the cover. I tore it off and, stepping out from behind our parapet, advanced to the rock which covered my light-coloured opponent. I had not made two steps in advance when three spears struck me nearly at the same moment, one of which was thrown by him. I felt severely wounded in the hip, but knew not exactly where the others had struck me. The force of all knocked me down, and made me very giddy and faint, but as I fell I heard the savage yells of the natives' delight and triumph; these recalled me to myself and, roused by momentary rage and indignation, I made a strong effort, rallied, and in a moment was on my legs; the spear was wrenched from my wound, and my haversack drawn closely over it, that neither my own party nor the natives might see it, and I advanced again steadily to the rock.

The man became alarmed, and threatened me with his club, yelling most furiously; but as I neared the rock, behind which all but his head and arm was covered, he fled towards an adjoining one, dodging dexterously according to the native manner of confusing an assailant and avoiding the cast of his spear; but he was scarcely uncovered in his flight when my rifle ball pierced him through the back, between the shoulders, and he fell heavily on his face with a deep groan.

The effect was electrical. The tumult of the combat had ceased: not another spear was thrown, not another yell was uttered. Native after native dropped away, and noiselessly disappeared. I stood alone with the wretched savage dying before me, and my two men close to me behind the rocks, in the attitude of deep attention; and as I looked round upon the dark rocks and forests, now suddenly silent and lifeless, but for the sight of the unhappy being who lay on the ground before me, I could have thought that the whole affair had been a horrid dream.

WARRUP
Onwards, Onwards, 1839

 Trust George Grey to give us what is probably the earliest first-hand Aboriginal account of exploration in Australia. In April 1839 Grey's expedition came to grief seeking an overland route south from Shark Bay. Grey split his party and struggled on to Perth with a handful of men. Here, Warrup, a Noongar man, memorably describes the journey of the relief expedition sent in search of the men who had been left behind, south of where Geraldton stands today.

1st day—At Dundalup we eat fish; then onwards, onwards, onwards, till we slept at Neerroba.

2nd day—Onwards, onwards, till we reached Nowergoop, where the horses drank water; then onwards, onwards, onwards, until Manbabee, where we eat flesh and bread. Onwards, onwards, onwards, until Yungee, where we shot ducks, and the horses drank water. Onwards, onwards, onwards, onwards, to Boongarrup, where we slept one *sleep*.

3rd day—Onwards through a forest, onwards through a forest, onwards through a forest. We slept at Neergammy, a pleasant resting-place; the land was good, the herbage good; pleasant was our resting-place, and our hut was good.

4th day—Onwards, onwards, onwards, we entered a woody country. Onwards, through a forest, onwards through a forest; we now see the waters of Kajeelup; we eat flesh and bread. Onwards through the forest, onwards through the forest, onwards through the forest. We see the tracks of natives; we shout aloud, and then proceed conversing with natives; they sit down. Onwards go we, onwards, onwards, onwards; the horses drink water; by and by, we see tracks. Onwards, onwards, onwards; we see a large water; we shoot ducks. On the one side we see two waters, on the other side one water we see. Onwards, onwards, onwards, onwards, onwards; we see no other water. Onwards through the forest, onwards through the forest, onwards through the forest; we see a river. You had here eaten freshwater mussels: at this river we sleep. Barramba is the place's name.

5th day—Onwards through the forest, through the forest, through the forest, through the forest onwards; water we see not. Through the forest onwards; through the forest onwards; we see a water, but a worthless water. Yours and Kaiber's footsteps we see. Here there is no grass. You had here shot a bird—a cockatoo you shot. Maribara was this place's name.

Onwards through the forest, through the forest onwards, through the forest onwards; we see no other water; the herbage is worthless. We still go onwards, onwards through the forest. We see natives; a few natives we see: the men are two, the women one, the children two. We see the place called Nowergup.

We say, 'Where is there water? Here the water is bad.'

The natives say, 'Yonder the water is good—here it is bad. At Boranyup the water is good.'

We go onwards, onwards, onwards; at Boranyup we sleep— rain falls as we sleep at Boranyup.

6th day—Onwards through the forest, onwards through the forest, onwards through the forest; some of the others sit down; Auger sits down; Hunt sits down. Mr Roe, Mr Spofforth and I on horseback go onwards, onwards, onwards, onwards, through the forest onwards, through the forest onwards, through the forest onwards, through the forest onwards. We see the sea; then onwards, onwards, onwards; along the seashore onwards, along the seashore onwards, along the seashore onwards. We see the tracks of white men.

Then we turn back again, away we go back again, back again away; through the forest away, through the forest away, through the forest away; back again. We move, move, till we sit at Boranyup; we then eat kangaroo; Hunt and Auger had brought it in. At Boranyup we lie down; we sleep.

7th day—The next day away, away, away, away, returning, returning, on our tracks returning, on our tracks returning, on our tracks returning. At Barramba we sit down: we eat bread and meat; they eat freshwater mussels; the natives eat not freshwater mussels.

Away, away, away, away, away; we see the water of Djunjup; we shoot game. Away, away, away, through a forest away, through a forest away; we see no water. Through a forest away; along our tracks away, along our tracks away, along our tracks away, along our tracks away. We sleep at Ka-jil-up; rain falls; the water here is good: the horses feed—well did the horses feed.

8th day—Away, away; along our tracks away, along our tracks away; hills ascending: then pleasantly away, pleasantly away, away; through a forest away, through a forest away, through a forest away; we see a water—the water of Goonmarrarup. Along the river away, along the river away; a short distance along the river we go; then away, away, away, through a forest away; a short distance through a forest we go.

Then along another river away, away; we cross the river; away, a short distance away. At Neergammy we sleep, raising huts.

The others continue returning; we go away, away: in the forest we see no water; we see no footsteps; we see some papers—the papers put by Mr Mortimer we see: still we go onwards, along the sea away, along the sea away, along the sea away: through the bush away, through the bush away; then along the sea away, along the sea away. We see white men—three of them we see. They cry out, 'Where is water?' Water we give them—brandy and water we give them. We sleep near the sea.

Away, away go we (I, Mr Roe and Kinchela), along the shore away, along the shore away, along the shore away. We see no fresh water; along the shore away, along the shore away. We see a paper, the paper of Mortimer and Spofforth. Away we go, away, away, along the shore away, away, away, a long distance we go. I see Mr Smith's footsteps ascending a sandhill, onwards I go regarding his footsteps. I see Mr Smith dead. We commence digging the earth.

Two *sleeps* had he been dead; greatly did I weep, and much I grieved. In his blanket folding him, we scraped away the earth.

We scrape earth into the grave, we scrape the earth into the grave, a little wood we place in it. Much earth we heap upon it—much earth we throw up. No dogs can dig there, so much earth we throw up. The sun had just inclined to the westward as we laid him in the ground.

EDWARD JOHN EYRE
Oh Massa, Oh Massa, Come Here, 1841

Edward Eyre's crossing of southern Australia in 1840–41, in the company of Wylie (an Aborigine from the Albany area), is one of the most compelling stories in Australian exploration. Eyre's overseer, James Baxter, and two Aboriginal youths, Joey and Yarry, who accompanied the expedition, were destined not to complete the journey. Eyre's brooding account illustrates the point that Aboriginal 'guides' were not always willing participants and reliable companions. When their interests conflicted with those of their white leaders, they had few means of being heard. Sometimes, frustration, fear and continual displays of white superiority would lead to an outburst—even to murder.

Eyre and Wylie trudged on to Albany where they had long been given up for dead. As they stood above the town in dismal weather Eyre wept, remembering the disasters of the journey. Wylie, on the other hand, was welcomed home by his people with wild joyous cries.

April 29—Three miles from where we had halted during the heat of the day, we passed some tolerable grass, though dry, scattered at intervals among the scrub which grew here in dense belts, but with occasional openings between. The character of the ground was very rocky, of an oolitic limestone, and having many hollows on its surface. Although we had only travelled eighteen miles during the day, the overseer requested I would stop here, as he said he thought the clouds would again gather and that rain might fall tonight; that here we had large sheets of rock and many hollows in which the rainwater could be collected; but that if we proceeded onwards we might again advance into a sandy country and be unable to derive any advantage from the rain, even should it fall.

I intended to have travelled nearly the whole of this night to make up for the time we had lost in the heat of the day, and I was the more inclined to do this now that the violence of the storm had in some measure abated, and the appearance of rain had almost disappeared. The overseer was so earnest, however, and so anxious for me to stop for the night that, greatly against my own wishes, and in opposition to my better judgment, I gave way to him and yielded. The native boys too had made the same request, seconding the overseer's application, and stating that the violence of the wind made it difficult for them to walk against it.

The horses having been all hobbled and turned out to feed, the whole party proceeded to make break-winds of boughs to form a shelter from the wind, preparatory to laying down for the night. We had taken a meal in the middle of the day, which ought to have been deferred until night, and our circumstances did not admit of our having another now, so that there remained only to arrange the watching of the horses before going to sleep. The native boys had watched them last night, and this duty of course fell to myself and the overseer this evening. The first watch was from six o'clock p.m. to eleven, the second from eleven until 4 a.m., at which hour the whole party usually arose and made preparations for moving on with the first streak of daylight.

Tonight the overseer asked me which of the watches I would keep, and as I was not sleepy, though tired, I chose the first. At a quarter before six, I went to take charge of the horses, having previously seen the overseer and the natives lay down to sleep, at their respective break-winds, ten or twelve yards apart from one another. The arms and provisions, as was our custom, were piled up under an oilskin between my break-wind and that of the overseer, with the exception of one gun, which I always kept at my own sleeping place. I have been thus minute in detailing the position and arrangement of our encampment this evening, because of the fearful consequences that followed, and to show the very slight circumstances upon which the destinies of life sometimes hinge. Trifling as the arrangement of the watches might seem, and unimportant as I thought it at the time, whether I undertook the first or the second, yet was my choice, in this respect, the means under God's providence of my life being saved, and the cause of the loss of that of my overseer.

The night was cold, and the wind blowing hard from the south-west, whilst scud and nimbus were passing very rapidly by the moon. The horses fed tolerably well, but rambled a good deal, threading in and out among the many belts of scrub which intersected the grassy openings, until at last I hardly knew exactly where our camp was, the fires having apparently expired some time ago. It was now half past ten, and I headed the horses back in the direction in which I thought the camp lay, that I might be ready to call the overseer to relieve me at eleven. Whilst thus engaged, and looking steadfastly around among the scrub to see if I could anywhere detect the embers of our fires, I was startled by a sudden flash, followed by the report of a gun, not a quarter of a mile away from me.

Imagining that the overseer had mistaken the hour of the night and, not being able to find me or the horses, had taken that method to attract my attention, I immediately called out, but as no answer was returned I got alarmed and, leaving the horses, hurried up towards the camp as rapidly as I could. About a hundred yards from it, I met the King George's Sound native (Wylie), running towards me, and in great alarm crying out, 'Oh massa, oh massa, come here'—but could gain no information from him as to what had occurred. Upon reaching the encampment, which I did in about five minutes after the shot was fired, I was horror-struck to find my poor overseer lying on the ground, weltering in his blood and in the last agonies of death.

Glancing hastily around the camp I found it deserted by the two younger native boys, whilst the scattered fragments of our baggage, which I left carefully piled under the oilskin, lay thrown about in wild disorder, and at once revealed the cause of the harrowing scene before me.

Upon raising the body of my faithful but ill-fated follower, I found that he was beyond all human aid. He had been shot through the left breast with a ball, the last convulsions of death were upon him and he expired almost immediately after our arrival.

The frightful, the appalling truth now burst upon me, that I was alone in the desert. He who had faithfully served me for many years, who had followed my fortunes in adversity and in prosperity, who had accompanied me in all my wanderings, and whose attachment to me had been his sole inducement to remain with me in this last, and to him, alas, fatal journey, was now no more. For an instant, I was almost tempted to wish that it had been my own fate instead of his. The horrors of my situation glared upon me in such startling reality as for an instant almost to paralyse the mind. At the dead hour of night, in the wildest and most inhospitable wastes of Australia, with the fierce wind raging in unison with the scene of violence before me, I was left with a single native, whose fidelity I could not rely upon, and who for aught I knew might be in league with the other two, who perhaps were even now lurking about with the view of taking away my life as they had done that of the overseer. Three days had passed away since we left the last water, and it was very doubtful when we might find any more. Six hundred miles of country had to be traversed before I could hope to obtain the slightest aid or assistance of any kind, whilst I knew not that a single drop of water or an ounce of flour had been left by these murderers from a stock that had previously been so small.

With such thoughts rapidly passing through my mind, I turned to search for my double-barrelled gun which I had left covered with an oilskin at the head of my own break-wind. It was gone, as was also the double-barrelled gun that had belonged to the overseer. These were the only weapons at the time that were in serviceable condition, for though there were a brace of pistols they had been packed away, as there were no cartridges for them, and my rifle was useless, from having a ball sticking fast in the breech, and which we had in vain endeavoured to extract. A few days' previous to our leaving the last water, the overseer had attempted to wash out the rifle not knowing it was loaded, and the consequence was that the powder became wetted and partly washed away, so that we could neither fire it off nor get out the ball. I was, therefore, temporarily defenceless, and quite at the mercy of the natives, had they at this time come upon me.

Having hastily ripped open the bag in which the pistols had been sewn up, I got them out, together with my powder flask, and a bag containing a little shot and some large balls. The rifle

I found where it had been left, but the ramrod had been taken out by the boys to load my double-barrelled gun with, its own ramrod being too short for that purpose; I found it, however, together with several loose cartridges, lying about near the place where the boys had slept, so that it was evident they had deliberately loaded the firearms before they tried to move away with the things they had stolen; one barrel only of my gun had been previously loaded, and I believe neither barrel in that of the overseer.

After obtaining possession of all the remaining arms, useless as they were at the moment, with some ammunition, I made no further examination then, but hurried away from the fearful scene, accompanied by the King George's Sound native, to search for the horses, knowing that if they got away now no chance whatever would remain of saving our lives. Already the wretched animals had wandered to a considerable distance; and although the night was moonlight, yet the belts of scrub intersecting the plains were so numerous and dense that for a long time we could not find them; having succeeded in doing so at last, Wylie and I remained with them, watching them during the remainder of the night; but they were very restless, and gave us a great deal of trouble.

With an aching heart, and in most painful reflections, I passed this dreadful night. Every moment appeared to be protracted to an hour, and it seemed as if the daylight would never appear. About midnight the wind ceased, and the weather became bitterly cold and frosty. I had nothing on but a shirt and a pair of trousers, and suffered most acutely from the cold; to mental anguish was now added intense bodily pain. Suffering and distress had well nigh overwhelmed me, and life seemed hardly worth the effort necessary to prolong it. Ages can never efface the horrors of this single night, nor would the wealth of the world ever tempt me to go through similar ones again.

April 30—At last, by God's blessing, daylight dawned once more, but sad and heart-rending was the scene it presented to my view, upon driving the horses to what had been our last night's camp. The corpse of my poor companion lay extended on the ground, with the eyes open but cold and glazed in death. The same stern resolution and fearless open look which had characterised him when living stamped the expression of his countenance even now. He had fallen upon his breast four or five yards from where he had been sleeping, and was dressed only in his shirt. In all probability, the noise made by the natives in plundering the camp had awoke him; and upon his jumping up with a view of stopping them they had fired upon and killed him.

Around the camp lay scattered the harness of the horses, and the remains of the stores that had been the temptation to this fatal deed.

As soon as the horses were caught and secured, I left Wylie to make a fire, whilst I proceeded to examine into the state of our baggage, that I might decide upon our future proceedings. Among the principal things carried off by the natives were the whole of our baked bread, amounting to twenty pounds weight, some mutton, tea and sugar, the overseer's tobacco and pipes, a one-gallon keg full of water, some clothes, two double-barrelled guns, some ammunition and a few other small articles.

There were still left forty pounds of flour, a little tea and sugar, and four gallons of water, besides the arms and ammunition I had secured last night.

From the state of our horses, and the dreadful circumstances we were placed in, I was now obliged to abandon everything but the bare necessaries of life. The few books and instruments I had still left, with many of the specimens I had collected, a saddle and some other things, were thrown aside to lighten somewhat more the trifling loads our animals had to carry. A little bread was then baked, and I endeavoured once more to put the rifle in serviceable condition, as it was the only weapon we should have to depend upon in any dangers that might beset us. Unable in any way to take out the breech, or to extract the ball, I determined to melt it out, and for that purpose took the barrel off the stock and put the breech in the fire, holding the muzzle in my hand. Whilst thus engaged, the rifle went off, the ball whizzing close past my head; the fire, it seems, had dried the powder, which had been wetted, not washed out; and when the barrel was sufficiently heated the piece had gone off, to the imminent danger of my life from the incautious way in which I held it. The gun, however, was again serviceable; and after carefully loading it I felt a degree of confidence and security I had before been a stranger to.

At eight o'clock we were ready to proceed; there remained but to perform the last sad offices of humanity towards him whose career had been cut short in so untimely a manner. This duty was rendered even more than ordinarily painful by the nature of the country where we happened to have been encamped. One vast unbroken surface of sheet rock extended for miles in every direction, and rendered it impossible to make a grave. We were some miles away from the seashore, and even had we been nearer could not have got down the cliffs to bury the corpse in the sand. I could only, therefore, wrap a blanket around the body of the overseer and, leaving it enshrouded where he fell, escape from the melancholy scene accompanied by Wylie, under the influence of feelings which neither time nor circumstances will ever obliterate. Though years have now passed away since the enactment of this tragedy, the dreadful horrors of that time and scene are recalled before me with frightful vividness, and make me shudder even now when I think of them. A lifetime was crowded into those few short hours, and death alone may blot out the impressions they produced.

For some time we travelled slowly and silently onwards, Wylie preceding, leading one of the horses, myself following behind and driving the others after him, through a country consisting still of the same alternations of scrub and open intervals as before. The day became very warm, and at eleven, after travelling ten miles to the west, I determined to halt until the cool of the evening.

After baking some bread and getting our dinners, I questioned Wylie as to what he knew of the sad occurrence of yesterday.

He positively denied all knowledge of it—said he had been asleep and was awoke by the report of the gun, and that upon seeing the overseer lying on the ground he ran off to meet me. He admitted, however, that after the unsuccessful attempt to leave us and proceed alone to King George's Sound the elder of the other two natives had proposed to him again to quit the party, and try to go back to Fowler's Bay to the provisions buried there. But he had heard or knew nothing, he said, of either robbery or murder being first contemplated.

My own impression was that Wylie had agreed with the other two to rob the camp and leave us—that he had been cognisant of all their proceedings and preparations, but that when, upon the eve of their departure, the overseer had unexpectedly awoke and been murdered, he was shocked and frightened at the deed and, instead of accompanying them, had run down to meet me. My opinion upon this point received additional confirmation from the subsequent events of this day; but I never could get Wylie to admit even the slightest knowledge of the fatal occurrence, or that he had even intended to have united with them in plundering the camp and deserting. He had now become truly alarmed; and independently of the fear of the consequences which would attach to the crime, should we ever reach a civilised community again, he had become very apprehensive that the other natives, who belonged to quite a different part of Australia to himself and who spoke a totally different language, would murder him as unhesitatingly as they had done the white man.

We remained in camp until four o'clock, and were again preparing to advance when my attention was called by Wylie to two white objects among the scrub at no great distance from us, and I at once recognised the native boys, covered with their blankets only, and advancing towards us. From Wylie's account of their proposal to go back towards Fowler's Bay I fully hoped that they had taken that direction, and left us to pursue our way to the Sound unmolested. I was therefore surprised and somewhat alarmed at finding them so near us. With my rifle and pistols I felt myself sufficiently a match for them in an open country or by daylight. Yet I knew that as long as they followed like bloodhounds on our tracks our lives would be in their power at any moment that they chose to take them, whilst we were passing through a scrubby country or by night. Whatever their intention might be, I knew that if we travelled in the same direction with them our lives could only be safe by their destruction. Although they had taken fully one-third of the whole stock of our provisions, their appetites were so ravenous and their habits so improvident that this would soon be consumed, and then they must either starve or plunder us; for they had already tried to subsist themselves in the bush and had failed.

As these impressions rapidly passed through my mind, there appeared to me but one resource left to save my own life and that of the native with me: that was to shoot the elder of the two. Painful as this would be, I saw no other alternative if they still persisted in following us. After packing up our few things, and putting them upon the horses, I gave the bridles to Wylie to hold whilst I advanced alone with my rifle towards the two natives. They were now tolerably near, each carrying a double-barrelled gun, which was pointed towards me, elevated across the left arm and held by the right hand. As I attempted to approach nearer they gradually retreated.

Finding that I was not likely to gain ground upon them in this way, I threw down my weapons and advanced unarmed, hoping that if they let me near them I might suddenly close with the eldest and wrest his gun from him. After advancing about sixty or seventy yards towards them, I found that they again began to retreat, evidently determined not to let me approach any nearer, either armed or unarmed.

Upon this I halted and endeavoured to enter into parley with them, with a view to persuading them to return towards Fowler's Bay, and thus obviate the painful necessity I should have been under of endeavouring, for my own security, to take away the life of the eldest whenever I met with him, should they still persist in going the same road as myself. The distance we were apart was almost too great for parley, and I know not whether they heard me or not; though they halted and appeared to listen, they did not reply to what I said, and plainly wished to avoid all closer contact. They now began to call incessantly to Wylie and, in answer to my repeated efforts to get them to speak to me, only would say, 'Oh massa, we don't want you, we want Wylie'—thus fully confirming me in the opinion I had formed that Wylie had agreed to go with them before the deed of violence was committed. It was now apparent to me that their only present object in following us had been to look for Wylie and get him to join them. In this they were unsuccessful; for he still remained quietly where I left him holding the horses, and evidently afraid to go near them. There was no use wasting further time, as I could not get them to listen to me. The sun, too, was fast sinking in the horizon, we had been four days without finding water, and the probability was we had very far still to go before we could hope to procure any; every moment, therefore, was precious.

Having returned to Wylie, I made him lead one of the horses in advance, and I followed behind, driving the rest after him, according to the system of march I had adopted in the morning. As soon as the two natives saw us moving on, and found Wylie did not join them, they set up a wild and plaintive cry, still following along the brush parallel to our line of route, and never ceasing in their importunities to Wylie, until the denseness of the scrub and the closing in of night concealed us from each other.

I was now resolved to make the most of the opportunity afforded me, and by travelling steadily onwards to gain so much distance in advance of the two natives as to preclude the possibility of their again overtaking us until we had reached the water, if indeed we were ever destined to reach water again. I knew that they would never travel more than a few miles before lying down, especially if carrying all the bread they had taken, the keg of water, guns, and other articles. We had, however, seen none of these things with them, except the firearms.

Our road was over scrubby and stony undulations, with

patches of dry grass here and there; in other parts we passed over a very sandy soil of a red colour, and overrun by immense tufts of prickly grass (spinifex), many of which were three and four yards in diameter. After pushing on for eighteen miles, I felt satisfied we had left the natives far behind and, finding a patch of grass for the horses, halted for the remainder of the night. It was quite impossible, after all we had gone through, to think of watching the horses, and my only means of preventing them from straying was to close the chains of their hobbles so tight that they could not go far; having thus secured them, we lay down, and for a few hours enjoyed uninterrupted and refreshing sleep.

Moving on again on the 1st of May, as the sun was above the horizon, we passed through a continuation of the same kind of country for sixteen miles, and then halted for a few hours during the heat of the day. We had passed many recent traces of natives both yesterday and today, who appeared to be travelling to the westward. After dividing a pot of tea between us, we again pushed on for twelve miles, completing a stage of twenty-eight miles, and halting, with a little dry grass for the horses. It was impossible they could endure this much longer; they had already been five days without water, and I did not expect to meet with any for two days more, a period which I did not think they could survive.

As yet no very great change had taken place in the country; it was still scrubby and rocky, but the surface stone now consisted of a cream-coloured limestone of a fine compact character, and full of shells. The cliffs, parallel with which we were travelling, were still of about the same height, appearance and formation as before, whilst the inland country increased in elevation, forming scrubby ridges to the back, with a few open grassy patches here and there.

One circumstance in our route today cheered me greatly, and led me shortly to expect some important and decisive change in the character and formation of the country. It was the appearance for the first time of the banksia, a shrub which I had never before found to the westward of Spencer's Gulf, but which I knew to abound in the vicinity of King George's Sound, and that description of country generally. Those only who have looked out with the eagerness and anxiety of a person in my situation, to note any change in the vegetation or physical appearance of a country, can appreciate the degree of satisfaction with which I recognised and welcomed the first appearance of the banksia. Isolated as it was amidst the scrub, and insignificant as the stunted specimens were that I first met with, they led to an inference that I could not be mistaken in, and added, in a tenfold degree, to the interest and expectation with which every mile of our route had now become invested.

During the day the weather had been again cloudy with the appearance of rain; but the night turned out cold and frosty, and both I and the native suffered extremely. We had little to protect us from the severity of the season, never being able to procure firewood of a description that would keep burning long at once, so that between cold and fatigue we were rarely able to get more than a few moments rest at a time; and were always glad when daylight dawned to cheer us, although it only aroused us to the renewal of our unceasing toil.

May 2—We again moved away at dawn, through a country which gradually became more scrubby, hilly and sandy. The horses crawled on for twenty-one miles, when I halted for an hour to rest, and to have a little tea from our now scanty stock of water. The change which I had noticed yesterday in the vegetation of the country was greater and more cheering every mile we went, although as yet the country itself was as desolate and inhospitable as ever. The smaller banksias now abounded, whilst the *Banksia grandis*, and many other shrubs common at King George's Sound, were frequently met with.

The natives whose tracks we had so frequently met with, taking the same course as ourselves to the westward, seemed now to be behind us; during the morning we had passed many freshly lit fires, but the people themselves remained concealed; we had now lost all traces of them and the country seemed untrodden and untenanted. In the course of our journey this morning, we met with many holes in the sheets of limestone which occasionally coated the surface of the ground; in these holes the natives appeared to procure an abundance of water after rains, but it was so long since any had fallen that all were dry and empty now. In one deep hole only did we find the least trace of moisture; this had at the bottom of it perhaps a couple of wine glasses full of mud and water, and was most carefully blocked up from the birds with huge stones; it had evidently been visited by natives not an hour before we arrived at it, but I suspect they were as much disappointed as we were, upon rolling away all the stones, to find nothing in it.

After our scanty meal, we again moved onwards, but the road became so scrubby and rocky, or so sandy and hilly, that we could make no progress at all by night, and at eight miles from where we dined we were compelled to halt after a day's journey of twenty-nine miles; but without a blade even of withered grass for our horses, which was the more grievous because for the first time since we left the last water a very heavy dew fell, and would have enabled them to feed a little, had there been grass. We had now traversed 138 miles of country from the last water and, according to my estimate of the distance we had to go, ought to be within a few miles of the termination of the cliffs of the Great Bight.

May 3—The seventh day's dawn found us early commencing our journey. The poor horses still crawled on, though slowly. I was surprised that they were still alive, after the continued sufferings and privations they had been subject to. As for ourselves, we were both getting very weak and worn out, as well as lame, and it was with the greatest difficulty I could get Wylie to move, if he once sat down. I had myself the same kind of apathetic feeling, and would gladly have laid down and slept forever. Nothing but a strong sense of duty prevented me from giving way to this pleasing but fatal indulgence.

The road today became worse than ever, being one continued succession of sandy, scrubby and rocky ridges, and hollows formed on the top of the cliffs along which our course lay. After travelling two and a half miles, however, we were cheered and encouraged by the sight of sandy hills, and a low coast stretching beyond the cliffs to the south-west, though they were still some distance from us. At ten miles from where we had slept, a native road led us down a very steep part of the cliffs, and we descended to the beach. The wretched horses could scarcely move. It was with the greatest difficulty we got them down the hill; and now, although within sight of our goal, I feared two of them would never reach it. By perseverance we still got them slowly along for two miles from the base of the cliffs and then, turning in among the sand-drifts, to our great joy and relief, found a place where the natives had dug for water. Thus at twelve o'clock on the seventh day since leaving the last depot we were again encamped at water, after having crossed 150 miles of a rocky, barren and scrubby tableland...

July 7—...Having turned our horses loose, and piled up our baggage, now again greatly reduced, I took my journals and charts, and with Wylie forded the river about breast high. We were soon on the other side, and rapidly advancing towards the termination of our journey. The rain was falling in torrents, and we had not a dry shred about us, whilst the whole country through which we passed had, from the long-continued and excessive rains, become almost an uninterrupted chain of puddles. For a great part of the way we walked up to our ankles in water. This made our progress slow, and rendered our last day's march a very cold and disagreeable one.

Before reaching the Sound, we met a native who at once recognised Wylie, and greeted him most cordially. From him we learnt that we had been expected at the Sound some months ago but had long been given up for lost, whilst Wylie had been mourned for and lamented as dead by his friends and his tribe. The rain still continued falling heavily as we ascended to the brow of the hill immediately overlooking the town of Albany— not a soul was to be seen—not an animal of any kind—the place looked deserted and uninhabited, so completely had the inclemency of the weather driven both man and beast to seek shelter from the storm.

For a moment I stood gazing at the town below me—that goal I had so long looked forward to, had so laboriously toiled to attain, was at last before me. A thousand confused images and reflections crowded through my mind, and the events of the past year were recalled in rapid succession. The contrast between the circumstances under which I had commenced and terminated my labours stood in strong relief before me. The gay and gallant cavalcade that accompanied me on my way at starting, the small but enterprising band that I then commanded, the goodly array of horses and drays, with all their well-ordered appointments and equipment, were conjured up in all their circumstances of pride and pleasure; and I could not restrain a tear as I called to mind the embarrassing difficulties and sad disasters that had broken up my party, and left myself and Wylie the two sole wanderers remaining at the close of an undertaking entered upon under such hopeful auspices.

Whilst standing thus upon the brow overlooking the town, and buried in reflection, I was startled by the loud shrill cry of the native we had met on the road and who still kept with us: clearly and powerfully that voice rang through the recesses of the settlement beneath, whilst the blended name of Wylie told me of the information it conveyed. For an instant there was a silence still almost as death—then a single repetition of that wild joyous cry, a confused hum of many voices, a hurrying to and fro of human feet, and the streets which had appeared so shortly before gloomy and untenanted were now alive with natives— men, women, and children, old and young, rushing rapidly up the hill to welcome the wanderer on his return and to receive their lost one almost from the grave.

It was an interesting and touching sight to witness the meeting between Wylie and his friends. Affection's strongest ties could not have produced a more affecting and melting scene—the wordless, weeping pleasure, too deep for utterance, with which he was embraced by his relatives, the cordial and hearty reception given him by his friends, and the joyous greeting bestowed upon him by all, might well have put to the blush those heartless calumniators who, branding the savage as the creature only of unbridled passions, deny to him any of those better feelings and affections which are implanted in the breast of all mankind, and which nature has not denied to any colour or to any race.

WILLIAM WALL
Bad Is the Bush, 1844

 William Wall, Irish 'Collector and Preserver' at the Australian Museum, lacked the stiff upper lip so often encountered in explorers' writings. In 1844 he was sent on a collecting expedition with a bullock team from Sydney to the Murrumbidgee River. Reading Wall's account gives the idea that he was pushing into the deepest wilds, but in fact he was journeying down what was to become the Hume Highway—and even then a weekly coach ran the route.

Wall had a unique way with words. I have left his spelling and punctuation entirely as I found them, not least because I found it difficult to divine the state of Mr Clark, who was, Wall tells us, 'compleatly punalised when he saw us'!

Friday Septr. 13th.—The Morning very gloomy likely to rain left Hurley's at 6 oclock for Camden. Had a wreatched night no sleep full of anxiety. Paid 5/- for bed and Tea also 3/- coach hire to Camden—arrived at Camden at 8 ock. had breakfast payed 1/6—left for Brownlow Hill accompanied by Mr Lakeman the propicitor of the Camden Inn in a Spring Cart got lost in the Bush about 11 ock. after driving about for 4 hours we came in sight of a farm which he believed to be Mr M. McLeay...It rained on us all day so that we arrived in a dreadfull mess wet through.

Saturday Septr. 14th.—Got my cloths dry the weather still very Bad so wet that we are obliged to remain untill Monday casterated a young Cock for Mr McLeay...

Wednesday Septr. 18th.—The weather still favourable I leave here to accompany the Teams which are wating a short distance at a place called Mount Hunter left Mount Hunter this Morning at 9 ock...the Roads not the best and the Bullocks young and troublesome in travelling i collected a few Insects...I slept in a Team with an old Tarpolian over me, I must say it was anything but comfortable night fine shot nothing...

Friday Septr. 20th.—The morng. very gloomy and likely to rain had a smart shower...shot 1 mock Diamond Bird 1 yellow-eared Honey sucker and 2 common Birds saw nothing rare— one of our Bullocks droped on the Road which prevents us from going any further...

Monday Septr. 23rd.—Up at sunrise the morning fine but stormy we start from here about 7 oclk. feel Rather bettor in health *thank god* during the day I got very Ill so much so that I am determined to return by the mail tomorrow morng. Toward Evening we reached Luctam's Publick House and I their made enquiries about my fair to Sydney I thought by leaving my Box and other things that he might forward me on the Coach but the answer I received from him was dam his Eyes if he would forward his mother...

Wednesday Septr. 25th.—The morning very dark and likely to rain we are obliged to remane here all day as our Bullocks are compleatly nocked up for want of food some of them are not able to walk...my stomach very raw and sore attribute it solely to makeing use of the damper which is half of it raw Badly Baked I have longily this last week for a Potatoe and I put on a bold face and Begged a few on the Road which I found to do me a great deal of good...

Thursday Septr. 26th.—The morning fine saw a Black Satin Bird took a long ramble in the Bush saw nothing uncommon returned about 12 oclock one of our best Bullocks lost and 3 or 4 compleatly shook so that we cannot stir to day Woolingong is only 20 miles from us. I am quite tired of this mode of collecting in fact it is a very great loss of time as to get anything new along the Roads it is impossible I account for it in this way the Birds and animals are compleatly driven into Bush for miles oweing to the number of Teams and other vaicles going the Road many Persons with teams I notice carry guns and shoot every thing the *see*, worth haveing whether they have any *use* for it or not so that I consider this mode of collecting will never answer I am compleatly sick of Bullock driving and Bullock drivers their company is anything but edifying...

Saturday Septr. 28th.—...during the day we had a visit from a Bush Rainger one of the men fortunately was with me he demanded Tobacco but was told by the man that we had but very little when we started...the Bush Rainger not finding Tobacco was just in the act of putting his hands on the Gun which was lying against a tree when the man took it and placed it in one of our drays greatly against the wishes of the Bush Rainger no doubt as he might with eas '*Bailed*' us up and helpt himself to what he pleased I had a long walk in the morning and shot 1 sattin Bird male, 2 Black headed shrikes males and 1 Kangaroo rat female, with young the night very dark no Moon.

Sunday Septr. 29th.—...made 12 miles in all this was the best days travelling we had sinse we started = *Bad is the Bush* = we met a tribe of Blacks returning from the Berama Races...

Saturday October 5th.—We left Medigang eirly this morng. and proceeded on our journey for Browlow Hill where we expect to reach with smart walking and a *Gods assistenec* by Sundown it is a distance of 33 miles Parts of the day very wet and the Road very Bad and hevey we arrived late at night when I arrived I was compleatly stiffened and suffered a great deel of Pain in my legs in fact I thought I should have droped before I got their. Mr Clark the overseer was compleatly punalised when he saw us and sayed the cattle must have been illused as they never would have Died on the Road...I went to bed and scarcely able to go that far the night wet and very dark never saw one Bird on my journey or anything else worth collecting.

Sunday October 6th.—The morning fine when I awoke could scarsely stand with Pains in my legs but during the day I got a diel better I thought to borrow as much money as would take me to Sydney but a man might as well expect to fly as get a shilling from anyone on the farm...

Sunday October 13th.—No change has taken place in the weather as yet raning all last night and continues to do so today during the day in rane fell in torrens everything I have is in a mess of wet Bed clothing and all in fact my situation at pressent is anything but eviable to describe the miseary which I am placed in is impossible. Some portions of the day I go to a few burning lims wich are collected together for a fire or at least intended for one and their stand looking at the smoke as if it could warm or dry me when I grow tired of that *Move* I go to the dray and sit under it for an hour or so and in this way I spend the day...

Thursday October 17th.—This morning the weather chainged and I am extremely happy to say for the better we have at last a fine day the sun during the day very warm so that we were able to get our bed and bedding dried had the Rain continued much longer everything we had must have perrished everything we had in the Team was wet through and must have wrotted in another day or two this day we were without provisions of any sort and had to go to bed with nothing but a drink of sugar and water this day we had to go and beg but unfortunately for us we were unsuccessfull in our attempt all we could get was a promise for tomorrow I went out into the Bush for several hours but could see nothing but magpies and Crows not a single specimen worth shooting either for Eating or Preserving such a miserable place as this for specimens I never was in...

Friday October 18th.—Still in the same place this morning I went out eirly into the Bush in hope of collecting the Eirly Worm but the worm provied to be a snake wich was the only thing I saw...during the day the other two men came up with the Team and they brought with them a little provision about as much as will last two days with care so that we are here to a peg...

Tuesday October 22nd.—A glorious morning everything right

and Start eirly. This is my birthday I am 29 years of age today— we had an excellent day travelling 25 miles we went through Goulbourn and campt at a place called the Run of Waters. Goulbourn is a beautiful inland town by far the pretiest I have seen in the Colony it is built on a plain which extends for several miles with a splendid river running through the center previous to our arriving at Goulbourn our team got stuck in a mud hole...

Thursday October 24th.—The day extremely hot I finde it very tiresome travelling yesterday we traveled 22 miles and today we expect to go as many more I have to walk all the way as we have a very heavy load and only 2 horses my feet are cut and my Boots have no souls...

Saturday October 26th.—The morning dark and very cold. Soon after we started it commenced to rane and continued to rain hail and snow all day part of the day the men amused themselves throwing snow Balls...

Wednesday October 30th.—The morning fine started at sun rise and reached the station about 8 oclock had to swim the horses and Team over 2 Creeks which wet everything we had on our arrival we met Mr George McLeay and Mr Gunn the overseer who were delighted to see us and seemed surprised at our making the journey in so short a time I have now compleated my long and tiresome journey of 350 miles thank god in good health and trust with *gods blessing* to finde some new specimens—

LUDWIG LEICHHARDT
Commandant! Come Here, Very Good, 1844

 Ludwig Leichhardt, Prussian by birth and educated in Paris, arrived in Australia in 1840, and died somewhere in the vast outback sometime after 26 February 1848. Attempts to solve the mystery of Leichhardt's disappearance did much to spur further exploration.

His greatest work was the expedition from Brisbane to Port Essington, north-east of Darwin, in 1844–45. Here we join him in the vicinity of what is now Kakadu National Park, on the final leg home. He encounters not only Aborigines who speak English, but water buffaloes escaped from the abandoned settlement at Raffles Bay. Leichhardt was a culinary explorer; his willingness to experiment with native foods doubtless contributed to his success.

December 2—Whilst we were waiting for our bullock, which had returned to the running brook, a fine native stepped out of the forest with the ease and grace of an Apollo, with a smiling countenance, and with the confidence of a man to whom the white face was perfectly familiar. He was unarmed, but a great number of his companions were keeping back to watch the reception he should meet with. We received him, of course, most cordially; and upon being joined by another good-looking little man, we heard him utter distinctly the words, 'Commandant!', 'Come here!', 'Very good!', 'What's your name?'

If my readers have at all identified themselves with my feelings throughout this trying journey, if they have only imagined a tithe of the difficulties we have encountered, they will readily imagine the startling effect which these, as it were, magic words produced—we were electrified—our joy knew no limits, and I was ready to embrace the fellows who, seeing the happiness with which they inspired us, joined, with a most merry grin, in the loud expression of our feelings. We gave them various presents, particularly leather belts, and received in return a great number of bunches of goose feathers, which the natives use to brush away the flies. They know the white people of Victoria, and called them Balanda, which is nothing more than 'Hollanders', a name used by the Malays from whom they received it.[†]

We had most fortunately a small collection of words, made

---

† Victoria: the settlement at Port Essington.

by Mr Gilbert when at Port Essington, so that we were enabled to ask for water (*obert*); for the road (*allun*); for *limbo cardja*, which was the name of the harbour. I wished very much to induce them to become our guides; and the two principal men, Eooanberry and Minorelli, promised to accompany us, but they afterwards changed their minds.

My first object was to find good water, and our sable friends guided us with the greatest care, pointing out to us the most shady road to some wells surrounded with ferns which were situated in some tea-tree hollows at the confines of the plains and the forest. These wells, however, were so small that our horses could not approach to drink, so that we had to go to another set of wells, where I was obliged to stop, as one of our horses refused to go any farther. This place was about four miles ENE from our last camp. The wells were about six or eight feet deep, and dug through a sandy clay to a stiff bed of clay, on which the water collected. It would appear that the stiff clay of the plains had been covered by the sandy detritus of the ridges, from which the water slowly drained to the wells.

It was evident, from the pains which the natives had taken in digging them, that the supply of fresh water was very precarious. In many instances, however, I observed that they had been induced to do so simply by the want of surface water in the immediate neighbourhood of places where they obtained their principal supply of food. This was particularly the case near the sea-coast, where no surface water is found; whilst the various fish, and even vegetable productions, attract the natives who will, in such a case, even contract the habit of going the longest possible time without water or, at least, with very little, as is well shown in Mr Eyre's journey round the Australian Bight. We had to water our horses and the bullock with the stew pot; and had to hobble the latter, to prevent his straying and attacking the natives.

The natives were remarkably kind and attentive and offered us the rind of the rose-coloured eugenia apple, the cabbage of the seaforthia palm, a fruit which I did not know, and the nut-like swelling of the rhizoma of either a grass or a sedge. The last had a sweet taste, was very mealy and nourishing, and the best article of the food of the natives we had yet tasted. They called it *allamurr* (the natives of Port Essington, *murnatt*) and were extremely fond of it. The plant grew in depressions of the plains, where the boys and young men were occupied the whole day in digging for it. The women went in search of other food; either to the sea-coast to collect shellfish—and many were the broad paths which led across the plains from the forest land to the salt water—or to the brushes to gather the fruits of the season, and the cabbage of the palms.

The men, armed with a wommala, and with a bundle of goose spears, made of a strong reed or bamboo (?), gave up their time to hunting.[†] It seemed that they speared the geese only when flying, and would crouch down whenever they saw a flight of them approaching: the geese, however, knew their enemies so well that they immediately turned upon seeing a native rise to put his spear into the throwing stick. Some of my companions asserted that they had seen them hit their object at the almost incredible distance of 200 yards: but, making all due allowance for the guess, I could not help thinking how formidable they would have been had they been enemies instead of friends.

They remained with us the whole afternoon, all the tribe and many visitors, in all about seventy persons, squatting down with crossed legs in the narrow shades of the trunks of trees, and shifting their position as the sun advanced. Their wives were out in search of food but many of their children were with them, which they duly introduced to us. They were fine, stout, well-made men, with pleasing and intelligent countenances. One or two attempts were made to rob us of some trifles; but I was careful; and we avoided the unpleasant necessity of showing any discontent on that head. As it grew late and they became hungry, they rose, and explained that they were under the necessity of

† Wommala: woomera.

leaving us, to go and satisfy their hunger; but that they would shortly return, and admire, and talk again.

They went to the digging ground, about half a mile in the plain, where the boys were collecting *allamurr*, and brought us a good supply of it; in return for which various presents were made to them. We became very fond of this little tuber: and I dare say the feast of *allamurr* with Eooanberry's and Minorelli's tribe will long remain in the recollection of my companions. They brought us also a thin grey snake, about four feet long, which they put on the coals and roasted. It was poisonous, and was called *yullo*. At nightfall, after filling their coolamons with water, there being none at their camp, they took their leave, and retired to their camping place on the opposite hill where a plentiful dinner awaited them. They were very urgent in inviting us to accompany them and, by way of inducement, most unequivocally offered us their sable partners.

We had to take great care of our bullock, as the beast invariably charged the natives whenever he obtained a sight of them, and he would alone have prevented their attacking us; for the whole tribe were so much afraid of him that, upon our calling out, 'The bullock,' they were immediately ready to bolt— with the exception of Eooanberry and Minorelli, who looked to us for protection. I had not, however, the slightest fear and apprehension of any treachery on the part of the natives; for my frequent intercourse with the natives of Australia had taught me to distinguish easily between the smooth tongue of deceit, with which they try to ensnare their victim, and the open expression of kind and friendly feelings, or those of confidence and respect. I remember several instances of the most cold-blooded smooth-tongued treachery, and of the most extraordinary gullibility of the natives; but I am sure that a careful observer is more than a match for these simple children of nature, and that he can easily read the bad intention in their unsteady, greedy, glistening eyes.

Dec. 3—The natives visited us very early in the morning, with their wives and children, whom they introduced to us.

There could not have been less than 200 of them present; they were all well made, active, generally well-looking, with an intelligent countenance: they had in fact all the characters of the coast blacks of a good country, but without their treacherous dispositions. I started in a north-east direction and, as we were accompanied by the natives, I led our bullock by the nose-rope behind my horse. After crossing a plain, we were stopped by a large sheet of salt water, about three or four miles broad, at the opposite side of which a low range was visible; when Eooanberry explained that we had to go far to the south-east and south, before we could cross the river, and that we had to follow it down again at the other side. He expressed his great attachment to his wife and child, and obtained leave of us to return to his tribe, which had already retired before him.

Seeing the necessity of heading the river, which I considered to be the East Alligator—the longitude of which was, where we first came to it, 132° 40' according to reckoning—I returned to the forest land, and travelled along its belt of pandanus, to obtain a better ground for our cattle, and to avoid the scorching heat of the forenoon sun. Observing some singularly formed mountains rising abruptly out of the plains and many pillars of smoke behind them, I tried to get to them, but was again prevented by the broad salt water. We now steered for a distant smoke to the south-east by east, and had travelled fully seventeen miles on or along extensive plains, when we perceived seven natives returning on a beaten footpath from the salt water to the forest.

We cooeed—they ran! But when we had passed, and Charley stopped behind alone, they came up to him and, having received some presents, they showed us some miserable wells between two tea-tree groves; after which they hastened home. Our cattle were tired and thirsty, but we could give them nothing to drink except about six quarts of brackish water which fell to the share of our bullock. The feed, however, was rich and young, and during the night a heavy dew was deposited. Many flocks of geese came flying low over the plains, which made us hope that water was not very distant. Whilst we were passing the head of a small mangrove creek, four native dogs started out of a shady hole; but we looked in vain for fresh water...

Dec. 4—The natives returned very early to our camp. I went up to them and made them some presents, in return for which they offered me bunches of goose feathers, and the roasted leg of a goose, which they were pleased to see me eat with a voracious appetite. I asked for *allamurr*, and they expressed themselves sorry in not having any left, and gave us to understand that they would supply us, if we would stay a day. Neither these natives nor the tribe of Eooanberry would touch our green hide or meat: they took it, but could not overcome their repugnance, and tried to drop it without being seen by us. Poor fellows! They did not know how gladly we should have received it back! They were the stoutest and fattest men we had met.

We travelled at first to the east, in the direction from which the geese had come last night, but arriving at ridges covered with scrubby forest we turned to the north-east and continued in that direction about seven miles and a half, over ironstone ridges, when we again entered upon the plains of the river. Mountains and columns of smoke were seen all along its northern banks, but we afterwards found that most of those supposed columns of smoke were dust raised by whirlwinds. We now followed the river until a vine brush approached close to its bank, into the cool shade of which our bullock rushed and lay down, refusing to go any farther; our packhorse and most of our riding horses were also equally tired. The bed of the river had become very narrow, and the water was not quite brine, which made me hope that we should soon come to fresh water. Charley, Brown and John had gone into the brush to a camp of flying-foxes, and returned with twelve, which we prepared for luncheon, which allowed our bullock time to recover. They gave an almost incredible account of the enormous numbers of flying-foxes, all clustering round the branches of low trees, which drooped by the weight so near to the ground that the animals could easily be killed by cudgels. The seaforthia palm raised its elegant crown far above the patches of vine brush which we passed at the river side of the ridges.

After a delay of two hours, we again started, and travelled in a due south direction towards some thick smoke rising between two steep and apparently isolated rocky hills: they were about four miles distant and, when we arrived at their base, we enjoyed the pleasing sight of large lagoons surrounded with mangrove myrtles (*Stravadium*), with pandanus, and with a belt of reeds and nelumbiums. Man, horse and bullock rushed most eagerly into the fine water, determined to make up for the privation and suffering of the three last days. The lagoons were crowded with geese and, as the close vegetation allowed a near approach, Brown made good use of the few slugs that were still left, and shot ten of them, which allowed a goose to every man; a great treat to my hungry party.

Dec. 5—I determined upon stopping for a day, to allow our cattle to recover. Everybody was anxious to procure geese or flying-foxes; and, whilst three of my companions went to the flying-fox camp which we had visited yesterday, loaded with ironstone pebbles for shot, and full of the most sanguine expectations, Brown was busy at the lagoons, and even Mr Roper stirred to try his good luck. The two met with a party of natives, who immediately retreated at sight of Mr Roper; but during the afternoon they came to the other side of the lagoon opposite to our camp, and offered us some fish, a silurus and a tench (?) which they had speared in the lagoons.[†]

I made a sign for them to come over and to receive, as presents in exchange, some small pieces of iron, tin canisters and leather belts, which they did; but they became exceedingly noisy, and one of them, an old rogue, tried to possess himself quietly and openly of everything he saw, from my red blanket to the spade and stew pot. I consequently sent Brown for a horse, whose appearance quickly sent them to the other side of the lagoon, where they remained until nightfall. Brown offered them half a goose, which, however, they refused, probably because it

---

[†] Silurus: a catfish.

was not prepared by themselves, as they were very desirous of getting some of the geese which we had not yet cooked. Brown had shot nine geese, and our fox hunters returned with forty-four of the small species...

Dec. 6—The natives visited us again this morning, and it was evident that they had not been with their gins. They invited us to come to their camp, but I wished to find a crossing place and, after having tried in vain to pass at the foot of the rocky hills, we found a passage between the lagoons, and entered into a most beautiful valley, bounded on the west, east and south by abrupt hills, ranges and rocks rising abruptly out of an almost treeless plain clothed with the most luxuriant verdure, and diversified by large nymphaea lagoons, and a belt of trees along the creek which meandered through it. The natives now became our guides, and pointed out to us a sound crossing place of the creek, which proved to be the head of the saltwater branch of the East Alligator River. We observed a great number of long conical fish and crab traps at the crossing place of the creek and in many of the tributary saltwater channels; they were made apparently of flagellaria.

Here I took leave of our guides, the leader of whom appeared to be Apirk, a young and slender, but an intelligent and most active man. We now travelled again to the northward, following the outline of the rocky ridges at the right side of the creek and, having again entered upon the plains, we encamped at a very broad, shallow, sedgy, boggy lagoon...

Dec. 7—Apirk, with seven other natives, visited us again in the morning, and it seemed that they had examined the camp we had last left. They gave us to understand that we could travel safely to the northward without meeting any other creek. Apirk carried a little pointed stick, and a flat piece of wood with a small hole in it, for the purpose of obtaining fire. I directed my course to a distant mountain, due north from the camp, and travelled seven or eight miles over a large plain, which was composed of a rich dark soil, and clothed with a great variety of excellent grasses. We saw many columns of dust raised by whirlwinds and again mistook them for the smoke of so many fires of the natives. But we soon observed that they moved in a certain direction, and that new columns rose as those already formed drew off; and when we came nearer and passed between them, it seemed as if the giant spirits of the plain were holding a stately corroboree around us. They originated on a patch of ground divested of its vegetation by a late fire. There was a belt of forest to the northward, and the current of the sea breeze coming up the valley of the river from NNW seemed to eddy round the forest, and to whirl the unsheltered loose earth into the air...

At this time we were all sadly distressed with boils and with a prickly heat; early lancing of the former saved much pain. The cuts and sores of the hands festered quickly, but this depended much more on the want of cleanliness than anything else. A most dangerous enemy grew up amongst us in the irresistible impatience to come to the end of our journey; and I cannot help considering it a great blessing that we did not meet with natives who knew the settlement of Port Essington at an earlier part of our journey, or I am afraid we should have been exposed to the greatest misery, if not destruction, by an inconsiderate, thoughtless desire of pushing onward.

Dec. 8—...We encamped at a fine lagoon, occupied, as usual, with geese and ducks, and teeming with large fish, which were splashing about during the whole night. The situation of these lagoons was, by an observation of Castor, in latitude 12° 6' 2", and about nine miles north-west from our last camp. Immediately after our arrival, Brown went to shoot some geese, and met with two natives who were cooking some roots, but they withdrew in great haste as soon as they saw him. Soon afterwards, however, a great number of them came to the opposite side of the lagoon, and requested a parley.

I went down to them with some presents, and a young man came over in a canoe to meet me. I gave him a tin canister, and was agreeably surprised that the stock of English words increased considerably, that very few things we had were new to him, and that he himself had been at the settlement. His name was Bilge. He called me Commandant, and presented several old men to me under the same title. Several natives joined us, either using the canoe or swimming across the lagoon and, after having been duly introduced to me, I took four of them to the camp, where they examined everything with great intelligence, without expressing the least desire of possessing it.

They were the most confiding, intelligent, inquisitive natives I had ever met before. Bilge himself took me by the hand and went to the different horses, and to the bullock and asked their names and who rode them. The natives had always been very curious to know the names of our horses, and repeated 'Jim Crow', 'Flourbag', 'Caleb', 'Irongrey', as well as they could, with the greatest merriment. Bilge frequently mentioned 'Devil devil', in referring to the bullock, and I think he alluded to the wild buffaloes, the tracks of which we soon afterwards saw. We asked him for *allamurr*, and they expressed their readiness to bring it, as soon as the children and women, who both went under the denomination of piccaninnies, returned to the camp. The day being far advanced, and their camp a good way off, they left us, after inviting us to accompany them: but this I declined.

About ten o'clock at night, three lads came to us with *allamurr*; but they were very near suffering for their kindness and confidence, as the alarm of 'blackfellows' at night was a call to immediate and desperate defence. Suspecting, however, the true cause of this untimely visit, I walked up to them and led them into the camp, where I divided their *allamurr* between us; allowing them a place of honour on a tarpaulin near me for the remainder of the night, with which attention they appeared highly pleased. The night was clear and dewy, but became cloudy with the setting of the moon.

Dec. 9—The natives came to our camp at break of day, and Bilge introduced several old warriors of a different tribe, adding always the number of piccaninnies that each of them had; they appeared very particular about the latter, and one of the gentlemen corrected Bilge very seriously when he mentioned only two instead of three. Bilge had promised to go with us to Balanda but, having probably talked the matter over during the night with his wife, he changed his intentions; but invited us in the most urgent manner to stay a day at their camp. Although no place could be found more favourable for feed and water, and a day's rest would have proved very beneficial to our cattle, yet our meat bags, on which we now solely depended, were so much reduced that every day of travelling was of the greatest importance; as the natives told us that four days would bring us to the peninsula, and two more to Balanda.

We crossed the plain to the westward, in order to avoid the low rocks and rocky walls which bounded this fine country to the north and east. After about three miles, however, we turned to the northward, and travelled with ease through an open undulating forest, interrupted by some tea-tree hollows. Just before entering the forest, Brown observed the track of a buffalo on the rich grassy inlets between the rocks...

Dec. 10—We travelled about seven miles to the northward, but kept for the first three miles in a NNW direction from our camp, when we came to a small plain with a mangrove creek going to the westward; scarcely two miles farther, we crossed a drooping tea-tree swamp, of which a pandanus creek formed the outlet; and, two miles farther still, a large plain opened upon us in which we saw a great number of natives occupied in burning the grass, and digging for roots. All the country intervening between the creeks and the plain was undulating stringybark forest.

I left my companions in the shady belt of drooping tea-trees, and rode with Charley towards the natives in order to obtain information. They were, however, only women and children, and they withdrew at my approach, although I had dismounted and left my horse far behind with Charley. They had, however, allowed me to come near enough to make them understand my incessant calls for *obeit*, water, adding occasionally, 'Balanda; very good; no good.' When they had disappeared in the forest, Charley came with the horse, and we reconnoitred along the boundaries of the plain to find water but, not succeeding, we returned; and, when opposite to the place where I had left my companions, I cooeed for them to come over with me.

My cooee was answered by natives within the forest, and shortly afterwards four men came running out of it, and approached us most familiarly. They spoke English tolerably, knew the pipe, tobacco, bread, rice, ponies, guns etc., and guided us to a fine lagoon which I named, after the leading man of their tribe, Nyuall's Lagoon. Two of them promised to pilot us to Balanda and to *rambal*, which meant houses. They were very confiding, and women and children entered for the first time freely into our camp.

They examined everything, but made not the slightest attempt to rob us even of a trifle. When the women returned at night, they did not bring *allamurr* or, as it was here called, *murnatt*, but plenty of *imberbi*, the root of convolvulus, which grow abundantly in the plain. They gave us a very seasonable supply of it, but would not taste our dried beef, which they turned, broke, smelled, and then with a feeling of pity and disgust returned to us. Nyuall gave an amusing account of our state: 'You no bread, no flour, no rice, no backi—you no good! Balanda plenty bread, plenty flour, plenty rice, plenty backi! Balanda very good!'

He, Gnarrangan and Carbaret promised to go with us; and the first intended to take his wife with him. They imitated with surprising accuracy the noises of the various domesticated animals they had seen at the settlement; and it was amusing to hear the crowing of the cock, the cackling of the hens, the quacking of ducks, grunting of pigs, mewing of the cat etc., evident proofs that these natives had been in Victoria.

A heavy thunderstorm passed over at six o'clock and the natives either crowded into my tent, or covered their backs with sheets of tea-tree bark, turning them to the storm, like a herd of horses or cattle surprised by a heavy shower in the middle of a plain. Imaru lay close to me during the night and, in order to keep entire possession of my blanket, I had to allow him a tarpaulin.

Dec. 11—We travelled about seven miles NNW over an

immense plain, with forest land and rising ground to the eastward, in which direction four prominent hills were seen, one of which had the abrupt peak form of Biroa in Moreton Bay. The plain appeared to be unbounded to the westward. When we approached the forest, several tracks of buffaloes were seen; and, upon the natives conducting us along a small creek which came into the plain from the NNE, we found a well-beaten path and several places where these animals were accustomed to camp. We encamped at a good-sized waterhole in the bed of this creek, the water of which was covered with a green scum.

As the dung and tracks of the buffaloes were fresh, Charley went to track them, whilst Brown tried to shoot some ibises, which had been at the water and were now perched on a tree about 300 yards off. At the discharge of the gun a buffalo started out of a thicket, but did not seem inclined to go far. Brown returned, loaded his gun with ball, went after the buffalo and wounded him in the shoulder. When Charley came back to the camp, he, Brown and Mr Roper pursued the buffalo on horseback and, after a long run, and some charges, succeeded in killing it. It was a young bull, about three years old, and in most excellent condition. This was a great, a most fortunate event for us; for our meat bags were almost empty and, as we did not wish to kill Redmond, our good companion, we had the prospect of some days of starvation before us.

We could now share freely with our black friends, and they had not the slightest objection to eat the fresh meat, after baking it in their usual manner. They called the buffalo *anaborro*, and stated that the country before us was full of them. These buffaloes are the offspring of the stock which had either strayed from the settlement at Raffles Bay, or had been left behind when the establishment was broken up. They were originally introduced from the Malay islands. I was struck with the remarkable thickness of their skin (almost an inch) and with the solidity of their bones, which contained little marrow; but that little was extremely savoury.

We had a heavy thunderstorm at ten o'clock at night from the southward.

Dec. 12—Part of the meat was cut up and dried, and part of it was roasted to take with us; a great part of it was given to the natives who were baking and eating the whole day; and when they could eat no more meat, they went into the plains to collect *imberbi* and *murnatt* to add the necessary quantum of vegetable matter to their diet. The sultry weather, however, caused a great part of the meat to become tainted and maggoty. Our friend Nyuall became ill, and complained of a violent headache, which he tried to cure by tying a string tightly round his head.

CHARLES STURT
At Noon I Took a Thermometer, 1845

 In 1844, aged forty-nine and partially blind from earlier expeditionary work, Charles Sturt left his beloved wife Charlotte and started on a third and final expedition—this time aimed straight at the heart of the continent. There, he believed he would find 'a large body of inland waters', so he equipped the expedition with a boat for sailing on this mythical sea. Instead, he discovered a sea of seemingly endless sand dunes—the Simpson Desert—and temperatures so extreme they shrivelled his supplies, prostrated his horses and burst his thermometer.

Sturt was possessed by an almost manic obsession. Scurvy was turning his men's skin black, and large pieces of spongy flesh hung from the roofs of their mouths. They were rotting where they stood, but still Sturt, now all but blind, pushed on. He wrote that he preferred death to defeat by this terrible land.

Sturt survived. At midnight on 19 January 1846, ten days in advance of the rest of the party, the defeated and skeletal explorer rode up to his isolated seaside house in Adelaide and knocked on the door. Charlotte, answering the unexpected call, had all but given him up for dead.

This account begins with Sturt's thoughts about the grand

quest he was to undertake. We then join him in November 1845 retracing his steps towards where Innamincka is today.

To that man who is really earnest in the performance of his duty to the last, and who has set his heart on the accomplishment of a great object, the attainment of which would place his name high up in the roll of fame; to him who had well nigh reached the topmost step of the ladder, and whose hand had all but grasped the pinnacle, the necessity must be great, and the struggle of feeling severe, that forces him to bear back, and abandon his task.

Let any man lay the map of Australia before him, and regard the blank upon its surface, and then let me ask him if it would not be an honourable achievement to be the first to place foot in its centre.

Men of undoubted perseverance and energy in vain had tried to work their way to that distant and shrouded spot. A veil hung over Central Australia that could neither be pierced or raised. Girt round about by deserts, it almost appeared as if nature had intentionally closed it upon civilised man, that she might have one domain on the earth's wide field over which the savage might roam in freedom.

I had traced down almost every inland river of the continent, and had followed their courses for hundreds of miles, but they had not led me to its central regions. I had run the Castlereagh, the Macquarie, the Lachlan, the Murrumbidgee, the Hume, the Darling and the Murray down to their respective terminations, but beyond them I had not passed—yet—I looked upon Central Australia as a legitimate field, to explore which no man had a greater claim than myself, and the first wish of my heart was to close my services in the cause of Geography by dispelling the mists that hung over it...

The drought had now continued so long, and the heat been so severe, that I apprehended we might be obliged to remain another summer in these fearful solitudes. The weather was terrifically hot, and appeared to have set in unusually early.

Under such circumstances, and with so many causes to render my mind anxious, the reader will believe I did not sleep much. The men were as restless as myself, so that we commenced our journey before the sun had risen on the morning of the 10th of November, to give the horses time to take their journey leisurely. Slowly we retraced our steps, nor did I stop for a moment until we had got to within five miles of our destination, at which distance we saw a single native running after us and, taking it into my head that he might be a messenger from Mr Browne, I pulled up to wait for him; but curiosity alone had induced him to come forward.† When he got to within a hundred yards, he stopped and approached no nearer. This little delay made it after sunset before we reached the upper pool (not the one Mr Browne and I had discovered), and were relieved from present anxiety by finding a thick puddle still remaining in it, so that I halted for the night. Slommy, Bawley and the colt had hard work to keep up with the other horses, and it really grieved me to see them so reduced. My own horse was even now beginning to give way, but I had carried a great load upon him.

As we approached the water, three ducks flew up and went off down the creek southwards, so I was cheered all night by the hope that water still remained at the lower pool, and that we should be in time to benefit by it. On the 11th, therefore, early we pushed on, as I intended to stop and breakfast at that place before I started for the depot.

We had scarcely got there, however, when the wind, which had been blowing all the morning hot from the NE, increased to a heavy gale, and I shall never forget its withering effect. I sought shelter behind a large gum tree, but the blasts of heat were so terrific that I wondered the very grass did not take fire. This really was nothing ideal: everything, both animate and inanimate,

---

† J. H. Browne was medical officer to the expedition. He had been left in charge of the depot when Sturt and his party advanced.

gave way before it; the horses stood with their backs to the wind, and their noses to the ground, without the muscular strength to raise their heads; the birds were mute, and the leaves of the trees, under which we were sitting, fell like a snow shower around us.

At noon I took a thermometer, graduated to 127°, out of my box, and observed that the mercury was up to 125°. Thinking that it had been unduly influenced, I put it in the fork of a tree close to me, sheltered alike from the wind and the sun. In this position I went to examine it about an hour afterwards, when I found that the mercury had risen to the top of the instrument, and that its further expansion had burst the bulb, a circumstance that I believe no traveller has ever before had to record. I cannot find language to convey to the reader's mind an idea of the intense and oppressive nature of the heat that prevailed. We had reached our destination, however, before the worst of the hot wind set in; but all the water that now remained in the once broad and capacious pool to which I have had such frequent occasion to call the attention of the reader was a shining patch of mud nearly in the centre. We were obliged to dig a trench for the water to filter into during the night, and by this means obtained a scanty supply for our horses and ourselves.

About sunset the wind shifted to the west, a cloud passed over us and we had heavy thunder; but a few drops of rain only fell. They partially cooled the temperature, and the night was less oppressive than the day had been. We had now a journey of eighty-six miles before us: to its results I looked with great anxiety and doubt. I took every precaution to fortify the horses, and again reduced the loads, keeping barely a supply of flour for a day or two. Before dawn we were up, and drained the last drop of water, if so it could be called, out of the little trench we had made and, reserving a gallon for the first horse that should fall, divided the residue among them.

Just as the morning was breaking, we left the creek and travelled for thirty-six miles. I then halted until the moon should rise, and was glad to see that the horses stood it well. At seven we resumed the journey, and got on tolerably well until midnight, when poor Bawley, my favourite horse, fell; but we got him up again and, abandoning his saddle, proceeded onwards. At a mile, however, he again fell, when I stopped, and the water revived him. I now hoped he would struggle on, but in about an hour he again fell. I was exceedingly fond of this poor animal, and intended to have purchased him at the sale of the remnants of the expedition, as a present to my wife. We sat down and lit a fire by him, but he seemed fairly worn out.

I then determined to ride on to the depot and, if Mr Browne should still be there, to send a dray with water to the relief of the men. I told them, therefore, to come slowly on, and with Mr Stuart pushed for the camp. We reached the plain just as the sun was descending, without having dismounted from our horses for more than fifteen hours and, as we rode down the embankment into it, looked around for the cattle, but none were to be seen. We looked towards the little sandy mound on which the tents had stood, but no white object there met our eye; we rode slowly up to the stockade, and found it silent and deserted.

I was quite sure that Mr Browne had had urgent reasons for retiring. I had indeed anticipated the measure: I hardly hoped to find him at the fort, and had given him instructions on the subject of his removal, yet a sickening feeling came over me when I saw that he was really gone; not on my own account for, with the bitter feelings of disappointment with which I was returning home, I could calmly have laid my head on that desert, never to raise it again. The feeling was natural, and had no mixture whatever of reproach towards my excellent companion.

We dismounted and led our horses down to water before I went to the tree under which I had directed Mr Browne to deposit a letter for me. A good deal of water still remained in the channel, but nevertheless a large pit had been dug in it as I had desired. I did not drink, nor did Mr Stuart—the surface of the water was quite green, and the water itself was of a red colour, but I believe we were both thinking of anything but ourselves at that moment.[†] As soon as we had unsaddled the horses, we went to the tree and dug up the bottle into which, as agreed upon, Mr Browne had put a letter; informing me that he had been most reluctantly obliged to retreat; the water at the depot having turned putrid, and seriously disagreed with the men; he said that he should fall back on the old depot along the same line on which we had advanced, and expressed his fears that the water in Strzelecki's Creek would have dried, on the permanence of which he knew our safety depended.

Under present circumstances the fate of poor Bawley, if not of more of our horses, was sealed. Mr Stuart and I sat down by the stockade, and as night closed in lit a fire to guide Morgan and Mack on their approach to the plain. They came up about 2 p.m., having left Bawley on a little stony plain, and the colt on the sand ridges nearer to us, and in the confusion and darkness had left all the provisions behind; it therefore became necessary to send for some, as we had not had anything for many hours. The horses Morgan and Mack had ridden were too knocked up for further work, but I sent the latter on my own horse with a leather bottle that had been left behind by the party, full of water for poor Bawley, if he should still find him alive. Mack returned late in the afternoon, having passed the colt on his way to the depot, towards which he dragged himself with difficulty, but Bawley was beyond recovery; he gave the poor animal the water, however, for he was a humane man, and then left him to die.

We had remained during the day under a scorching heat, but could hardly venture to drink the water of the creek without first purifying it by boiling, and as we had no vessel until Mack should come up we had to wait patiently for his arrival at 7 p.m. About nine we had a damper baked, and broke our fast for the first time for more than two days.

[†] Mr Stuart: The thirty-year-old John McDouall Stuart who accompanied Sturt on this expedition.

While sitting under a tree in the forenoon Mr Stuart had observed a crow pitch in the little garden we had made, but which never benefited us, since the sun burnt up every plant the moment it appeared above the ground. This bird scratched for a short time in one of the soft beds, and then flew away with something in his bill. On going to the spot Mr Stuart scraped up a piece of bacon and some suet, which the dogs of course had buried. These choice morsels were washed and cooked, and Mr Stuart brought me a small piece of bacon, certainly not larger than a dollar, which he assured me had been cut out of the centre and was perfectly clean. I had not tasted the bacon since February, nor did I now feel any desire to do so, but I ate it because I thought I really wanted it in the weak state in which I was.

Perhaps a physician would laugh at me for ascribing the pains I felt the next morning to so trifling a cause, but I was attacked with pains at the bottom of my heels and in my back. Although lying down I felt as if I was standing balanced on stones; these pains increased during the day, insomuch that I anticipated some more violent attack, and determined on getting to the old depot as soon as possible; but as the horses had not had sufficient rest I put off my journey to 5 p.m. on the following day, when I left Fort Grey with Mr Stuart, directing Mack and Morgan to follow at the same hour on the following day, and promising that I would send a dray with water to meet them.

I rode all that night until 3 p.m. of the 17th, when we reached the tents, which Mr Browne had pitched about two miles below the spot we had formerly occupied. If I except two or three occasions on which I was obliged to dismount to rest my back for a few minutes, we rode without stopping, and might truly be said to have been twenty hours on horseback.

Sincere I believe was the joy of Mr Browne, and indeed of all hands, at seeing us return, for they had taken it for granted that our retreat would have been cut off. I too was gratified to find that Mr Browne was better, and to learn that everything had gone on well. Davenport had recently been taken ill, but the other men had recovered on their removal from the cause of their malady.

When I dismounted I had nearly fallen forward. Thinking that one of the kangaroo dogs in his greeting had pushed me between the legs, I turned round to give him a slap, but no dog was there, and I soon found out that what I had felt was nothing more than strong muscular action brought on by hard riding.

As I had promised I sent Jones with a dray load of water to meet Morgan and Mack, who came up on the 19th with the rest of the horses.

Mr Browne informed me that the natives had frequently visited the camp during my absence. He had given them to understand that we were going over the hills again, on which they told him that if he did not make haste all the water would be gone. It now behoved us therefore to effect our retreat upon the Darling with all expedition. Our situation was very critical, for the effects of the drought were more visible now than before the July rain—no more indeed had since fallen, and the water in the depot creek was so much reduced that we had good reason to fear that none remained anywhere else.

On the 18th I sent Flood to a small creek, between us and the pine forest, but he returned on the following day with information that it had long been dry. Thus then were my fears verified, and our retreat to the Darling apparently cut off. About this time too the very elements, against which we had so long been contending, seemed to unite their energies to render our stay in that dreadful region still more intolerable. The heat was greater than that of the previous summer; the thermometer ranging between 110° and 123° every day; the wind blowing heavily from NE to ESE filled the air with impalpable red dust, giving the sun the most foreboding and lurid appearance as we looked upon him. The ground was so heated that our matches, falling on it, ignited; and, having occasion to make a night signal, I found the whole of our rockets had been rendered useless, as on being lit they exploded at once without rising from the ground...

When we first arrived on the 27th of January, 1845, the cereal grasses had ripened their seed, and the larger shrubs were fast maturing their fruit; the trees were full of birds, and the plains were covered with pigeons—having nests under every bush. At the close of November of the same year—that is to say six weeks earlier—not an herb had sprung from the ground, not a bud had swelled, and, where the season before the feathered tribes had swarmed in hundreds on the creek, scarcely a bird was now to be seen. Our cattle wandered about in search for food, and the silence of the grave reigned around us day and night.

Was it instinct that warned the feathered races to shun a region in which the ordinary course of nature had been arrested, and over which the wrath of the Omnipotent appeared to hang? Or was it that a more genial season in the country to which they migrate rendered their desertion of it at the usual period unnecessary? Most sincerely do I hope that the latter was the case, and that a successful destiny will await the bold and ardent traveller who is now crossing those regions.[†]

On the 20th I sent Flood down the creek to ascertain if water remained in it or the farther holes mentioned by the natives, thinking that in such a case we might work our way to the eastward; but on the 23rd he returned without having seen a drop of water from the moment he left us. The deep and narrow channel I had so frequently visited, and which I had hoped might still contain water, had long been dry, and thus was our retreat cut off in that quarter also. There was apparently no hope for us—its last spark had been extinguished by this last disappointment; but the idea of a detention in that horrid desert was worse than death itself.

On the morning of the 22nd the sky was cloudy and the sun obscure, and there was every appearance of rain. The wind was somewhat to the south of west, the clouds came up from the north, and at ten a few drops fell; but before noon the sky was

† Sturt is referring to Leichhardt's expedition to Port Essington.

clear, and a strong and hot wind was blowing from the west: the dust was flying in clouds around us, and the flies were insupportable.

At this time Mr Stuart was taken ill with pains similar to my own, and Davenport had an attack of dysentery.

On the 23rd it blew a fierce gale and a hot wind from west by north, which rendered us still more uncomfortable: nothing indeed could be done without risk in such a temperature and such a climate. The fearful position in which we were placed caused me great uneasiness; the men began to sicken, and I felt assured that if we remained much longer the most serious consequences might be apprehended.

On the 24th, Mr Browne went with Flood to examine a stony creek about sixteen miles to the south, and on our way homewards. We had little hope that he would find any water in it but, if he did, a plan had suggested itself by which we trusted to effect our escape. It being impossible to stand the outer heat, the men were obliged to take whatever things wanted repair to our underground room, and I was happy to learn from Mr Stuart, who I sent up to superintend them, that the natives had not in the least disturbed Mr Poole's grave.[†]

On the 25th Mr Browne returned, and returned unsuccessful; he could find no water anywhere, and told me it was fearful to ride down the creeks and to witness their present state.

We were now aware that there could be no water nearer to us than 118 miles, i.e., at Flood's Creek, and even there it was doubtful if water any longer remained. To have moved the party on the chance of finding it would have been madness: the weather was so foreboding, the heat so excessive and the horses so weak that I did not dare to trust them on such a journey, or to risk the life of any man in such an undertaking. I was myself laid up, a helpless being, for I had gradually sunk under the attack of scurvy which had so long hung upon me. The day after I

[†] Some months earlier James Poole, Sturt's second-in-command, had died of scurvy.

arrived in camp I was unable to walk: in a day or two more, my muscles became rigid, my limbs contracted and I was unable to stir; gradually also my skin blackened, the least movement put me to torture, and I was reduced to a state of perfect prostration.

Thus stricken down, when my example and energies were so much required for the welfare and safety of others, I found the value of Mr Browne's services and counsel. He had already volunteered to go to Flood's Creek to ascertain if water was still to be procured in it, but I had not felt justified in availing myself of his offer. My mind, however, dwelling on the critical posture of our affairs, and knowing and feeling as I did the value of time, and that the burning sun would lick up any shallow pool that might be left exposed, and that three or four days might determine our captivity or our release, I sent for Mr Browne, to consult with him as to the best course to be adopted in the trying situation in which we were placed, and a plan at length occurred by which I hoped he might venture on the journey to Flood's Creek without risk.

This plan was to shoot one of the bullocks, and to fill his hide with water. We determined on sending this in a dray, a day in advance, to enable the bullock driver to get as far as possible on the road; we then arranged that Mr Browne should take the light cart, with thirty-six gallons of water, and one horse only; that on reaching the dray, he should give his horse as much water as he would drink from the skin, leaving that in the cart untouched until he should arrive at the termination of his second day's journey, when I proposed he should give his horse half the water and, leaving the rest until the period of his return, ride the remainder of the distance he had to go.

I saw little risk in this plan, and we accordingly acted upon it immediately: the hide was prepared and answered well, since it easily contained 150 gallons of water. Jones proceeded on the morning of the 27th, and on the 28th Mr Browne left me on this anxious and to us important journey accompanied by Flood. We calculated on his return on the eighth day, and the reader will judge how anxiously those days passed. On the day Mr Browne left me, Jones returned, after having deposited the skin at the distance of thirty-two miles.

On the eighth day from his departure, every eye but my own was turned to the point at which they had seen him disappear. About 3 p.m., one of the men came to inform me that Mr Browne was crossing the creek, the camp being on its left bank, and in a few minutes afterwards he entered my tent. 'Well, Browne,' said I, 'what news? Is it to be good or bad?'

'There is still water in the creek,' said he, 'but that is all I can say. What there is is as black as ink, and we must make haste, for in a week it will be gone.'

JOHN AINSWORTH HORROCKS
Shot by Camel, 1846

 In July 1846 John Ainsworth Horrocks set out towards Lake Torrens in search of good pastoral land. He took with him a veritable menagerie, but relations between the humans and the grazing species were strained from the very start. Indeed, open warfare seems to have broken out between them. At one point Horrocks 'killed a goat—the one that has given us so much trouble, and which Jimmy [an Aborigine] was delighted to see slaughtered, having in his hatred of the animal promised Garlick, the tent-keeper, a pint of ale if he would kill it next'.

But one member of Horrocks' expedition was trouble from the very start—Harry the cantankerous camel who bit Garlick severely on the head leaving 'two wounds of great length above his temples and another severe gash on his cheeks'. Earlier, Harry had attempted to eat an expedition goat.

The goats had their own strategy, for they became 'with the exception of one...very lame. They amused themselves last night by leaping on our tent, and tearing it in several places'.

But worse was to come, for the errant dromedary bit through the flour bags, wasting the expedition supplies, and was eventually to have the ultimate revenge when it shot Horrocks.

Horrocks dictated this letter to the expedition secretary on 8 September 1846. How he managed to transmit it despite severe wounds to his right hand and mouth, and how he maintained such a calm, detached tone, remain mysterious. He died on 23 September. Harry, incidentally, was the first camel used in inland Australia. After Horrocks' death, it took two bullets to kill him, and he managed to bite a stockman on the head before succumbing.

It is with the greatest regret I have to inform the committee and my fellow-colonists who subscribed towards the expenses of the expedition of its untimely and unfortunate termination. Having made an excursion, accompanied by Mr Gill, to the tableland on the west of Lake Torrens, to ascertain if it were practicable to form a depot in that neighbourhood, and not succeeding in finding either water or grass, I returned to Depot Creek, determined to make an excursion with the camel, as it was impracticable to take horses sufficiently far, from what I saw of the desolate and barren country.[†]

Having ascertained the morning previous to our departure, from the summit of the range behind Depot Creek, the bearings of the high land seen by Messrs Eyre and Darke to be 32 degrees north of west by compass, and the distance I considered about eight miles, I determined to make straight for that land.

With this view I started on the 28th of August, accompanied by Mr Gill and Bernard Kilroy, with provisions sufficient for three weeks and ten gallons of water, the camel being loaded with about 356 pounds. Our first day's journey brought us to one of the creeks running from Lake Torrens into the Gulf,

† Mr Gill: this was S. T. Gill who was to earn fame for his drawings and lithographs of colonial Australia.

distance about ten miles. The last six miles was over red sandhills, partially covered with oaten grass.

The second day's journey we camped on the west side of the tableland, distance fifteen miles. The first eight miles over a continuation of sandhills, the last seven miles over a country covered with stones and salsolaceous plants.

The next day we entered a light scrub and very heavy sandhills, fifteen miles.

The day following scrub and very heavy sandhills, and plain all covered with salsolaceous plants.

The day after, having made six miles, we reached a large saltwater lake about ten miles long and five miles broad. The land we were making for we distinctly saw I supposed about twenty-five miles distant. In rounding this lake, which I named Lake Gill, Bernard Kilroy, who was walking ahead of the party, stopped, saying he saw a beautiful bird which he recommended me to shoot to add to the collection.

My gun being loaded with slugs in one barrel and ball in the other, I stopped the camel to get at the shot belt, which I could not get without his laying down.

Whilst Mr Gill was unfastening it I was screwing the ramrod into the wad over the slugs, standing close alongside of the camel. At this moment the camel gave a lurch to one side, and caught his pack in the cock of my gun, which discharged the barrel I was unloading, the contents of which first took off the middle fingers of my right hand between the second and third joints, and entered my left cheek by my lower jaw, knocking out a row of teeth from my upper jaw.

In this dilemma I was fortunate in having two most excellent companions. We were now sixty-five miles from the depot or any water that we knew of, and all the water remaining was about five gallons. With very great reluctance I consented to Bernard Kilroy's entreaty for him to return back and fetch Mr Theatstone and two horses, as I knew part of the country was inhabited by a fierce lot of natives, as they had attacked Mr Gill and myself on my previous excursion. He said he was not afraid.

Therefore he left and reached the depot the next morning by about nine o'clock. Having missed the tracks during the night, he could not have walked less than 100 miles from the morning of the accident to the time he reached the depot, having most bravely accomplished his task.

Mr Gill stopped to nurse me and his attention and kindness were not to be surpassed. Considering the distance we were away and the uncertainty of Kilroy's reaching the depot, Mr Gill showed himself to be a brave and steady companion by remaining with me. He has taken several sketches of this country, which will show to those interested how very improbable it is that any stations can be made to the west of Lake Torrens. All the drainage is into freshwater ponds and salt lakes. The ponds are apparently dry in a very few days after rain, and the water which is in them being of a dark red ochreous color, the size of them varying from half an acre to five acres, and when full not more than six inches in depth.

The hill we were making for is table-topped, with precipitous sides, about seven miles in length. To the NNE are three smaller hills, and continuing on from them is a low land, gradually diminishing in height until it gains the land running from Lake Torrens. I did not find a spot where there was any probability of finding a spring. Grass there is none except a little wild oaten grass, which grows in the sand here and there, and that not sufficient to feed a horse.

It is with extreme sorrow I am obliged to terminate the expedition, as the two that were with me, the camel and myself were in excellent working condition; and had it not been for this accident it was my intention to have followed down this low land running to the NNE, and returned by Lake Torrens, a distance of between 300 and 400 miles; and would then have been able to have given a more accurate account, although I am convinced we should not have found one acre of ground to make a station on, judging from the land I have gone over and what I could discern with my eye, there being a sterile sameness throughout.

Had it been earlier in the season and my wounds healed up I should have started again.

On Sunday last I returned to the depot, horses, myself and party all completely knocked up.

I remain, yours truly,

J. HORROCKS.

JACKEY JACKEY
I Turned Round Myself and Cried, 1848

 Jackey Jackey's tale of the tragic end of John Kennedy's Cape York expedition forms one of the most moving narratives in Australian exploration history. It is beautifully and economically told—a riveting piece of literature.

Jackey Jackey, a native of the Hunter Valley, was a born leader who slowly assumed command as the crisis deepened. His account reveals an individual of exceptional resourcefulness and humanity, for he stayed with Kennedy to the very end.

After he was rescued, Jackey Jackey led a relief party to the spot where eight members of the original expedition had been left behind. He should be remembered among the first rank of Australian explorers.

I started with Mr Kennedy from Weymouth Bay for Cape York, on the 13th November, 1848, accompanied by Costigan, Dunn and Luff, leaving eight men at the camp at Weymouth Bay. We went on till we came to a river which empties itself into Weymouth Bay. A little further north we crossed the river; next morning a lot of natives camped on the other side of the river. Mr Kennedy and the rest of us went on a very high hill and came to a flat on the other side and camped there. I went on a good way next day; a horse fell down a creek; the flour we took with us lasted three days; we had much trouble in getting the horse out of the creek; we went on, and came out, and camped on the ridges; we had no water.

Next morning we went on and Luff was taken ill with a very bad knee. We left him behind, and Dunn went back again and brought him on; Luff was riding a horse named Fiddler; then we went on and camped at a little creek; the flour being out this day we commenced eating horse flesh, which Carron gave us when we left Weymouth Bay; as we went on we came on a small river, and saw no blacks there; as we proceeded we gathered nondas, and lived upon them and the meat. We stopped at a little creek and it came on raining, and Costigan shot himself; in putting his saddle under the tarpaulin, a string caught the trigger and the ball went in under the right arm and came out at his back under the shoulder.

We went on this morning all of us, and stopped at another creek in the evening, and the next morning we killed a horse named Browney, smoked him that night and went on next day, taking as much of the horse as we could with us, and went on about a mile and then turned back again to where we killed the horse, because Costigan was very bad and in much pain; we went back again because there was no water; then Mr Kennedy and I had dinner there, and went on in the afternoon leaving Dunn, Costigan and Luff at the creek.

This was at Pudding-pan Hill, near Shelburne Bay. Mr Kennedy called it Pudding-pan Hill.

We left some horse meat with the three men at Pudding-pan Hill, and carried some with us on a pack horse. Mr Kennedy wanted to make great haste when he left this place, in order to get the doctor to go down to the men that were ill. This was about three weeks after leaving Weymouth Bay. One horse was left with the three men at Pudding-pan Hill, and we (Kennedy and myself) took with us three horses. The three men were to remain there until Mr Kennedy and myself had gone to and returned from Cape York for them. Mr Kennedy told Luff and Dunn when he left them if Costigan died they were to come along the beach till they saw the ship, and then to fire a gun;

he told them he would not be long away, so it was not likely they would move from there for some time. They stopped to take care of the man that was shot; we (me and Mr Kennedy) killed a horse for them before we came away.

Having left these three men, we camped that night where there was no water; next morning Mr Kennedy and me went on with the four horses, two pack horses, and two saddle horses; one horse got bogged in a swamp. We tried to get him out all day, but could not; we left him there, and camped at another creek. The next day Mr Kennedy and I went on again, and passed up a ridge very scrubby, and had to turn back again, and went along gullies to get clear of the creek and scrub. Now it rained, and we camped; there were plenty of blacks here, but we did not see them, but plenty of fresh tracks, and camps and smoke.

Next morning we went on and camped at another creek, and on the following morning we continued going on, and camped in the evening close to a scrub; it rained in the night. Next day we went on in the scrub, but could not get through. I cut and cleared away, and it was near sundown before we got through the scrub—there we camped. It was heavy rain next morning, and we went on in the rain, then I changed horses and rode a black colt, to spell the other, and rode him all day, and in the afternoon we got on clear ground, and the horse fell down, me and all; the horse lay upon my right hip.

Here Mr Kennedy got off his horse and moved my horse from my thigh; we stopped there that night, and could not get the horse up; we looked to him in the morning and he was dead; we left him there; we had some horse meat left to eat and went on that day and crossed a little river and camped. The next day we went a good way; Mr Kennedy told me to go up a tree to see a sandy hill somewhere; I went up a tree, and saw a sandy hill a little way down from Port Albany. That day we camped near a swamp; it was a very rainy day.

The next morning we went on, and Mr Kennedy told me we should get round to Port Albany in a day; we travelled on all day till twelve o'clock (noon), and then we saw Port Albany;

then he said, 'There is Port Albany, Jackey—a ship is there—
you see that island there,' pointing to Albany Island; this was
when we were at the mouth of Escape River. We stopped there
a little while; all the meat was gone; I tried to get some fish but
could not; we went on in the afternoon half a mile along the
riverside, and met a good lot of blacks, and we camped. The
blacks all cried out '*powad, powad,*' and rubbed their bellies; and
we thought they were friendly, and Mr Kennedy gave them fish
hooks all round.

Everyone asked me if I had anything to give away, and I
said, 'No?' And Mr Kennedy said, 'Give them your knife, Jackey.'
This fellow on board was the man I gave the knife to, I am sure
of it; I know him well; the black that was shot in the canoe was
the most active in urging all the others on to spear Mr Kennedy;
I gave the man on board my knife. We went on this day, and I
looked behind, and they were getting up their spears, and ran
all round the camp which we had left; I told Mr Kennedy that
very likely those blackfellows would follow us, and he said, 'No,
Jackey, those blacks are very friendly.'

I said to him, 'I know these blackfellows well; they too much
speak.'

We went on some two or three miles and camped; I and Mr
Kennedy watched them that night, taking it in turns every hour
all night; by and by I saw the blackfellows; it was a moonlight
night; and I walked up to Mr Kennedy, and said to him, 'There
is plenty of blackfellows now.'

This was in the middle of the night; Mr Kennedy told me to
get my gun ready; the blacks did not know where we slept, as we
did not make a fire; we both sat up all night; after this, daylight
came, and I fetched the horses and saddled them; then we went
on a good way up the river, and then we sat down a little while,
and we saw three blackfellows coming along our track, and they
saw us, and one fellow ran back as hard as he could run, and
fetched up plenty more, like a flock of sheep almost; I told Mr
Kennedy to put the saddles on the two horses and go on, and the
blacks came up, and they followed us all the day; all along it was

244

raining, and I now told him to leave the horses and come on without them, that the horses made too much track.

Mr Kennedy was too weak, and would not leave the horses. We went on this day till towards evening, raining hard, and the blacks followed us all the day, some behind, some planted before; in fact, blacks all around following us. Now we went on into a little bit of a scrub, and I told Mr Kennedy to look behind always; sometimes he would do so, and sometimes he would not look behind to look out for the blacks. Then a good many blackfellows came behind in the scrub, and threw plenty of spears, and hit Mr Kennedy in the back first. Mr Kennedy said to me, 'Oh! Jackey, Jackey! shoot 'em, shoot 'em.'

Then I pulled out my gun and fired, and hit one fellow all over the face with buckshot; he tumbled down, and got up again and again and wheeled right round, and two blackfellows picked him up and carried him away. They went away then a little way, and came back again, throwing spears all around, more than they did before: very large spears. I pulled out the spear at once from Mr Kennedy's back, and cut out the jag with Mr Kennedy's knife; then Mr Kennedy got his gun and snapped, but the gun would not go off. The blacks sneaked all along by the trees, and speared Mr Kennedy again in the right leg, above the knee a little, and I got speared over the eye, and the blacks were now throwing their spears all ways, never giving over, and shortly again speared Mr Kennedy in the right side; there were large jags to the spears, and I cut them out and put them into my pocket. At the same time we got speared, the horses got speared too, and jumped and bucked all about, and got into the swamp.

I now told Mr Kennedy to sit down, while I looked after the saddle-bags, which I did; and when I came back again, I saw blacks along with Mr Kennedy; I then asked him if he saw the blacks with him, he was stupid with the spear wounds, and said, 'No.' Then I asked, where was his watch? I saw the blacks taking away watch and hat as I was returning to Mr Kennedy; then I carried Mr Kennedy into the scrub. He said, 'Don't carry me a good way,' then Mr Kennedy looked this way, very bad (Jackey rolling his eyes).

I said to him, 'Don't look far away,' as I thought he would be frightened; I asked him often, 'Are you well now?' and he said, 'I don't care for the spear wound in my leg, Jackey, but for the other two spear wounds in my side and back,' and said, 'I am bad inside, Jackey.'

I told him blackfellow always die when he got spear in there (the back); he said, 'I am out of wind, Jackey.' I asked him, 'Mr Kennedy, are you going to leave me?' and he said, 'Yes, my boy, I am going to leave you.' He said, 'I am very bad, Jackey; you take the books, Jackey, to the captain, but not the big ones— the governor will give anything for them.' I then tied up the papers. He then said, 'Jackey, give me paper and I will write.'

I gave him paper and pencil, and he tried to write, and then he fell back and died, and I caught him as he fell back and held him, and I then turned round myself and cried. I was crying a good while until I got well; that was about an hour, and then I buried him; I digged up the ground with a tomahawk, and covered him over with logs, then grass, and my shirt and trousers.

That night I left him near dark; I would go through the scrub, and the blacks threw spears at me, a good many, and I went back again into the scrub; then I went down the creek which runs into Escape River, and I walked along the water in the creek very easy, with my head only above water, to avoid the blacks, and get out of their way; in this way I went half a mile; then I got out of the creek, and got clear of them, and walked on all night nearly, and slept in the bush without a fire.

I went on next morning, and felt very bad, and I spelled for two days; I lived on nothing but salt water; next day I went on and camped one mile away from where I left, and ate one of the pandanus fruits; next morning I went on two miles, and sat down there, and I wanted to spell a little there, and go on; but when I tried to get up, I could not, but fell down again very tired and cramped, and I spelled here two days; then I went on again one mile, and got nothing to eat but one nonda; and I went on that day and camped, and on again next morning, about half a mile, and sat down where there was good water, and remained all day.

On the following morning, I went a good way, went round a great swamp and mangroves, and got a good way by sundown; the next morning I went and saw a very large track of blackfellows; I went clear of the track and of swamp or sandy ground; then I came to a very large river and a large lagoon; plenty of alligators in the lagoon, about ten miles from Port Albany. I now got into the ridges by sundown, and went up a tree and saw Albany Island; then next morning at four o'clock, I went on as hard as I could go all the way down, over fine clear ground, fine ironbark timber, and plenty of good grass; I went on round the point (this was towards Cape York, north of Albany Island) and went on and followed a creek down, and went on top of the hill, and saw Cape York; I knew it was Cape York, because the sand did not go on further.

I sat down then a good while; I said to myself, this is Port Albany, I believe inside somewhere; Mr Kennedy also told me that the ship was inside, close up to the mainland; I went on a little way, and saw the ship and boat; I met close up here two black gins and a good many piccaninnies; one said to me, '*Powad, powad.*' Then I asked her for eggs, she gave me turtle's eggs, and I gave her a burning glass; she pointed to the ship which I had seen before; I was very frightened of seeing the black men all along here, and when I was on the rock cooeeing, and murry murry glad when the boat came for me.

JOHN MACGILLIVRAY
Sir, I Am a Christian, 1848

 Just eight years after Eliza Fraser's experience, Barbara Thomson was shipwrecked and adopted by the Aborigines of Muralag Island, Torres Strait. There she lived as a wife of Boroto until she was 'rescued' four years later by the crew of the HMS *Rattlesnake*, commanded by Captain Owen Stanley. Speaking a mixture of English and the Kowrárega language she told of being well-treated by the Muralag men, if not the women. John MacGillivray, the naturalist on the *Rattlesnake* expedition, recorded her story of life beyond the frontier.

On the day after our arrival at Cape York the vessel from Sydney with our supplies anchored beside us and, besides provisions and stores, we had the additional pleasure of receiving five months' news from home.

On Oct. 16th, a startling incident occurred to break the monotony of our stay. In the afternoon some of our people on shore were surprised to see a young white woman come up to claim their protection from a party of natives from whom she had recently made her escape and who, she thought, would otherwise bring her back. Of course she received every attention, and was taken on board the ship by the first boat, when she told her story, which is briefly as follows.

Her name is Barbara Thomson: she was born at Aberdeen in Scotland and, along with her parents, emigrated to New South Wales. About four years and a half ago she left Moreton Bay with her husband in a small cutter (called the *America*), of which he was owner, for the purpose of picking up some of the oil from the wreck of a whaler, lost on the Bampton Shoal, to which place one of her late crew undertook to guide them; their ultimate intention was to go on to Port Essington. The man who acted as pilot was unable to find the wreck and, after much quarrelling on board in consequence, and the loss of two men by drowning, and of another who was left upon a small uninhabited island, they made their way up to Torres Strait, where, during a gale of wind, their vessel struck upon a reef on the eastern Prince of Wales Island.

The two remaining men were lost in attempting to swim on shore through the surf, but the woman was afterwards rescued by a party of natives on a turtling excursion, who when the gale subsided swam on board, and supported her on shore between two of their number. One of these blacks, Boroto by name, took possession of the woman as his share of the plunder; she was compelled to live with him, but was well treated by all the men, although many of the women, jealous of the attention shown her, for a long time evinced anything but kindness.

A curious circumstance secured for her the protection of one of the principal men of the tribe, a party from which had been the fortunate means of rescuing her and which she afterwards found to be the Kowrárega, chiefly inhabiting Múralug, or the western Prince of Wales Island. This person, named Piaquai, acting upon the belief (universal throughout Australia and the islands of Torres Strait so far as hitherto known) that white people are the ghosts of the Aborigines, fancied that in the stranger he recognised a long-lost daughter of the name of Gi(a)om, and at once admitted her to the relationship which he thought had formerly subsisted between them; she was immediately acknowledged by the whole tribe as one of themselves, thus ensuring an extensive connection in relatives of all denominations.

From the headquarters of the tribe, with which Gi'om thus became associated, being upon an island which all vessels passing through Torres Strait from the eastward must approach within two or three miles, she had the mortification of seeing from twenty to thirty or more ships go through every summer without anchoring in the neighbourhood, so as to afford the slightest opportunity of making her escape. Last year she heard of our two vessels (described as two war canoes, a big and a little one) being at Cape York—only twenty miles distant—from some of the tribe who had communicated with us and been well treated, but they would not take her over, and even watched her more narrowly than before. On our second and present visit, however, which the Cape York people immediately announced by smoke signals to their friends in Múralug, she was successful in persuading some of her more immediate friends to bring her across to the mainland within a short distance of where the vessels lay.

The blacks were credulous enough to believe that 'as she had been so long with them, and had been so well treated, she did not intend to leave them—only she felt a strong desire to see the white people once more and shake hands with them'; adding that she would be certain to procure some axes, knives, tobacco, and other much prized articles. This appeal to their cupidity decided the question at once. After landing at the sandy bay on the western side of Cape York, she hurried across to Evans Bay as quickly as her lameness would allow, fearful that the blacks might change their mind; and well it was that she did so, as a small party of men followed to detain her, but arrived too late. Three of these people were brought on board at her own request and, as they had been instrumental in saving her from the wreck, they were presented with an axe apiece, and other presents.

Upon being asked by Captain Stanley whether she really preferred remaining with us to accompanying the natives back to their island, as she would be allowed her free choice in the matter, she was so much agitated as to find difficulty in expressing her thankfulness, making use of scraps of English alternately with the Kowrárega language, and then, suddenly awaking to the recollection that she was not understood, the poor creature blushed all over, and with downcast eyes beat her forehead with her hand, as if to assist in collecting her scattered thoughts.

At length, after a pause, she found words to say, 'Sir, I am a Christian, and would rather go back to my own friends.'

At the same time, it was remarked by everyone that she had not lost the feelings of womanly modesty—even after having lived so long among naked blacks, she seemed acutely to feel the singularity of her position—dressed only in a couple of shirts, in the midst of a crowd of her own countrymen.

When first seen on shore our new shipmate presented so dirty and wretched an appearance that some people who were out shooting at first mistook her for a gin, and were passing by without taking further notice, when she called out to them in English, 'I am a white woman, why do you leave me?' With the exception of a narrow fringe of leaves in front, she wore no clothing, and her skin was tanned and blistered with the sun, and showed the marks of several large burns which had been received from sleeping too near the fire on cold nights; besides, she was suffering from ophthalmia, which had previously deprived her of the sight of one eye.[†] But good living, and every comfort (for Captain Stanley kindly provided her with a cabin and a seat at his table), combined with medical attention, very soon restored her health, and she was eventually handed over to her parents in Sydney in excellent condition.

Although perfectly illiterate, Mrs Thomson had made good use of her powers of observation, and evinced much shrewdness in her remarks upon various subjects connected with her residence among the blacks, joined to great willingness to communicate any information which she possessed...Several hundred words of the Kowrárega language, and a portion of its grammar, were also obtained from time to time, and most of these were subsequently verified. And, although she did not understand the language spoken at Cape York, yet, as some of the Gúdang people there knew the Kowrárega, through its medium I was usually able to make myself tolerably well understood, and thus obtain an explanation of some matters which had formerly puzzled me, and correct various errors into which I had fallen. It was well, too, that I took an early opportunity of procuring these words, for my informant afterwards forgot much of her lately acquired language, and her value as an authority on that subject gradually diminished.

Gi'om was evidently a great favourite with the blacks, and hardly a day passed on which she was not obliged to hold a levee in her cabin for the reception of friends from the shore, while other visitors, less favoured, were content to talk to her through the port. They occasionally brought presents of fish and turtle, but always expected an equivalent of some kind.

Her friend Boroto, the nature of the intimacy with whom was

[†] Although Patrick White based his novel *A Fringe of Leaves* on the story of Eliza Fraser, it is Barbara Thomson who gave him his title.

not at first understood, after in vain attempting by smooth words and fair promises to induce her to go back to live with him, left the ship in a rage, and we were not sorry to get rid of so impudent and troublesome a visitor as he had become. Previous to leaving, he had threatened that, should he or any of his friends ever catch his faithless spouse on shore, they would take off her head to carry back with them to Múralug; and so likely to be fulfilled did she consider this threat, being in perfect accordance with their customs, that she never afterwards ventured on shore at Cape York.

GERARD KREFFT
They Are Very Good Eating, 1857

 Gerard Krefft is one of the great unsung heroes of Australian biological exploration. He was appointed director of the Australian Museum but, following rumours that he was profiting from the sale of risqué postcards and problems with the museum trust, he was eventually dismissed. He refused to go quietly, however, and two bully-boys were employed to carry him out of his office—still in his director's chair—and eject him unceremoniously into Sydney's William Street.

Here we join him in happier times, on the Blandowski expedition to the junction of the Murray and Darling rivers in 1857. He is brought two *landwang*, as the local Aborigines knew the pig-footed bandicoot, *Chaeropus occidentalis* (now called *Chaeropus ecaudatus*). The species is today extinct and much of what we know about it comes from these notes. Unfortunately, Krefft was so hungry that he ate his precious specimens.

4 October 1857—After returning from a short excursion into the scrub, I fell in with a party of natives who had succeeded, at last, in securing a pair of the *Chaeropus* (male and female). They wanted

all manner of things for them, from a pair of blankets to a cutty pipe; and as I was very anxious to sketch them from life I emptied my pockets there and then, and promised a grand entertainment for the night with plenty of damper and sugar and tea.

On arrival at the camp, the two animals were secured in a birdcage; and I was busy for several hours sketching my charges in different positions.

Gould's figures of *Chaeropus occidentalis* are spiritless, being taken from dry skins.[†] I was in the habit of showing a copy of Sir Thomas Mitchell's tail-less specimen to the natives, urging them to procure animals of that description; of course, they did not recognise it as a *landwang* and I was furnished in consequence with a large number of the common bandicoot (*Perameles obesula*) minus the tail, which, to please me, had been screwed clean out.[††]

About sundown, when I was about to secure my animals for the night, one of the nimblest made its escape, jumping clean through the wires of the cage.

At a quick pace it ran up one of the sandstone cliffs, followed by myself, all of the blackfellows, men, women and children, and their dogs.

Here was a splendid opportunity for observing the motions of the animal; and I availed myself of it. The *Chaeropus* progressed like a broken-down hack in a canter, apparently dragging the hindquarters after it; we kept in sight of the fugitive and, after a splendid run up and down the sandhills, our pointer, who had been let loose, brought it to bay in a saltbush.

A large tin case was fitted up for the habitation of these animals, and provided with coarse barley grass, upon which, as the natives informed me, they feed. Insects, particularly grass-hoppers, were also put into the box, and though they were rather restless at first, and made vain attempts to jump out, they

† John Gould: the great animal illustrator.
†† Bandicoots often lose their tails. The original specimen of the pig-footed bandicoot had suffered such a loss.

appeared snug enough in the morning, having constructed a completely covered nest with the grass and some dried leaves.

During the daytime, they always kept in their hiding-places and, when disturbed, quickly returned to them; but as soon as the sun was down they became lively, jumping about and scratching the bottom of the case in their attempts to regain liberty. I kept these animals upon lettuces, barley grass, bread, and some bulbous roots for six weeks, until the camp was broken up, when they were killed for the sake of their skins.

I think that about eight specimens of this species were secured during our stay; several of which proved to be females with good-sized young ones in the pouch, which is very deep and runs upwards, not like that of a kangaroo. All were provided with eight teats, and bore two young ones, only one pair of teats being drawn.

I may mention here that the *Chaeropus* drinks a good deal of water, but will neither touch meat nor attack or eat mice, as the other members of this family do.

Their dung, which I often examined when out hunting, was entirely composed of grass, very dry, about the size of a sheep's trundles, but much longer, so that I believe that in a state of nature they feed principally upon vegetables. They are very good eating, and I am sorry to confess that my appetite more than once over-ruled my love for science.

JOHN MCDOUALL STUART
What He Imagined I Was, 1858–60

 Stuart was an independent, even lonely man with a fierce pride. He had a reputation as a hard drinker but achieved great things. His lasting innovation was to eschew large overland expeditions in favour of exploration by small, mobile parties. Stuart's great ambition was to cross the continent from south to north.

We first meet him here at a rather comic moment in 1858 in the vicinity of Lake Torrens when he asks directions from a solitary Aboriginal hunter. Then we join him two years later at his celebrations upon reaching the geographic centre of Australia.

Thursday, 24th June [1858], Sandhills—At 8.30 we left on a course of 340°, commencing with about two miles of rather heavy sandhills. At eight miles these sandhills diminished, and the valleys between them became much wider—both sandhills and valleys being well covered with grass and saltbush, with courses of lime and ironstone cropping out and running east and west. At twelve miles changed our course to 79° to examine a gum creek (Yarraout), which we ran down for water, but did not obtain it before four miles, when we found a small hole of rainwater. This creek seems to be a hunting ground of the natives, as we saw a great many summer wurleys on its banks.[†]

They had evidently been here today, for a little above where we first struck the creek we saw some smoke, but on following it up we found they had gone; mostly likely they had seen us and run away. The latter part of our journey today was over a stony plain, bounded on the west by the stony tableland with the sandhills on the top. All this country seems to have been under water, and is mostly likely the bed of Lake Torrens, or Captain Sturt's inland sea. In travelling over the plains, one is reminded of going over a rough, gravelly beach; the stones are all rounded and smooth. Distance today, thirty miles.

Friday, 25th June, Yarraout Gum Creek—Started at 9.40 from the point where we first struck the creek last night, bearing 20° for two miles, thence 61° for one mile to a high sandhill, thence 39° for one mile to a stony rise. My doubt of the blackfellow's knowledge of the country is now confirmed; he seems to be quite lost and knows nothing of the country, except

† Wurley: Aboriginal shelter.

what he has heard other blacks relate; he is quite bewildered and points all round when I ask him the direction of Wingillpin. I have determined to push into the westward, keeping a little north of west. Bearing 292° for five miles, sandhills; thence 327° to a table-hill nine miles. Camped without water. Our route today has been through sandhills, with a few miles of stones and dry reedy swamp, all well grassed, but no water.

We came across some natives who kept a long distance off. I sent our black up to them to ask in which direction Wingillpin lay. They pointed to the course I was then steering, and said, 'Five sleeps.' They would not come near to us. About three-quarters of an hour afterwards I came suddenly upon another native who was hunting in the sandhills. My attention being engaged in keeping the bearing, I did not observe him until he moved, but I pulled up at once, lest he should run away, and called to him. What he imagined I was I do not know; but when he turned round and saw me I never beheld a finer picture of astonishment and fear. He was a fine muscular fellow, about six feet in height, and stood as if riveted to the spot, with his mouth wide open, and his eyes staring.

I sent our black forward to speak with him, but omitted to tell him to dismount. The terrified native remained motionless, allowing our black to ride within a few yards of him, when, in an instant, he threw down his waddies, and jumped up into a mulga bush as high as he could, one foot being about three feet from the ground, and the other about two feet higher, and kept waving us off with his hand as we advanced. I expected every moment to see the bush break with his weight. When close under the bush, I told our black to inquire if he were a Wingillpin native.

He was so frightened he could not utter a word, and trembled from head to foot. We then asked him where Wingillpin was. He mustered courage to let go one hand and, emphatically snapping his fingers in a north-west direction, again waved us off. I take this emphatic snapping of his fingers to mean a long distance. Probably this Wingillpin may be Cooper's Creek. We then left him, and proceeded on our way through the sandhills...Distance today, twenty-four miles.

Sunday, 22nd April [1860], Small Gum Creek, under Mount Stuart, Centre of Australia—Today I find from my observations of the sun, 111° 00' 30", that I am now camped in the centre of Australia. I have marked a tree and planted the British flag there. There is a high mount about two miles and a half to the north-north-east. I wish it had been in the centre; but on it tomorrow I will raise a cone of stones, and plant the flag there, and name it Central Mount Stuart. We have been in search of permanent water today but cannot find any. I hope from the top of Central Mount Stuart to find something good to the north-west. Wind south. Examined a large creek; can find no surface water, but got some by scratching in the sand. It is a large creek divided into many channels, but they are all filled with sand; splendid grass all round this camp.

Monday, 23rd April, Centre—Took Kekwick and the flag, and went to the top of the mount, but found it to be much higher and more difficult of ascent than I anticipated. After a deal of labour, slips and knocks, we at last arrived on the top. It is quite as high as Mount Serle, if not higher. The view to the north is over a large plain of gums, mulga and spinifex, with watercourses running through it. The large gum creek that we crossed winds round this hill in a north-east direction; at about ten miles it is joined by another. After joining they take a course more north, and I lost sight of them in the far-distant plain. To the north-north-east is the termination of the hills; to the north-east, east and south-east are broken ranges, and to the north-north-west the ranges on the west side of the plain terminate. To the north-west are broken ranges; and to the west is a very high peak, between which and this place to the south-west are a number of isolated hills. Built a large cone of stones, in the centre of which I placed a pole with the British flag nailed to it. Near the top of the cone I placed a small bottle, in which there is a slip of paper, with our signatures to it, stating by whom it was raised. We then gave three hearty cheers for the flag, the emblem of civil and religious liberty, and may it be a sign to the natives that the dawn of liberty, civilisation, and Christianity is about to break upon them. We can see no water from the top.

WILLIAM WILLS
My Pulse Is at Forty-Eight, 1861

 William Wills' father was heartbroken by the failure of his son to return from the tragically incompetent expedition in which he and Robert O'Hara Burke, together with John King and Charles Gray, became the first men to cross the continent from south to north. Two years after their deaths, Wills senior published a book stubbornly titled *A Successful Exploration through the Interior of Australia.* In it he lovingly describes the future explorer as a babe in arms, then as a growing young man whom he treated as his friend and equal. I wonder what it cost this very un-Victorian father to read these entries from his son's diary? The young Wills reserved the last of his strength to write a farewell letter to his father.

Stranded at Cooper Creek after the depot party stationed there left for Menindie on the very day the explorers struggled back into camp, Wills describes the peculiar fate of one destined to die of starvation on a full stomach. Uncertainty still surrounds his condition: was it the nardoo or the greens he was eating that decided his fate? Gray was already dead; Burke and King had gone along the creek to find the Aborigines who were their only hope of survival. Back in Melbourne, Wills senior was desperately trying to raise the alarm to organise a rescue.

Monday, 3rd June 1861—Started at seven o'clock, and keeping on the south bank of the creek was rather encouraged at about three miles by the sound of numerous crows ahead; presently fancied I could see smoke, and was shortly afterwards set at my ease by hearing a cooee from Pitchery, who stood on the opposite bank, and directed me round the lower end of the waterhole, continually repeating his assurance of abundance of fish and bread. Having with some considerable difficulty managed to ascend the sandy path that led to the camp, I was conducted by the chief to a fire where a large pile of fish were just being cooked in the most approved style. These I imagined to be for the general consumption of the half-dozen natives gathered around, but it turned out that they had already had their breakfast. I was expected to dispose of this lot—a task which, to my own astonishment, I soon accomplished, keeping two or three blacks pretty steadily at work extracting the bones for me. The fish being disposed of, next came a supply of nardoo cake and water until I was so full as to be unable to eat any more; when Pitchery, allowing me a short time to recover myself, fetched a large bowl of the raw nardoo flour mixed to a thin paste, a most insinuating article, and one that they appear to esteem a great delicacy.[†] I was then invited to stop the night there, but this I declined, and proceeded on my way home.

Tuesday, 4th June 1861—Started for the blacks' camp intending to test the practicability of living with them, and to see what I could learn as to their ways and manners.

Wednesday, 5th June 1861—Remained with the blacks. Light rain during the greater part of the night, and more or less throughout the day in showers. Wind blowing in squalls from south.

Thursday, 6th June 1861—Returned to our own camp: found that Mr Burke and King had been well supplied with fish by the blacks. Made preparation for shifting our camp nearer theirs on the morrow...

Friday, 7th June 1861—Started in the afternoon for the

---

† Nardoo is the spore bundle of an aquatic fern which resembles a four-leafed clover.

blacks' camp with such things as we could take; found ourselves all very weak in spite of the abundant supply of fish that we have lately had. I, myself, could scarcely get along, although carrying the lightest swag, only about thirty pounds. Found that the blacks had decamped, so determined on proceeding tomorrow up to the next camp, near the nardoo field.

Saturday, 8th June 1861—With the greatest fatigue and difficulty we reached the nardoo camp. No blacks, greatly to our disappointment; took possession of their best mia-mia and rested for the remainder of the day.

Sunday, 9th June 1861—King and I proceeded to collect nardoo, leaving Mr Burke at home.

Monday, 10th June 1861—Mr Burke and King collecting nardoo; self at home too weak to go out; was fortunate enough to shoot a crow...

Tuesday, 11th June 1861—King out for nardoo; Mr Burke up the creek to look for the blacks.

Wednesday, 12th June 1861—King out collecting nardoo; Mr Burke and I at home pounding and cleaning. I still feel myself, if anything, weaker in the legs, although the nardoo appears to be more thoroughly digested.

Thursday, 13th June 1861—Last night the sky was pretty clear, and the air rather cold, but nearly calm, a few cir. st. hung about the NE horizon during the first part of the night. Mr Burke and King out for nardoo; self weaker than ever; scarcely able to go to the waterhole for water. Towards afternoon, cir. cum. and cir. st. begin to appear moving northward. Scarcely any wind all day.[†]

Friday, 14th June 1861—Night alternately clear and cloudy; cir. cum. and cum. st. moving northwards; no wind; beautifully mild for the time of year; in the morning some heavy clouds on the horizon. King out for nardoo; brought in a good supply. Mr Burke and I at home, pounding and cleaning seed. I feel weaker

† Wills' abbreviations refer to cloud formations: cirrus, stratus, cumulus.

than ever, and both Mr B. and King are beginning to feel very unsteady in the legs.

Saturday, 15th June 1861—Night clear, calm and cold; morning very fine, with a light breath of air from NE. King out for nardoo; brought in a fine supply. Mr Burke and I pounding and cleaning; he finds himself getting very weak, and I am not a bit stronger.

I have determined on beginning to chew tobacco and eat less nardoo, in hopes that it may induce some change in the system. I have never yet recovered from the constipation, the effect of which continues to be exceedingly painful.

Sunday, 16th June 1861—Wind shifted to north; clouds moving from west to east; thunder audible two or three times to the southward: sky becoming densely overcast, with an occasional shower about 9 a.m.

We finished up the remains of the camel Rajah yesterday, for dinner; King was fortunate enough to shoot a crow this morning.

The rain kept all hands in, pounding and cleaning seed during the morning. The weather cleared up towards the middle of the day, and a brisk breeze sprang up in the south, lasting till near sunset, but rather irregular in its force. Distant thunder was audible to westward and southward frequently during the afternoon...

Wednesday, 19th June 1861—Night calm; sky during first part overcast with cirro-cumulus clouds, most of which cleared away towards morning, leaving the air much colder; but the sky remained more or less hazy all night, and it was not nearly as cold as last night.

About eight o'clock a strong southerly wind sprang up, which enabled King to blow the dust out of our nardoo seed, but made me too weak to render him any assistance.

Thursday, 20th June 1861—Night and morning very cold, sky clear. I am completely reduced by the effects of the cold and starvation. King gone out for nardoo; Mr Burke at home pounding seed; he finds himself getting very weak in the legs. King holds out by far the best; the food seems to agree with him pretty well.

Finding the sun come out pretty warm towards noon, I took a sponging all over; but it seemed to do little good beyond the cleaning effects, for my weakness is so great that I could not do it with proper expedition.

I cannot understand this nardoo at all—it certainly will not agree with me in any form; we are now reduced to it alone, and we manage to consume from four to five pounds per day between us; it appears to be quite indigestible, and cannot possibly be sufficiently nutritious to sustain life by itself.

Friday, 21st June 1861—Last night was cold and clear, winding up with a strong wind from NE in the morning. I feel much weaker than ever and can scarcely crawl out of the mia-mia. Unless relief comes in some form or other, I cannot possibly last more than a fortnight.

It is a great consolation, at least, in this position of ours, to know that we have done all we could, and that our deaths will rather be the result of the mismanagement of others than of any rash acts of our own. Had we come to grief elsewhere, we could only have blamed ourselves; but here we are returned to Cooper's Creek, where we had every reason to look for provisions and clothing; and yet we have to die of starvation, in spite of the explicit instructions given by Mr Burke: 'That the depot party should await our return'; and the strong recommendation to the committee 'that we should be followed up by a party from Menindie'.

About noon a change of wind took place, and it blew almost as hard from the west as it did previously from the NE. A few cir. cum. continued to pass over towards east.

Saturday, 22nd June 1861—Night cloudy and warm; every appearance of rain; thunder once or twice during the night; clouds moving in an easterly direction; lower atmosphere perfectly calm. There were a few drops of rain during the night, and in the morning, about 9 a.m., there was every prospect of more rain until towards noon, when the sky cleared up for a time.

Mr Burke and King out for nardoo; the former returned much fatigued. I am so weak today as to be unable to get on my feet.

Sunday, 23rd June 1861—All hands at home. I am so weak as to be incapable of crawling out of the mia-mia. King holds out well, but Mr Burke finds himself weaker every day.

Monday, 24th June 1861—A fearful night. At about an hour before sunset, a southerly gale sprung up and continued throughout the greater portion of the night; the cold was intense, and it seemed as if one would be shrivelled up. Towards morning it fortunately lulled a little, but a strong cold breeze continued till near sunset, after which it became perfectly calm.

King went out for nardoo in spite of the wind, and came in with a good load; but he himself terribly cut up. He says that he can no longer keep up the work and, as he and Mr Burke are both getting rapidly weaker, we have but a slight chance of anything but starvation, unless we can get hold of some blacks.

Tuesday, 25th June 1861—Night calm, clear and intensely cold, especially towards morning. Near daybreak, King reported seeing a moon in the east, with a haze of light stretching up from it; he declared it to be quite as large as the moon, and not dim at the edges. I am so weak that any attempt to get a sight of it was out of the question; but I think it must have been Venus in the zodiacal light that he saw, with a corona around her.

26th—Mr Burke and King remain at home cleaning and pounding seed; they are both getting weaker every day; the cold plays the deuce with us, from the small amount of clothing we have: my wardrobe consists of a wide-awake, a merino shirt, a regatta shirt without sleeves, the remains of a pair of flannel trousers, two pairs of socks in rags, and a waistcoat, of which I have managed to keep the pockets together.[†] The others are no better off. Besides these, we have between us, for bedding, two small camel pads, some horse-hair, two or three little bits of rag, and pieces of oilcloth saved from the fire.

The day turned out nice and warm.

† Wide-awake: a felt hat.

Wednesday, 27th June 1861—Calm night; sky overcast with hazy cum. strat. clouds; an easterly breeze sprung up towards morning, making the air much colder. After sunrise there were indications of a clearing up of the sky, but it soon clouded in again, the upper current continuing to move in an easterly direction, whilst a breeze from the N and NE blew pretty regularly throughout the day. Mr Burke and King are preparing to go up the creek in search of the blacks. They will leave me some nardoo, wood and water, with which I must do the best I can until they return. *I think this is almost our only chance.* I feel myself, if anything, rather better, but I cannot say stronger: the nardoo is beginning to agree better with me; but without some change I see little chance for any of us. They have both shown great hesitation and reluctance with regard to leaving me, and have repeatedly desired my candid opinion in the matter. I could only repeat, however, that I considered it our only chance, for I could not last long on the nardoo, even if a supply could be kept up.

Thursday, 28th June 1861—Cloudy, calm and comparatively warm night, clouds almost stationary; in the morning a gentle breeze from east. Sky partially cleared up during the day, making it pleasantly warm and bright; it remained clear during the afternoon and evening, offering every prospect of a clear cold night.

Friday, 29th June 1861—Clear cold night, slight breeze from the east, day beautifully warm and pleasant. Mr Burke suffers greatly from the cold and is getting extremely weak; he and King start tomorrow up the creek to look for the blacks; it is the only chance we have of being saved from starvation. I am weaker than ever, although I have a good appetite and relish the nardoo much; but it seems to give us no nutriment, and the birds here are so shy as not to be got at. Even if we got a good supply of fish, I doubt whether we could do much work on them and the nardoo alone.

Nothing now but the greatest good luck can save any of us; and as for myself I may live four or five days if the weather continues warm. My pulse is at forty-eight, and very weak, and my legs and arms are nearly skin and bone. I can only look out, like Mr

Micawber, 'for something to turn up'.† Starvation on nardoo is by no means very unpleasant, but for the weakness one feels, and the utter inability to move one's self; for as far as appetite is concerned it gives the greatest satisfaction. Certainly fat and sugar would be more to one's taste; in fact those seem to me to be the great stand-by for one in this extraordinary continent: not that I mean to depreciate the farinaceous food, but the want of sugar and fat in all substances obtainable here is so great that they become almost valueless to us as articles of food, without the addition of something else.

W. J. WILLS

JOHN KING
They Looked upon Me As One of Themselves, 1861

 The Burke and Wills expedition had set out to discover 'if there really existed within their great continent a Sahara...great lakes...or watered plains which might tempt men to build new cities'. The expedition foundered, near the centre of the continent, in good if dry country, on the ignorance and prejudice of its leader Burke. He feared the Aborigines, and the constant use of his revolver in turn inspired fear in them.

John King was a young Irishman, an ex-soldier who had served in India and came to Australia specifically to join the expedition. As the sole survivor, cared for by the Aborigines, King is a fascinating figure. He was barely twenty when the relief party found him 'half-demented by starvation and loneliness'. Here King tells us what happened after he and Burke left Wills to search for the Aborigines. This account is

---

† Mr Micawber: the incurable optimist from Dickens' *David Copperfield* who after many failed schemes migrated to Australia and made his fortune at last.

taken from the evidence he presented to the subsequent royal commission into the disaster.

Mr Wills having returned, it was decided to go up the creek and live with the natives if possible, as Mr Wills thought we should have but little difficulty in obtaining provisions from them if we camped on the opposite side of the creek to them. He said he knew where they were gone, so we packed up and started. Coming to the gunyahs where we expected to have found them, we were disappointed, and seeing a nardoo field close by halted, intending to make it our camp.

For some time we were employed gathering nardoo, and laying up a supply. Mr Wills and I used to collect and carry home a bag each day, and Mr Burke generally pounded sufficient for our dinner during our absence; but Mr Wills found himself getting very weak, and was shortly unable to go out to gather nardoo as before, or even strong enough to pound it, so that in a few days he became almost helpless. I still continued gathering, and Mr Burke now also began to feel very weak, and said he could be of very little use in pounding; I had now to gather and pound for all three of us. I continued to do this for a few days; but finding my strength rapidly failing, my legs being very weak and painful, I was unable to go out for several days, and we were compelled to consume six days' stock which we had laid by.

Mr Burke now proposed that I should gather as much as possible in three days, and that with this supply we should go in search of the natives—a plan which had been urged upon us by Mr Wills as the only chance of saving him and ourselves as well, as he clearly saw that I was no longer able to collect sufficient for our wants. Having collected the seed as proposed, and having pounded sufficient to last Mr Wills for eight days, and two days for ourselves, we placed water and firewood within his reach and started; before leaving him, however, Mr Burke asked him whether he still wished it, as under no other circumstance would he leave him, and Mr Wills again said that he looked on it as our only chance. He then gave Mr Burke a letter and his watch for his father, and we buried the remainder of the field-books near the gunyah. Mr Wills said that, in case of my surviving Mr Burke, he hoped that I would carry out his last wishes, in giving the watch and letter to his father.

In travelling the first day, Mr Burke seemed very weak, and complained of great pain in his legs and back. On the second day he seemed to be better, and said that he thought he was getting stronger, but on starting did not go two miles before he said he could go no further. I persisted in his trying to go on, and managed to get him along several times, until I saw that he was almost knocked up, when he said he could not carry his swag, and threw all he had away. I also reduced mine, taking nothing but a gun and some powder and shot, and a small pouch and some matches. In starting again, we did not go far before Mr Burke said we should halt for the night; but as the place was close to a large sheet of water and exposed to the wind, I prevailed on him to go a little further, to the next reach of water, where we camped.

We searched about and found a few small patches of nardoo, which I collected and pounded, and with a crow, which I shot, made a good evening's meal. From the time we halted Mr Burke seemed to be getting worse, although he ate his supper; he said he felt convinced he could not last many hours, and gave me his watch, which he said belonged to the committee, and a pocketbook to give to Sir William Stawell, and in which he wrote some notes.[†] He then said to me, 'I hope you will remain with me here till I am quite dead—it is a comfort to know that someone is by; but, when I am dying, it is my wish that you should place the pistol in my right hand, and that you leave me unburied as I lie.'

That night he spoke very little, and the following morning I found him speechless, or nearly so, and about eight o'clock he

† Sir William Stawell: chairman of the Exploration Fund Committee.

expired. I remained a few hours there, but as I saw there was no use in remaining longer I went up the creek in search of the natives. I felt very lonely, and at night usually slept in deserted wurleys belonging to the natives. Two days after leaving the spot where Mr Burke died, I found some gunyahs where the natives had deposited a bag of nardoo, sufficient to last me a fortnight, and three bundles containing various articles. I also shot a crow that evening; but was in great dread that the natives would come and deprive me of the nardoo.

I remained there two days to recover my strength, and then returned to Mr Wills. I took back three crows; but found him lying dead in his gunyah, and the natives had been there and had taken away some of his clothes. I buried the corpse with sand and remained there some days but, finding that my stock of nardoo was running short, and as I was unable to gather it, I tracked the natives who had been to the camp by their footprints in the sand, and went some distance down the creek shooting crows and hawks on the road. The natives, hearing the report of the gun, came to meet me, and took me with them to their camp, giving me nardoo and fish; they took the birds I had shot and cooked them for me, and afterwards showed me a gunyah where I was to sleep with three of the single men. The following morning they commenced talking to me, and putting one finger on the ground and covering it with sand, at the same time pointing up the creek saying 'whitefellow', which I understood to mean that one white man was dead.

From this I knew that they were the tribe who had taken Mr Wills's clothes. They then asked me where the third white man was, and I also made the sign of putting two fingers on the ground and covering them with sand, at the same time pointing up the creek. They appeared to feel great compassion for me when they understood that I was alone on the creek, and gave me plenty to eat. After being four days with them, I saw that they were becoming tired of me, and they made signs that they were going up the creek and that I had better go downwards; but I pretended not to understand them. The same day they shifted camp and I followed them, and on reaching their camp I shot some crows, which pleased them so much that they made me a break-wind in the centre of their camp, and came and sat round me until such time as the crows were cooked, when they assisted me to eat them.

The same day one of the women, to whom I had given part of a crow, came and gave me a ball of nardoo, saying that she would give me more only she had such a sore arm that she was unable to pound. She showed me a sore on her arm, and the thought struck me that I would boil some water in the billy and wash her arm with a sponge. During the operation, the whole tribe sat round and were muttering one to another. Her husband sat down by her side, and she was crying all the time. After I had washed it, I touched it with some nitrate of silver, when she began to yell, and ran off, crying out, '*Mokow! Mokow!*' (Fire! Fire!)

From this time, she and her husband used to give me a small quantity of nardoo both night and morning, and whenever the tribe was about going on a fishing excursion he used to give me notice to go with them. They also used to assist me in making a wurley or break-wind whenever they shifted camp. I generally shot a crow or a hawk, and gave it to them in return for these little services. Every four or five days the tribe would surround me and ask whether I intended going up or down the creek; at last I made them understand that if they went up I should go up the creek, and if they went down I should also go down; and from this time they seemed to look upon me as one of themselves, and supplied me with fish and nardoo regularly. They were very anxious, however, to know where Mr Burke lay, and one day, when we were fishing in the waterholes close by, I took them to the spot. On seeing his remains, the whole party wept bitterly, and covered them with bushes.

After this, they were much kinder to me than before, and I always told them that the white men would be here before two moons; and in the evening when they came with nardoo and fish they used to talk about the 'whitefellows' coming, at the same time pointing to the moon. I also told them they would receive many presents, and they constantly asked me for tomahawks, called by them *bomay ko*. From this time to when the relief party arrived, a period of about a month, they treated me with uniform kindness, and looked upon me as one of themselves.

ALFRED HOWITT
Our Black Friends, 1861

 It was a search party led by Alfred Howitt, explorer, magistrate, geologist and ethnographer, which finally located John King. Howitt enjoyed the company of Aborigines and was intrigued by their culture. They in turn esteemed and trusted him. If Howitt had led the great expedition in place of the bellicose Burke, how different would have been the outcome.

September 15th—...I crossed at a neck of sand, and at a little distance again came on the track of a camel going up the creek; at the same time I found a native, who began to gesticulate in a very excited manner, and to point down the creek, bawling out, '*Gow, gow!*' as loud as he could. When I went towards him he ran away, and finding it impossible to get him to come to me I turned back to follow a camel track, and to look after my party. The track was visible in sandy places, and was evidently the same I had seen for the last two days. I also found horse traces in places, but very old.

Crossing the creek, I cut our track and rode after the party. In doing so I came upon three pounds of tobacco, which had lain where I saw it for some time. This, together with a knife-handle, fresh horse tracks and the camel track going eastward, puzzled me extremely, and led me into a hundred conjectures. At the lower end of the large reach of water before mentioned,

I met Sandy and Frank looking for me, with the intelligence that King, the only survivor of Mr Burke's party, had been found.

A little further on I found the party halted, and immediately went across to the blacks' wurleys, where I found King sitting in a hut which the natives had made for him. He presented a melancholy appearance—wasted to a shadow, and hardly to be distinguished as a civilised being but by the remnants of clothes upon him. He seemed exceedingly weak, and I found it occasionally difficult to follow what he said. The natives were all gathered round, seated on the ground, looking with a most gratified and delighted expression...

September 18th—Left camp this morning with Messrs Brahe, Welsh, Wheeler and King to perform a melancholy duty, which has weighed on my mind ever since we have encamped here, and which I have only put off until King should be well enough to accompany us. We proceeded down the creek for seven miles, crossing a branch running to the southward, and followed a native track leading to that part of the creek where Mr Burke, Mr Wills and King encamped after their unsuccessful attempt to reach Mount Hopeless and the northern settlements of South Australia, and where poor Wills died.

We found the two gunyahs situated on a sandbank between two waterholes and about a mile from the flat where they procured nardoo seed, on which they managed to exist so long. Poor Wills's remains we found lying in the wurley in which he died, and where King, after his return from seeking for the natives, had buried him with sand and rushes. We carefully collected the remains and interred them where they lay; and, not having a prayer-book, I read chap. xv of 1 Cor., that we might at least feel a melancholy satisfaction in having shown the last respect to his remains. We heaped sand over the grave, and laid branches upon it, that the natives might understand by their own tokens not to disturb the last repose of a fellow-being. I cut the following inscription on a tree close by, to mark the spot:

```
W. J. WILLS,
V. YDS.
W.N.W.
A. H.
```

The fieldbooks, a notebook belonging to Mr Burke, various small articles lying about, of no value in themselves but now invested with a deep interest from the circumstances connected with them, and some of the nardoo seed on which they had subsisted, with the small wooden trough in which it had been cleaned, I have now in my possession...

September 21st—Finding that it would not be prudent for King to go out for two or three days, I could no longer defer making a search for the spot where Mr Burke died, and with such directions as King could give I went up to the creek this morning with Messrs Brahe, Welsh, Wheeler and Aitkin. We searched the creek upwards for eight miles, and at length, strange to say, found the remains of Mr Burke lying among tall plants under a clump of box-trees, within two hundred yards of our last camp, and not thirty paces from our track. It was still more extraordinary that three or four of the party and the two black boys had been close to the spot without noticing it.

The bones were entire, with the exception of the hands and feet; and the body had been removed from the spot where it first lay, and where the natives had placed branches over it, to about five paces' distance. I found the revolver which Mr Burke held in his hand when he expired partly covered with leaves and earth, and corroded with rust. It was loaded and capped. We dug a grave close to the spot, and interred the remains wrapped in the Union Jack—the most fitting covering in which the bones of a brave but unfortunate man could take their last rest. On a box-tree, at the head of the grave, the following inscription is cut in a similar manner to the above:

```
┌─────────────────┐
│   R. O'H. B.    │
│   21 | 9 | 61   │
│     A. H.       │
└─────────────────┘
```

September 23rd—Went down the creek today in search of the natives...I could not think of leaving without showing them that we could appreciate and reward the kindness they had shown to Burke's party and particularly to King...Passed the first feeder of Strzelecki's Creek, going to the southward, and at a large reach of water below found the natives camped.

They made a great commotion when we rode up, but seemed very friendly. I unpacked my blanket, and took out specimens of the things I intended giving them—a tomahawk, a knife, beads, a looking-glass, comb and flour and sugar. The tomahawk was the great object of attraction, after that the knife, but I think the looking-glass surprised them most. On seeing their faces reflected, some seemed dazzled, others opened their eyes like saucers and made a rattling noise with their tongues expressive of wonder. We had quite a friendly palaver, and my watch amused them immensely. I made them understand that they were to bring the whole tribe up next morning to our camp to receive their presents, and we parted the best of friends.

September 24th—This morning, about ten o'clock, our black friends appeared in a long procession, men, women and children or, as they here also call them, piccaninnies; and at a mile distance they commenced bawling at the top of their voices as usual. When collected all together on a little flat, just below our camp, they must have numbered between thirty and forty, and the uproar was deafening. With the aid of King, I at last got them all seated before me and distributed the presents— tomahawks, knives, necklaces, looking-glasses, combs—amongst them. I think no people were ever so happy before, and it was very interesting to see how they pointed out one or another whom they thought might be overlooked. The piccaninnies were brought forward by their parents to have red ribbon tied round their dirty little heads. An old woman, Carrawaw, who had been particularly kind to King, was loaded with things.

I then divided fifty pounds of sugar between them, each one taking his share in a Union-Jack pocket-handkerchief, which they were very proud of. The sugar soon found its way into their mouths; the flour, fifty pounds of which I gave them, they at once called 'whitefellow nardoo', and explained that they understood that these things were given to them for having fed King. Some old clothes were then put on some of the men and women, and the affair ended in several of our party and several of the blackfellows having an impromptu 'corroboree', to the intense delight of the natives, and I must say, very much to our amusement.

They left, making signs expressive of friendship, carrying their presents with them. The men all wore a net girdle; and of the women some wore one of leaves, others of feathers. I feel confident that we have left the best impression behind us, and that the 'whitefellows', as they have already learned to call us, will be looked on henceforth as friends, and that, in case of emergency, anyone will receive the kindest treatment at their hands.

W. P. AULD
Where Are You Going?, 1862

 Although Burke and Wills had beaten him to the Gulf, Stuart remained determined to make the trek for himself. Pat Auld was twenty-one, working in the South Australian survey office, when he joined Sturt's expedition on 24 October 1861. He recalled that:

> At about four o'clock Stephen King called on me at the office to say goodbye.
> 'Where are you going?' I enquired.

'Out with Stuart.'

'Stuart! Where's he going?'

'To the Victoria River.'

'Oh, I'll go too.'

'I wish you could, old boy; but we start tomorrow, everything is fixed up.'

'Oh, I'll go.'

And so Auld set out to cross the continent from south to north. Here we find him, thirty years later, recalling his golden days. His reminiscences have the flavour of the beery hotels, salons and dining rooms of colonial Adelaide, but they still sparkle with a freshness that dust, starvation and sheer exhaustion sometimes stripped from accounts written on the spot.

On 25 June we struck the Roper, a splendid navigable river. The difficulty now was not too little water, but too much. How were we to get over? Several natives were seen on the banks, and we rode steadily up to them. We tried our best to make them understand that we wanted to get to the other side of the river, and for them to tell us how best to do it. They could not understand us. I know not what they thought of us, for we made all sorts of gestures. We had some fun over the matter, though, with the natives, for one member of the party fancied he could make them understand, and so said, 'Hold on a minute: let *me* talk to them...Look here, old man; how can we get over there?'

The native immediately replied in the same manner, pointing: 'Look here, old man, how can we get over there?'

'You old fool, don't repeat what I say, but show us where we can get across.'

The moment he stopped speaking our listener in fair imitation said, 'You-old-fool-don't-repeat-what-I-say-but-show-us-where-we-can-get-across.'

The natives are wonderful mimics.

They were astonished at our horses, and when one of the party dismounted they appeared thunderstruck. We could not get them to go near the heads of the horses. They pointed to the teeth, but they would go quite close to the heels. Stuart finding that no information could be got from the blacks filled his pipe and struck a match. The moment the lucifer struck the blacks gave a yell and cleared out. We found the banks of the river lined with cabbage trees, bamboos and shrubs. We were in latitude 14° 5'. Next day we returned to the last camp.

On 27 June we succeeded in crossing the river by a ford. The country here is really splendid. One of the horses got into the river and we tried to get him out, but the rope broke and the horse was seen to be drowned. It being dark we cut his throat to save his life, and left him till morning. Next day we cut up the horse and dried the meat. This food supply made all hands happy, for we had three meals that day—meals, too, of freshly killed meat with native cucumbers as a relish. We thought that horse meat surpassed anything we had ever eaten.

The country we now passed over was splendid soil, well grassed, though with some rough stony hills. Frew picked up a small turtle alive, and this greatly improved the flavour of our breakfast soup. We ascended some very rough stony hills, and got on to the top of sandy tableland, thick with stringybark pines and the fan palm. Some of these were over fifteen feet high. There was also grass—very coarse, mixed with spinifex. When we had gone about twelve or thirteen miles on the tableland we were suddenly stopped. We found ourselves on the edge of a precipice two or three hundred feet. The scenery was simply grand. Underneath us was a creek thickly wooded with palm trees, which were as straight as an arrow and fifty feet high. Then there was stringybark with dense foliage and a range of hills lay to the north-west. We had much difficulty in finding a place to descend, but at last we succeeded.

The top of the tableland, Stuart stated, 'is a layer of magnetic ironstone which attracted my compass 20°. Underneath is a layer of red sandstone which is very soft, and crumbles away with the action of the atmosphere. In the valley is growing an immense crop of grass.'

Our difficulty now was not want of water, but how to get

across the numerous creeks we met with and the stony hills, and the work told severely on the horses. On 28 July Stuart and I were up nearly all night taking observations, and found the latitude 13° 22' 30". We started next morning at seven-thirty with the feeling that we should see the Indian Ocean about eleven o'clock. We crossed a plain, and then entered a dense scrub with a complete network of vines. We had to use our tomahawks to cut the interlacing branches. Thring was in the lead making a way for Stuart, when he exultantly cried out, 'The sea, the sea!' This put fresh energy into us, and in the rush amongst the thick scrub Kekwick was nearly hanged, rehearsing the fate of Absolom. Having got through this belt of scrub— about a quarter of a mile—we were delighted at seeing the Indian Ocean.

Every man and every horse stood on the beach. Stuart dismounted, lit his pipe—he always lit his pipe when he did anything—took his boots off, and washed his feet in the sea. The beach was very uninteresting—it was simply blue mud, too soft to travel on, over which were scattered a few shells, some of which were collected. We then returned to the plain, and King cut JMDS on a large tree, of which during recent years a photograph has been taken by Inspector Foelsche. We proceeded on a course for a mile and a half, and camped on the banks of a small creek named by Stuart Charles Creek, after the eldest son of John Chambers (latitude 12° 13' 10").

Next day we started with the intention of making the head of the Adelaide River. But it took us over two hours' hard work to get the horses over this creek. Stuart, knowing that we would meet with more boggy places, made for the coast, two miles from our last camp—course north-west. A fringe of mangroves ran along the beach. We chopped down trees and left one in the centre, which we stripped of its branches. We fixed the Union Jack on it, cut in the bark 'Dig one foot south', dug a hole and buried an airtight tin case with a paper with the following notice:

'South Australian Great Northern Exploring Expedition. The exploring party, under the command of John McDouall Stuart, arrived at this spot on 25 July 1862, having crossed the entire continent of Australia, from the Southern to the Indian Ocean, passing through the centre. They left the City of Adelaide 25 October 1861, and the most northern station of the colony on 21 January 1862. To commemorate this happy event they have raised this flag bearing his name. All well God save the Queen.'

GEORG NEUMAYER
Storm on Kosciusko, 1862

 The exploration of the Australian Alps seems inextricably linked with Germans and Poles: Lhotsky, Strzelecki, Neumayer and von Guérard. Georg Balthasar von Neumayer was a German-born scientist with a passion for terrestrial magnetism, hydrography and meteorology. He came to Australia in the 1850s, established an observatory in Melbourne and set about conducting a magnetic survey of Victoria. His account of his visit to the summit of Mt Kosciusko in the late spring of 1862, in the company of the artist Eugène von Guérard, provides a terrifying example of Australia's fickle alpine weather. Von Guérard went on to paint one of his most memorable works from the view he obtained on that dramatic November day.

It was a day which Edward Brinkmann, assistant to Neumayer, would certainly never have forgotten. In the storm that blew across the mountain he became separated from the party and was given up for dead. Neumayer continued on with his magnetic survey and three weeks later the expedition, having travelled hundreds of kilometres, was near Albury.

Thick fog in the valley on the morning of the 18th but sky clear. Preparing everything for the ascent of Mt Kosciusko. Left three horses at Groggan's and took only Tommy with me packed with all the blankets and rations. Crossed the creek till it led us to a bluff commanding a fine view towards Mts Hope, Haystack and Pilot. Descended a steep incline towards the valley of the Leather Jacket Creek (3184) where we arrived at 10.30 a.m.; temp. of the creek 56.7°; that of the air 84.5°.[†] Left the place and ascended the steep banks of the creek under much difficulty although the horse behaved admirably. Continued ascending till we arrived at the region of dead timber (4663). The weather was quite calm, but the sky very threatening.

About this time all of our party except myself felt very ill so that we were obliged to stop here for some time and take some brandy and water, which enabled them better to resist the effects of heat and fatigue. Crossed an extensive flat at 1.46 p.m., then after a continual ascent came to the upper limit of dwarf timber (6254) (*Eucalyptus*), and resolved to pitch our tents. The aneroid ceased to indicate the pressure of air since the last 1000 feet, the little compensation weight being fixed by the case of the instrument.

We arrived at this spot at 5 p.m.; it must be mentioned, however, that the ascent would not have taken all this time had we been able to keep up a proper pace, for with the exception of the crossing of the Leather Jacket the ascent of Mt Kosciusko from the Victorian side is an easy one when compared with that of some of the equally high mountains in other parts of the world; but, throughout, our progress was retarded partly by the necessity of clearing a path, and the illness of the men. The vegetation near the camping place reminds one very much of that of the Alps except that the strange look of the dwarf gum trees introduces rather a new feature.

Inspected the instruments and found to my great satisfaction that none of them had received any serious injury from the unavoidable knocking about during the ascent. The temp. of the boiling point 200.27°; 9 p.m., few drops of rain but calm and overcast. An immense number of Bogong moths about the

[†] Numbers in parentheses indicate feet above sea level.

camp. By 10 p.m. a strong breeze rose from the north, which continued in puffs nearly throughout the night. The flapping of the tent although very annoying did not seriously interfere with our sound rest.

November 19th at 5 a.m. threatening weather, the wind veering rather more to the west; bar 23.960", temp 54.9°. This place commands a fine view of the Manroo Plains and Thredbo River. Packed some of the magnetic instruments on Tommy and left our camp at 7 a.m. and after crossing some extensive snowfields arrived at what I named the Pinnacle Hill (7038) at 8 a.m. Resolved to make some observations on terrestrial magnetism and placed the theodolite on a hill, composed of granite boulders; the weather, however, becoming unsettled and the wind being still strong from the north, I deferred these observations until my return.

The instruments were consequently packed up again and as it evidently would be extremely difficult to take the horse any farther on, I ordered Edward to secure him properly and provide him with food for the time of our absence, and then started for what we supposed, and subsequently found to be, the highest point of Mt Kosciusko. Our path led us across ravines, snowfields and extensive marshes, covered with alpine vegetation, to a little lake at the foot of the highest summit. A few hundred feet higher up and we reached the watershed between the Murray and Snowy Rivers, the one flowing towards the Indian, the other into the Pacific Ocean. Passing over some snowfields of considerable extent, we arrived at the summit (7176) at 11 a.m.; temp. 54.5°.

As the wind blew very strong from the north and rain fell occasionally in showers, I gave Edward my maps to put under shelter during the observations, and I hurried them as much as possible in order that we might yet have time to ascend the Snowy Peak, another point of Mt Kosciusko, which from its being thickly covered with snow has frequently been believed to be its highest point. Descended into a flat and made a short halt for the purpose of taking dinner, during which I learned that my friend M. de Guérard celebrated his fiftieth birthday on this very day and we accordingly drank his health.

All at once Edward recollected that he had forgotten to bring my maps with him on leaving the last hill; not much importance was attached to this at the time, as I thought it an easy matter to go and fetch them on our return. At 1 p.m. we reached the Snowy Peak (7140), but the wind was so very strong and the granite boulders, of which the summit is composed, were so piled up that I did not think it prudent to take the barometers to the top and accordingly mounted them some forty feet lower down. Temp. of boiling point 198.62°.

M. de Guérard, meanwhile, had seated himself on the summit, which affords a beautiful view of the mountainous country of New South Wales and Victoria, as well as the plains of the Murray River, and was taking a sketch of the scenery when, just as I was completing my observations, he called out that it appeared to him a heavy storm was approaching from the New South Wales side. It was apparent from the barometrical readings that the pressure of air was rapidly decreasing, and on ascending to the top I became convinced there was no time to be lost and that we must hasten our return to camp as much as possible. Before leaving, I distinctly stated to our whole party that we were seven miles distant from our camp in a NNW direction, and that our course would therefore have to be SSE.

Left the Snowy Peak at 2.25 p.m. When we reached the snowfields at the foot of the summit, I told Edward to run up and fetch the maps he had forgotten and advised him to take our dog Hector with him. He had scarcely quitted our party five minutes when a terrific gale set in from west and the whole top of the mount was enveloped in dense clouds, the rain falling in torrents. Seeing the danger he was exposed to from the state of the weather, of becoming separated from our party, I cried out to him in order to recall him, but unfortunately this had the effect only of recalling the dog and thus leaving Edward to his own resources.

It was a very difficult task indeed to find our way against

wind and weather but, the watershed once crossed, we could scarcely fail to strike the camp, provided only we maintained ordinary presence of mind. I entertained the hope that perhaps Edward would succeed in making his way to the little lake above mentioned, but as the fog was so dense that we could hardly see each other and had to steer by the compass and the terrain, we ourselves could not make this lake and it was not till about half an hour later, on the weather clearing up for a moment, that we perceived we had passed it.

The roaring of the wind was at this time so loud that it was by no means an easy matter to communicate with each other, and thus it happened that another of our party, Weston, dropped off and could not be found. Another difficulty now was to find Pinnacle Hill that we might relieve the poor horse and fetch the instruments, and at times the attempt appeared almost hopeless, the more so from the chilly state of the atmosphere. Mr Twynham, now perfectly exhausted, became quite stiff and unable to move. By great good fortune, however, M. de Guérard and myself, dragging him between us through fog and mist, hit upon the very spot where horse and instruments had been left in the morning.

I had now to pack the horse—by no means an easy task as neither of my companions was able to assist me, and the animal, terrified by the storm, had become entangled in the rope by which he was tethered. Luckily, however, I succeeded in accomplishing it much sooner than I expected. After immense difficulties, it being now nearly dark, M. de Guérard and I—Mr Twynham had been lost a short time before—reached the camp by eight o'clock. We found it in a terrible state, everything wet through and torn. After fastening the horse and putting things a little in order we went back for Mr Twynham, who could hardly be more than half a mile from us, and were fortunate enough to recover him. Had to carry him as he was in a perfectly helpless state.

We were now most anxious to light a fire but, as Edward had the matchbox with him and we had but few left, it was no easy thing; but after an hour and a half we succeeded in kindling a fire, which was soon blown into a good blaze by the terrific gale now raging, the roaring of the wind interrupted occasionally only by the thunder. Lightning and rain continued the whole evening. By eleven o'clock we had the water in the kettle boiling and our tent roughly fixed again and, could we only have known something of the whereabouts of our companions, would have been tolerably comfortable, notwithstanding the rough state of the weather.

My delight can scarcely be imagined when the barking of the dog announced the return of one of our missing men. It was Weston, who said that, attracted by the light of our fire, he had made his last effort to reach the camp.

At 4 a.m. on the 20th, clear morning, so that I was able to have a good view of the whole country, climbed up a rock in order to fix a piece of canvas to serve as a flag, hoping this might perhaps direct Edward to the camp. Resolved to proceed at once in search of him, M. de Guérard volunteering to accompany me, neither of the other two men being in a fit state to do so, and even he, after walking with me for an hour, declared himself unable to proceed any farther.

The search was now left to me alone and my first care was to ascertain whether Edward had reached the summit and taken the maps with him; therefore, when crossing the snowfield, I looked carefully for his footprints, but though I could plainly make out those of the dog I could discover none of his. On reaching the top, I found my maps untouched and concluded that he had not succeeded in crossing the snowfield or in ascending the summit, and that, in his bewilderment, he had travelled down into the valley of the Snowy River.

After depositing some clear and precise directions with respect to the position of our camp, and the time I intended yet to stay on Mt Kosciusko, I turned back and reached the camp at twelve o'clock in a very depressed state, enhanced by finding that Edward had not returned during my absence. In the afternoon we could do nothing but rest and recover strength, hoping every moment to hear the footstep of our companion, but in vain. The gale was still blowing so hard from NNW that it was impossible to suspend and register the barometer Greiner; and Edward, having the only suitable instrument with him, we could not effect any observations. At 7 p.m., just as we had taken supper and it was already dark, our horse, who had been nibbling at some scanty herbage near the spot, made off and could not be found any more. It seems that the poor animal cared to stop no longer where he hardly could get anything to eat and had to suffer severely from a temperature of 37.5°.

Morning of the 21st cold and foggy. Got up at 4 a.m. and started with the intention of tracking the horse but without success. Weston, who went in another direction, returned at 7.45 a.m. without having seen a trace of him and it was now quite clear that he had tried to find his way to Groggan's station—no very pleasant prospect for us, being thus left without any means of transport and our stores fast running out. Sent Weston again with strict injunctions to descend towards the station till he found the horse. It was now my opinion that Edward must already have perished or, if he still survived, had taken such a course as to place him beyond all chance of assistance from us.

I therefore resolved to return to Groggan's station as soon as Weston should appear with the horse, which we had the satisfaction of seeing at 10 a.m. He had found him near the lower limit of the belt of dead timber; there is no doubt that, had it not been for the hobbles, he would have succeeded in reaching the station. In the course of the forenoon I made some few magnetic observations near the camp. On the track leading towards Groggan's station, the theodolite was fixed on a stone to the east of which there was a mass of granite.

Leaving all the provisions yet in our possession and exact instructions to Edward, should he ever return to the camp, how to follow our track, we packed the horse and started, after having given three cheers for the missing man. While descending I made it a point to blaze all the trees in such a manner that even a man in a reduced state of body would be able to follow the track. During all this time we were still in hope that our friend might have gained the station before us, thus rendering our labour useless.

Arrived at the Leather Jacket again by 4 p.m. Had great difficulty in getting the horse, in its exhausted state, up the Groggan's side of the banks of the creek. The brave animal tried it three times, and on each occasion succeeded in reaching a height of eighty feet, but rolled back again and there remained. There was no other course left but to unpack and carry the things ourselves to the top of the hill. Got to Groggan's station at last by 7.15 p.m., but heard nothing of our friend...

Strong winds from the NW accompanied by rain and dense fog seem to prevail here at times. On the first day the weather was tolerably fair and quite calm, but the sun being scarcely visible through the thick veil covering the sky indicated the approach of one of these gales. I regretted very much that in consequence of the absence of Edward, who carried the only suitable barometer for such occasions, it was impossible to record the oscillations in the pressure of the air during this NW gale, the comparison of which with observations made at the sea-level or in other localities of the mountainous part of the country would have proved of considerable interest.

The force of the wind was, at times, really fearful, so much so that it was thoroughly impossible to make any headway against it and I do not think I shall be far out in estimating it at from 40 to 45 pounds on the square foot. The unfortunate affair with Edward interfered greatly with the scientific objects during my stay on the mount, my time being entirely taken up in looking for him, and the idea continually preying on my mind that he would not be able to make for the settled districts and thus extricate himself from his very perilous position. I was therefore now determined to hurry to Omeo and secure the assistance of the police, for the purpose of instituting another search after the poor fellow...

[3 December 1862]—The day very hot, and a haze, caused by bushfires, over the whole sky, so that nothing of the fine mountain scenery was visible. Returned to the Devil's Creek and arrived at Porepankah, on the crossing place of the Ovens River at 5 p.m. At Sleeve's place got some information about the road to Yackandandah, twenty-five miles from here. After leaving Sleeve's place on the 4th, we went up a steep gap (1688); found it very fatiguing, the weather being fearfully hot, and then descended into the Happy Valley (918). The creek here spread out into a swamp of considerable width and the crossing of it was very difficult. Had to construct a sort of bridge of brushwood over which our horses, when unpacked, might venture.

Mr Twynham, notwithstanding, fell into the mud together with his horse and we found it hard work to extricate him. Had to carry all our instruments and other things on our backs. Missed Edward very much, for it was very hard for me to attend to such things as I have just described, and conduct my observations as well. Steering about NE along a swamp lying between granite hills 800 feet high, we reached Barwoodgee (1160) at 4 p.m. Had to stop here in consequence of M. de Guérard having lost some things on the road and being obliged to go back for them. Fixed upon a station and made some magnetical and astronomical observations.

A calm, dull morning with sky overcast on the 5th...Started early and, travelling on a very fair track, through a slightly undulating country, we reached Yackandandah at noon. Went on to Adam's Flat gold diggings, about four to five miles from Yackandandah. M. de Guérard remained here for the night, in order to have an opportunity of speaking to Mr Lane, the police magistrate, about Edward and asking his advice as to the best mode of instituting an inquiry after him. He overtook us on the road and we arrived together at Belvoir at 11 a.m. on the 6th.

Our anxiety on approaching this place may be imagined, for we still entertained the hope that Edward might have made for it, knowing that we had left our waggon there and would be sure to direct our course thither as soon as we could. Went to the police court, but could hear nothing of him, so that the last hope of his safety was now quite destroyed.

Sat down to dinner, and had hardly done so when the lost

man made his appearance in a most deplorable condition, having been without food and clothes for some time. My conjectures as to the route he had taken proved to be correct. Soon after leaving us on Mt Kosciusko, he endeavoured to return but missed the track to the camp and descended into the valley of the Thredbo River. For two days he wandered on, with scarcely anything to eat, until he fell in with some diggers in a lonely valley, who behaved most kindly to him and assisted him in making his way to Kiandra. From this place he worked his way to Albury, where he arrived on the same morning on which we reached Belvoir—a strange coincidence when we consider that we both had travelled upwards of 300 miles, in quite different directions, since parting on Mt Kosciusko.

I cannot quit this most annoying affair without expressing my appreciation of Edward's courageous behaviour, after separating from our party, and of the skill and care he bestowed upon the instruments entrusted to his charge; for the fine mountain barometer Fortin II did not receive the least injury during the whole of this rough and perilous journey.

ALEXANDER AND FRANK JARDINE
The Battle of the Mitchell, 1864

 During 1864–65, the Jardine brothers drove a small herd of cattle north from Rockhampton to Somerset at the tip of Cape York. Hailed at the time as 'a brilliant achievement in exploration', their travels today read as one of the most disgraceful episodes in Australian exploration history. The frankness with which their journal tells the story of the 'battle of the Mitchell', as they called their most brutal murder of local Aborigines, reveals much about the mores of frontier life in north Queensland in the last half of the nineteenth century. It makes shameful reading.

December 18—The river was followed down today for nine miles through a complete network of anabranches, gullies and vine scrubs to another branch which may be called the true stream. It was thirty yards wide, deep and running strongly. Here the party had to camp for about three hours whilst the brothers searched for a good crossing. The cattle and pack-horses were crossed in safety, but some of the pack-bags got wetted in the passage. They were travelled another mile over to a sandstone bar, crossing another deep sheet of water that had been previously found. This stream had been explored in search of a ford for four miles further up but without success. It continued of the same width and appeared to do so much further.

This day, Sunday, was marked by the severest conflict the travellers had yet had with the natives, one which may well be dignified by the name of the Battle of the Mitchell. On arriving at the running stream before mentioned, whilst the cattle halted, the brothers and Eulah, taking axes with them to clear the scrub, went down to find a safe crossing. At about a mile and a half they came on to a number of blacks fishing; these immediately crossed to the other side, but on their return swam across again in numbers, armed with large bundles of spears and some nullahs, and met them.

The horsemen, seeing they were in for another row, now cantered forward towards the camp, determined this time to give their assailants a severe lesson. This was interpreted into a flight by the savages, who set up a yell and redoubled their pursuit, sending in their spears thick and fast. These now coming much too close to be pleasant (for some of them were thrown a hundred yards), the three turned suddenly on their pursuers and, galloping up to them, poured in a volley, the report of which brought down their companions from the camp, when the skirmish became general.

The natives at first stood up courageously, but either by accident or through fear, despair or stupidity, they got huddled in a heap in and at the margin of the water, when ten carbines poured volley after volley into them from all directions, killing and wounding with every shot with very little return, nearly all their spears having been expended in the pursuit of the horsemen. About thirty being killed, the leader thought it prudent to hold his hand, and let the rest escape. Many more must have been wounded and probably drowned, for fifty-nine rounds were counted as discharged.

On the return of the party to the cattle an incident occurred which nearly cost one of them his life. One of the routed natives, probably burning with revengeful and impotent hate, got into the water under the river bank and waited for the returning party, and as they passed threw a spear at Scrutton, before anyone was aware of his proximity. The audacious savage had much better have left it alone, for he paid for his temerity with his life.

Although the travellers came off providentially without hurt, there were many narrow escapes, for which some of them might thank their good fortune. At the commencement of the fight, as Alexander Jardine was levelling his carbine, a spear struck the ground between his feet, causing him to drop his muzzle and lodge the bullet in the ground a few yards in front of him. His next shot told more successfully...This is one of the few instances in which the savages of Queensland have been known to stand up in fight with white men, and on this occasion they showed no sign of surprise or fear at the report and effect of firearms...

December 21—The rain of last night continuing through the morning, the party had to start in the downpour. They crossed another large shallow sandy creek at four miles, coming from the eastward, running south-east. The camp was formed on a lagoon about a mile from the river bank. The country traversed was sandy, growing only coarse wiry grasses and spinifex, sandstone rock cropping out occasionally above the surface. The river was here a quarter of a mile wide, salt, and running strongly.

Before the pack-horses came up, a mob of blacks approached the camp and, getting up in the trees, took a good survey of the white intruders, but on one of the party going towards them they scampered off over the open ground towards the river, the recollection of the affair at the crossing place probably quickening their movements. Just at sundown, however, the sharp eyes of the black boys detected some of them actually trying to stalk the whites, using green boughs for screens.

So the brothers, taking with them Scrutton and the four black boys, started in chase. They were in camp costume, that is to say, shirt and belt, and all in excellent condition and wind; and now a hunt commenced which perhaps stands alone in the annals of nature warfare. On being detected the natives again decamped, but this time closely pursued. The party could at any time overtake or outstep the fugitives, but they contented themselves with pressing steadily on them, in open order, without firing a shot, occasionally making a spurt, which had the effect of causing the blacks to drop nearly all their spears.

They fairly hunted them for two miles into the scrub when, as darkness was coming on, they left their dingy assailants to recover their wind, and returned to camp laughing heartily at their 'blank run' and taking with them as many of the abandoned spears as they could carry...

December 25—The rain came down all last night...The leader wished his companions the compliments of the season, and pushed on. The country decidedly improved if the weather did not. The tail end of some scrubs were passed in the first five miles, chiefly tea-tree and oak and, half a mile further on, a fine creek of sandstone rock, permanently watered. At seven miles another similar, but larger, was named Christmas Creek. Here, whilst Mr Jardine was halting in wait for the cattle, he marked a tree XMAS 1864, in square.

PETER EGERTON WARBURTON
Enema by Shotgun, 1873

 Bearded, gaunt, with deeply set yet penetrating eyes, Colonel Peter Egerton Warburton looked like an explorer, and he suffered like one. His passage across the western interior of Australia, with his son Richard, Afghans and Aborigines, was one of the toughest journeys ever made by an Australian explorer.

Fly-blown camels whose sores had to be emptied of maggots with a pint-pot, constipated camels which had to be relieved by enemas administered through double-barrelled shotguns, demented Afghan camel-drivers, and festering scorpion bites were just a few of the expedition's tribulations. A week or two before the expedition reached safety, Warburton matter-of-factly remarked of his camel-driver: 'Sahleh's finger is very bad indeed from the scorpion sting...If it continues to get worse without any prospect of surgical aid, someone (not I) will have to chop his finger off with a tomahawk.'

October 19th—Started at daylight, and reached No. 98 at 9.15 a.m. We here feel the advantage of not travelling very far from our last water, whilst any uncertainty exists of our finding any before us.

One camel-man quite unable to move from a bad leg. He had an old sore on his ankle, and one of the camels struck him upon it last night; it is an ugly wound. I have plastered it as well as I can, and hope it will be better in a few days.

This is Sunday. How unlike one at home!

Half a quart of flour and water, at 4 a.m.; a hard, sinewy bit of raw, that is, sun-dried, but uncooked, camel meat for dinner at 2 p.m. Supper uncertain, perhaps some roasted acacia seeds; this is our bill of fare. These seeds are not bad, but very small and very hard; they are on bushes, not trees, and the natives use them roasted and pounded.

20th—Got a pigeon, and some flour and water for breakfast. We can only allow ourselves a spoonful of flour each at a time, and it won't last many days even at this rate.

Killed a large camel for food at sunset. We would rather have killed a worse one, but this bull had in the early part of our journey got a very bad back, and was unable to work for a long time. His wound was not quite healed when we were compelled to load him, in consequence of the loss of our master bull, and so the sore had broken out again, and would have rendered him unfit for work in a day or two; and he might have fallen a prey to the maggots, as a former sore-backed camel did, for they breed in these sores with such wonderful rapidity and in such prodigious numbers that they eat the camel up in a short time.*

21st—Cutting up and jerking camel-meat. The inside has given us a good supper and breakfast. This is a much better beast than the old, worn-out cow we killed before, and we have utilised every scrap, having had a sharp lesson as to the value of anything we can masticate.

22nd—A very hot day. Sent two men out with three days' provisions to look for water to the southward. I hope they may succeed, as they will be able to get a distance of twenty or thirty miles. It is now a fortnight since we first came to the water; all our efforts to get away have as yet failed; we are imprisoned for the present as safely as we should be in jail, only we are much worse fed.

I begin to think it is just possible we may be stopped here till the summer tropical rains fall in January. The heat is now so fierce, that neither we nor our camels could live long without an abundant supply of water; but such a contingency as this would only be a prolongation of our sufferings, it would not save us. I don't want to go south, for it increases the difficulty of crossing the sandhills, without diminishing the distance from the Oakover River, but if we can find water, any direction (except east) is better than staying here; we are all sick of the place.

---

* The number of flies in Australia, and the rapidity with which they breed, are quite horrible. Nothing in the shape of meat can be left exposed for a moment, otherwise a swarm of flies descend and seem to emit living maggots on the flesh. They assail the ears, nostrils and eyes of the traveller, who is unable to stir without a veil, and in Colonel Warburton's expedition the additional precaution of rubbing Holloway's ointment round the eye had to be taken. Owing to the flies and the impoverished condition of the blood, the slightest abrasion of the skin led to its festering and becoming an ugly wound. A little scratch, that under other circumstances would pass unnoticed, here becomes a troublesome, ulcerous sore. Some idea of the condition of the camel's back may be imagined when the reader hears that the maggots were *scooped out with a pint pot*! [Charles Eden]

23rd—Another roasting day.

24th—A close, cloudy heat; it looks like rain...

28th—Had hoped to have started this evening, but one of the camels lately out looks in want of a longer rest. I dare not move a tired camel from here; they will need all the strength we can give them...

29th—A short rain squall passed over us last evening; it has cooled the ground a little. Economy is of course the order of the day in provisions. My son and I have managed to hoard up about one pound of flour and a pinch of tea; all our sugar is gone. Now and then we afford ourselves a couple of spoonfuls of flour, made into paste. When we indulge in tea the leaves are boiled twice over. I eat my sun-dried camel-meat uncooked, as far as I can bite it; what I cannot bite goes into the quart-pot, and is boiled down to a sort of poor-house broth. When we get a bird we dare not clean it, less we should lose anything.

More disasters this morning. One of our largest camels very ill; the only thing we could do for it was to pound four boxes of Holloway's pills, and drench the animal. I hope it may recover, for its loss would be ruinous, leaving us with only five camels, and two of them very weak and uncertain.

One of the Afghans apparently wrong in his head; but it would answer no good purpose to enter into details; he has caused us much inconvenience and trouble.

In the evening the camel was still very sick. When once ill there is little hope of them without suitable medicine, which we have not got, and long rest, which we cannot give.

Very cloudy, but no rain, though it appears to be falling to the southward.

30th—Camel still very bad; going to try an enema from the double-barrelled breech-loader. Our difficulty of getting on will be greatly increased by the loss of this camel, which carries two men. We shall only have five indifferent camels to carry seven men, with provisions and water, the former light enough; but the water is very heavy, yet quite indispensable. Should the animal be unable to travel, we must kill it, and cut off as much fresh meat as we can carry.

The camel-man all right again, and the camel much better this evening. A very cloudy and close night.

31st—Half a gale from the eastward; most disagreeable, as it blows the sand over everything; and prevents us lighting a fire.

We started from camp No. 98 at 4.15 a.m., our general course being slightly to the westward of south for eleven miles. The camels did the journey well. The wind choked up the well, but it answers our purpose when cleared. We are all most thankful to have got away from No. 98 at last. We have now two known waters to the southward, which will give us all the southing we want; but unfortunately no westing, and leaves us a longer distance for our rush than I like; but I fear we must try it.

The weather being a little cooler, and the camels well watered, we started again at 3.30 p.m. Reached our first well, over heavy sandhills, at 7.30. There is not much water, but enough for our uses. We are now in latitude 20° 20', and longitude by account 123° 10'; so our position is good.

November 1st—Moderately cool; sent to try the western well. If good enough for us to camp a day or two upon, we shall go to it this morning; if not, we must camp at the middle one, and get what water we can for the camels out of the three wells, distant about a mile or two from each other. Camped at the middle well; the other one having too much sand in it for a man to clear out. Tormented all night by the ants.*

---

* A small black ant seems to have been the avowed enemy of this expedition. The ground literally swarmed with them, and a stamp of the foot brought them up in thousands. When the wearied men threw themselves down under the shade of a bush, to snatch the half-hour's slumber their exhausted frames required, the merciless little insects attacked them, and not only effectually routed sleep, but even rendered a recumbent position impossible. The scanty clothing possessed by the travellers was no protection; so feeble a bulwark was speedily under-run by the enemy, and their successful invasion announced by sharp painful nips from their powerful mandibles. Often, when the vertical sun poured down in full fierceness on their heads, and the poor shade afforded even by a bush would have been an inestimable blessing, the

2nd—The well affords sufficient for us, and I send the camels to the others. The ants prevent our doing anything; they leave us no peace. I am afraid of losing the moon, and the comparatively cool nights; we are also eating up our small stock of camel-meat, so I must try to commence our flight on the 4th.

The gale of adversity sends us scudding under bare poles; but it seems our only chance to make a rush for the Oakover. We cannot hit upon any water more to the westward to start from, so we must take our chance of finding a little somewhere in the 150 miles of desert which separate us from that river. We had the misfortune to lose our bottomless bucket by the falling in of our well yesterday; fortunately no one was down it at the time, or he would have been instantly killed, and we should have known nothing about it for a long time. The depth of this well was unusually great, being over nine feet.

3rd—Hot day. The camels' well is a good one, and sufficient for their wants.

4th—We are to commence our flight to the Oakover at sunset. God grant us strength to get through! Richard is very weak, and so am I. To get rid of a small box, we selected a few bottles of homoeopathic medicines for use and ate up all the rest. How much of our property we had thrown away before we resorted to this expedient of lightening the loads may be guessed. I started later than we intended; our course about west by south. The sandhills are more troublesome than we have had them for some time. When we wanted to look north and south for water, the sandhills generally ran east and west; now, when we particularly wish to avoid crossing them, we are compelled to do so from their running north-west by west. The eclipse of the moon darkened our journey for several hours, but we made a favourable stretch westward for the last few miles of our night's journey. I

---

travellers were driven away from the shelter by their relentless persecutors, and in despair flung themselves down on the burning sand, where it was too hot even for an ant. By day or by night the little insects gave them no respite. [Charles Eden]

could not go so far as I had hoped, from the fatiguing character of the country. Camped at 3.15 a.m.

5th—A strong east wind is blowing. We are compelled to give up smoking whilst on short allowance of water. It is a deprivation, for smoke and water stand in the place of food. We started west-south-west at 6.30 p.m., and made twenty-five miles, though we had most trying sandhills to cross. I became quite unable to continue the journey, being reduced to a skeleton by thirst, famine and fatigue. I was so emaciated and weak I could scarcely rise from the ground, or stagger half a dozen steps when up.

Charley had been absent all day, and we were alarmed about him when he did not return at sunset. I know not what to do. Delay was death to us all, as we had not water enough to carry us through; on the other hand, to leave the camp without the lad seemed an inhuman act, as he must then perish. It was six against one, so I waited till the moon was well up, and started at 9 p.m. We made about eight miles and whilst crossing a flat heard, to our intense delight, a cooee, and Charley joined us. Poor lad, how rejoiced we were to see him again so unexpectedly! The lad had actually walked about twenty miles after all the fatigue of the previous night's travelling; he had run up a large party of natives, and gone to their water. This news of more water permitted us to use at once what we had with us, and the recovery of Charley put us in good spirits.

It may, I think, be admitted that the hand of providence was distinctly visible in this instance. I had deferred starting until 9 p.m, to give the absent boy a chance of regaining the camp. It turned out afterwards that had we expedited our departure by ten minutes, or postponed it for the same length of time, Charley would have missed us; and had this happened there is little doubt that not only myself, but probably other members of the expedition would have perished from thirst. The route pursued by us was at right angles with the course taken by the boy, and the chances of our stumbling up against each other in the dark were infinitesimally small. Providence mercifully directed it otherwise, and our departure was so timed that, after travelling from two to two hours and a half, when all hope of the recovery of the wanderer was almost abandoned, I was gladdened by the cooee of the brave lad, whose keen ears had caught the sound of the bells attached to the camels' necks. To the energy and courage of this untutored native may, under the guidance of the Almighty, be attributed the salvation of the party.

It was by no accident that he encountered the friendly well. For fourteen miles he followed up the tracks of some blacks, though fatigued by a day of severe work; and, receiving a kindly welcome from the natives, he had hurried back, unmindful of his own exhausted condition, to apprise his companions of the important discovery he had made. We turned towards the native camp, and halted a short distance from it, that we might not frighten them away. I was so utterly exhausted when we camped, at 3 a.m., that it was evident I never could have gone on after that night without more food and water. I would therefore thankfully acknowledge the goodness and mercy of God in saving my life by guiding us to a place where we got both.

7th—Reached the well at 6 a.m. The natives fled at our approach, but returned after a little time. Wallaby were procured from them by barter. The fresh meat and plenty of water restored me for a time from my forlorn condition. There are so many natives that they drink more of their own water than we can well spare them. We obtained here the rest we all so much needed.

8th—The natives all disappeared at daylight, and our hope of more food goes with them. I have invariably throughout the journey carried my pistol in my belt, but for the last few days its weight was too much for me, and I had put it in my bag. Whilst lying under the shade of a blanket, with my head on the bag, one barrel unaccountably went off and, had not the muzzle been turned from me, I should have had the ball through my head. My life has again been given to me...

9th—Started west at 6.15 p.m. Crossed a few sand-ridges and wide plains thickly covered with spinifex, also two or three water-courses (what a delight it is to see one again!) running, so far as we could judge in the dark, from south to north. The ground seems to be rising. Travelled about twenty-two miles.

10th—...Started at 5.40 p.m. crossing a succession of very high sandhills. At 8.00 p.m. saw what we took for a native fire to our left; turned towards it, but in a couple of miles it disappeared and we renewed our course. Latterly sandhills have become more distant from each other and less high. Travelled over a good deal of burnt ground, but got on pretty well. Camped at 3 a.m.

11th—With all the care we can take of the camels, and with the lightest possible loads, they can barely do twenty miles in the whole night, so we have yet a good stretch of country between us and the river.

We killed our last meat on the 20th October; a large bull-camel has therefore fed us for three weeks. It must be remembered that we have no flour, tea or sugar, neither have we an atom of salt, so we cannot salt our meat. We are seven in all, and are living entirely upon sun-dried slips of meat, which are as tasteless and innutritious as a piece of dead bark. Unless the game drops into our hands in great abundance we must kill another camel directly we get to water. Most of us are nearly exhausted from starvation, and our only resource is a camel, which would disappear from before us in a twinkling.

Started at 6.15 p.m. Travelled five hours, then took a latitude, which put us in 21° 2', so we turned west for three hours more, completing twenty miles over very hard country and heavy sandhills.

12th—We find no appearance of change in the country, and suppose that we are either more to the eastward than we suppose, or else the head of the Oakover is laid down more to the eastward than it is. The error is most probably mine, as it is difficult to keep the longitude quite correct after travelling so many months on a general westerly course. Our position is most critical in consequence of the weakness of the camels. They cannot get over this terrible country and stand the fierce heat without frequent watering and rest. Without water we are helpless.

Three p.m. I have decided to send Lewis, the two camel-men and the black boy on ahead with the best and strongest camels, to try and reach the river, returning to us with water if successful. My son and Dennis White and myself remain behind, but following the first party as fast as our jaded camels can take us. We have abandoned everything but our small supply of water and meat, and each party has a gun.

Lewis and his party started at 6 p.m. We left ourselves at 6.30. We could only make about four miles, when we lay down till 2 a.m. Starting again, we had made about eight miles when we were surprised by a voice, and found we had overtaken the advance party, one of whose camels had knocked up on the previous night. This was a death-blow to our hopes of getting relief by sending them on first. We are hemmed in on every side; every trail we make fails, and I can now only hope that some one or more of the party may reach water sooner or later. As for myself, I can see no hope of life, for I cannot hold up without food and water.

I have given Lewis written instructions to justify his leaving me, should I die, and have made such arrangement as I can for the preservation of my journal and maps. The advance party has started again, and we followed till a little after sunrise, when our camels showed signs of distress, and we camped. Should the advance party see likely smokes they are to turn to them.

My party at least are now in that state that, unless it please God to save us, we cannot live more than twenty-four hours. We are at our last drop of water, and the smallest bit of dried meat chokes me. I fear my son must share my fate, as he will not leave me. God have mercy upon us, for we are brought very low, and by the time death reaches us we shall not regret exchanging our present misery for that state in which the weary are at rest.

We have tried to do our duty, and have been disappointed in all our expectations. I have been in excellent health during the whole journey, and am so still, being merely worn out from want of food and water. Let no self-reproaches afflict anyone respecting me. I undertook the journey for the benefit of my family, and I was quite equal to it under all the circumstances that could be reasonably anticipated, but difficulties and losses have come upon us so thickly for the last few months that we have not been able to move; thus our provisions are gone, but this would not have stopped us could we have found water without such laborious search. The country is terrible. I do not believe men ever traversed so vast an extent of continuous desert.

We follow this afternoon on the advance tracks as far as our camels can take us. Richard shot me a little bird. It was only about the size of a sparrow, but it did me good. If the country would only give any single thing we could eat, I should do very well, but we cannot find a snake, kite or crow. There are a few wallabies in the spinifex, but we cannot get them. Our miseries are not a little increased by the ants. We cannot get a moment's rest, night or day, for them.

13th—My rear party could only advance eight miles, when the camels gave in. Our food is scanty enough, but our great want is water. We have a little, but dare not take more than a spoonful at a time, whilst the heat is so great that the slightest exposure and exertion bring on a parching thirst. We are as low and weak as living men well can be, and our only hope of prolonging our lives is in the advance party finding some native camp; we have seen smokes, but are in too crippled a state to go to them.

14th—Early this morning my son took our man White, and started in the direction of the smoke we had last seen. At midday, whilst I was sipping in solitude a drop of water out of a spoon, Lewis came up with a bag of water.

Never shall I forget the draught of water I then got, but I was so weak that I almost fainted shortly after drinking it. The advance party had run up a smoke and found a well about twelve miles off. Our lives were saved, but poor Charley was nearly killed. He had gone forward alone (at his own request, and as he had done before) to the native camp, the remainder of the party with the camels keeping out of sight. The blacks treated Charley kindly, and gave him water, but when he cooeed for the party to come up, and the camels appeared, then I suppose the men were frightened, and supposed Charley had entrapped them; they instantly speared him in the back and arm, cut his skull with a waddy, and nearly broke his jaw.

I do not think this attack was made with any premeditated malice, but doubtless they would have killed the lad, had not the remainder of the party, rushing to his rescue, frightened them away. Unfortunately, the few medicines we had not eaten had, by some oversight, been left behind at the camp, where we had abandoned almost everything but the clothes we happened to stand up in. Lewis returned to the well, and was to come out and meet us next day with more water. We started at sunset, but could not keep on the tracks for more than two miles when we camped.

15th—We made another effort at daylight to get on, but one of the camels broke down, though it had not carried a saddle. The poor beast had become quite blind, and staggered about in a most alarming way. We could not get her beyond a mile and a half, when she knocked up under the shade of a bush, and would go no farther. We therefore also sat down to await the water to be sent out to us. The heat was intense, and my son, having been obliged to walk because the camel could not carry him, suffered very greatly from thirst, and had not water been brought us before midday, it would have gone ill with him. Between 10 and 11 a.m. Lewis returned with water from the well.

The camel, though we gave it some water, could not move from the shade of the bush. We tried to drive it, and to drag it, but to no purpose, therefore we shot it.

ERNEST GILES
Living, Raw, Dying, 1874

Ernest Giles was retrenched from the Victorian Post Office in 1854 during an austerity drive. The post office's loss was our gain, for Giles went on to become one of the most audacious and eloquent explorers in the history of the continent. For Giles, exploration was a huge and irresistible game of brinkmanship. It was a game in which he gambled his life, the lives of his horses, and even his men. Here in the waterless wasteland later known as the Gibson Desert, we see Giles face his nadir. Yet even when things are at their most desperate, when the explorers are a hundred miles from nowhere, with just a few pints of water and one exhausted horse between them, all Giles can think of is the quest. 'Oh, how ardently I longed for a camel,' he writes, as he sees the distant and untouchable ranges on the horizon.

And then, when Giles is alone, without water and horse, he hangs grimly on in conditions that would have killed a lesser man. The tiny wallaby he eats alive, and which perhaps tips the balance from death to life, is a meal that few could have written about so enthusiastically.

20th April 1874—Gibson and I, having got all the gear we required, took a week's supply of smoked horse, and four excellent horses, two to ride and two to carry water, all in fine condition. I rode the Fair Maid of Perth, an excellent walker; I gave Gibson the big ambling horse, Badger, and we packed the big cob, a splendid bay horse and fine weight-carrier, with a pair of water-bags that contained twenty gallons at starting. The other horse was Darkie, a fine, strong, nuggetty-black horse, who carried two five-gallon kegs of water and our stock of smoked horse, rugs etc. We reached the Circus, at twenty miles, early, and the horses had time to feed and fill themselves after being watered, though the grass was very poor.

21st—While I went for the horses Gibson topped up the water-bags and kegs, and poured a quantity of water out of the hole on to a shallow place, so that if we turned any horses back, they could drink without precipitating themselves into the deep and slippery hole when they returned here. As we rode away, I remarked to Gibson that the day was the anniversary of Burke and Wills's return to their depot at Cooper's Creek, and then recited to him, as he did not appear to know anything whatever about it, the hardships they endured, their desperate struggles for existence, and death there, and I casually remarked that Wills had a brother who also lost his life in the field of discovery. He had gone out with Sir John Franklin in 1845.[†]

Gibson then said, 'Oh! I had a brother who died with Franklin at the North Pole, and my father had a deal of trouble to get his pay from government.' He seemed in a very jocular vein this morning, which was not often the case, for he was usually rather sulky, sometimes for days together, and he said, 'How is it, that in all these exploring expeditions a lot of people go and die?'

I said, 'I don't know, Gibson, how it is, but there are many dangers in exploring, besides accidents and attacks from the natives, that may at any time cause the death of some of the people engaged in it; but I believe want of judgment or knowledge or courage in individuals often brought about their deaths. Death, however, is a thing that must occur to everyone sooner or later.'

To this he replied, 'Well, I shouldn't like to die in this part of the country, anyhow.'

In this sentiment I quite agreed with him, and the subject dropped. At eleven miles we were not only clear of the range, but had crossed to the western side of Lake Christopher, and were fairly enclosed in the sandhills, which were of course covered with triodia.[†] Numerous fine casuarinas grew in the hollows between them, and some stunted bloodwood trees (red gum) ornamented the tops of some of the sandhills. At twenty-two miles, on a west course, we turned the horses out for an hour. It was very warm, there was no grass. The horses rested in the shade of a desert-oak tree, while we remained under another. These trees are very handsome, with round umbrageous tops; the leaves are round and fringe-like.

---

† Exploration must have run in the family. Wills' brother had joined Franklin's expedition to the Arctic, which vanished without trace until the grisly remains were found in 1857.
† Triodia: spinifex.

We had a meal of smoked horse; and here I discovered that the bag with our supply of horseflesh in it held but a most inadequate supply for two of us for a week, there being scarcely sufficient for one. Gibson had packed it at starting, and I had not previously seen it. The afternoon was oppressively hot—at least it always seems so when one is away from water. We got over an additional eighteen miles, making a day's stage of forty.

The country was all sandhills. The Rawlinson Range completely disappeared from view, even from the tops of the highest sandhills, at thirty-five miles. The travelling, though heavy enough, had not been so frightful as I had anticipated, for the lines of sandhills mostly ran east and west, and by turning about a bit we got several hollows between them to travel in. Had we been going north or south, north-easterly or south-westerly, it would have been dreadfully severe.

The triodia here reigns supreme, growing in enormous bunches and plots, and standing three and four feet high, while many of the long dry tops are as high as a man. This gives the country the appearance of dry grassy downs; and as it is dotted here and there with casuarina and bloodwood trees, and small patches of desert shrubs, its general appearance is by no means displeasing to the eye, though frightful to the touch. No sign of the recent presence of natives was anywhere visible, nor had the triodia been burnt for probably many years. At night we got what we in this region may be excused for calling a grass flat, there being some bunches of a thin and wiry kind of grass, though white and dry as a chip. I never saw the horses eat more than a mouthful or two of it anywhere, but there was nothing else, and no water.

22nd—The ants were so troublesome last night, I had to shift my bed several times. Gibson was not at all affected by them and slept well. We were in our saddles immediately after daylight. I was in hopes that a few miles might bring about a change of country, and so it did, but not an advantageous one to us. At ten miles from camp the horizon became flatter, the sandhills fell off, and the undulations became covered with brown gravel, at first very fine. At fifty-five miles it became coarser, and at sixty miles it was evident the country was becoming firmer, if not actually stony. Here we turned the horses out, having come twenty miles.

I found one of our large water-bags leaked more than I expected, and our supply of water was diminishing with distance. Here Gibson preferred to keep the big cob to ride, against my advice, instead of Badger, so, after giving Badger and Darkie a few pints of water each, Gibson drove them back on the tracks about a mile and let them go, to take their own time and find their own way back to the Circus. They both looked terribly hollow and fatigued, and went away very slowly. Sixty miles through such a country as this tells fearfully upon a horse. The poor brutes were very unwilling to leave us, as they knew we had some water, and they also knew what a fearful region they had before them to reach the Circus again.

We gave the two remaining horses all the water contained in the two large water-bags, except a quart or two for ourselves. This allowed them a pretty fair drink, though not a circumstance to what they would have swallowed. They fed a little while we remained here. The day was warm enough. The two five-gallon kegs with water we hung in the branches of a tree, with the pack-saddles, empty water-bags etc. of the other two horses.

Leaving the Kegs—I always called this place by that name—we travelled another twenty miles by night, the country being still covered with small stones and thickly clothed with the tall triodia. There were thin patches of mulga and mallee scrub occasionally. No view could be obtained to the west; all around us, north, south, east and west, were alike, the undulations forming the horizons were not generally more than seven or eight miles distant from one another, and when we reached the rim or top of one we obtained exactly the same view for the next seven or eight miles. The country still retained all the appearance of fine, open, dry, grassy downs, and the triodia tops waving in the heated breeze had all the semblance of good grass. The afternoon had been very oppressive, and the horses were greatly disinclined to exert themselves, though my mare went very well.

It was late by the time we encamped, and the horses were much in want of water, especially the big cob, who kept coming up to the camp all night, and tried to get at our water-bags, pannikins etc. The instinct of a horse, when in the first stage of thirst in getting hold of any utensil that ever had water in it, is surprising and most annoying, but teaching us by most persuasive reasons how akin they are to human beings. We had one small water-bag hung in a tree. I did not think of this just at the moment when my mare came straight up to it and took it in her teeth, forcing out the cork and sending the water up, which we were both dying to drink, in a beautiful jet which, descending to earth, was irrevocably lost.

We now had only a pint or two left. Gibson was now very sorry he had exchanged Badger for the cob, as he found the cob very dull and heavy to get on; this was not usual, for he was generally a most willing animal, but he would only go at a jog while my mare was a fine walker. There had been a hot wind from the north all day. The following morning (23rd) there was a most strange dampness in the air, and I had a vague feeling, such as must have been felt by augurs, and seers of old, who trembled as they told events to come; for this was the last day on which I ever saw Gibson. It was a lamentable day in the history of this expedition. The horizon to the west was hid in clouds. We left the camp even before daylight, and as we had camped on the top of a rim we knew we had seven or eight miles to go before another view could be obtained. The next rim was at least ten miles from the camp, and there was some slight indications of a change.

We were now ninety miles from the Circus water, and 110 from Fort McKellar. The horizon to the west was still obstructed by another rise three or four miles away; but to the west-north-west I could see a line of low stony ridges, ten miles off. To the south was an isolated little hill, six or seven miles away. I determined to go to the ridges, when Gibson complained that his horse could never reach them, and suggested that the next rise to the west might reveal something better in front. The ridges were five miles away, and there were others still farther preventing a view. When we reached them we had come ninety-eight miles from the Circus. Here Gibson, who was always behind, called out and said his horse was going to die, or knock up, which are synonymous terms in this region.

Now we had reached a point where at last a different view was presented to us, and I believed a change of country was at hand, for the whole western, down to the south-western, horizon was broken by lines of ranges, being most elevated at the south-western end. They were all notched and irregular, and I believed formed the eastern extreme of a more elevated and probably mountainous region to the west. The ground we now stood upon, and for a mile or two past, was almost a stony hill itself, and for the first time in all the distance we had come we had reached a spot where water might run during rain, though we had not seen any place where it could lodge.

Between us and the hilly horizon to the west the country seemed to fall into a kind of long valley, and it looked dark, and seemed to have timber in it, and here also the natives had formerly burnt the spinifex, but not recently. The hills to the west were twenty-five to thirty miles away, and it was with extreme regret I was compelled to relinquish a farther attempt to reach them. Oh, how ardently I longed for a camel! How ardently I gazed upon this scene! At this moment I would even my jewel eternal have sold for power to span the gulf that lay between! But it could not be, situated as I was; compelled to retreat—of course with the intention of coming again with a larger supply of water—now the sooner I retreated the better.

These far-off hills were named the Alfred and Marie Range, in honour of their Royal Highnesses the Duke and Duchess of Edinburgh. Gibson's horse having got so bad had placed us both in a great dilemma; indeed, ours was a most critical position. We turned back upon our tracks, when the cob refused to carry his rider any farther, and tried to lie down. We drove him another mile on foot, and down he fell to die. My mare, the Fair Maid of Perth, was only too willing to return; she had now to carry Gibson's saddle and things, and we went away walking and riding by turns of half an hour. The cob, no doubt, died where he fell; not a second thought could be bestowed upon him.

When we got back to about thirty miles from the Kegs I was walking and, having concluded in my mind what course to pursue, I called to Gibson to halt till I walked up to him. We were both excessively thirsty, for walking had made us so, and we had scarcely a pint of water left between us. However, of what we had we each took a mouthful, which finished the supply, and I then said—for I couldn't speak before—'Look here, Gibson, you see we are in a most terrible fix with only one horse, therefore only one can ride, and one must remain behind. I shall remain: and now listen to me. If the mare does not get water soon she will die; therefore ride right on; get to the Kegs if possible tonight, and give her water. Now the cob is dead there'll be all the more for her; let her rest for an hour or two, then get over a few more miles by morning, so that early tomorrow you will sight the Rawlinson, at twenty-five miles from the Kegs. Stick to the tracks, and never leave them. Leave as much water in one keg for me as you can afford after watering the mare and filling up your own bags, and, remember, I depend upon you to bring me relief. Rouse Mr Tietkens, get fresh horses and more water-bags, and return as soon as you possibly can. I shall of course endeavour to get down the tracks also.'

He then said if he had a compass he thought he could go better at night. I knew he didn't understand anything about compasses, as I had often tried to explain them to him. The one I had was a Gregory's Patent, of a totally different construction from ordinary instruments of the kind, and I was very loath to part with it, as it was the only one I had. However, he was so anxious for it that I gave it him, and he departed. I sent one final shout after him to stick to the tracks, to which he replied, 'All right,' and the mare carried him out of sight almost immediately. That was the last ever seen of Gibson.

I walked slowly on, and the further I walked the more thirsty I became. I had thirty miles to go to reach the Kegs, which I could not reach until late tomorrow at the rate I was travelling, and I did not feel sure that I could keep on at that. The afternoon was very hot. I continued following the tracks until the moon went down, and then had to stop. The night was reasonably cool, but I was parched and choking for water. How I longed again for morning! I hoped Gibson had reached the Kegs, and that he and the mare were all right. I could not sleep for thirst, although towards morning it became almost cold. How I wished this planet would for once accelerate its movements and turn upon its axis in twelve instead of twenty-four hours, or rather that it would complete its revolution in six hours.

24th April to 1st May—So soon as it was light I was again upon the horse tracks, and reached the Kegs about the middle of the day. Gibson had been here, and watered the mare, and gone on. He had left me a little over two gallons of water in one keg, and it may be imagined how glad I was to get a drink. I could have drunk my whole supply in half an hour, but was compelled to economy, for I could not tell how many days would elapse before assistance could come: it could not be less than five, it might be many more. After quenching my thirst a little I felt ravenously hungry and, on searching among the bags, all the food I could find was eleven sticks of dirty, sandy, smoked horse, averaging about an ounce and a half each, at the bottom of a pack-bag. I was rather staggered to find that I had a little more than a pound weight of meat to last me until assistance came. However, I was compelled to eat some at once, and devoured two sticks raw, as I had no water to spare to boil them in.

After this I sat in what shade the trees afforded, and reflected on the precariousness of my position. I was sixty miles from water, and eighty from food, my messenger could hardly return before six days, and I began to think it highly probable that I should be dead of hunger and thirst long before anybody could possibly arrive. I looked at the keg; it was an awkward thing to carry empty. There was nothing else to carry water in, as Gibson had taken all the smaller water-bags, and the large ones would require several gallons of water to soak the canvas before they began to tighten enough to hold water. The keg when empty, with its rings and straps, weighed fifteen pounds, and now it had twenty pounds of water in it. I could not carry it without a blanket for a pad for my shoulder, so that with my revolver and cartridge-pouch, knife, and one or two other small things on my belt, I staggered under a weight of about fifty pounds when I put the keg on my back. I only had fourteen matches.

After I had thoroughly digested all points of my situation, I concluded that if I did not help myself providence wouldn't help me. I started, bent double by the keg, and could only travel so slowly that I thought it scarcely worth while to travel at all. I became so thirsty at each step I took that I longed to drink up every drop of water I had in the keg, but it was the elixir of death I was burdened with, and to drink it was to die, so I restrained myself. By next morning I had only got about three miles away from the Kegs, and to do that I travelled mostly in the moonlight. The next few days I can only pass over as they seemed to pass with me, for I was quite unconscious half the time, and I only got over about five miles a day.

To people who cannot comprehend such a region it may seem absurd that a man could not travel faster than that. All I can say is, there may be men who could do so, but most men in the position I was in would simply have died of hunger and thirst, for by the third or fourth day—I couldn't tell which—my horse meat was all gone. I had to remain in what scanty shade I could find during the day, and I could only travel by night.

When I lay down in the shade in the morning I lost all consciousness, and when I recovered my senses I could not tell whether one day or two or three had passed. At one place I am sure I must have remained over forty-eight hours. At a certain place on the road—that is to say, on the horse tracks—at about fifteen miles from the Kegs—at twenty-five miles the Rawlinson could again be sighted—I saw that the tracks of the two loose horses we had turned back from there had left the main line of tracks, which ran east and west, and had turned about east-south-east, and the tracks of the Fair Maid of Perth, I was grieved to see, had gone on them also. I felt sure Gibson would soon find his error, and return to the main line. I was unable to investigate this any farther in my present position. I followed them about a mile, and then returned to the proper line, anxiously looking at every step to see if Gibson's horse tracks returned into them.

They never did, nor did the loose horse tracks either. Generally speaking, whenever I saw a shady desert-oak tree there was an enormous bulldog ants' nest under it, and I was prevented from sitting in its shade. On what I thought was the 27th I almost gave up the thought of walking any farther, for the exertion in this dreadful region, where the triodia was almost as high as myself, and as thick as it could grow, was quite overpowering and, being starved, I felt quite light-headed. After sitting down, on every occasion when I tried to get up again, my head would swim round, and I would fall down oblivious for some time. Being in a chronic state of burning thirst, my general plight was dreadful in the extreme. A bare and level sandy waste would have been paradise to walk over compared to this. My arms, legs, thighs, both before and behind, were so punctured with spines, it was agony only to exist; the slightest movement and in went more spines, where they broke off in the clothes and flesh, causing the whole of the body that was punctured to gather into minute pustules, which were continually growing and bursting. My clothes, especially inside my trousers, were a perfect mass of prickly points.

My great hope and consolation now was that I might soon meet the relief party. But where was the relief party? Echo could only answer—where? About the 29th I had emptied the keg, and was still over twenty miles from the Circus. Ah! who can imagine what twenty miles means in such a case? But in this April's ivory moonlight I plodded on, desolate indeed, but all undaunted, on this lone, unhallowed shore.

At last I reached the Circus, just at the dawn of the day. Oh, how I drank! How I reeled! How hungry I was! How thankful I was that I had so far at least escaped from the jaws of that howling wilderness, for I was once more upon the range, though still twenty miles from home.

There was no sign of the tracks, of anyone having been here since I left it. The water was all but gone. The solitary eagle still was there. I wondered what could have become of Gibson; he certainly had never come here, and how could he reach the fort without doing so?

I was in such a miserable state of mind and body that I refrained from more vexatious speculations as to what had delayed him: I stayed here, drinking and drinking, until about 10 a.m., when I crawled away over the stones down from the water. I was very footsore, and could only go at a snail's pace. Just as I got clear of the bank of the creek, I heard a faint squeak, and looking about I saw, and immediately caught, a small dying wallaby, whose marsupial mother had evidently thrown it from her pouch. It only weighed about two ounces, and was scarcely furnished yet with fur. The instant I saw it, like an eagle I pounced upon it and ate it, living, raw, dying— fur, skin, bones, skull and all. The delicious taste of that creature I shall never forget. I only wished I had its mother and father to serve in the same way.

I had become so weak that by late at night I had only accomplished eleven miles, and I lay down about five miles from the Gorge of Tarns, again choking for water. While lying down here, I thought I heard the sound of the footfalls of a galloping horse going campwards, and vague ideas of Gibson on the Fair Maid—or she without him—entered my head. I stood up, and listened, but the sound had died away upon the midnight air. On the 1st of May, as I afterwards found, at one o'clock in the morning, I was walking again, and reached the Gorge of Tarns long before daylight, and could again indulge in as much water as I desired; but it was exhaustion I suffered from, and I could hardly move.

My reader may imagine with what intense feelings of relief I stepped over the little bridge across the water, staggered into the camp at daylight, and woke Mr Tietkens, who stared at me as though I had been one new risen from the dead. I asked him had he seen Gibson, and to give me some food. I was of course prepared to hear that Gibson had never reached the camp; indeed I could see but two people in their blankets the moment I entered the fort, and by that I knew he could not be there. None of the horses had come back, and it appeared that I was the only one of six living creatures—two men and four horses— that had returned, or were now ever likely to return, from that desert, for it was now, as I found, nine days since I last saw Gibson.

JOHN FORREST
Fight for Water, 1874

 Such arrogance! To turn up at a waterhole in a remote part of the driest continent, to name it as if it was a new discovery, then camp by it and be *surprised* when you are told, in no uncertain terms, to clear off by those who have owned it for 50,000 years. John Forrest, who made his discovery near the Carnarvon Range in central Western Australia, was quick to see evidence of cannibalism among the Aborigines in a burned skull. Perhaps this made it a little easier to pull the trigger.

Forrest was a frontiersman, born and bred in the bush. The first city he ever saw was Melbourne, yet even its great sights failed to stir his imagination, for it seems that the only thing he rushed to see was the monument to Burke and Wills. Exploration, perhaps, was all to him.

June 1st—Barometer 28.38; thermometer 45° at 8 a.m. In collecting the horses we came on an old native camp and found the skull of a native, much charred, evidently the remains of one who had been eaten. Continued on about NE along a grassy flat, and at five miles passed some claypans of water, after which we encountered spinifex, which continued for fifteen miles, when we got to a rocky range, covered with more spinifex. Myself and Windich were in advance, and after reaching the range we followed down a flat about north for six miles, when it joined another large watercourse, both trending NNW and NW. We followed down this river for about seven miles, in hopes of finding water, without success...

2nd—Early this morning went with Pierre to look for water, while my brother and Windich went on the same errand. We followed up the brook about south for seven miles, when we left it and followed another branch about SSE, ascending which, Pierre drew my attention to swarms of birds, parakeets etc., about half a mile ahead.

We hastened on, and to our delight found one of the best springs in the colony. It ran down the gully for twenty chains, and is as clear and fresh as possible, while the supply is unlimited. Overjoyed at our good fortune, we hastened back and, finding that my brother and Windich had not returned, packed up and shifted over to the springs, leaving a note telling them the good news. After reaching the springs we were soon joined by them. They had only found sufficient water to give their own horses a drink; they also rejoiced to find so fine a spot. Named the springs the Weld Springs, after His Excellency Governor Weld, who has always taken such great interest in exploration, and without whose influence and assistance this expedition would not have been organised.[†] There is splendid feed all around. I intend giving the horses a week's rest here, as they are much in want of it, and are getting very poor and tired. Barometer 28.24; thermometer 71° at 5 p.m. Shot a kangaroo...

7th (Sunday)—Pierre shot an emu, and the others shot several

† Sir Frederick Weld was governor of Western Australia between 1869 and 1875.

pigeons. This is a splendid spot; emus and kangaroos numerous, pigeons and birds innumerable, literally covering the entire surface all round the place in the evenings. We have been living on game ever since we have been here. Intend taking a flying trip tomorrow; party to follow on our tracks on Tuesday. Read Divine Service. Barometer 28.38; thermometer 55° at 7 p.m.

8th—Started with Tommy Pierre to explore the country ENE for water, leaving instructions for my brother to follow after us tomorrow with the party. We travelled generally ENE for twenty miles over spinifex and undulating sandhills, without seeing water. We turned east for ten miles to a range, which we found to be covered with spinifex. Everywhere nothing else was to be seen; no feed, destitute of water; while a few small gullies ran out of the low range, but all were dry. Another range about twenty-four miles distant was the extent of our view, to which we bore. At twenty miles, over red sandy hills covered with spinifex and of the most miserable nature, we came to a narrow samphire flat, following which south, for two miles, we camped without water and scarcely any feed. Our horses were knocked up, having come over heavy ground more than fifty miles. The whole of the country passed over today is covered with spinifex, and is a barren worthless desert...

10th—We travelled on to the springs, which were only about three miles from where we slept last night, and camped. I intend staying here for some time, until I find water ahead or we get some rain. We are very fortunate in having such a good depot, as the feed is very good. We found that about a dozen natives had been to the springs while we were away. They had collected some of the emu feathers, which were all lying about. Natives appear to be very numerous, and I have no doubt that there are springs in the spinifex or valleys close to it. Barometer 28.08; thermometer 62° at 5.30 p.m....

12th—My brother and Windich started in search of water; myself and Pierre accompanied them about twelve miles with water to give their horses a drink. About ten o'clock we left them and returned to camp.

13th—About one o'clock Pierre saw a flock of emus coming to water, and went off to get a shot. Kennedy followed with the rifle. I climbed up on a small tree to watch them. I was surprised to hear natives' voices, and looking towards the hill I saw from forty to sixty natives running towards the camp, all plumed up and armed with spears and shields. I was cool, and told Sweeney to bring out the revolvers; descended from the tree and got my gun and cooeed to Pierre and Kennedy, who came running. By this time they were within sixty yards, and halted.

One advanced to meet me and stood twenty yards off; I made friendly signs; he did not appear very hostile. All at once one from behind (probably a chief) came rushing forward, and made many feints to throw spears. He went through many manoeuvres, and gave a signal, when the whole number made a rush towards us, yelling and shouting, with their spears shipped. When within thirty yards I gave the word to fire: we all fired as one man, only one report being heard. I think the natives got a few shots, but they all ran up the hill and there stood, talking and haranguing and appearing very angry.

We reloaded our guns, and got everything ready for a second attack, which I was sure they would make. We were not long left in suspense. They all descended from the hill and came on slowly towards us. When they were about 150 yards off I fired my rifle, and we saw one of them fall, but he got up again and was assisted away. On examining the spot we found the ball had cut in two the two spears he was carrying; he also dropped his woomera which was covered with blood. We could follow the blood-drops for a long way over the stones. I am afraid he got a severe wound.

My brother and Windich being away we were short-handed. The natives seem determined to take our lives, and therefore I shall not hesitate to fire on them should they attack us again. I thus decide and write in all humility, considering it a necessity, as the only way of saving our lives. I write this at 4 p.m., just after the occurrence, so that, should anything happen to us, my brother will know how and when it occurred.

5 p.m. The natives appear to have made off. We intend sleeping in the thicket close to camp, and keeping a strict watch, so as to be ready for them should they return to the attack this evening. At 7.30 my brother and Windich returned, and were surprised to hear of our adventure. They had been over fifty miles from camp ESE, and had passed over some good feeding country, but had not found a drop of water. They and their horses had been over thirty hours without water.

14th (Sunday)—The natives did not return to the attack last night. In looking round camp we found the traces of blood where one of the natives had been lying down. This must have been the foremost man, who was in the act of throwing his spear, and who urged the others on. Two therefore, at least, are wounded, and will have cause to remember the time they made their murderous attack upon us.

We worked all day putting up a stone hut, ten by nine feet, and seven feet high, thatched with boughs. We finished it; it will make us safe at night. Being a very fair hut, it will be a great source of defence. Barometer 28.09; thermometer 68° at 5 p.m. Hope to have rain, as without it we cannot proceed.

ROBERT LOGAN JACK
Each Caught Hold of Her Breasts, 1879

 Robert Jack was one of Australia's most prolific field geologists. In 1879–80 he undertook geological exploration for the Queensland government in Cape York. On several occasions he encountered Aborigines who were unaccustomed to Europeans, and I'm afraid he showed them scant respect. One meeting was so remarkable, however, that I still puzzle over its significance. Aborigines showered many explorers with the milk of human kindness. Here Jack certainly gets the milk, but I don't know about the kindness.

August 26—The horses had gone back a good way in the night, owing to the poorness of the grass, and it was about nine o'clock before we made a start. In ten miles (W 6° N) through desert country exactly like that of the previous day...We found some grass and water in a marshy bottom and camped for the night. There was a thunderstorm with heavy rain during the night.

August 27—Having dried our tents, we continued on the same course. In eight miles we came on two gins carrying a baby—mother, daughter and grandchild probably—the first natives we had seen near enough to speak to. The elder woman was hideous by nature and was rendered still more so by having her cheeks daubed with clay. The best that could be said of the younger was that she was less repulsive. She wore a fringe about four inches square, but her mother had no covering but mud. They were very much scared at first, but soon became very loquacious. Neither of our black boys understood a word of their language. We made known by signs our anxiety to find water, and the gins pointed to the west.

As the gins had more luggage than two could carry, they probably had companions who may have seen us and hidden themselves. We had the curiosity to overhaul their swags, but I was careful that the boys should take nothing. They had a well-made fishing net and line, about a score of long, thin bamboos for making fish-spears, and a net full of miscellanies, including two old jam-tins, some seashells (for drinking cups) and part of an old tent or fly. The European articles were probably spoils from the deserted Coen diggings. I was interested in seeing that the gins had distinctly the instinct of sexual modesty, as they kept getting behind trees and hiding behind one another during their parley with us. When we turned to leave, they followed us till we warned them that we did not desire their company. They seemed pleased at getting permission to retire, and I fancy they had in some way got it into their heads that they were bound to follow us as prisoners of war.

A low, table-topped hill of sandstone now appeared about a mile ahead of us, to W 26° N, and I made for it in order to have a look out for landmarks. We had scarcely started when Macdonald informed me that two of the horses were getting weak, while a third had fallen a long way behind, and was in a lather of perspiration and could hardly be pulled and pushed along by Grainer and Willie on foot. They had taken off his very light pack and put it on another horse. I was under the impression that the horses must have eaten some poisonous grass or herb. The superiority of such of the horses as have youth and breeding on their side comes out conspicuously in such a strait as we were now in. Not much could be expected from the best of them, however.

The country we had travelled over for three days was nothing but a wooded Sahara. The blacks had just burned what grass it usually bears. Once in ten miles or so we crossed a wet bottom with a little grass which had escaped the fire. But for these grassy patches the horses must have died of starvation.

It will be readily understood that I gazed from the hill with feelings of considerable anxiety for some change in the nature of the country. Westward (our proposed course) as far as the eye could reach, nothing but low, flat land was to be seen, and there was nothing to indicate an improvement in the character of the vegetation. With a heavy heart I admitted that to carry out my programme had become impossible, and made up my mind that the first thing to be done was to find water and camp, to save the failing horses; and the second, to strike the Normanby River or the Coen track and go back to the nearest point of the Palmer Road, spell the horses, and perhaps buy a few more to replace those that were unfit to travel.

Turning to the south-west (magnetic), in which direction I hoped to find the Normanby at its nearest point, we came in one mile to a waterhole in a sandy gully, with a little green picking for the horses.

August 28—...Half a mile above our camp there had been a native fishing station last wet season. The mouth of a gully (still retaining a few waterholes) had been stopped by a fence of stakes and twisted branches. The blacks must have got a good many large barramundi, judging from the heaps of large scales lying about. Six dome-shaped gunyahs, four feet high and six in diameter, were still standing. They were strongly built of flakes of tea-tree bark, secured with vines and tea-tree bark ropes to a framework of boughs. Every cranny was carefully stopped up with straw. The access was by a door fourteen inches square, stopped up with a wisp of straw. A heap of ashes lay inside each gunyah, opposite the door. I thought the buildings were designed for smoking fish, but the boys assured me that they were only for protection in the season when 'bigfellow rain come up'. It is an undeniable fact that Queensland natives can live where white men would be suffocated.

The next day (August 29), Brusher and Willie having been sent out with a shotgun and rifle to get game and report if they saw the Coen track, were attacked by natives while eating their lunch, about five miles down the river. One spear (barbed with kangaroo bone) lighted at Willie's feet, and a fishing-spear (a bamboo lance with four bloodwood prongs) broke in a tree above his head. The boys saw five natives in all, two of whom they shot dead—one of them while in the act of aiming a spear. The rest fled. Such, at least, was the boys' story, and I failed to shake it in any essential point by a long cross-examination. They brought home two spears in support of the story. I regret the circumstance, as I hoped to accomplish my peaceful mission without bloodshed; but I could not blame the boys for doing what I should have done myself had I been attacked.

In view of possible retaliation we kept a watch all night. It was clear moonlight, and it would have been easy for the natives to track the boys to the camp and treat us to a *camisade*. I did not doubt our joint ability to defend ourselves, but what was to prevent the natives wreaking their revenge (as is their custom) on the horses feeding out of our sight? Brusher insisted that the blacks would not start in pursuit till they had eaten the last of their two friends. We were not disturbed, which gives a colour to this theory; but my mind was not so easy as Brusher's. The boys, who do not usually watch with a good grace, were on the alert all night, even when 'their watch was below'—a circumstance which, I think, corroborates their story to some extent...

September 1—...In two miles NNW, we passed a large lagoon on the left. Five gins were surprised here engaged in digging lily-roots on the edge of the lagoon. They ran away at first, one gin leaving her child behind, but they shortly approached and jabbered volubly. The women had straight hair. One of them had a child about three days old, and it was interesting to note that it was marked with the boiled-lobster tint common among white children of the same age. The women stood in line and pointed with their left hands along the track, reminding me of the witches in *Macbeth*. They were understood by the boys to mean that their men were in that direction, and that we should go another way to avoid a collision.

One gesture of the 'weird sisters' surprised and puzzled us all. All at once each caught hold of her breasts and squirted milk towards us in copious streams. Perhaps they meant that they were entitled to our consideration as women and mothers. The party we met before had distinctly a sense of modesty, but this party had absolutely none.

EMILY CAROLINE CREAGHE
The Little Explorer's Diary, 1883

 'E. Carrie Creaghe. The Little Explorer's Diary'. Thus did Emily Caroline Creaghe sign the title page of her extraordinary, unpublished diary of frontier adventure. Accompanying her husband Harry, Creaghe was the only female member of Ernest Favenc's exploring expedition, which pushed deep into the Gulf country in 1882–83. Her account is of especial interest because of her perspective on Australia's barbarous northern frontier—well illustrated when she enters a settler's hut to see forty pairs of Aboriginal ears nailed to the walls. We drop in on her just as

an expedition member dies of sunstroke, and later at first
contact with some Aborigines.

18 January 1883—Found today that Mrs Favenc is not strong
enough to go out to the exploring expedition so, much to our
disgust, we have to give up all idea of going. She is going back
to Sydney with Mr Favenc and I am going to Mr Shadforth's
station 220 miles inland with Harry. When Mr Favenc returns
in March the two will go out with one man and get the work
done in three months instead of four and a half as they would
have done if we had gone...

20 January—Left Normanton at half past three p.m. for
'Magowrah', Mr Trimble's station, a distance of sixteen miles.
Arrived there at seven, about a dozen men camped all night and
eight of us belonging to the party going inland. Mr Shadforth,
Mr Murray, McNaught, Power, two men and ourselves. Being
the only female except one in the kitchen I felt decidedly queer
amongst such a number of men.

21 January—Left Magowrah, at nine a.m. passed the Bynoe
River, Flinders River and had dinner at Armstrong Creek. The
men left almost immediately after dinner for L Creek, a distance
of thirty-two miles, called after Leichhardt the explorer whose
initials are on a tree on the bank of the creek. I felt nearly done
up when we got to Armstrong Creek, having come sixteen miles
(and not yet being accustomed to long riding and poor food).
Managed to get to the end of the second stage but was nearly
knocked up. Got into camp at half past seven p.m. Rather hot,
scarcely anything but bare plains all the way.

22 January—Made a start at half past six a.m. Arrived at
camp a mile and a half this side of M Lagoon, twenty-two miles
from L Creek, called after Morrel—Leichhardt's companion—
at about noon. We, Harry and I, did intend remaining in camp
at L Creek all today as I am nearly 'finished' but there is every
appearance of rain, so we must push on to cross the River
Leichhardt before it is flooded. The hottest weather I have ever
felt today; the flies are something dreadful. Mr McNaught and

his man left the camp in the afternoon. Still the country is level and bare.

23 January—Left M Lagoon at half past five a.m. Passed Diary Creek and camped on Packsaddle Creek where the mosquitoes were something terrible...Diary Creek gets its name from an old diary being found there, and Packsaddle Creek from an old saddle being found there, both articles supposed to have belonged to Leichhardt's party. Nicely timbered country.

24 January—Left Packsaddle at half past eight a.m., the horses having got away and the men were from half past five looking for them. Travelled all the morning, passed Margaret Lagoon and are now camped on the banks of the River Leichhardt. There is an old tumbled-down public house close to the river crossing. The country is again plains and not much timber. The heat is intense, no rain yet but every appearance of it. Yesterday we did about twenty miles and today eighteen. There are plenty of crocodiles in the rivers but I have not seen many. Mr Warner had a fearful headache when we got to camp and we hope he has not had a touch of the sun.

25 January—Left the Leichhardt camp at 7 a.m. and arrived at 'The Rocky' at half past ten, a distance of fourteen or fifteen miles. Warner (Mr Murray's man) who had not been well last night got some terrible fits and has evidently had a sunstroke. He managed to drive the packhorses into camp but got ill immediately on arrival. Mr Watson and two men from his station twelve miles distant came up and he, being a friend of Harry's, stopped all day and night with us. He gave us an account of his being speared by the blacks some little time ago. He was of great assistance in trying to hold Warner during his fits. We are afraid Warner won't get over it, as he is still unconscious.

26 January—A plague of beetles last night. Warner is slightly better and has not had a return of the fits, but our going any further this morning is quite out of the question. We did not put up the tents last night for the first time as it looked so very unlike rain and it was too hot to sleep in it, so when a thunderstorm broke in the middle of the night, we all had to

turn out and put them up as fast as we could and only just put the finishing touches when down it came. Mr Watson went off before we were up. It is fine and very hot today (evening). Warner is much worse this evening. He is quite unconscious and has been so since 10 a.m. It is most painful to hear his groans. A terrific thunderstorm this evening at eight, got a little wet.

27 January—Warner died at three this morning. He never became conscious but his groans were something terrible at night. Poor Mr Murray sat with him. A death in a camping party is an awful thing. Mr Murray went away at 7 a.m. to Augustus Downs and brought back Mr Watson and two men with pick and shovel to dig a grave. Harry and I spent a miserable day until half past three by ourselves in camp guarding the body from native dogs. They have just sewn up his body in his blanket in the midst of a heavy thunderstorm, while some of the others are digging the grave. The poor fellow was quite young, strong, tall and healthy three days ago. 'In the midst of life we are in death.' Mr Watson and men will camp all night with us, and we shall leave early tomorrow morning.

Mr Watson brought us some milk, bread, plain cake and a watermelon which were great treats; at least the milk was. I have got into that state from not eating that I could not manage even cake. Our food in camp consists of nasty dirty hairy dried salt beef, dark brown sugar (half dust) and hard dry damper. There are some tinned meats, but the jolting has made them uneatable. There is some jam, but who can eat it with hard dry damper and no butter.

28 January—They finished the grave at 2 a.m. and so poor Warner was buried in the dead of night. The horses were troublesome so we did not start till twenty to nine this morning. Only went seven miles as the heat became so intense it was dangerous to travel, and camped till five o'clock at the side of a waterhole. Travelled till half past eight and them camped at the Ridgepoll on Fiery Creek about nineteen miles from the Rocky. The food we are living upon is something horrible, and I have scarcely touched a thing since we left Normanton; just two or

three mouthfuls at each meal, but make up for the want of food by drinking any amount of tea (without milk) which is detestable...

20 February—The rainy season seems to have set in properly. Mr Shadforth and Ernest came home...They brought a new black gin with them who can't speak a word of English. The usual method here of bringing in a new wild gin is to put a rope around her neck and drag her along from horseback, the gin on foot.

21 February—The new gin whom they call Bella is chained up to a tree a few yards from the house, and is not to be loosed until they think she is tamed.

23 February—Still raining heavily. The new gin Bella made Topsy (an old one) jealous and the latter threw a firestick at her and said she would kill her. The stick flew past Mrs Shadforth's face, so Madame Topsy got a thrashing.

24 February—Bella, the new gin, decamped in the night, whether it was because of Topsy's threat to kill her, or discontent at this life we don't know. They tracked her as far as the O'Shanassy but that river is a 'banker' so they could not afford to go after her any further. There is no mail expected for two months owing to the floods...

2 May—Mr Favenc and Mr Crawford took the horses back to the waterhole we were at yesterday to get a drink as they could not go on, as it was so probable we might be some time in finding more water. They left at half past six and returned at three and we packed up immediately after they had had a hurried lunch and left at four. Harry and I remained about the camp doing odd jobs all the morning. We are reduced to damper and honey as we have finished our cooked meat and have no water with which to boil the one piece that remains. We have some anchovy paste, but are afraid to eat it owing to its tendency to create thirst. We came on until about eight tonight, Mr Favenc carrying the lantern as on the previous night. We have not come upon water, but the horses can do without it for some hours

tomorrow and we trust we shall come upon it soon.

I had a tiny scrap of water spared me this morning to rinse my hands and face, but I feel extremely 'grubby'. We came over very rough country this afternoon, and at times we all had narrow escapes from being thrown off our horses, for the holes were so numerous and deep that it was only by holding on tightly and being on our guard that we managed to stay in our saddles when the horses stumbled into the holes.

3 May—It has been a very eventful day. We left camp soon after 8 a.m., anxious to hurry on as much as possible to reach water early. We continued our right course (west) for an hour and seeing no signs of water (viz. emus and native dog tracks or flocks of birds), we changed our course north. We went on till 2 p.m. and were despairing of getting water, when we saw not three miles straight ahead of us a blacks' fire (or smoke rather) and we made for it in desperation, knowing there would be water where niggers were.

We reached the fire and were going round it, when Favenc made a gallop and Crawford followed from behind with us, and we knew they must have seen blacks. Presently we got up to them and saw Favenc holding a man with one hand and in the other pointing his revolver at him, and Crawford holding a gin. They were a peculiar sight. The blacks had never seen a white man before, we soon found out by their showing no fear when Favenc pulled out his revolver.

When Mr Favenc came upon them, they climbed a small tree, and when he made signs for them to come down the nigger threw his gin down, thinking that might satisfy him, and it was some time before the black was induced to come down himself. Favenc tied him with a strap to prevent his running away before he had led us to water.

We were not going to do them any harm, so they remained captives till we had shown them, by giving them some drops of water to drink (which we had kept specially for the purpose) and signing to them what we wanted them to do. They then went on with a great many gesticulations which we suppose meant fright, and after taking us about three miles we came upon the main blacks' camp and a waterhole. There were seven men and nine gins and some piccaninnies. The gins bolted at our appearance and we saw nothing of them. One poor little baby was left by the mother in her fright and it was toddling about crying.

The blacks wear no clothing of any sort, and one of them had a carpet snake which he had killed tied round his waist ready to cook for his supper. The poor things were quiet and frightened, but not having been molested by white men they did not attempt to do us any harm. When we went down to the waterhole they all took up their boomerangs, so Harry remained on the bank with his revolver ready to fire at the first throw. They soon put them down however and came and stood about twenty yards away while we had dinner. We gave them some damper and they seemed pleased.

We left their camp at 4 p.m. and came on till eight through a dreadful scrub. How we got through in the dark without accident I don't know. We soon had the fire lit and the billy boiling for our meagre supper. We saw spears and things lying on the ground in the blacks' camp, but we took nothing away as harm has been done so often by white men stealing the blacks' only means of gaining their food. The man we caught first had a white plaited string made of bark round his head, and he threw it down when Favenc let him loose, as a sign of submission and peace. All the men amongst these blacks are circumcised.

CARL LUMHOLTZ
I Was Perfectly Shocked, 1883

 A Norwegian student of theology, Carl Lumholtz travelled to the rainforests of north Queensland in 1880 in search of zoological and ethnographic specimens. His search was spectacularly successful, for he collected most of the larger mammals of the Atherton forests, many of which were then new to science, during his sojourns with the Aborigines. His account of the discovery, then loss, in March 1883 of the tree kangaroo which was eventually to bear his name, is a classic of Australian biological exploration.

The blacks had for several days been talking about a dance to be held in a remote valley.

A tribe had learned a new song and new dances, and was going to make an exhibition of what it had learned to a number of people. The Herbert Vale tribe had received a special invitation to be present, and the natives assured me that there would be great fun. My action was determined by the fact that Nilgora, who owned the splendid dog Balnglan...would be there. But I had my misgivings on account of the horses, for as we were in the midst of the rainy season I ran some risk of not being able to bring them back again.

Early one morning we set out, a large party of men, women and children. A short time before reaching our destination we were met by a number of natives, for they expected us that night. Some of the strangers were old acquaintances of my people, but this fact was not noticeable, for they exchanged no greetings. In fact an Australian native does not know what it is to extend a greeting. When two acquaintances meet, they act like total strangers, and do not even say 'good-day' to each other. Nor do they shake hands. After they have been together for some time they show the first signs of joy over their meeting.

If a black man desires to show how glad he is to meet his old friend, he sits down, takes his friend's head into his lap, and begins to look for the countless little animals that annoy the natives, and which they are fond of eating. When the one has had his head cleaned in this manner, the two change places, and the other is treated with the same politeness. I accustomed myself to many of the habits of the natives during my sojourn among these children of nature, but this revolting operation, I confess, was a great annoyance to me.

A more emphatic sign of joy at meeting again is given by uttering shrieks of lamentation on account of the arrival of strangers to the camp. I was frequently surprised at hearing shrieks of this sort in the evenings, and found upon examination that they were uttered in honour of some stranger who had arrived in the course of the day. This peculiar salutation did not last more than a few moments, but was repeated several evenings in succession during the visit of the stranger. The highest token of joy on such occasions is shown by cutting their bodies in some way or other.

Later in the afternoon we arrived in the valley where the dance was to be. Those who were to take part in the dance had already been encamped there for several days. We had also taken time by the forelock, for the festivities were not to begin before the next evening. Several new arrivals were expected in the course of the next day, among them Nilgora. A proposition was made that two men should be sent to meet him on the mountain and request him to look for boongary on the way down, and early the next morning before sunrise they actually started, after being supplied with a little tobacco.[†]

My men and I had encamped about 200 paces from the others. I made a larger and more substantial hut than was my usual custom. It did not reach higher than my chest, but the roof was made very thick and tight on account of the rain. At first the blacks were very timid, but gradually the bravest ones among them began to approach my hut. As was their wont, they examined everything with the greatest curiosity. Yokkai walked about in the most conscious manner possible, and assumed an air of knowing everything. He brought water from the brook, put the tin pail over the fire, and accompanied by one or two admirers went down to the brook to wash the salt out of some salt beef which was to be boiled. The matches, the great amount of tobacco, my pocket handkerchief, my clothes, and my boots—

† Boongary: Lumholtz's tree kangaroo (*Dendrolagus lumholtzi*).

all made the deepest impression upon the savages. After unpacking, a newspaper was left on the ground. One of the natives sat down and put it over his shoulders like a shawl, examining himself to see how he looked in it; but when he noticed the flimsy nature of the material, he carelessly let it slip down upon the ground again.

My white woollen blanket provoked their greatest admiration, which they expressed by smacking with their tongues, and exclaiming in ecstasy: *Tamin, tamin!*—that is, Fat, fat! The idea of 'excellent' is expressed by the natives, as in certain European languages, by the word 'fat'.

It is an interesting fact that, much as the civilised Australian blacks like fat, they can never be persuaded to eat pork. 'There is too much devil in it,' they say.

At noon I heard continuous lamentations, but as I supposed they were for someone deceased, I paid but little attention to them at first. Lamentations for the dead, however, usually take place in the evening, and so I decided to go and find out what was going on. Outside of a hut I found an old woman in the most miserable plight. She had torn and scratched her body with a sharp stone, so that the blood was running and became blended with the tears which were flowing down her cheeks as she sobbed aloud.

Uncertain as to the cause of all this lamentation, I entered the hut, and there I found a strong young woman, lying half on her back and half on her side, playing with a child. I approached her. She turned her handsome face toward me, and showed me a pair of roguish eyes and teeth as white as snow, a very pleasing but utterly incomprehensible contrast to the pitiful scene outside. I learned that the young woman inside was a daughter of the old woman, who had not seen her child for a long time, and now gave expression to her joy in this singular manner. I expressed my surprise that the old woman's face did not beam with joy, but this seemed to be strange language to them. These children of nature must howl when they desire to express deep feeling.

Night was approaching, the sun was already setting behind the horizon, the air was very hot and oppressive, and it was evident that there would soon be a thunderstorm. The blacks sat at home in their huts or sauntered lazily from place to place, waiting until it became cool enough for the dance to begin. I had just eaten my dinner and was enjoying the shade in my hut, while my men were lying round about smoking their pipes, when there was suddenly heard a shout from the camp of the natives. My companions rose, turned their faces towards the mountain, and shouted, *Boongary, boongary!* A few black men were seen coming out of the woods and down the green slope as fast as their legs could carry them. One of them had a large dark animal on his back.

Was it truly a boongary? I soon caught sight of the dog Balnglan running in advance and followed by Nilgora, a tall powerful man.

The dark animal was thrown on the ground at my feet, but none of the blacks spoke a word. They simply stood waiting for presents from me.

At last, then, I had a boongary, which I had been seeking so long. It is not necessary to describe my joy at having this animal, hitherto a stranger to science, at my feet. Of course I did not forget the natives who had brought me so great a prize. To Nilgora I gave a shirt, to the man who had carried the boongary, a handkerchief, and to all, food. Nor did I omit to distribute tobacco.

I at once began to skin the animal, but first I had to loosen the withies with which its legs had been tied for the men to carry it. The ends of these withies or bands rested against the man's forehead, while the animal hung down his back, so that, as is customary among the Australians, the whole weight rested on his head.

I at once saw that it was a tree kangaroo (*Dendrolagus*). It was very large, but still I had expected to find a larger animal, for according to the statements of the natives a full-grown specimen was larger than a wallaby—that is to say, about the size of a sheep. This one proved to be a young male.

The tree kangaroo is without comparison a better proportioned animal than the common kangaroo. The fore-feet, which are nearly as perfectly developed as the hind-feet, have large crooked claws, while the hind-feet are somewhat like those of a kangaroo, though not so powerful. The sole of the foot is somewhat broader and more elastic, on account of a thick layer of fat under the skin. In soft ground its footprints are very similar to those of a child. The ears are small and erect, and the tail is as long as the body of the animal. The skin is tough and the fur is very strong and beautiful. The colour of the male is a yellowish-brown, that of the female and of the young is greyish, but the head, the feet and the underside of the tail are black. Thus it will be seen that this tree kangaroo is more variegated in colour than those species which are found in New Guinea.

Upon the whole, the boongary is the most beautiful mammal I have seen in Australia. It is a marsupial and goes out only in the night. During the day it sleeps in the trees and feeds on the leaves. It is able to jump down from a great height and can run fast on the ground. So far as my observation goes, it seems to live exclusively in *one* very lofty kind of tree, which is very common on the coast mountains, but of which I do not know the name. During rainy weather the boongary prefers the young low trees, and always frequents the most rocky and inaccessible localities. It always stays near the summit of the mountains, and frequently far from water, and hence the natives assured me that it never went down to drink.

During the hot season it is much bothered with flies, and then, in accordance with statements made to me by the savages, it is discovered by the sound of the blow by which it kills the fly. In the night, they say, the boongary can be heard walking in the trees.

I had finished skinning the animal, and so I put a lot of arsenic on the skin and laid it away to dry in the roof of my hut, where I thought it would be safe, and placed the skin there in such a way that it was protected on all sides.

Meanwhile my men had gone down to witness the dance. Happy over my day's success I too decided to go thither and amuse myself, but before I had prepared the skin with arsenic and could get away, darkness had already set in, and the dancing was postponed until the moon was up. The natives had in the meantime retired to their camps until the dance was to begin again.

The tribe that was to give the dance had its camp farthest away, while the other tribes, who were simply spectators, had made their camps near mine. There was lively conversation among the huts. All were seated round the camp fires and had nothing to do, the women with their children in their laps, and those who had pipes smoking tobacco. I went from one group to the other and chatted with them; they liked to talk with me, for they invariably expected me to give them tobacco. Occasions like this are valuable for obtaining information from the natives. Still, it is difficult to get any trustworthy facts, for they are great liars, not to mention their tendency to exaggerate greatly when they attempt to describe anything. Besides, they have no patience to be examined, and they do not like to be asked the same thing twice. It takes time to learn to understand whether they are telling the truth or not, and how to coax information out of them. The best way is to mention the thing you want to know in the most indifferent manner possible. The best information is secured by paying attention to their own conversations. If you ask them questions, they simply try to guess what answers you would like, and then give such responses as they think will please you. This is the reason why so many have been deceived by the savages, and this is the source of all the absurd stories about the Australian blacks.

Among the huts the camp fires were burning, and outside of the camp it was dark as pitch, so that the figures of the natives were drawn like silhouette pictures in fantastic groups against the dark background.

It amused me to make these visits, but my thoughts were chiefly occupied with the great event of the day. In the camp there were several dingoes and, although the boongary skin was carefully put away, I did not feel perfectly safe in regard to it. I therefore returned at once to look after my treasure; I stepped quickly into my hut, and thrust my hand in among the leaves to see whether the skin was safe; but imagine my dismay when I found that it was gone.

I was perfectly shocked. Who could have taken the skin? I at once called the blacks, among whom the news spread like wildfire, and after looking for a short time one of them came running with a torn skin, which he had found outside the camp. The whole head, a part of the tail and legs were eaten. It was my poor boongary skin that one of the dingoes had stolen and abused in this manner. I had no better place to put it, so I laid it back again in the same part of the roof, and then, sad and dejected in spirits, I sauntered down to the natives again.

Here everyone tried to convince me that it was not *his* dog that was the culprit. All the dogs were produced, and each owner kept striking his dog's belly to show that it was empty, in his eagerness to prove its innocence. Finally a half-grown cur was produced. The owner laid it on its back, seized it by the belly once or twice, and exclaimed, *Ammery, ammery!*—that is, Hungry, hungry! But his abuse of the dog soon acted as an emetic, and presently a mass of skin-rags was strewed on the ground in front of it.

My first impulse was to gather them up, but they were chewed so fine that they were useless. As the skin had been thoroughly prepared with arsenic, it was of importance to me to save the life of the dog, otherwise I would never again be able to borrow another.

Besides, I had a rare opportunity of increasing the respect of the natives for me. I told them that the dog had eaten *kola*— that is, wrath—as they called poison, and as my men had gradually learned to look at it with great awe, it would elevate me in their eyes if I could save the life of the dog. I made haste to mix tobacco and water. This I poured into the dog, and thus caused it to vomit up the remainder of the poisoned skin. The life of the dog was saved, and all joined in the loudest praises of what I had done. They promised me the loan of Balnglan again, and thus I had hopes of securing another boongary; of course they added as a condition that I must give them a lot of tobacco.

DAVID CARNEGIE
Sorry as I Was to Be Rude to a Lady, 1896

 David Carnegie began his career as an explorer somewhat compulsorily. He was a miner, but his searches took him so far from the beaten track that getting home again became a matter of life and death. Later, his yen for exploring seems to have got the better of his wish to become rich from gold, and carried him on a truly remarkable exploration through the centre of Western Australia.

We meet him here in the Gibson Desert, desperately tracking Aborigines so that he can force them to reveal the whereabouts of their waterholes. In this episode Carnegie treats an elderly Aboriginal woman abominably. Did he ever consider how he would react if someone had treated his own mother so?

The next morning [8 September] we were up betimes and ready to start as soon as ever the tracks were visible; presently a smoke, their first hunting-smoke of the day, rose close to us. Despatching Charlie on Satan and Godfrey on foot, with instructions to catch a native if possible, I hastened along the tracks followed by the rest of the party. We reached their camp just in time to see the late inmates disappear into a thicket of mulga close by. Neither Charlie nor Godfrey was able to come up with the lighters of the fire unseen, and these, too, fled into the scrub, where chase was almost impossible. Their camp deserves description, as it was the first (excepting travelling camps) we had seen of the desert blackfellow.

Facing the belt of mulga was a low wall of uprooted tussocks of spinifex built in a half circle and some two feet high. On the leeward side of this breakwind, inside the semicircle, half a dozen little hollows were scraped out in the sand. Between each of these nests lay a little heap of ashes, the remains of a fire which burns all night, replenished from time to time from a bundle of sticks kept handy for the purpose. The nest in the sand is the

335

bed, a double one, and not only double but treble and more; for in it, coiled up snugly, may lie several of the tribe, higgledy-piggledy, like pups in a basket. The fire takes the place of nightshirt, pyjamas or blankets—a poor substitute on a cold night!

Scattered about were several utensils, two wooden coolamons full of water and grass—this showing that the owners contemplated a journey, for the grass floating on the surface is used to prevent the water from spilling. Two more coolamons were filled with seed—a fine yellow seed from a plant like groundsel. Close by these were the flat stones (of granite, evidently traded from tribe to tribe) used for grinding the seed. In the spinifex wall were stuck numerous spears, varying from eight to ten feet in length, straight, thin and light, hardened by fire, fined down and scraped to a sharp point. Near these was a gin's yam-stick—a stout stick with a sharp, flat point on one end and charred at the other, used for digging up roots, stirring the fire, or chastising a dog or child. They serve, too, as a weapon of defence.

Quaintest of all these articles were the native 'portmanteaus', that is to say, bundles of treasures rolled up in bark, wound round and round with string—string made from human hair or from that of dingoes and opossums. In these 'portmanteaus' are found carved sticks, pieces of quartz, red ochre, feathers and a number of odds and ends. Of several that were in this camp I took two— my curiosity and desire to further knowledge of human beings, so unknown and so interesting, overcame my honesty, and since the owners had retired so rudely I could not barter with them. Without doubt the meat tins and odds and ends that we had left behind us have more than repaid them. One of these portmanteaus may be seen in the British Museum, the other I have still, unopened...

Between the camp and the well, which we easily found, there ran a well-beaten foot-pad, showing that this had been a favoured spot for some time past...We started at once to water the camels, which had had no drink since August 21st, a period of seventeen days, with the exception of two gallons apiece at Warri Well, where the parakeelya grew. By midnight all but three—Satan,

Redleap and Misery—had drunk as much as they could hold. These three had to be content with a small amount, for we could not get more without digging out the well, and this we proceeded to do. The night was hot and cloudy, and constant puffs of wind made work by the light of candles so impossible that we had perforce to bear the extra heat of a blazing fire...This was the second night without rest or food, and no more than a mouthful of water each, for on arrival we had given what our tanks contained to the thirsty camels...

It soon became clear that, labour as we would, the hole would yield but little so, leaving the rest to work, I took Warri, and continued the search for the natives...After a long, tedious day of tracking, we found ourselves back at our own camp. The natives—two bucks, two gins and three piccaninnies—travelled north to a dry well, and there split, the men going one way and the rest another. We chose the bucks to follow, and presently the rest joined in, and the whole family swung round until close to our camp. We could, by their tracks, see where they had herded together in fear under a beef-wood tree not one hundred yards from us. Just before sunset we again set forth, taking Czar and Satan as riding-camels, and were lucky in picking up tracks going in a fresh direction before night fell.

We camped on the tracks, and ran them in the morning, noticing two interesting things on the way: the first, several wooden sticks on which were skewered dried fruits, not unlike gooseberries; these were hidden in a bush and are remarkable, for they not only show that the natives have some forethought, but that they trade in edible goods as well as in weapons and ornaments. These fruits are from the *Solanum sodomeum*, and were only seen by us near the Sturt Creek (300 miles away).[†] The second, little heaps of the roots of a tree (known to me only as pine-mulga) stacked together, which had been sucked for water; we tried some but without result, and the tree the natives had

---

† *Solanum sodomeum*: a kind of bush tomato.

made use of did not seem to be different from others of its kind. This showed us, too, that they must be dry, and probably had had no water since our arrival at their well.

About midday we rode right on to their camp without warning. Again the scrub befriended them, but in spite of this I could have got ahead of them on Satan had his nose-line not snapped. Determined not to be baulked, I jumped down and gave chase, old Czar lumbering along behind, and Warri shouting with glee and excitement, 'Chase 'em—we catch 'em,' as if we were going through all this trouble for pleasure. Happy Warri! He never seemed to see gravity in anything.

It is almost incredible how quickly and completely a blackfellow can disappear; as if in a moment the whole family was out of sight. One black spot remained visible, and on it I centred my energies. Quickly overhauling, I overtook it, and found it to be an old and hideous gin, who, poor thing! had stopped behind to pick up some dingo puppies.

Sorry as I was to be rude to a lady, I had to make her prisoner, but not without a deal of trouble. 'Dah, dah, dah!' she shouted, scratching, biting, spitting, and tearing me with her horrid long nails, and using, I feel sure, the worst language that her tongue could command. I had to carry this unsavoury object back to her camp, she clutching at every bush we passed, when her hands were not engaged in clawing and scratching me. After her anger had somewhat abated she pointed out a rock-hole from which they had got their water. Securing the woman with a light rope, I put her in Warri's charge, who kept watch above, lest the natives should return and surprise us, whilst I descended the rock-hole to see what supply was there. A little water was visible, which I quickly baled into the canvas bags we had brought for the purpose.

The bottom of the hole was filled in with dead sticks, leaves, the rotting bodies of birds and lizards, bones of rats and dingoes. Into this ghastly mass of filth I sunk up to my middle, and never shall I forget the awful odour that arose as my feet stirred up the mess. Nevertheless water was there, and thankful I was to find it, even to drink it as it was. After half an hour's work in this stinking pit, sick from the combination of smells—distinguishable above every other being the all-pervading perfume of aboriginals—I was rewarded by some twelve gallons of water, or, more properly speaking, liquid.

I decided to take the gin back with us, as it had been clear to me for some time past that without the aid of natives we could not hope to find water. With our small caravan it was impossible to push on and trust to chance, or hope to reach the settled country still nearly 500 miles ahead in a bee-line. Even supposing the camels could do this enormous stage, it was beyond our power to carry sufficient water for ourselves. The country might improve or might get worse; in such weather as we now experienced no camel could go for more than a few days without water.

I felt myself justified, therefore, in unceremoniously making captives from what wandering tribes we might fall in with. And in light of after events I say unhesitatingly that, without having done so, and without having to a small extent used rough treatment to some natives so caught, we could not by any possibility have succeeded in crossing the desert, and should not only have lost our own lives, but possibly those of others who would have made search for us after.

'A man arms himself where his armour is weakest', so I have read; that, however, is not my case. I am not justifying myself to myself, or defending a line of action not yet assailed. I write this in answer to some who have unfavourably criticised my methods, and to those I would say, 'Put yourselves in our position, and when sitting in a comfortable armchair at home, in the centre of civilisation, do not, you who have never known want or suffered hardship, be so ready to judge others who, hundreds of miles from their fellow-men, threatened every day with possible death from thirst, were doing their best to lay bare the hidden secrets of an unknown region, as arid and desolate as any the world can show.'

On starting back for camp the gin refused to walk or move in any way, so we had to pack her on Czar, making her as comfortable as possible on Warri's blankets, with disastrous results thereto. Arrived at camp, I found that the rock-hole was bottomed, and now quite dry. Straining the putrid water brought by me through a flannel shirt, boiling it, adding ashes and Epsom salts, we concocted a serviceable beverage. This, blended with the few gallons of muddy water from the well, formed our supply, which we looked to augment under the guidance of the gin. After completing our work the well presented the appearance of a large rock-hole, thirty feet, deep, conical in shape, of which one half of the contents had been dug out. This confirmed my opinion that the native wells of these regions are nothing more than holes in the bed-rock, which have been covered over and in by the general deposit of sand. I had no time to observe for latitude at this spot, the position of which is fixed merely by dead reckoning. The rock-hole lies eight miles from it to the SE by E, and has no guide whatever to its situation. I christened the well 'Patience Well', and I think it was well named.

From September 8th, 9 a.m. until September 12th, 12.30 a.m. we had worked almost continuously, only taking in turn what sleep we could snatch when one could be spared; and the result, 140 gallons as sum total, inclusive of mud and other matter.

We left Patience Well on the 12th, at 10 a.m., taking the woman with us. Breaden was the only one in whose charge she would consent to be at all calm; to him therefore was allotted the duty of looking after her. At eleven we reached the dry well to which Warri and I had tracked the natives. The water we were forced to use was so uninviting that I decided to make another effort to find a supply in this locality. The gin was of no use whatever, and would only repeat whatever we said to her—*gabbi*, which King Billy had understood, was wasted on her. '*Gabbi, gabbi,*' she repeated, waving her arm all round the horizon.[†]

Leaving the rest to bottom the dry well, which might have water lower down, Warri and I again started off on the tracks of a buck, and these we followed due north on foot for four and

[†] King Billy: an Aborigine captured by Carnegie earlier in the expedition.

a half hours, hoping every moment to come on a well. Soon after starting, an apparently old track joined the other, and together they marched still north. Presently the old tracks changed into fresh ones, and close by I found two rough sandals made of strips of bark. One I kept, the other was nearly worn out. There was no change in the dreary appearance of the country; through scrubs, over stones and sand we held our way, until Warri, who was now a little way behind, called, 'No good, no more walk!' I could see the poor boy was knocked up, and felt little better myself; to go on did not guarantee water, and might end in disaster, so after a short rest we retraced our steps.

The night was now dark and oppressive, so hatless and shirtless we floundered through the spinifex, nearly exhausted from our walk, following so close on the last few days' work. I believe that but for Warri I should have been 'bushed'; my head was muddled and the stars not too clear. What a joyful sight met our eyes as we crested a rise of sand—a sight almost as reviving as the food and water we so anxiously looked forward to. Tongues of flame shot up in the air, a fire lit by our mates, but showing that, in spite of Warri's instinct, we had not been walking in quite the right direction.

No welcome news greeted our arrival—the well was dry, and the native obdurate. We all agreed she was useless, and since she refused all forms of nutriment I feared she would die on our hands, so she regained her liberty, and fled away with a rapidity not expected in one of her years.

LAWRENCE WELLS
Dried Like a Mummy, 1897

 Two young men, Charles Wells and George Jones, joined Albert Calvert's 1896 expedition to northern Australia, and never returned. Their mummified bodies, along with a pathetic notebook documenting their last days, were finally found the following year in the desert to the north of Separation Well, at the centre of the most forbidding part of Western Australia. A map of the area shows a trackless tangle of sand dunes, the well a tiny pinprick in the middle of nothingness.

The bodies were found by a party led by Lawrence Wells, Charles' cousin, who had sent the two men out into the desert to make their own discoveries. Despite the grief he must have felt at seeing his cousin's remains, his treatment of Aborigines was so abominable it is hard to empathise with him. We join the search party in the Great Sandy Desert.

Monday 24 May—Started Bejah with the camels, accompanied by Sandy and the tracker Ned, for Joanna Spring. Taking Ned's horse, I accompanied Mr Ord, Nicholson, and Bob. Bearing north 152° east in the direction where smokes were seen yesterday, we travelled over wretched desert sand ridges for ten miles, when smoke began to rise in several directions: one, which we made for, immediately on our bearing. Getting close to it, Bob crawled up a sand ridge to 'look out', and returning reported two natives some distance east along the ridge, which we followed down, and crossing over it, galloped down upon them, but discovered they were two gins, the elder almost a dwarf about thirty years of age, and the other a young gin, and good-looking for a native.

They were very frightened at first, but the younger soon recovered and, in answer to our inquiries, pointed on the course we were taking for a water called Djillill, thirteen miles from our camp, and took us to it. Here we surprised a wizard or doctor rejoicing in the name of Yallamerri. He rushed out of a bough wurley with a spear, shaking it at Bob who covered him with this rifle, and would have fired but for Mr Ord, who called to him to desist. There were also four small boys at the water. The wise man could not understand the horses, and was trembling with fear.

Searching the camp, we found several pieces of iron, including a large piece of a part of the bow of a camel riding saddle. It was sharpened at one end, evidently for use as an axe. Questioning the native about this, he said, '*Purrunng* whitefellow', pointing south-westerly. Noting smokes a few miles WNW, we took the wise man, gins and children in that direction. The old fellow pleaded lameness, but, being prodded occasionally with a spear, he soon forgot he was lame. He was most anxious to go for a number of smokes where he pointed saying, '*Jibir*', and counting ten on his fingers; but as we did not want ten more natives, we made him go for a single smoke bearing north 280° east for four miles, where we found a native, whom with Yallamerri's assistance we enticed to come up to us.

He was a bold-looking customer, and walked round the horses in astonishment, making peculiar noises with his tongue and lips. Informing them they must come on with us to Joanna Spring (Biggarong), they both pleaded lameness, afterwards pointing northwards in the direction of the smokes, saying Biggarong was there. Finding we were to have trouble, Mr Ord handcuffed them together. Sending the gins and children back to Djillill, I rode in advance, bearing north 247° east, whilst Mr Ord and Nicholson drove the natives after me, having to jostle them to make them follow up. After travelling eight miles, they ran up behind me and decided I was going in the right direction.

Reached the spring at ten miles and found that Bejah's party had arrived.

Travelled for day twenty-seven miles. We chained the natives to the tree I had previously marked here. They had visited this tree since I had marked it, and cut all the lettering off. The younger native, whose names is Pallarri, says *wanndanni* had done this, meaning the women. Being a descendant of Adam I suppose we must excuse him. We found the spring in the same condition as on our last visit, the supply being abundant. Hundreds of birds are now coming here to water.

This being the birthday of Her Majesty the Queen, we drank her health in whisky.

The natives are fastened to the tree by means of chains padlocked round their necks, and their legs are fastened with handcuffs. They have a break of bushes and some firewood, the nights being cold now. I was very anxious and could not rest, fearing the natives would get away. In the middle of the night I noticed a flicker of light and could see from behind my saddle where I was sleeping their dark eyes by the scanty firelight. For a long while I watched them trying to get the chain over their heads. Twice I called Mr Ord; the second time he was annoyed and administered a little chastisement to Master Yallamerri, telling them both to *lummbo*.

Tuesday 25 May—We bagged thirteen galahs and six pigeons this morning.

Spelled the camels here today, and filled kegs. During the afternoon Mr Ord and myself, each with a tracker, circled around the spring for some miles, to ascertain whether any other of the natives had come in, acting as spies; but we could see no signs of them.

We shall have difficulty in inducing these natives to conduct us to the spot where our comrades have perished. They say that two are dead and that the sun killed them, but they profess ignorance regarding the locality, and state that the women and children had found the remains and taken the goods. They are anxious to go north-west to some smokes where they say other natives are. No doubt they are afraid and naturally think we are in quest of the equipment our friends had and cannot understand our coming after the bodies or bones of dead men. Tomorrow, Wednesday, we purpose travelling westward.

Wednesday 26 May—Left Joanna Spring at 7.30 a.m., Bejah in advance with the camels, and following my old pad westerly, then the two natives handcuffed together, and Mr Ord with Nicholson, the trackers and myself bringing up the rear. We frequently asked the natives where the dead men were, but they were silent on this subject. We heard the elder native telling the younger something in whispers. They were very eager to go north and eventually said the dead men were in that direction. I could not stand this for it would not agree with statements made by the natives at other times.

At fifteen miles we reached the top of an unusually high sand ridge and halted to again question the natives. They pointed eagerly for Joanna Spring or other places, and also where other natives were, but on my suggesting the whereabouts of the dead white men they said nothing but walked on. It was most exasperating and Mr Ord, losing patience, cantered after them, and lifting Master Pallarri off his legs by a chignon (the style in which they dress the hair in these parts) shook him and brought them both back.

Pallarri angrily exclaimed *wah* at this treatment, and when I questioned him and spoke severely he laughed at me. Mr Ord then instructed Nicholson to administer a little moral suasion, whereupon Pallarri threw himself on the sand, partly dragging the wizard with him. Master Yallamerri, trembling and becoming afraid that his time had arrived, turned to me and eagerly snapping his fingers in a southerly direction exclaimed, '*Purrunng* whitefellow.'

Pallarri jumping up, they started off at a Chinaman's trot, exclaiming, '*Bah! bah!*' which I suppose means 'Go quickly'. Whistling to Bejah we gave him a sign to wheel round, and driving the natives we followed them for three miles when it was getting late, so we decided to camp for the night. Our last course was north 145° east. After the natives were chained up and fed and made comfortable I explained that if they did not take us to the dead men they would get neither food, water, nor fire. They replied, '*Mabu, mabu.*' As I feed them and have so far not hurt them they say I am good, but they have a wholesome dread of Nicholson, the chain, and handcuffs, and look with suspicion upon Mr Ord.

Thursday 27 May—After we had packed and mounted this morning, the natives, when loosened, again attempted to plead their ignorance, but upon Nicholson dismounting they ran off on the same bearing, exclaiming, '*Bah! Bah!*' At two miles on this course they halted on a high sand ridge and had a conversation together. Urging them on they then turned south-westerly for one and a half miles, when we came to a recently burnt patch of porcupine. Yallamerri then held his hand up, and moving his fingers about said, '*Purrunng* whitefellow.' Urging them forward again they ran along with their '*Bah! Bah!*'.

Immediately in front of us was a high point of sand ridge with a low saddle to the west. Being on my camel this morning I had a better view and, seeing a rope hanging from a small desert gum tree on the ridge, I drew Sub-Inspector Ord's attention to it. The natives, now at the foot of the ridge, exclaimed in one awed breath, '*Wah! Wah!*' I could then see my cousin's iron-grey beard, and we were at last at the scene of their terrible death, with its horrible surroundings:—

Where Nature is sombre and sear,
Midst Solitude's silent embrace;
In reflection—pray pardon a tear
For the heroes who died in this place.

Dismounting, Mr Ord and myself went to my cousin, whilst Nicholson and Bejah went where they saw some remnants of the camp equipment and found the body of Mr G. L. Jones, which was partly covered with drift sand.

Where Charles Wells lay, half-clothed and dried like a mummy, we found nothing but a rug, a piece of rope hanging from a tree, and some old straps hanging to some burnt bushes, which held the brass eyelets of a fly that had either been rifled by the natives or burnt by a fire which had been within a few feet of his body. Where Mr Jones lay and near his head was a notebook with a piece of paper fastened outside it by an elastic band. It was addressed to his father and mother.

On suggesting to Sub-Inspector Ord that we should not open the note, he pointed out that in his official capacity it was imperative that he should see the contents. Besides, the note might give us something to act upon out here. Amongst a heap of remnants of their equipment we also found a satchel containing a box of medicines, a prayer book, leather pouch, Mr Jones's compass and journal, which was kept from the time of their departure from Separation Well until they returned to that water.

He stated in his journal that they had gone WNW for five days, after separating from the main party, then travelling a short distance NE, and that both himself and Charles had felt the heat terribly and were both unwell. They then returned to the well, after an absence of nine days, rested at the water five days, and then started to follow our tracks northward. Afterwards one of their camels died, which obliged them to walk a great deal and they became very weak and exhausted by the intense heat. When writing he says that two days previously he attempted to follow their camels, which had strayed, but after walking half a mile felt too weak to go further and returned with difficulty.

Charles Wells, he then said, was very ill indeed. There was, at that time, but about two quarts of water remaining to them, and he did not think they could last long after that was finished.

The natives have rifled the spot of everything that would be of any service to them. They have by some means cut up and removed the whole of the iron from the riding saddle, and taken all the hoops from both pairs of water-kegs, firearms etc. Although we made a careful search we could not find any writing left by my cousin, nor his journal, plans, sextant, compass, artificial horizon or star charts etc. and, with the exception of the map I picked up at the well six miles south-west of this spot, we have not seen a sign of any of these articles amongst the different natives I have met with.

Looking at my cousin as he lay on the sand with features perfect and outstretched open hand, I recalled the time we last parted when I felt his hard, strong grip. I little thought then that this would be our next meeting! I remember we spent a lively evening, our last together, at Separation Well, when both he and Mr Jones were joking freely, hopeful and full of life. The lines of his favourite poet, Adam Lindsay Gordon, occur to me—

With the pistol clenched in his failing hand,
With the death mists spread o'er his fading eyes,
He saw the sun go down on the sand,
And he slept and never saw it rise.

God grant that whenever, soon or late,
Our course is run and our goal is reached,
We may meet our fate as steady and straight
As he whose bones on yon desert bleached.

This spot is six miles north-easterly from the well where we encountered natives in April last, with rifled goods in their possession, and my camel pad from that place to Joanna Spring passes within a quarter of a mile to the south-east of the scene.

Sub-Inspector Ord has taken charge of all articles found here, and the bodies are sewn up in sheets ready for removal to Derby.

Leaving this melancholy spot we followed my old pad *en route* for Joanna Spring, during the afternoon, travelling seven miles, and camped for the night. The natives are well fed, but still prisoners.

Friday 28 May—Travelling eight miles this morning, we returned to Joanna Spring, and camped to allow our horses to recruit.

Saturday 29 May—Myself, Mr Ord and two trackers, with Yallamerri as guide, started in a south-easterly direction to try and find Bundir Water, of which natives had previously informed me. Yallamerri explains that that water is at present dead—'Bundir purrunng napa'. But we could not make him understand that we merely wanted to see the place. After going eight miles, the whole distance having recently been burnt, he told us the waters round about were all dead and not springs—'Waddji tcharramarra'— that the only spring water was far away east-south-east, and it would take three sleeps to reach the spots.

Returning to Joanna Spring we questioned the natives, and they said there was another spring to the westward, but not in their country. They also knew nothing of a water called Lambeena which, in my opinion, must therefore be a considerable distance from here. Travelled sixteen miles per day.

Sunday 30 May—Started on return journey, travelling twenty miles along our old camel pad. The natives we have taken as far as this for our own safety. They both fairly broke down this morning, when they found the direction we were taking them. And crying 'Sunndai' they pretended great lameness. However, forcing them along for fourteen miles, they then forgot their ailments, and Yallamerri caught six bandicoots amongst the clumps of porcupine grass.

Monday 31 May—Presenting the natives with knives, hand-kerchiefs, some food and water, we liberated them, telling them they could go back again to Djillill. They stood on the first sand ridge and watched us out of sight.

LOUIS DE ROUGEMONT
Illywhacker, 1899

The wonderfully named Henri Louis Grin, alias Louis de Rougemont, provides the only fictitious account of exploration included in this anthology and earns his place because he is such an outrageous liar. The Swiss-born Grin arrived in Western Australia in 1875 as a butler but ultimately surfaced in Sydney where he sold real estate. After a stint in New Zealand as a spiritualist he returned to England in 1898 and published his imaginary adventures under the name Louis de Rougemont. Below, he tells of being besieged, along with his Aboriginal wife Yamba, by an extraordinary plague of rats.

One day as we were marching steadily along, Yamba startled me by calling out excitedly, 'Up a tree—quick! Up a tree!' And so saying she scampered up the nearest tree herself. Now, by this time I had become so accustomed to acting upon her advice unquestioningly that without waiting to hear any more I made a dash for the nearest likely tree and climbed into it as fast as I could. Had she called out to me, 'Leap into the river,' I should have done so without asking a question.

When I was safely in the branches, however, I called out to

her (her tree was only a few yards away), 'What is the matter?'

She did not reply, but pointed to a vast stretch of undulating country over which we had just come; it was fairly well wooded. It lingers in my mind as a region in which one was able to see a fairly long way in every direction—a very unusual feature in the land of 'Never Never'.

I looked, but at first could see nothing. Presently, however, it seemed to me that the whole country in the far distance was covered with a black mantle, *which appeared to be made up of living creatures.*

Steadily and rapidly this great mysterious wave swept along towards us and, seeing that I was both puzzled and alarmed, Yamba gave me to understand that *we should presently be surrounded by myriads of rats*, stretching away in every direction like a living sea. The phenomenon was evidently known to Yamba and she went on to explain that these creatures were migrating from the lowlands to the mountains, knowing by instinct that the season of the great floods was at hand. That weird and extraordinary sight will live in my memory for ever. I question whether a spectacle so fantastic and awe-inspiring was ever dealt with, even in the pages of quasi-scientific fiction.

It was impossible for me to observe in what order the rats were advancing, on account of the great stretch of country which they covered. Soon, however, their shrill squeals were distinctly heard, and a few minutes later the edge of that strange tide struck our tree and swept past us with a force impossible to realise. No living thing was spared. Snakes, lizards—ay, even the biggest kangaroos—succumbed after an ineffectual struggle. The rats actually ate those of their fellows who seemed to hesitate or stumble. The curious thing was that the great army never seemed to stand still. It appeared to me that each rat simply took a bite at whatever prey came his way, and then passed on with the rest.

I am unable to say how long the rats were in passing—it might have been an hour. Yamba told me that there would have been no help for us had we been overtaken on foot by these migratory rodents. It is my opinion that no creature in nature, from the elephant downwards, could have lived in that sea of rats. I could not see the ground between them, so closely were they packed. The only creatures that escaped them were birds.

The incessant squealing and the patter of their little feet made an extraordinary sound, comparable only to the sighing of the wind or the beat of a great rainstorm. I ought to mention, though, that I was unable accurately to determine the sound made by the advancing rats owing to my partial deafness, which you will remember was caused by the great wave which dashed me on to the deck of the *Veielland,* just before landing on the sand-spit in the Sea of Timor. I often found this deafness a very serious drawback, especially when hunting. I was sometimes at a loss to hear the 'cooee' or call of my natives. Fortunate men! *They* did not even understand what deafness meant.

Lunacy also was unknown among them, and such a thing as suicide no native can possibly grasp or understand. In all my wanderings I only met one idiot or demented person. He had been struck by a falling tree, and was worshipped as a demigod!

When the rats had passed by, we watched them enter a large creek and swim across, after which they disappeared in the direction of some ranges which were not very far away. They never seemed to break their ranks; even when swimming, one beheld the same level brownish mass on the surface of the water. Yamba told me that this migration of rats was not at all uncommon, but that the creatures rarely moved about in such vast armies as the one that had just passed.

I also learned that isolated parties of migrating rats were responsible for the horrible deaths of many native children, who had, perhaps, been left behind in camp by their parents, who had gone in search of water.

HEDLEY HERBERT FINLAYSON
Oolacunta, 1931

 In December 1931 Hedley Herbert Finlayson made an extraordinary discovery. A chemist with a passion for the mammals of his native South Australia, Finlayson had heard rumours that a kind of rat-kangaroo, known to the Aborigines as oolacunta, existed in the far north of the state. He undertook an 1100-kilometre trek from Adelaide to investigate. Upon arriving at Appamunna station, among the gibber plains and sand ridges, he found that the oolacunta was no other than the Desert rat kangaroo, a species described by John Gould in 1843 but never recorded again until Finlayson's rediscovery. Remarkably, although Finlayson found the species to be common in northern South Australia and south-western Queensland between 1931 and 1935, this mysterious animal has never been heard of since.

We 'pulled off' finally on a little stony plain with scattered saltbush, and made our depot camp under some corkwoods. We were five miles from water, but the boys seemed so assured that the country was 'right', that we decided to endure the discomforts of a waterless camp for the benefit of being near the coveted *Caloprymnus*. But I had grave misgivings. All the five bettongs that are the nearest allies of the oolacunta, I have seen in the country of their choice, and anything less promising than this stony, shelterless plain in the blaze of midsummer would be difficult to imagine. But the blacks were right.

The plan of campaign had been anxiously debated all the way in from Appamunna. The great open sweep of the country is so immense that all methods of procedure partook somewhat of hunting for a needle in a haystack. Snaring and trapping were out of the question, shooting was too damaging to skeletons, and the most practicable method (while the horses lasted) seemed to be for the whole party to beat up the country mounted, and gallop anything which was put up.

At this juncture Butcher created a sensation by announcing that he could catch oolacuntas by hand. When questioned, he explained that many years ago when 'big mob jump up alonga Barcoo', the blacks used to locate the grass nests and then, determining the direction in which the opening lay, would, if the wind were right, sneak up behind and, silently slipping a coolamon or their hands over the top, bag the occupant! Some jealousy existed between Butcher and Jimmy, and Reese and I were inclined to attribute this account to a desire to shine. Moreover, there was a certain Alice-in-Wonderlandish touch about this method of capture by the 'laying on of hands'. So much so that Reese, on reflection, was constrained to administer a grave rebuke to Butcher, suggesting indeed that he was a sanguinary liar. But in this we wronged him.

Seldom do the things one keenly desires come easily. But on our very first cast we got a prize. The six of us rode east in the early morning, and on a sandhill picked up fresh oolacunta tracks crossing to a flat on the far side. We followed them out till we lost them in the gibbers; then we opened out to a half-mile front and rode slowly south, each man scanning every lump and tussock for a possible nest. We had ridden less than half an hour when there came a shrill excited '*Yuchai*' from the horse-boy farthest out, and the chase was on. The pre-arranged plan was for each of us to take up the galloping in turn, the rat being headed whenever possible and turned in towards the rest of the party who remained in a group. When the first horse showed signs of losing heart, the next man took the first opportunity of replacing him, and so on.

Following the yell, Tommy came heading back down the line towards the sandhill, but it was only after much straining of eyes that the oolacunta could be distinguished—a mere speck, thirty or forty yards ahead. At that distance it seemed scarcely to touch the ground; it almost floated ahead in an eerie, effortless way that made the thundering horse behind seem, by comparison, like a coal hulk wallowing in a heavy sea.

They were great moments as it came nearer; moments filled

with curiosity and excitement, but with a steady undercurrent of relief and satisfaction. It was here!

Caloprymnus bears a strong external resemblance to five or six other related species and from a distance there was little to distinguish that which was approaching from either of two other marsupials known to occur in adjoining tracts. But as it came down the flat towards me, a little pale ghost from the 1840s, all doubt fled. The thing was holding itself very differently from the bettongs. As I watched it through the shimmering heat haze, some sense of the incongruous brought back a vivid memory of a very different scene, two years before, when I had sought the nearest living relative of *Caloprymnus*, above the snowline on a Tasmanian range.

Imagine a little animal about the bulk of a rabbit, but built like a kangaroo, with long spindly hind legs, tiny forelegs folded tight on its chest, and a tail half as long again as the body but not much thicker than a lead pencil, and you have it in the rough. But its head, short and blunt and wide, is very different from that of any kangaroo or wallaby, and its coat is uniformly coloured a clear pale yellowish ochre—exactly like the great clay-pans and floodplains.

As it came up to us I galloped alongside to keep it under observation as long as possible. Its speed, for such an atom, was wonderful, and its endurance amazing. We had considerable difficulty in heading it with fresh horses. When we finally got it, it had taken the starch out of three mounts and run us twelve miles; all under such adverse conditions of heat and rough going, as to make it almost incredible that so small a frame should be capable of such an immense output of energy. All examples obtained subsequently by this method behaved similarly; they persisted to the very limit of their strength, and quite literally, they paused only to die.

Back at the camp all was jubilation. The afternoon and most of the next day were spent in examining, sketching, photographing, measuring, dissecting, and preserving—for luck is not to be trusted. And I wanted to make the very most of the first specimen lest it be also the last. We rode out each day, sometimes to success, sometimes not. In the afternoons we worked on the rats which the 'rat boss' had dug, while the heat under the corkwoods grew ever worse and worse. Even the old hands, reared under the grim old tradition of 'salt beef, damper, and constipation', who love to hark back to the summers when it really *was* hot, admitted subsequently that it had been bad. I had thought the still days bad, but when the hot winds came I thought again. When the flies and ants and heat and sand could be endured no longer, we left the skinning and spelled. And while we gazed out over the white-hot flats and sandhills, we sipped boiling tea, and had torturing visions of iced Quellthaler in an old-time shady garden.

On the day before we broke camp to start on the long ride to Cordilla and the Innamincka track, Butcher quashed for ever the soft impeachment which Reese had made on his veracity and covered himself with glory.

It was usual for two of the boys to take the horses to water each evening near sundown, and fill the canteens at the hole five miles away. On this afternoon they had been gone no more than half an hour when Butcher rode back into camp alone. With impassive face and in dignified silence, he handed over a bag tied at the mouth. Very cautious investigation showed it to contain a beautiful fully adult oolacunta and a half-grown joey— both alive and undamaged. Those we had run down were too exhausted to make good life-studies for a camera, but here were fitting subjects at last.

In riding over the country, we had had ample confirmation of Butcher's statement about the nest-building habit of *Caloprymnus*. In a fiery land, where a burrowing habit is the chief factor in the survival of most species, the oolacunta clings pathetically to a flimsy shelter of grass and leaves, which it makes in a shallow depression scratched out of the loam. And now, here was a splendid proof of his second claim. The Yalliyanda boy had, while riding with the others, spotted a nest and noted the head of the occupant in the opening, watching the party. He rode on without pause for a quarter of a mile, then, leaving his horse, made a rapid stalk up the wind and grabbed both mother and babe from behind.

The laying on of hands was no myth!

MICHAEL TERRY
Like a Gun Going Off, 1932

 Michael Terry was a prospector who has been characterised as 'the last explorer', and in a sense he was, for in the 1930s he pushed deep into the uncharted and hostile deserts of Western Australia on camel back. There he encountered 'warramulla blacks' in meetings and confrontations reminiscent of those experienced by Sturt and others a century before. He also had a wonderful sense of humour, and an impeccable sense of when to turn back. We first encounter him west of Alice Springs as he gets to know his camels, and then at Lake Mackay where he gives up the chase for his el dorado.

Having selected a dead bush for firewood, and two less than usually denuded tress for shade, the camels were wooshed down.

'Quiet feller Lockey, and quiet feller Jack,' Ben admonished the boys not to hurry them. Nothing irritates a camel more than to have its noseline jerked. One light pull, perhaps a tap on its knee with your foot is enough. It may look round a bit as though composing itself for descent; that's its style so leave it alone and move on to the next.

In a jiffy Stan had dried timber in flame. The boys mustered the quart pots, their own and ours, filled them from a tap in a canteen, put them by the fire. Ben and I undid a flap on one of the kitchen boxes, pulled out the tucker box, carried it over to the tree, spread a piece of cloth on the table (the ground) and set out the rations.

A chunk of corned beef on a slab of damper and a lump of

brownie* for the boys. Carved corned beef and slices of damper
with butter on a plate for us—what we had they had.

'Boil-oh; up and at it,' sang out Stan from the fire, 'bring
over the tea.'

'Tucker ready, Lockey. Come up.'

The boys walked over from their own shade, stood at the
table whilst I handed them their rations, walked to the fire to
collect their quart pots of tea, brought them to me for sugar,
and returned to their own camp whilst we settled down in ours.

Barely had we begun to feed when Dolly, for no apparent
reason, stood up. Down went Ben's plate, up went his hand to
her noseline, down went Dolly.

That's the trial of crib time. Some days the team sits quietly;
other days one after another they get up and destroy the peace
and rest of the hour.

Now whilst we sat at food, my riding camel, Rocket, so far
unnamed, sort of christened himself. We noticed a habit peculiar
in that his stomach gases seemed to ricochet through his body.
Watching him, we went into hoots of laughter.

He would open his mouth and belch noisily. Then almost
immediately up would go his tail as a sort of rebound of internal
gases issued beneath. That was nothing special, but what was
peculiar was the odd pellet or two ejected at the same time. He
had a range of six to eight feet and hit the camel behind!

'My word, that's marvellous, never seen it before. Like a gun
going off. No, it's not, it's like... it's like... I know what—one of
those weird rocket cars some cranky Hun invented.' So Rocket
got his name...

How interesting it was to gaze, about ten miles west, on the vast
white expanse of Lake Mackay, knowing we were probably the
first of our kind to see it from the ground as Mackay reported
it from the air only two years before.

* Bush cake.

Shimmering in the mirage, its brilliant glare threw up into strong relief the redness of the desert, the sombre hue of such herbage as crept to its shores. Samphire flats dense with low saline-loving shrubs and stunted ti-tree lined the lake edge. In the distance this border, almost black to the eye, became an irregular line of cleavage, a third component in a colour scheme hitherto predominated by the mingled hue of spinifex and sand. Sharp and clear were the nearest shores of the lake; the further ones quite indistinguishable, for a screen of ghostly white vapour, the mirage curtain, hid all sights a few miles out. Low promontories of scrub-covered sand protruded into the lake, deep bays between, and like long palsied fingers seeking to clutch the unwary, attenuated arms of this dead white sea ran out from the main bed. Islands here, islands there, some mere dots, others many acres in extent, one in particular seemingly dense with tall dark trees, took monotony from the scene, which, though not at all of beauty, possessed a certain wild majestic grandeur, a ferocity, a savagery wholly in keeping with the scene of which it was but a part.

Once possibly deep with calm sweet waters, forest bound where curious animals and quaint folk may have dwelt before the skies became pitiless, this vast lake gave one to ponder on its first happiness. For though geology is not an exact science it does admit this huge hinterland to have become its present deadened self beneath the merciless inquisition of its agents. Denudation by frost and wind and rain, aridity resultant from the change of climate and other agents in all powerful array have conquered and remodelled such a place as this. Deserts have not existed in their present shapes and places through the world since the dawn of time—time and nature have evolved them as partners to the present easy lands in a scheme beyond the true conception of enlightened man.

Which, after all, to those who gazed upon this scene was of interest great and strong—but of no comfort at all. We had to live, and pondering would not deepen native wells nor quench the thirst of dry-throated camels...

Soon Lake Mackay, probably larger than Lake Amadeus, hitherto regarded as largest of all west of the Overland Telegraph line, was reached.

We took the camels on to the surface, but the test was far from satisfactory. The briny character of the surface caused their large pads to slip. They slithered about, broke noselines, ran dire risk of tumbling over altogether, being not built by nature for boggy places.

'No good, we'll have to stick to the shore.'

So northwards we moved till the sun was low. Over each high sandhill which ran to the very edge of the lake the camels struggled slowly, then across the loose incompact surface of a samphire swamp to the next sandhill. Their pads sank in six inches; laboriously they made each step, at times refusing altogether to go ahead, fearful always of ground at all treacherous. We had to beat the riding camels to make them lead the way and break the track, an exertion which made one sweat profusely, for of late the weather had warmed up considerably; the air had a distinct touch of summer and, as the lonely outfit struggled along, a dust of fine briny particles rose all about to make matters worse. Eyes smarted; throats became dry, the voice hoarse. Thirsty and filthy, begrimed and without any hope of a wash, we slept uncleansed. An evil odour pervaded each man; he hated it but in philosophy disregarded it. Arms, necks, faces, dust-coated on top of sunburnt flesh a mixture of white from the swamp and black from the camp fires, where sweat had streaked down. Eyes sticky and gummy with unwashed lids, clothes whitened in the folds where perspiration had dried, we must have looked a pretty sight. But cheerful withal for, being absorbed by the task, thoughts ever ahead on the far horizon, one was able to rise above dirt and discomfort, the ever present flies and the hard tucker, to see the purpose behind these trials, to understand the reason of our tribulations. And able to laugh as well (which the leader should always encourage, no matter what the subject) for if one loses that golden faculty then life becomes a serious matter, and as I once heard a man say in this type of country, 'It seems to be clutching at me.' That is the start of 'cafard', the beginning of a desert madness with which one unfitted for this task can be seized, lose his balance, become panicky, and a misery to his mates. Incidentally, he may perish himself for no just reason.

That night was the first warm one of the trip, even sultry, and flickers of lightning played about the southern horizon. Oh! for a thunderstorm—how I prayed for it before sleep, deep and refreshing, banished care till piccaninny daylight.

By crib time we had encircled the north-east corner of the lake and had made some progress westwards. Having eaten, we climbed a high sandhill, for the time of decision had arrived. All camels were dry, Rocket in particular was causing me anxiety and by his crying made matters far worse for himself.

Gathered in a little group we studied the horizon, the landscape near and far with eyes and glasses until...

'My word look at that!'

'Isn't it a beauty!'

'Something to look at anyway.'

The spectacle which riveted the attention of all hands was a new range, a tall imposing one, even at that distance strong in the mirage. Far away to the west, distant no more than thirty miles (although it seemed to be fifty miles, but that was distortion by mirage) stood this feature whose high points appeared to be 800 feet above the surrounding country.

'Might'em spring that way,' said the boys.

'What do you think about it, Stan?'

'I'm willing to go ahead—should be a good water there.'

'What about you, Ben?'

'No, too great a risk. Looks a sure thing if it wasn't for the drought.'

'What've you got to say, Boss?' they asked.

For a while I gazed through the glasses, put them down, smoked thoughtfully. It was indeed the hour of decision, an hour of particular difficulty by reason of that cursed new range which, like the finger of a devilish siren, beckoned, oh so temptingly!

almost mocked one's courage to proceed where each man so fervently desired. Without this sight the decision to retreat, already partly formed, would have been so easy, so obvious.

'Well, boys, here's where each man has his say. You've had yours; mine's the casting vote. And this is how I sum it up. It's darned easy to walk into a tragedy, and a hell of a scramble to get out. In fact, it's pretty clear if we go ahead and that range lets us down none of us'll ever see home and mother again. If the camels don't get a drink in a very little over three days we're going to have a smash. The risk isn't good enough, so I vote no.'

Silent, depressed, we turned down the sandhill. What a miserable decision, right on the border of Western Australia, with rocks to tempt for hope of water and gold, far far out from our base, deep in the arid desert, to have to turn our backs on the promised land for a few miserable, invaluable, essential gallons of water. But life is very sweet; and judgment, experience, appreciation of all factors, is the unseen hand which places the weights correctly to determine the true values, keeps wisely poised the balance between life and death.†

OLIVE PINK
Stabbed in Back by Fates, 1933

 Miss Olive Pink was a formidable individual who, in the early 1930s, left depression-struck Sydney for life as a field anthropologist among the Walbiri of central Australia. Her letters to her doctoral supervisor, Professor A. P. Elkin of Sydney University, are numerous and lengthy, her mounting frustration at delays in

---

† A year later Terry learned from Aborigines that the range in question, the Ross Range, was dry when he saw it. To have gone on would have meant certain death.

receiving funding indicated first by capitals, then red under-
lining, and finally by entirely vermilion missives. She is the
only explorer in this anthology who sends a telegram. Ill with
severe dysentery, she wired Elkin: 'STABBED IN BACK BY FATES'.
On 30 October 1933 she headed a letter: 'Oonmundjee, Central
Australia, about 280 miles W of Alice Springs (perhaps 230
only, am not sure until I return).'

A lost explorer maybe, but one who returned with fascinating
insights. She scribbled into her notebook this list of items
carried by an Aboriginal woman. It is a detailed inventory of
a kind never made by male explorers.

A WOMAN'S POSSESSIONS & REQUIREMENTS

Domestic Utensils

four types of wooden vessels (sometimes more than one of a
kind)

two grinding stones, one large and flat, one small

old digging sticks for pokers and loosening earth

fine grass or fine vine used to prevent water slopping over...

Personal Use

yam stick (digging-stick) used like spade

fire stick (i.e., a short piece of wood with smouldering embers
still attached)

ligatures and bandages of vine

a waddi (have not seen it in use)

flints for cutting food (now European knives)

native tobacco (chewed now, but whether prior to whites'
introduction to their tobacco I don't know)

improvised handkerchiefs (of grass or leaves)

? pubic apron only used at certain periods (if at all?) (This is quite
uncertain. I have never seen one worn. Whether adults wear this
is uncertain. A bride does on her wedding night apparently.)

fur string upper chest protector

rabbit-bandicoot tails (for head)

neck bands of fur string

head bands of fur string

nose bone, whether of wood or bone (uncertain for women).
Men use both.
Cosmetics etc
larvae of termites
grease from animals and lizards
red ochre
yellow ochre
white lime
(charcoal—for women—uncertain. I think not used.)
For Babies
wooden scraps used as cradle and perambulator
dusting powder (the sandy soil) and perhaps powdered charcoal
handkerchiefs (leaves and grass)
paperbark in place of baby's blanket

CECIL MADIGAN
Across the Simpson, 1939

Some Australian terrain is so forbidding that the
jet age had arrived before it was conquered. The
east–west transect of the Simpson Desert, crossing
against the grain of the great dunes, was one
such conquest. Cecil Madigan, geologist and lecturer at the
University of Adelaide, perused the region by air before
attempting to lead his scientific expedition across by the best
means then available—camel. We join him here in the heart
of the desert, where the dunes are tallest and the feed scarcest.
I had never guessed at the difficulty of obtaining astronomical
observations before reading Madigan.

Next day we were still in giant sand ridges, the biggest yet. They
must have reached 100 feet. They were more symmetrical, with
the approach side steeper, and there were sometimes short
transverse dunes on the top of them. We made rather a late

start owing to the dew, but got in our six hours of travel, and it was quite enough. The going was very heavy. The wider crests with more loose sand greatly increased the camels' tasks. We passed a few little patches of munyeroo during the day, but otherwise it was very barren. In the afternoon some of the camels began to stumble and fall. We pushed on, hoping to find some feed and firewood to camp on, but it became worse. At last I had to stop. There was some dead needlebush for the fire but no feed at all. Again Jack criticised me for not stopping earlier where was a little feed, but it was my way to hope for something better ahead and to put the miles behind. The only satisfaction I had that day was to travel hopefully. I reckoned we had made eleven miles, in which we had climbed over forty great masses of sand. They were the highest sand ridges we had seen. There was nothing but sand and spinifex between the ridges, no feed, no signs of claypans. A few finches were noticed, a hawk, and a flock of nineteen crows. I wondered if they were the same crows as we had seen the day before, following us. Something sinister about these carrion birds.

It was a quiet and sober camp that night. Things were beginning to look serious. The day's march had definitely given cause for some misgiving. We were not yet halfway across the desert, and the camels were beginning to fail. One was developing mange and seemed almost done. There was still over 100 miles to go to reach the Mulligan, but there could be no question of turning back, for returning was now no easier than go o'er, but on the contrary would be much more difficult if one's expectations about the country ahead proved correct. Jack Bejah was depressed. He spoke of leaving one or two camels behind to follow us if they could, but this would have been against all the principles of exploration. Once you begin to abandon your gear it is a sign of approaching collapse. You should not have any gear you can do without. I told him to redistribute the loads but to keep the string together. It was no good spreading ourselves over the desert. We must come into that Queensland feed any day now...

It was a clear night again at last, and I was able to take star observations. This careful navigation was not really essential, as there had been no features worth fixing since we left the Hale, but there was satisfaction in it. We could go east and strike the Mulligan without even the aid of compasses, but we would not know which side of the old Kaliduwarry Station we were on, and might have difficulty in finding it and waste time in locating ourselves before setting a course for Birdsville. Also I expected to find the course of the Hay River, if nothing else, where no one had seen it before, and this was worth fixing. If disaster should befall us and aeroplanes had to be sent out, we should be able to say exactly where we were; so I took my observations as opportunity offered. This was the first clear night since leaving the Hale, and our first opportunity to fix our position since then. The night was cold, the light poor. Papers, books, maps and instruments were soon wet with dew. Sitting out in the open among the spinifex under these conditions, not to mention considerable physical fatigue, did not help the accuracy of the calculations. I kept making mistakes and finding myself in the Pacific Ocean, which was no place to go to bed in. At last I got it right and was able to pinpoint our position on the map. It was 24° 44' south and 136° 59' east. We had come seventy-eight miles from the Hale in thirty-five and three-quarter hours, giving an average rate of just over two miles an hour. My daily dead reckoning had made it seventy-nine miles, one mile out in seventy-eight. This was the reward for a late night, an aching back and a shivering frame. We might be in considerable difficulty in the worst place in the world, but we knew just where it was. My companions had long ago turned in, quiet and somewhat worried, and were now all fast asleep. I got into my pyjamas as usual, distributed all my clothing along the side of the sleeping bag on the ground sheet, not forgetting boots and socks and hat, else they would be soaking wet in the morning, covered and tucked everything in with the other half of the sheet, and crawled under. I was pleased with the results of my calculations. That feed couldn't be far away now! It was a little bit fuggy shut up in this waterproof and almost air-tight groundsheet, but very warm and comfortable. The camels couldn't stand many more days like today, but we could take easier stages. The chronometer was wound and put away in the bottom of Jack's big box—must get a better fastening for that, the piece of stick came out today. Nice the way the wireless was working—we must all send more messages home—been neglecting that. We'd be in that feed any day now...

Next morning there was some readjustment of loads, but soon the damp packages were heaved up and the wet cordage knotted, the camels jerked themselves on to their feet, and the long string began to wind slowly over the first sand ridge. How were we going to fare today? Across the valley and on to the top of the next sand ridge—and there before us lay a small claypan covered with water. Down into the valley, to find the clayey soil was carpeted with munyeroo! No waiting for something better this time. There were a few low mulga bushes at the end of the claypan, a suitable place to camp. Round to these, and down went the camels, and off came the loads laboriously put on a quarter of an hour before. We would let the camels graze here all day. If we had only come on another half mile last night it would have saved us a lot of work and some anxiety! This water and the green munyeroo must mean the edge of the rain country. Anyway, we would give the camels all the feed they wanted and a spell before tackling the sand ridges again. They were soon chewing at great mats of munyeroo pulled up from the ground and dangling from their mouths.

It was a beautiful sunny day. We opened up the baggage and spread everything out to dry, then took a walk round the camp. Two sand ridges away to the north-east there was a group of five claypans with gidgee trees, the first gidgee we had seen since leaving the Hale. This certainly looked like the edge of the rain belt. There was more clay here in the soil between the sand ridges, and a thinner cover over the underlying rock. Nodules of ironstone lay around, and pieces of chalcedony. Crocker discovered a small rock outcrop of chalcedonised sandstone. More interesting still was the discovery of signs of the former presence of aboriginals, the only such indications seen in the whole desert crossing. These were chips of chalcedony, typical of aboriginal workshop sites where knives, scrapers and spearheads have been made, and also parts of grinding stones, one a piece of schist that must have come from the MacDonnells. This disproved my theory and Winnecke's that aboriginals never entered any part of the desert.

ROBYN DAVIDSON
Panic and Shake, 1977

 Robyn Davidson undertook one of the most remarkable journeys ever made in contemporary Australia—from Alice Springs to Shark Bay, alone and on camel back. Her account is bone-chillingly honest. The terror of isolation, of not knowing where water can be found, is something every explorer must have felt but would never admit to. Davidson's confrontations with wild bull camels also add a codicil to camel exploration in Australia. It will be even more difficult now that feral camels have become so widespread.

We join Davidson setting out from Docker River, several hundred kilometres west of Uluru.

As I left the settlement, alone, I was aware only of a flatness, a lack of substance in everything. My steps felt achingly slow, small and leaden. They led me nowhere. Step after step after step, the interminable walking dragged out, pulling my thoughts downwards into spirals. The country seemed alien, faded, muted, the silence hostile, overwhelming.

I was twenty miles out, tired and thirsty. I drank some beer. I was about to turn off and make camp when through the beer-hazed afternoon heat came striding three large strong male camels in full season.

Panic and shake. Panic and shake. They attack and kill, remember. Remember now, one—tie up Bub securely, two—whoosh him down, three—take rifle from scabbard, four—load rifle, five—cock, aim and fire rifle. They were just thirty yards away and one was spurting a cylindrical arch of red blood. He didn't seem to notice it. They all came forward again.

I was scared deep in my bones. First, I could not believe it was happening, then I believed it was never going to stop. My ears thumped, cold sweat stuck to the hollow of my back. My vision was distorted by fear. Then I was past it, not thinking any more, just doing it.

Zzzzt. This time just behind his head and he turned and ambled away. Zzzt. Near the heart again, he slumped down but just sat there. Zzzt. In the head, dead. The other two trundled off into the scrub. Shake and sweat, shake and sweat. You've won for now.

I unsaddled the camels and hobbled them close, glancing around constantly. It was getting dark. They came back. Braver now, I shot one, but only wounded it. Night came too quickly.

The fire flickered on white moonstruck sand, the sky was black onyx. The rumbling sound of bulls circled the camp very close until I fell asleep. In the moonlight, I woke up and maybe twenty yards away was a beast standing in full profile. I didn't want to harm it. It was beautiful, proud. Not interested in me at all. I slept again. drifting off to the sound of bells on camels, peacefully chewing their cud.

Came dawn, I was already stalking, gun loaded and ready. They were both still there. I had to kill the wounded one. I tried to. Another cylinder of blood and he ran away nipping at his wound. I could not follow, I had my own survival to think of. There he was, the last young bull, a beautiful thing, a moonlight camel. I made a decision. This one of the three would be allowed to live until he did something directly to jeopardise my safety. Happy decision. 'Yes, maybe he'll tag along right to Carnarvon. And I'll call him Aldebaran and isn't he magnificent, Diggity, what a match for Dookie. I don't have to kill him at all.' I snuck around to catch the camels. He watched me. Now, last camel to catch, Bub. Off he galloped in his hobbles, the new bull pacing lazily beside him. I couldn't catch him with the other bull so close. I tried for an hour, I was exhausted, I wanted to kill Bubby, to dismember him, rip his balls out, but they'd already gone. I took the rifle and walked to within thirty feet of the now excited and burbling young bull. I put a slug right where I knew it would kill him. It did not, and he bit and roared at his wound. He didn't understand this pain, I was crying. I fired again into his head and he sat down, gurgling through his own blood. I walked up to his head, we stared at one another— he knew then. He looked at me, I shot him in the brain, point blank.

Bubby was puzzled. He walked up to the carcass and drank some blood. It was all over his nose, like clown's lipstick, and he threw his lips around. He allowed himself to be caught, I didn't hit him. I walked on.

I entered a new time, space, dimension. A thousand years fitted into a day and aeons into each step. The desert oaks sighed and bent down to me, as if trying to grab at me. Sandhills came and sandhills went. Hills rose up and hills slipped away. Clouds rolled in and clouds rolled out and always the road, always the road, always the road.

So tired, I slept in the creek and thought of nothing but failure. I could not even light a fire. I wanted to hide in the dark. I thought it was surely longer than two days, I had walked so far. But time was different here, it was stretched by step after step and in each step a century of circular thought. I didn't want to think like this, was ashamed of my thoughts but I could not stop them. The moon, cold marble and cruel, pushed down on me, sucked at me, I could not hide from it, even in dream.

And the next day and the next day too, the road and the sandhills and the cold wind sucked at my thoughts and nothing happened but walking.

The country was dry. How could the camels be so thirsty and thin. At night, they came into camp and tried to knock over the water drums. I hadn't enough to spare, I rationed them. The map said 'rockhole'. Thank god. I turned off the track somewhere in that haze of elastic time and walked in. More sandhills, then a stretch of gibberflat, wide and dry and desolate with one dead bird, and two empty holes. Some string somewhere inside me was starting to unravel. An important string, the one that held down panic. I walked on, That night I camped in those sandhills.

The sky was leaden and thick. All day it had been grey, smooth, translucent, like the belly of a frog. Spots of rain pattered on me but not enough to lay the dust. The sky was washing me out, emptying me. I was cold as I hunched over my meagre fire. And somewhere, between frozen sandhills, in a haunted and forgotten desert, where time is always measured by the interminable roll of constellations, or the chill call of a crow waking, I lay down on my dirty bundle of blankets. The frost clung like brittle cobwebs to the black bushes around me, while the sky turned thick with glitter. It was very still. I slept. The hour before the sun spills thin colour on the sand, I woke suddenly and tried to gather myself from a dream I could not remember. I was split. I woke into limbo and could not find myself. There were no reference points, nothing to keep the world controlled and bound together. There was nothing but chaos and the voices.

The strong one, the hating one, the powerful one was mocking me, laughing at me.

'You've gone too far this time. I've got you now and I hate you. You're disgusting, aren't you? You're nothing. And I have you now, I knew it would come, sooner or later. There's no use fighting me you know, there's no one to help you. I've got you, I've got you.'

Another voice was calm and warm. She commanded me to lie down and be calm. She instructed me to not let go, not give in. She reassured me that I would find myself again if I could just hold on, be quiet and lie down.

The third voice was screaming.

Diggity woke me at dawn. I was some distance from camp, cramped, and cold to my bones. The sky was cold, pale blue and pitiless, like an Austrian psychopath's eyes. I walked out into the time warp again. I was only half there, like an automaton. I knew what I had to do. 'You must do this, it will keep you alive. Remember.' I walked out into that evil whispering sea. Like an animal, I sensed a menace, everything was quite still, but threatening, icy, beneath the sun's heat. I felt it watching me, following me, waiting for me.

I tried to conquer the presence with my own voice. It croaked out into the silence and was swallowed by it. 'All we have to do,' it said, 'is reach Mount Fanny, and there is certain to be water there. Just one step and another, that's all I have to do, I must not panic.' I could see what had to be Mount Fanny in the hot blue distance, and I wanted to be there, protected by those rocks, more than anything I'd ever wanted. I knew I was being unreasonable. There was more than enough water to get by on to Wingelinna. But the camels, I'd been so sure they'd do a week comfortably. I hadn't planned on the sudden dryness— the lack of green feed. 'But there'll be water there, of course there will. Haven't they told me so? What if there's not? What if the mill's run dry? What if I miss it? What if this thin little piece of string that keeps me tied to my camels breaks? What then? Walk walk walk, sandhills for ever, they all looked the same. I walked as if on a treadmill—no progress, no change. The hill came closer so slowly. 'How long is it now? A day? This is the longest day. Careful. Remember, it's just a day. Hold on, mustn't let go. Maybe a car will come. No cars. What if there's no water, what will I do? Must stop this. Must stop. Just keep walking. Just one step at a time, that's all it takes.' And on and on and on went that dialogue in my head. Over and over and round and round.

Late in the afternoon—long creeping shadows. The hill was close. 'Please please let me be there before night. Please don't let me be here in the dark. It will engulf me.'

It must be over the next sandhill surely. No, then the next one. OK, all right, the next, no the next, no the next. Please god, am I mad. The hill is there, I can almost touch it. I started to yell. I started to shout stupidly at the dunes. Diggity licked my hand and whined but I could not stop. I had being doing this for ever. I walked in slow motion. Everything was slowing down.

And then, over the last sandhill, I was out of the dunes. I crouched on the rocks, weeping, feeling their substance with my hands. I climbed steadily, up the rocky escarpment, away from that terrible ocean of sand. The rocks were heavy and dark and strong. They rose up like an island. I crawled over this giant spine, where it emerged from the waves in a fuzz of green. I looked back to the immensity of where I had been. Already the memory was receding—the time, the aching time of it. Already, I had forgotten most of the days. They had sunk away from memory, leaving only a few peaks that I could recall. I was safe.

W. J. PEASLEY
A Frontier Closes, 1977

 The great drought of the late 1970s had the Aboriginal people of Wiluna worried. They knew that there was still one old couple 'out there' in the western Gibson Desert, living as their people had always done. But could they survive, alone, in the extreme conditions of the drought? Their concern prompted Western Australian doctor W. J. Peasley to undertake his epic search by four-wheel drive for 'The Last of the Nomads'. Its successful conclusion ended a major phase of Australian exploration, for with the removal of Warri and Yatungka from the desert, the frontier between autonomous Aboriginal and European cultures had vanished, just 189 years after it opened in Sydney Cove.

Soon after leaving the depot we crossed an area of burnt country and Mudjon again found the footprints of Warri and Yatungka. They were moving towards the east-north-east, heading towards the waterhole that existed out in that direction.

Nine and a half kilometres further on we came to a well known as Ngargin, located amongst some rather pathetic looking mulga trees. Several small windbreaks had been erected in the vicinity, suggesting that Warri and Yatungka had been able to obtain a little water and had remained there until the well was dry.

We continued to the east-north-east for another twenty-one kilometres to the well of Wangabaddi. Mudjon was our navigator, we relied on his knowledge of the country to guide us. He was leading us from one waterhole to another through almost featureless country, without tracks to guide him or a compass to assist him. He shrugged his shoulders, as was his fashion, when we commented on his skill, saying it 'was nothing,' that he was following the 'main road.' By this he meant we were travelling the same paths that his people had trodden for centuries as they moved between the wells. But one associates a main road with a broad track of cleared country along which vehicles of all descriptions can travel, while the 'road' we moved along was unmarked by a single vehicle. There was not even the faintest suggestion of a footpath to indicate that the desert people once moved to and fro across the land.

Wangabaddi soak was located in the centre of a flat stony clearing about a hundred metres in diameter. A few spindly mulga trees struggled to survive in the rocky ground, although on the northern edge of the clearing grew a little clump of healthier looking specimens.

The well was three and a half metres deep, and it would have been an extremely difficult and even dangerous undertaking to climb into, and out of, the shaft, especially if one was in a weakened condition. The well was dry and not even the slightest moisture could be found after extensive digging.

Warri and Yatungka had camped at Wangabaddi on many occasions in the past. The remains of many fires and several windbreaks were discovered, and at one of their old campsites was a spear, a digging stick, several old cans and a grinding stone. What was of special interest was something wrapped in a piece of ancient canvas wedged in the fork of a mulga tree about forty-six metres from the well. Mudjon appeared not to notice the object and made no comment although I was certain his keen eyes would have seen it long before we did. We were fascinated by it but as Mudjon was acting in a peculiar manner we did not wish to investigate immediately for fear of offending him.

Our first thought was that either Warri or Yatungka had died and the remains had been placed in the tree, and Mudjon's actions reinforced that assumption. We waited until he had moved off to the north, past the clump of mulga and out onto the sandy spinifex plain to search for footprints before we attempted to examine it.

John Hanrahan climbed the tree and passed the bundle down for inspection. The covering was a piece of tattered canvas, possibly the remains of a groundsheet that Warri had been given long ago. It was unfolded carefully and with some trepidation, and the contents were found to be not human remains as we expected, but the bones of an animal! What on earth was the reason for wrapping animal bones in canvas and placing them high in a mulga tree at Wangabaddi? Was it possible that one of the Aboriginal couple's dogs had died and they had given it a tree burial? Closer examination showed the remains to be those of a kangaroo, but the mystery remained.

When Mudjon returned from his excursion out on the plain the bundle had been replaced in position in the tree and once more he made no reference to it, passing close by without a glance towards it. Anxious to hear his explanation I mentioned our discovery to him. His eyes remained on the ground, indicating that he was fully aware of its presence and that he was a little afraid of it.

We did not inform him that we had taken it down and had some knowledge of the contents because, again, we did not wish to offend him. He offered no suggestion as to what the bundle might contain but in response to my question as to whether it might be 'secret business' he replied, 'Might be,' and did not wish to talk about the matter any further.

Ninety metres south of the well was a semicircle composed of five stones of the same type of greyish-white quartz we had seen at Walloogoobal. They were firmly set into the ground and a distance of six metres separated the two ends of the arrangement. These, too, were the work of Warrida of the Dreamtime. He had found water at Wangabaddi, he had camped there and had left the mysterious stones to indicate he had passed that way.

A little further to the south was a small cleared area with several artefacts on the periphery. The place, said Mudjon, was a little dancing ground where formerly his people, when camped at the well, would dance and follow a path that wound past the stones of Warrida towards the waterhole.

On leaving Wangabaddi we continued in an easterly direction towards the sandhills to the north, and after travelling twenty-four kilometres a remarkable little hill capped with yellow-pink sandstone was visible a little to the south-east. Although it was off the 'main road' it had often been visited by the Mandildjara in the past, for near its base was a rockhole, and the waterhole and hill were together known as Birri Birri.

Here, at Mudjon's request, we halted in a clearing for he wished to fire some high spinifex and scrub which grew in a shallow depression running across the open space. The tinder-dry grass burned with an intense heat, igniting the green scrub and sending enormous columns of black smoke skywards.

From the top of the vehicle we looked towards Ngarinarri, about thirty kilometres distant, but the sky remained clear. Mudjon did not appear at all surprised for, he said, Warri and Yatungka had not replied to our earlier signals and he did not expect an answer on that occasion. They did not send up smoke because they could not and he again indicated that they were dead.

We pushed on towards Ngarinarri and after going six and a half kilometres further to the east, we rounded the eastern extremity of the sandhills and turned to the north-east. There were sandhills still to be crossed before we could reach the well but they were no longer an obstacle to our progress.

In the cabin of the vehicle it was hot and noisy as we ground along for another nine and a half kilometres. There was little talk, for all us had been affected by Mudjon's profound depression: we wanted desperately to get to Ngarinarri but feared what we might discover there. It was late afternoon and we knew we could not reach the well that day and we were pleased, for it would be better to approach it in the morning, rather than stumble onto it in the darkness.

The vehicle heaved itself up a low sand ridge and as we reached the crest Mudjon, who had been sitting quietly beside me, apparently uninterested in the world about him, suddenly shouted and pointed excitedly to the north. There was smoke out there, he said, he was sure he had seen smoke. We peered in the direction he indicated and there it was, a faint wisp of smoke spiralling into the blue-grey sky of that late hour of the day.

There were great cries of joy from all members of the party. There was somebody alive out there, somebody had survived the long walk to Ngarinarri. Was it Warri or was it Yatungka or were, by some miracle, both of them alive? Mudjon was overjoyed that at least one of his people would be found alive after having convinced himself that his old friends had perished.

I took a fix on the smoke and found it bore two degrees from north, and on looking at the map I found that the spot that Mudjon had indicated previously as being Ngarinarri's position, was within half a degree of that bearing.

We wanted to press on with all speed to reach the well but it was an impossible task and darkness forced us to make camp in a valley between sand ridges where there was a little wood for our fire. On top of the ridge to the north grew a large and rather gnarled tree and Mudjon, who was now in a euphoric mood, said that it had been growing for a very long time. He had seen it many times before on his journeys between Ngarinarri and Wangabaddi and the old people had told him it had always been there, that it had been planted there in the Dreamtime.

As we sat round our camp fire that night, Mudjon spoke

animatedly of the times that he had roamed the desert with Warri, where they had hunted and what they had hunted. He was obviously tremendously relieved by the sighting a few hours previously and he talked about his people far into the night.

We were all excited at the prospect of finding the Aboriginal couple alive, but at the same time I had a strange feeling of uneasiness, perhaps it was sadness. I could not help feeling that that night would be the last that Warri and Yatungka (presuming both were alive) would spend alone in the desert together if they chose to return to Wiluna with us. The long years they had spent together without the company of other human beings, wandering their ancestral land, might come to an end within a few short hours. We were about to intrude into the lives of the last nomadic people in the Western Gibson Desert, and in doing so it was possible that we might be responsible for bringing to an end a way of life that had gone on for several thousand years.

Ever since Wati Kudjarra had moved through the land creating the features on the landscape, there had been Aboriginal people in the desert. If tomorrow Warri and Yatungka decided to leave with us then, for the first time since the Dreamtime, there would not be a single Aborigine in the country of the Mandildjara or, indeed, in the whole of the Western Gibson Desert. That was a sobering thought, one that weighed heavily on me and one that greatly disturbed my sleep that night.

I wondered why our smoke signals, which certainly had been seen, had not been answered earlier. Was it possible that Warri and Yatungka did not wish to leave their country and had no desire to make contact with us? Our progress across the land could be gauged by our signals and it would be apparent to them that we were moving along the 'main road' between waterholes, and that somebody was leading the party towards them, and who else but Mudjon would be guiding such a party? At his last meeting with Warri, Mudjon had told his friend that one day he would return to lead them out of the desert, that with advancing age they could not remain alone in their country. Was it possible that Warri and Yatungka feared Mudjon's return and refrained from sending up smoke to indicate their position? But surely they must be in dire straits if the country we had passed through in the preceding two weeks was any indication, there being little game of any kind, and not one of the waterholes we had encountered in well over 100 kilometres of travel had contained a drop of water. Mudjon believed they must be in very poor physical condition and would be prepared to leave the desert, at least until the rains came and the long drought ended.

Perhaps Warri and Yatungka were determined to spend their last days in their own country rather than be removed to a strange and, to them, frightening way of life. Was there a change of heart at the last minute and a decision made to acknowledge our last signal when they realised we were heading towards Ngarinarri and would find them even if they did not send smoke?

We had no wish to disturb them or to interfere with their way of life and should they desire to remain in their homeland and were in reasonable physical condition we would leave provisions with them and on our return to Wiluna would arrange for contact to be made at intervals to offer any assistance they required. However if they were weak and ill and wished to remain, could we just drive away and leave them, knowing they would surely die without adequate food and without medical attention? We sincerely hoped that such a situation would not present itself.

On the other hand, if they chose to go out with us, we would be haunted by the knowledge that we had removed the last of the nomads from the desert.

Those were the thoughts that weighed so heavily on me that night near Ngarinarri.

We rose early, for we were eager to make contact with the man or woman who had signalled us. Travelling almost due north on the bearing we had obtained the previous evening, we had gone eight kilometres when Mudjon called a halt and proceeded to fire spinifex once more. Almost immediately an answering smoke rose on a bearing of thirty-five degrees and we changed direction towards it. Two and a half kilometres on, our new course brought us to the crest of a long sand ridge which ran roughly east-west to the horizon and there, on the wide open plain between the sandhills, were flames and smoke rising from a long trail of burning spinifex.

From our observation point there was a distance of one kilometre to a sand ridge to the north, the intervening flat country being covered with spinifex and occasional low scrub. Almost due north of our position and about four hundred metres distant, another sand ridge, which had its origins away to the east, terminated on the plain. With binoculars I searched the plain for a human being amongst the burning spinifex, but without success. It was obvious that somebody was moving out there, for at intervals there would be a sudden burst of flame as a new patch of grass was ignited. A long trail of smoke rose slowly in the still air of the morning and a blackened strip of burnt country denoted the burner's progress across the plain.

Then I saw the figure, moving slowly eastwards, unaware of our presence on the sand ridge to the south. We were disturbed that only one person was visible. Was it Warri or was it Yatungka? A highly excited Mudjon said that, without doubt, it was Warri. We searched the plain and the sandhills beyond with our glasses but there was no sign of Yatungka. Had she perished, leaving Warri alone in the desert? Mudjon did not know but he intended to answer that question as soon as possible. He could contain himself no longer and plunging down the northern face of the sand ridge he strode briskly out to intercept Warri, who still continued moving eastwards, intently firing the country, still not aware that he was being observed.

As Mudjon walked rapidly through the spinifex he, too, fired the grass to attract attention, but Warri continued on to the east. It was not until Mudjon was within one hundred metres that Warri caught sight of him. During the time that Mudjon had been seeking to intercept him, Warri had moved off the flat country onto the southern side of the sand ridge which terminated on the plain, and it was from that elevated position that he first became aware of Mudjon's presence.

Through my glasses I saw Warri stop abruptly to stare at Mudjon, then move down off the sand ridge towards him. The two old friends met, but there was no demonstration of joy, no handshakes, no clasping of one to the other. Instead they faced each other from a distance of six metres for at least half a minute, each apparently making a quick appraisal of the other. Presumably some words were then spoken, the gap between the two men closed, and immediately they began to walk back towards our position.

There was still no sign of Yatungka, and Warri did not appear to be looking for her as he followed Mudjon through the clumps of spinifex. It was indeed strange that the two nomads had not been walking together that morning and I feared the worst.

On reaching the base of the sand ridge on which we stood, Warri halted whilst Mudjon continued up the incline to our position. Where was Yatungka? Was she still alive? we hurriedly asked. To our immense relief Mudjon explained that she was indeed alive and was, at that moment, gathering food out to the east where the quandong trees grew and would return to Ngarinarri later in the day.†

† Tragically, both Warri and Yatungka died shortly after leaving the desert.

SOURCES AND FURTHER READING

W. P. Auld, *Recollections of McDouall Stuart*, Sullivan's Cove, Adelaide, 1984, 46–51.

Joseph Banks, from *The Journal of Joseph Banks in the* Endeavour, with a commentary by A. M. Lysaght, facsimile edition, Rigby, Adelaide, 1980.

Francis Barrallier, 'Barrallier's Journal', *Historical Records of New South Wales*, vol. v, ed. F. M. Bladen, William Applegate Gullick, Government Printer, Sydney, 1897, 753–59.

John Batman, from 'Journal', 10 May–11 June 1835, MS 13181, and 'The Batman Deed', Latrobe Australian Manuscripts Collection, State Library of Victoria.

Gregory Blaxland, *A Journal of a Tour of Discovery across the Blue Mountains in New South Wales*, from *Blaxland–Lawson–Wentworth 1813*, ed. Joanna Armour Richards, Blubber Head Press, Hobart, 1979, 67–77. First published London, 1823.

The Journal of Arthur Bowes Smyth: Surgeon, Lady Penrhyn, 1787–1789, ed. Paul Fidlon and R. J. Ryan, Australian Documents Library, Sydney, 1979, 82–84.

David W. Carnegie, *Spinifex and Sand*, Hesperian Press, Victoria Park, 1989, 130–35. First published C. Arthur Pearson Ltd, London, 1898.

Jan Carstensz, 'Voyage By the *Pera* By Herself under Carstensz...', *The Part Borne by the Dutch in the Discovery of Australia 1606–1765*, ed. J. E. Heeres, Luzac & Co., London, 1899, 39–41.

James Cook, from the original journal of Captain James Cook on the voyage of HMS *Endeavour*, 6 May 1770, National Library of Australia, MS 1.

Emily Caroline Creaghe, 'The Little Explorer's Diary', unpublished typescript, 1883, Mitchell Library MSS 2982, State Library of New South Wales. Donated by Mr E. R. Barrett.

William Dampier, *Dampier's Voyages*, ed. John Masefield, E. Grant Richards, London, 1906, vol. i, 452–56; vol. ii, 437–40. *A New Voyage Round the World* first published 1697; *A Voyage to New Holland* first published 1703.

Robyn Davidson, *Tracks*, Picador, London, 1998, 148–53. First published London, 1980. Reproduced with permission.

Louis de Rougemont, *The Adventures of Louis de Rougemont As Told by Himself*, J. B. Lippincott, Philadelphia, 1900, 257–59.

Willem de Vlamingh, *Voyage to the Great South Land: Willem de Vlamingh 1696–1697*, ed. Günter Schilder, trans. C. de Heer, Royal Australian Historical Society, History House, 133 Macquarie Street, Sydney, 1985, 153–58.

Jules Dumont d'Urville, *An Account in Two Volumes of Two Voyages to the South Seas*, trans. and ed. Helen Rosenman, Melbourne University Press, 1987, 42–45.

George Evans, 'Assistant-Surveyor Evans' Journal', from *Historical Records of Australia*, series 1, vol. viii, Library Committee of the Commonwealth Parliament, Sydney, 1916, 174.

Edward John Eyre, *Journals of Expeditions of Discovery into Central Australia and Overland from Adelaide to King George's Sound in the Years 1840–1*, T. & W. Boone, London, 1845, vol. i, 398–402, vol. ii, 1–17, 107–10. Facsimile edition published by Libraries Board of South Australia, Adelaide, 1966.

H. H. Finlayson, *The Red Centre*, Angus and Robertson, Sydney, 1935, 99–104.

Matthew Flinders, *A Voyage to Terra Australis*, G. & W. Nicol, London, 1814, vol. i, 169–70, vol. ii, 228–33, 238–39. Facsimile edition published by Libraries Board of South Australia, Adelaide, 1966.

John Forrest, *Explorations in Australia*, Sampson Low, Marston, Low & Searle, London, 1875, 183–90. Facsimile edition published by Libraries Board of South Australia, Adelaide, 1969.

George Frankland, *The Narrative of an Expedition to the Head of the Derwent and to the Countries Bordering the Huon in 1835*, Sullivan's Cove, Adelaide, 1983, 17–25.

Ernest Giles, *Australia Twice Traversed*, vol. ii, Sampson Low, Marston, Searle & Rivington, London, 1889, 27–43. Facsimile edition published by Libraries Board of South Australia, Adelaide, 1964.

John Graham, from Archives Office of New South Wales, 4/2325.5 reproduced as Appendix 5 in *The Rescue of Eliza Fraser*, Barry Dwyer and Neil Buchanan, Gympie, 1986, 30–32.

George Grey, *Journals of Two Expeditions of Discovery in North-West and Western Australia*, vol. i, T. & W. Boone, London, 1841, 146–51.

John Ainsworth Horrocks, from *Proceedings of the Royal Geographical Society of Australasia: South Australian Branch*, vol. viii, Vardon & Sons, Adelaide, 1906, 44–46.

Alfred Howitt, from *A Successful Exploration through the Interior of Australia*, ed. William Wills, Richard Bentley, London, 1863, 321–26. Facsimile edition published by The Friends of the State Library of South Australia, Adelaide, 1996.

Hamilton Hume, *A Brief Statement of Facts in Connection with an Overland Expedition from Lake George to Port Phillip in 1824*, Third Edition with Addenda, J. J. Brown, Yass, 1874, 36–44.

Robert Logan Jack, *Northmost Australia*, vol. ii, George Robertson & Co., Melbourne, 1922, 486–91.

Jackey Jackey, from John MacGillivray, *Narrative of the Voyage of HMS Rattlesnake*, vol. ii, T. & W. Boone, London, 1852, 228–36.

Willem Jansz, 'Voyage of the Ship *Duifken* under Command of Willem Jansz(oon)...', *The Part Borne by the Dutch in the Discovery of Australia 1606–1765*, ed. J. E. Heeres, Luzac & Co., London, 1899, 5–6.

F. and A. Jardine, *Narrative of the Overland Expedition of the Messrs. Jardine from Rockhampton to Cape York*, ed. Frederick J. Byerley, J. W. Buxton, Brisbane, 1867, 35–38.

John King, from *A Successful Exploration through the Interior of Australia*, ed. William Wills, Richard Bentley, London, 1863, 312–18. Facsimile edition published by The Friends of the State Library of South Australia, Adelaide, 1996.

Gerard Krefft, *Transactions of the Philosophical Society of New South Wales*, Reading and Wellbank, Sydney, 1866, 12–14.

Ludwig Leichhardt, *Journal of an Overland Expedition in Australia from Moreton Bay to Port Essington*, T. & W. Boone, London, 1847, 502–25.

John Lhotsky, *A Journey from Sydney to the Australian Alps*, ed. Alan E. J. Andrews, Blubber Head Press, Hobart, 1979, 67–79. First published Sydney, 1835.

Carl Lumholtz, *Among Cannibals*, John Murray, London, 1889, 242–50. Facsimile edition published by Caliban Books, Sussex, 1979.

John MacGillivray, *Narrative of the Voyage of HMS Rattlesnake*, vol. i, T. & W. Boone, London, 1852, 301–07.

Cecil T. Madigan, *Crossing the Dead Heart*, Georgian House, Melbourne, 1946, 61–65.

Páloo Máta Môigna source, 'Transactions at the Tonga Islands', *Constable's Miscellany of Original and Selected Publications in the Various Departments of Literature, Science & the Arts*, vol. xiii, Constable & Co., Edinburgh, 1827, 210–14.

Thomas Livingstone Mitchell, *Three Expeditions into the Interior of Eastern Australia*, vol. ii, T. & W. Boone, London, 1839, 210–13, 238–43.

Georg Neumayer, *Results of the Magnetic Survey of the Colony of Victoria*, J. Schneider, Mannheim, 1869, 76–80, 84–85.

John Oxley, *Journals of Two Expeditions into the Interior of New South Wales*, John Murray, London, 1820, 138–41, 287–92.

Nicholas Pateshall, *A Short Account of a Voyage Round the Globe in H.M.S Calcutta 1803–1804*, ed. Marjorie Tipping, Queensberry Hill Press, Melbourne, 1980, 56–64.

W. J. Peasley, *The Last of the Nomads*, Fremantle Arts Centre Press, 1983, 126–37.

François Pelsaert, 'Woeful Diurnal Annotations Touching the Loss of Our Ship *Batavia*...', *The Part Borne by the Dutch in the Discovery of Australia 1606–1765*, ed. J. E. Heeres, Luzac & Co., London, 1899, 55, 60–61.

François Péron, *A Voyage of Discovery to the Southern Hemisphere*, Marsh Walsh Publishing, Melbourne, 1975, 271–78. First published London, 1809.

Arthur Phillip, *The Voyage of Governor Phillip to Botany Bay*, John Stockdale, London, 1789, 44–52. Facsimile edition published by Georgian House, Melbourne, 1950.

Olive Pink, from 'The Personal Papers of Elkin', P130, University of Sydney Archives.

John Price, 'Journey into the Interior of the Country', *Historical Records of New South Wales*, vol. iii, ed. F. M. Bladen, Charles Potter, Government Printer, Sydney, 1895, 820–23.

George Augustus Robinson, *Friendly Mission: The Tasmanian Journals and Papers of George Augustus Robinson 1829–1834*, ed. N. J. B. Plomley, Tasmanian Historical Research Association, Hobart, 1996, 490–93.

John McDouall Stuart, *The Journals of John McDouall Stuart*, ed. William Hardman, Saunders, Otley and Co., London, 1865, 10–12, 164–66.

Charles Sturt, *Two Expeditions into the Interior of Southern Australia*, vol. ii, Smith, Elder and Co., London, 1833, 88–110. Facsimile edition published by Doubleday Australia, Sydney, 1982.

Charles Sturt, *Narrative of an Expedition into Central Australia*, vol. ii, T. & W. Boone, London, 1849, 1–2, 89–102.

Abel Tasman, *Abel Janszoon Tasman's Journal of his Discovery of Van Diemen's Land and New Zealand*, ed. J. E. Heeres, Amsterdam, 1898. Republished by N. A. Kovach, Los Angeles, 1965, 11–12, 14–15.

Watkin Tench, *A Complete Account of the Settlement at Port Jackson*, London, 1793, republished in *1788*, ed. and intr. Tim Flannery, Text Publishing, Melbourne, 1996, 186–97.

Michael Terry, *Sand and Sun*, Michael Joseph, London, 1937, 38–39, 103–10.

Te Pahi sources, *Historical Records of New South Wales*, vol. vi, ed. F. M. Bladen, William Applegate Gullick, Government Printer, Sydney, 1898, 2–9; *Sydney Gazette*, Sunday, 22 December 1805, *A Facsimile Reproduction of Volume Three*, Trustees of the Public Library of New South Wales, Sydney, 1996.

William Wall, from Australian Museum Archives: series 265; W. S. Wall, 'Notes of a Journey from Sydney to the Murrimbigi River in Pursuite of Specimens of Natural History', 1844 (original handwritten manuscript and typescript copy).

Peter Egerton Warburton, *Journey across the Western Interior of Australia*, ed. H. W. Bates, Sampson Low, Marston, Low and Searle, London, 1875, 238–61.

Warrup, from George Grey, *Journals of Two Expeditions of Discovery in North-West and Western Australia*, vol. ii, T. & W. Boone, London, 1841, 346–50.

Lawrence Wells, from 'Journal of the Calvert Scientific Exploring Expedition 1896–7' *Parliamentary Paper, Western Australia 1902*, No. 46, W. M. Alfred Watson, Government Printer, Perth, 1902, 59–62.

William John Wills, *A Successful Exploration through the Interior of Australia*, ed. William Wills, Richard Bentley, London, 1863, 292–303. Facsimile edition published by The Friends of the State Library of South Australia, Adelaide, 1996.

Readers interested in discovering more about the world of Australian exploration might also want to seek out these books:

Jan Bassett, *Great Explorations: An Australian Anthology*, Oxford University Press, Melbourne, 1996.

Michael Cannon, *The Exploration of Australia*, Reader's Digest, Sydney, 1987.

Kathleen Fitzpatrick, *Australian Explorers: A Selection from Their Writings*, Oxford University Press, London, 1958.

Robin Hanbury-Tenison, *The Oxford Book of Exploration*, Oxford University Press, Oxford, 1994.